Lecture Notes of the Institute for Computer Sciences, Social Informatics and Telecommunications Engineering 158

More information about this series at http://www.springer.com/series/8197

Ramón Agüero · Thomas Zinner
Mario García-Lozano · Bernd-Ludwig Wenning
Andreas Timm-Giel (Eds.)

Mobile Networks and Management

7th International Conference, MONAMI 2015
Santander, Spain, September 16–18, 2015
Revised Selected Papers

 Springer

Editors
Ramón Agüero
Dpto. Ingeniería de Comunicaciones
Universidad de Cantabria
Santander
Spain

Thomas Zinner
Lehrstuhl für Informatik III
University of Würzburg
Würzburg
Germany

Mario García-Lozano
Dpt. de Teoria del Senyal i Comunicacions
Universitat Politècnica de Catalunya -
BarcelonaTech
Castelldefels
Spain

Bernd-Ludwig Wenning
Cork Institute of Technology
Cork
Ireland

Andreas Timm-Giel
Institute of Communication Networks
Hamburg University of Technology
Hamburg
Germany

ISSN 1867-8211   ISSN 1867-822X (electronic)
Lecture Notes of the Institute for Computer Sciences, Social Informatics
and Telecommunications Engineering
ISBN 978-3-319-26924-5   ISBN 978-3-319-26925-2 (eBook)
DOI 10.1007/978-3-319-26925-2

Library of Congress Control Number: 2015954986

Springer Cham Heidelberg New York Dordrecht London

Printed on acid-free paper

Springer International Publishing AG Switzerland is part of Springer Science+Business Media
(www.springer.com)

Preface

This volume is the result of the 7th EAI International Conference on Mobile Networks and Management (MONAMI), which was held in Santander, Spain, during September 16–18, 2015, hosted by University of Cantabria.

The MONAMI conference series aims at bringing together top researchers, academics, and practitioners specializing in the area of mobile network management, service management, virtualization and object management. Multiaccess and resource management, mobility management, and network management have emerged as core topics in the design, deployment, and operation of current and future networks. Yet, they are treated as separate, isolated domains with very little interaction between the experts in these fields and a lack of cross-pollination. Recently, new avant-garde techniques and solutions have emerged; as notable examples, network function virtualization, software-defined networking, network virtualization, and the cloud paradigm have taken roots. All in all, these techniques bring about new requirements and scientific challenges, and migration strategies are required to provide a smooth transition from today's legacy systems to future systems. At the same time, new wireless broadband access technologies, in what has been referred to as 5G, are posing new challenges and requirements that need to be taken into account; energy efficiency, densification, and offloading are examples of the new issues the scientific community is currently addressing.

The conference started with a half-day tutorial, "HTTP Adaptive Video Streaming and Quality of Experience," presented by Michael Seufert, Chair of Communication Networks, Julius-Maximilians-Universität Würzburg. Dr. Milos Tesanovic, from Samsung Electronics R&D Institute UK (SRUK), officially opened the conference with his vision on "5G Network Architecture Challenges - Towards Distributed, Flat, Heterogeneous Systems of the Future." Finally, Josep Mangues, from the Centre Tecnològic de Telecomunicacions de Catalunya (CTTC), opened the second day of the conference with his keynote entitled "Programmable Mobile Networks: Why? What? How?"

After a thorough peer review process, 15 papers were selected for inclusion in the main track of the technical program. Each paper was reviewed by at least three competent researchers, including at least one Technical Program Committee member. In addition, MONAMI 2015 hosted a well-received special session on "Future Research Directions," which featured six papers. All in all, 21 peer-reviewed papers were orally presented at the conference. This volume includes the revised versions of all papers that were presented at MONAMI 2015 in a single-track format. All MONAMI 2015 newcomers acknowledged the collegial atmosphere that characterizes the conference making it an excellent venue, not only to present novel research work, but also to foster stimulating discussions between the attendees.

This volume is organized thematically in five parts, starting with cellular network management and self-organizing networks in Part I. Radio resource management in LTE and 5G networks aspects are discussed in Part II. Part III presents novel techniques and algorithms for wireless networks, while Part IV deals with video streaming over wireless networks. Part V includes papers presenting avant-garde research on applications and services and, finally, Part VI features two papers introducing novel architectural approaches for wireless sensor networks.

We close this short preface to the volume by acknowledging the vital role that the Technical Program Committee members and additional reviewers played during the review process. Their efforts ensured that all submitted papers received a proper evaluation. We thank EAI and ICST for assisting with organization matters, and the University of Cantabria for hosting MONAMI 2015. The team that put together this year's event is large and required the sincere commitment of many folks. Although too many to recognize here by name, their effort should be highlighted. We particularly thank Barbara Fertalova, Ivana Allen, and Lucia Kisova for their administrative support on behalf of EAI, and Prof. Imrich Chlamtac of CREATE-NET for his continuous support of the conference. Finally, we thank all delegates for attending MONAMI 2015 and making it such a vibrant conference!

September 2015

Ramón Agüero
Thomas Zinner
Mario García-Lozano
Bernd-Ludwig Wenning
Andreas Timm-Giel

Organization

General Chairs

Ramón Agüero   University of Cantabria, Spain
Thomas Zinner   University of Würzburg, Germany

TPC Chairs

Mario García-Lozano   Technical University of Catalunya, Spain
Bernd-Ludwig Wenning   Cork Institute of Technology, Ireland

Publications Chair

Andreas Timm-Giel   Hamburg University of Technology, Germany

Web and Publicity Chair

Jarno Pinola   VTT, Finland

Contents

Wireless Sensor Networks and IoT Architecures

Cellular Network Management
and Self-Organizing Networks

A Scoring Method for the Verification of Configuration Changes in Self-Organizing Networks

Szabolcs Nováczki[1], Tsvetko Tsvetkov[2], Henning Sanneck[3],
and Stephen S. Mwanje[3（✉）]

[1] Nokia, Budapest, Hungary
szabolcs.novaczki@nokia.com
[2] Department of Computer Science, Technische Universität München,
Munich, Germany
tsvetko.tsvetkov@in.tum.de
[3] Nokia, Munich, Germany
{henning.sanneck,stephen.mwanje}@nokia.com

Abstract. In today's mobile communication networks the increasing reliance on Self-Organizing Network(SON) features to perform the correct optimization tasks adds a new set of challenges. In a SON-enabled network, the impact of each function's action on the environment depends upon the actions of other functions as well. Therefore, the concept of pre-action coordination has been introduced to detect and resolve known conflicts between SON function instances. Furthermore, the idea of post-action SON verification has been proposed which is often understood as a special type of anomaly detection. It computes statistical measures on performance indicators at a relevant spatial and temporal aggregation level to assess the impact of a set of (SON-evoked) Configuration Management (CM) changes.

In this paper, we present such a verification technique, which utilizes Key Performance Indicator (KPI) normalization, aggregation and statistical processing for dynamically changing areas of the network. In addition, the introduced approach rewards or punishes CM changes based on their impact on the network and generates a recommendation to accept or undo them. A Coverage and Capacity Optimization (CCO) case study based on real Performance Management (PM) and CM data from an operator's Wideband Code Division Multiple Access (WCDMA) network is presented.

1 Introduction

Mobile SONs contain a potentially large number of concurrently operating SON function instances that need to be managed in order to achieve system-level operational goals [1]. Typically, this task is delegated to pre-action SON coordination, which defines rules used to prevent *known* conflicts [2,3]. One type of conflicts includes such that occur when instances of SON functions operate on

© Institute for Computer Sciences, Social Informatics and Telecommunications Engineering 2015
R. Agüero et al. (Eds.): MONAMI 2015, LNICST 158, pp. 3–15, 2015.
DOI: 10.1007/978-3-319-26925-2_1

shared CM parameters. Another type consists of those where the activity of one SON function instance affects the input measurements of another one. In addition to that, we can face situations where two function instances are in a direct conflict, e.g., both try to change the cell coverage area of two neighboring cells, or in a logical dependency, e.g., one changes the coverage area and the other one adjusts the handover parameters for that area.

In addition to using existing engineering knowledge to manage and coordinate SON function instances, it has been proposed to also verify the automated operation of the set of SON function instances [4]. This type of verification can be considered as a special type of anomaly detection that allows detecting previously *unknown* problems. The verification process itself comprises of three steps [5]: (1) defining the verification area, (2) running an anomaly detection algorithm, and (3) performing diagnosis on the impacted network elements. During the first step the network is partitioned in sets of cells, also sometimes called observation areas or scopes of verification, that are being under assessment. During the second step several KPIs are aggregated for each of those network regions and an anomaly detector is triggered to assess them. During the third step the decision is made to either accept the given changes or rollback bad performing areas to some previous network configuration.

In this paper we present verification method that follows those three steps. First of all, it divides the network in verification areas based on the CM changes that are occurring over a certain time span. Then, it starts an assessment interval during which it continuously monitors the performance impact of those changes and either rewards or punishes them based on whether they had a positive or negative influence on the network. As an outcome, our method generates a recommendation to either accept or reject the given CM change(s).

Our work is structured as follows. Section 2 describes how we assess CM changes occurring in the network and how our verification method works. In Sect. 3 we explain how we gather the performance data and how we compute the statistics that allow us to detect an anomalous network behavior. Section 4 outlines the results after using our method on real network data. Our paper concludes with the related work and a summary.

2   Assessment of CM Changes

In this section we describe our CM assessment method used to evaluate CM changes from performance effects point of view and use its output to place recommendations to accept or undo the corresponding CM change. The high level overview of the mechanism is shown in Fig. 1. In the following we are going to introduce each step.

2.1   Assessment Request

Our assessment method can either be triggered by a SON coordinator after accepting a CM change request [4], or after analyzing the changes in tables of a CM history database. In the latter case we expect that there is no direct interface

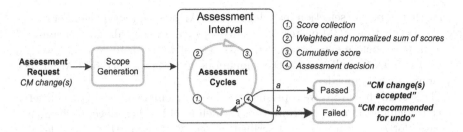

Fig. 1. Overview of the CM assessment method

between the assessment function and the initiator of the CM change. Typically, this happens when we perform manual CM changes or when we allow functions that are out of the scope of the coordinator to get active.

2.2 Scope Generation

The scope of a CM change is the set of cells that might be affected by the corresponding parameter adjustment. In research, several approaches of how to select the scope of verification (also called verification or observation area) have been introduced. A common technique is to compute a verification area by taking the impact area of the SON function instance whose activity is being under assessment [4]. Furthermore, areas of dense traffic, difficult environments and known trouble spots can be considered during the selection process as well [6]. Another possible solution is to consider the cell neighbor relations, e.g., by taking the first degree neighbors of the reconfigured cell [7]. In a mobile network two cells are neighbors when they have a common coverage area so that a handover of User Equipments (UEs) can be made.

After selecting the scope of a CM change, we observe the scopes of other CM changes and try to determine whether they can be combined. CM changes that are generating the same scope (or scopes with significant overlap) and within the same KPI granularity interval are merged. For example, if we have KPIs with hourly granularity the CM changes that have been generated within the same hour belong to the same scope. The resulting merges are handled as one entity during the rest of the process.

2.3 Assessment Interval Preparation

The first thing we do during the assessment interval preparation is the specification of the number of assessment cycles. It should be noted, however, that the interval does not have a fixed length for each set of CM changes, also called a *CM change group*. Instead, it depends on two CM parameter properties: (1) the time and (2) the type of the CM change. The first parameter allows us to make sure that only relevant system operation time is part of the assessment interval. For instance, we may have the desire to not only measure during the day but also at night. The second parameter, gives us the propagation time of the change.

Furthermore, the selection may depend on CM pattern knowledge. For example, if we know that a CM pattern is usually rejected, we may already recommend it for an undo before even starting the assessment interval. In this way, we can inform the SON Coordinator or the human operator that a harmful CM pattern is planned to be applied.

The second thing that we (optionally) do is to calculate a baseline cell level of the cells included in a scope. Note that the cell level is a high level performance indicator for the given cell, as described in Sect. 3. This particular cell level is used as a reference point to measure relative performance effects of the CM change group compared to the performance before the CM change was applied. Different methods of how this can be achieved have been described in [4,7,8].

2.4   Assessment Strategy Selection

The input of the scope generation step is the CM change group, and a set of cells composing the *scope of the CM assessment*. Since multiple parallel CM change groups can enter the assessment interval, we have decided to allow each CM change group to have its own assessment interval.

The assessment interval itself consists of assessment cycles which are driven by the selected assessment strategy. The goal of the assessment strategy is to collect and derive information about the performance impacts of the CM change so that the assessment can come to a decision. The output of the assessment cycle can either be that the CM change is *recommended to be accepted*, or to be *undone*. The CM change is accepted if it passes all the assessment cycles and rejected when it fails a single one.

2.5   Scoring of CM Changes

CM change(s) or change groups collect positive or negative scores based on the performance changes of cells in the scope. On the one hand we reward CM changes with positive scores that improve the performance of bad performing cells and/or do not impair the well performing ones. On the other hand we punish CM changes with negative scores that impair the performance of well performing cells and/or do not improve the performance of bad performing ones. CM changes accumulating significant negative scores are recommended for undo while CM changes accumulating positive scores are recommended to be accepted. In order to compute those scores, we need to perform the following steps:

- *Preparation*: calculate the baseline cell level B_{cl}, which is used as a performance reference point during the assessment.
- *Score collection*: each cell in the scope of a CM change is eligible to give assessment scores, which reflect the relative performance change of the cell since the CM change was applied.
- *Weighted average score computation*.
- *Cumulative scores*: the average score is added to the cumulative assessment score of the CM change.

– *Assessment decision*: the cumulative score is used to decide if the CM change passed or failed the actual assessment cycle.

During the preparation phase, B_{cl} is computed for all cells in the scope by taking the average cell level that has been reported during the last 24 h. The score collection phase is based on a *scoring function* used by each cell in the scope to provide feedback about the change of performance compared to the performance before the CM change was applied. The output of the function is the assessment score, which is defined as the function of the relative and signed difference of the actual cell level and the baseline cell level. In this paper we call this score the delta cell level D_{cl}.

As shown in Fig. 2(a), our scoring function has four zones: green, yellow, red, and gray zones. The green zone defines the score if the cell experiences significant performance improvements while the yellow and red zones define the score if it shows moderate or significant degradation. Furthermore, the scores defined by green, yellow, and red zones are the same for all cells in the scope. This, however, does not apply for gray zone scores which may differ for each cell in the scope. The main purpose why we have designed the function to have an additional zone is to observe changes when there is no significant change in performance. Contrary to the most common assumption, which tells that no change in performance is a "good thing" and we should reward or at least not punish it, we have a rather different opinion. If a cell shows good performance before the CM change is applied and the performance remains the same after the CM change, the scoring function should take this into account and award the CM change with positive scores. However, if a cell shows poor performance and the CM change that was applied does not improve the performance, it should be labeled as an ineffective and unnecessary change, and be punished by receiving negative scores. The reasons why we need to limit the number of unnecessary changes have been outlined in [4,5].

In Fig. 2(b) we show how scores are actually given. As long as B_{cl} is in the acceptable range between 0.7 and 1 (greed domain), positive scores are returned. However, if the cell shows poor performance and B_{cl} drops below 0.7 (red domain), we punish the CM change with negative scores.

3 Assessment of Cell Performance

The conceptual diagram of the performance assessment is shown in Fig. 3. This can be considered as an aggregation pyramid with low level, cell wise KPIs on the left and the cell level in the middle and the accumulate score value on the right. Note that in this paper we use the term KPI, however, we do not want to limit the proposed method only to KPIs but to any data source that reflects some aspect of the system's performance.

The raw KPI values are converted to KPI level values, which show how far individual cell KPIs are actually from the expectations when we compare them to the corresponding profiles. More precisely, the profiles determine the accepted domain of the raw KPI values, while the KPI level measures the distance of the

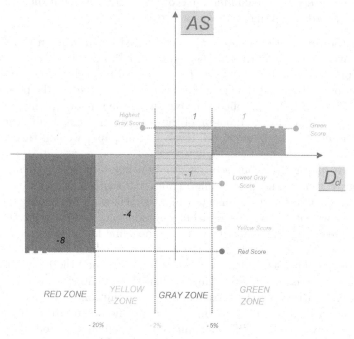

(a) Zones of the scoring function

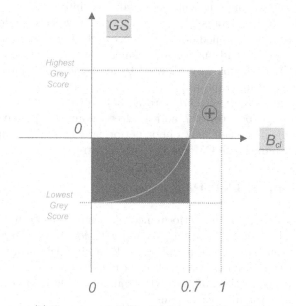

(b) Gray zone definition of the scoring function

Fig. 2. Properties of the scoring based assessment strategy (Color figure online)

actual raw KPI values from the profiles. The cell level is the aggregation of KPI levels and represent a cell's overall performance that reflects the overall behavior of the individual KPI level values. The more KPI levels are getting degraded, i.e., moving out of the acceptable domain, the more the cell level is getting degraded.

3.1 Profiling and KPI Level

The profile of a KPI is a mathematical model, which determines the acceptable domain of the KPI's values. Typical KPIs are the number of radio link failures, Call Setup Success Rate (CSSR), the Handover Success Rate (HOSR), the Channel Quality Indicator (CQI) and so on.

The profile is required to compute the *KPI level*, a value that depicts the deviation of a KPI from its expectation. To do so, the profile includes a training phase during which we collect samples $X_1 \ldots X_t$ for each KPI (t marks a training period). During this particular phase the network has to show an expected behavior. Furthermore, the duration of a training period depends on the granularity for gathering PM data from the network. For instance, it can correspond to an hour if KPIs are exported on hourly basis as presented in [7].

Then, we standardize the gathered data by computing the z-score of each data point $X_1 \ldots X_t, X_{t+1}$. Here, X_{t+1} corresponds to the current sample that we are going to observe. The level of a KPI corresponds to the z-score of X_{t+1}. It should be noted here that the KPI level can be considered as an anomaly value as well.

Let us give an example of how this may look like when we observe the CSSR for a given cell. Suppose that a cell has reported a success rate of 99.9 %, 99.9 %, 99.1 %, 99.7 %, 99.8 %, and 99.6 % during the training phase. Moreover, let us assume 90.2 % is the result from the current sampling period. The normalized result of all four samples would be 0.44, 0.44, 0.21, 0.38, 0.41, 0.35, and −2.26. The CSSR level equals to −2.26, which is the z-score of the current sampling period.

3.2 Cell Level

The cell level function creates an overall performance metric of individual cells. The output is the sum of the weighted KPI levels which we have named the *cell level*. The ability to change those weighting factors allows us to test a cell for different anomaly types. For example, we may take only handover related KPI levels into consideration when we assess the adjustments made by the Mobility Load Balancing (MLB) function.

The cell level has to fall within an acceptable range defined by two constants: c_{min} and c_{max}. Typical values for those two constants are −2.0 and 2.0, respectively. Any data-point that has a z-score higher than 2.0 or lower than −2.0 is an outlier, and likely to be an anomaly.

In addition to that, a detector is attached to this output to generate alarms if the cell levels get below a threshold. Moreover, a diagnosis module is activated by

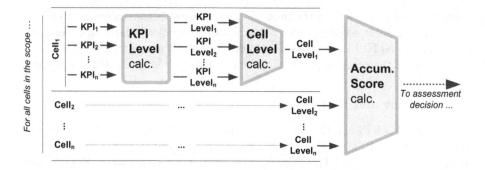

Fig. 3. Performance data aggregation overview

the detector and is used to generate detailed reports about the detected degradation. A report contains information about the worst performing cells (e.g., those having the lowest 10 % cell level values), the worst performing KPIs (i.e., the KPI levels aggregated in the observed scope, or among the worst performing cells), degradation patterns among the worst performing cells (i.e., identify groups of cells with a significantly different set of degraded KPIs).

4 Evaluation

As the next step of SON verification research work the assessment algorithm has been put in action to automatically verify the performance effect of antenna tilt optimizations in a WCDMA network.

4.1 Context and Environment

The main objective was to test the performance of the CCO capabilities of the network. Based on KPI analysis results the CCO algorithm identified some cells to be optimized by either increasing or decreasing the tilt angle of the serving antenna, i.e., down-tilting or up-tilting respectively. The recommended tilt changes have been accepted and deployed in the network by the network operations personnel on 4th of September 2014 between 09:00 and 09:15. The optimization impacted 21 WCDMA cells, 11 of which were down-tilted and 10 up-tilted. In order to be able to study the effects of these tilt changes on the performance of the corresponding part of the network (referred to as optimization area), a performance measurement dataset was created. The dataset contained the hourly resolution values of 90 KPIs (covering the most important performance aspects of a WCDMA network) collected in the optimized cells as well as in their neighbors (400 cells in total) between 5th of August 2014 and 7th of September, 2014. Note that the indicated time period contains data, which shows performance of the optimization area before as well as after the tilt changes were applied. This dataset was used as the input of the verification study.

The tilt changes are deployed by using Remote Electrical Tilt (RET) modules connected to antennas. However, there are usually more than one antenna

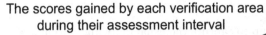

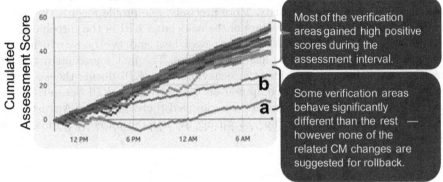

(a) The CM assessment result

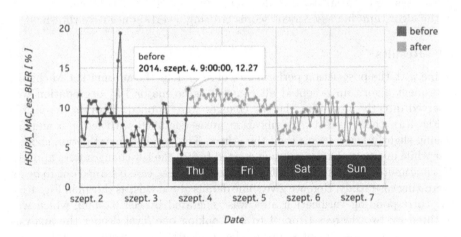

(b) The block error rate in the HSUPA MAC layer of cell W43072

Fig. 4. Impact of the CCO changes and their verification

connected to a single RET module, also called a shared RET module. In case of shared RET modules it is not possible to change the tilt angle of the connected cells independently. Consequently, in the scope of this study if the CCO algorithm suggested to change the tilt angle of a cell, which shares a single RET module with other cells, the tilt angel of all the other cells connected to the same RET module is changed. As a result we had to take 11 addition cells into account and verify the performance effects of the corresponding "forced" tilt changes. Finally, 32 tilt change events were taken into account during the study: 21 suggested by the CCO algorithm and 11 forced by the shared RET constraint.

4.2   Profiling Setup

In this study, a profile is set up to capture the usual daily fluctuation of a KPI of every cell with hourly granularity. More precisely, one profile records the mean and standard deviation of the values of the associated KPI in the corresponding cell. In addition, we distinguish between weekdays and weekends, which as a consequence leads each KPI to have two profiles. The first represents a typical weekday and other one describes the behavior of the KPI during the weekend. Furthermore, the profiles are computed on the part of the KPI dataset, which was collected before the tilt changes were applied (between 5th of August 2014 and 3rd of September 2014), thus, capturing the non-optimized performance of the optimization area.

4.3   Cell Level Computation

KPI levels are directly fed into the scoring algorithm, i.e., cell levels are not computed. This enables the system to drill down to the lowest possible level when explaining CM assessment decisions, e.g., a certain CM change is rejected by the algorithm due assessment scores crossing a certain negative threshold.

4.4   Results

In line with the post-action performance observations the automatic CM change assessment algorithm accepted all changes as no major PM degradation was observed directly after that the tilt changes were applied. However, as visible in Fig. 4(a), there were two verification areas (signified with letter a and b), gaining slightly lower scores than the others. The detailed investigation showed that while in case a the degradation started before the tilt changes were applied, thus not interesting from the verification point of view, case b turned out to be an interesting case study. Here we give some details about this, as shown in Fig. 4(b). The corresponding verification area was generated by cell W29598, which was up-tilted by two degrees (from 4 to 2). Looking one level deeper the analysis showed that the assessment scores of the verification area were pulled down by degradation of performance in one cell (W43072), which is the handover neighbor of W29598. We have analyzed the KPIs of this cell and observed that W43072 shows increased values of KPI measuring the block error rate in the HSUPA MAC layer (HSUPA_MAC_es_BLER) after cell W28598 was up-tilted as shown on the bottom left of Fig. 4(b). W28598's up-tilting was, however, not suggested by the CCO algorithm but was forced as W28598 is on the same RET module as cell W13107, which was selected by the CCO algorithm as candidate for a 2 degree up-tilt. Consequently, the CM assessment algorithm could reveal the hidden effect of an unintended tilt modification due to shared RET constraint, which was not taken into account by the CCO algorithm.

5   Related Work

While this paper is focused on applying our CM scoring method, SON verification itself is relevant from a broader use case point of view. One example is network acceptance [6] where typically fixed performance thresholds, fixed scopes (the area around a network element), and simple actions like an alarm to the network operator can be generated.

Another example is the deployment of CM undo actions. In [5], the problem of scheduling of conflicting CM undo actions has been introduced. According to the authors, a SON coordinator does not have the knowledge to resolve them and may, therefore, prevent them from being deployed. The presented approach of scheduling such undo actions makes use of minimum graph coloring in order to identify the sets of cells whose configuration can be safely rolled back. The network is partitioned in verification areas which are used as nodes during the coloring process. An edge between two nodes is added only when the two represented areas share anomalous cells that have not been reconfigured, also called a verification collision. The nodes getting the most frequently used color are marked for a CM undo.

Within the SOCRATES project [9] an idea has been introduced of how undesired network behavior can be potentially detected and resolved in a SON. The presented approach is realized by two functions: a Guard and an Alignment function. The purpose of the first one is to detect unusual network behavior like CM parameter oscillations or unexpected KPI combinations like a high Random Access Channel (RACH) rate and a low amount of carried traffic. The second one is responsible for taking countermeasures like undoing configuration changes assembled by a SON function and even suggesting SON function parameter adjustment.

In literature, several approaches have been presented of how to apply anomaly detection in mobile communication networks. In [10] topic modeling is applied to the PM data from all cells within the scope leading to the computation of topic model clusters that can be seen as indicators of the network state. Depending on the semantic interpretation, those clusters are classified as either normal or abnormal. In [11] a technique is presented that is based on an extended version of the incremental clustering algorithm Growing Neural Gas (GNG). This algorithm is known as Merge Growing Neural Gas (MGNG) and is focused on the capturing of input data behavior by taking the history data into account. Furthermore, it allows the learning of common sequences of input data and the prediction of their future values.

6   Conclusion

The existing pre-action Self-Organizing Network (SON) coordination scheme can be seen as a pessimistic approach where existing engineering knowledge is encoded into simple rules to avoid known issues in concurrently executing SON function instances. The trade-off is here that using a rule-based pro-active approach is relatively simple to implement into legacy systems, yet the knowledge implemented in the rules is rather simple. Therefore, the system may miss some relevant conditions and may enforce some coordination actions which may not be required for the specific condition. In a complementary way, SON verification is an optimistic (i.e., post-action) approach which evaluates the performance after each "round" of SON-induced actions being deployed to the network. The technical approach to realize SON verification is a type of anomaly detection and diagnosis tailored to the specific requirements. The trade-off is here that the verification is only getting active for really relevant conditions and can react also to previously *unknown* conditions which deviate significantly from the normal state. However, identifying those conditions reactively and even diagnosing their root causes is significantly more complex than just executing a set of rules.

In this paper, we addressed the problem of identifying such unknown conditions and finding at the same time the cause for them to occur. Our approach observes deployed Configuration Management (CM) changes, either computed by a SON function or manually set by the human operator. At first, we partition the network in so-called verification areas, also referred to as observation areas or scopes of verification. Then, we create an overall performance metric for each cell within a given scope, which we have named the cell level. This particular value is computed by aggregating a cell's Key Performance Indicator (KPI) levels which depict how far the KPI values actually are from their optimal domains. The computed values are used during the CM assessment interval which consists of one or more assessment cycles. During those cycles we reward or punish CM changes by giving them positive or negative scores. A key feature here, however, is the accumulation of the scores over time and punish unnecessary CM changes that did improve the network performance in case of a low cell level. The output of our approach is a recommendation to either accept or reject, i.e., undo the given configuration changes. We managed to evaluate it on real Wideband Code Division Multiple Access (WCDMA) data and outline a Coverage and Capacity Optimization (CCO) change that has led a certain part of the network to experience an anomalous behavior. This could not be foreseen by the CCO algorithm due to the shared Remote Electrical Tilt (RET) module.

References

1. Hämäläinen, S., Sanneck, H., Sartori, C. (eds.): LTE Self-Organising Networks (SON): Network Management Automation for Operational Efficiency. Wiley, Chichester (2011)
2. Bandh, T.: Coordination of autonomic function execution in Self-Organizing Networks. Ph.D. thesis, Technische Universität München, April 2013
3. Romeikat, R., Sanneck, H., Bandh, T.: Efficient, dynamic coordination of request batches in C-SON systems. In: IEEE Vehicular Technology Conference (VTC Spring 2013), Dresden, Germany, June 2013
4. Tsvetkov, T., Nováczki, S., Sanneck, H., Carle, G.: A post-action verification approach for automatic configuration parameter changes in self-organizing networks. In: Agüero, R., Zinner, T., Goleva, R., Timm-Giel, A., Tran-Gia, P. (eds.) MONAMI 2014. LNICST, vol. 141, pp. 135–148. Springer, Heidelberg (2015)
5. Tsvetkov, T., Sanneck, H., Carle, G.: A graph coloring approach for scheduling undo actions in self-organizing networks. In: IFIP/IEEE International Symposium on Integrated Network Management (IM 2015), Ottawa, Canada, May 2015

6. Ericsson: Transparent Network-Performance Verification for LTE Rollouts. White Paper, 284 23–3179 Uen, September 2012
7. Tsvetkov, T., Nováczki, S., Sanneck, H., Carle, G.: A configuration management assessment method for SON verification. In: International Workshop on Self-Organizing Networks (IWSON 2014), Barcelona, Spain, August 2014
8. Ciocarlie, G., Lindqvist, U., Nitz, K., Nováczki, S., Sanneck, H.: On the feasibility of deploying cell anomaly detection in operational cellular networks. In: IEEE/IFIP Network Operations and Management Symposium (NOMS 2014), Krakow, Poland, May 2014
9. Kürner, T., Amirijoo, M., Balan, I., van den Berg, H., Eisenblätter, A., et al.: Final Report on Self-Organisation and its Implications in Wireless Access Networks. Deliverable d5.9, Self-Optimisation and self-ConfiguRATion in wirelEss networkS (SOCRATES), January 2010
10. Ciocarlie, G.F., Connolly, C., Cheng, C.-C., Lindqvist, U., Nováczki, S., Sanneck, H., Naseer-ul-Islam, M.: Anomaly detection and diagnosis for automatic radio network verification. In: Agüero, R., Zinner, T., Goleva, R., Timm-Giel, A., Tran-Gia, P. (eds.) MONAMI 2014. LNICST, vol. 141, pp. 163–176. Springer, Heidelberg (2015)
11. Gajic, B., Nováczki, S., Mwanje, S.: An improved anomaly detection in mobile networks by using incremental time-aware clustering. In: IFIP/IEEE Workshop on Cognitive Network and Service Management (CogMan 2015), Ottawa, Canada, May 2015

The Shared Spectrum Service, Technology and Network Provision in Mobile Communication

Esko Luttinen[1(✉)] and Marcos Katz[2]

[1] University of Oulu, Oulu, Finland
eskok.luttinen@elisanet.fi
[2] Wireless Communications Department of Communication Engineering,
University of Oulu, Oulu, Finland
marcos.katz@ee.oulu.fi

Abstract. This text describes some developments of an explosive growth in mobile traffic demand. The growth has led to market driven approaches and need for more effective spectrum access and management. Regulatory, technology and economic issues have led to innovative strategic approaches and policies for more effective spectrum usages. This text seeks factors and possibilities to influence spectrum sharing and use of additional spectrum in mobile communication. Wireless network architecture defines functionalities, which impact on mobile subscriber's behavior both technically and economically. If telecommunication services fit together, interfaces between elements and services are the key. Economic assets form a new shared spectrum access, which means ubiquitous technical functionality, new service architectures and interfaces between different radio networks in the value-added chains. The modern radio networks form bit-pipes for added value services. For different stakeholders there are technology environment, economic environment and content wish environment in search for additional spectrum utility.

Keywords: Spectrum sharing and management · Additional spectrum · Cognitive radio · Mobile service · Technology and network provision

1 Introduction

Growth of mobile broadband will be significant in future. Mobile access, development of broadband networks, is increased especially in urban (U) and dense urban (DU) areas [1]. Planning of mobile needs requires efficient network planning, counting of engineering and strategic values. Communication markets are based on information technology (IT), cloud technology, big data handling and social communication technologies. The mobile communication changes customers' behavior: The questions are how to understand changes in mobile communication, how different operators are challenging it, and how subscribers challenge mobility possibilities. Current core competences, which are needed or should be mastered, mean features, which may become critical in future. Some of the competencies should be hold and some should be outsourced. Facilities of mobile telecommunication consist of mastering the

© Institute for Computer Sciences, Social Informatics and Telecommunications Engineering 2015
R. Agüero et al. (Eds.): MONAMI 2015, LNICST 158, pp. 16–27, 2015.
DOI: 10.1007/978-3-319-26925-2_2

technology, management all the services, logical chains and subscribers' wishes. Subscribers of mobile communication buy mobile products to solve their communication problems, regulators to serve nationwide needs and operators to make communication network and services profitable. Mobile system coverage, capacity, applications and modern devices facilitate demands for private and enterprise usages as well as in rural and metropolitan areas. Additional spectrum availability and agreement may fulfil coverage and capacity needs, if all quality issues (Quality of Services, QoS) are fulfilled [2].

Spectrum is an important asset and resource for mobile network operators (MNOs) and additional spectrum could provide significant business opportunities. The spectrum sharing concept has been understood in many international discussions meaning the idea of where MNOs could share spectrum from another type of spectrum users (incumbent) under the permission of the (national) spectrum regulator. On regulator point of view spectrum resourcing requires good management [3]. European RSPG (Radio Spectrum Policy group) search activities how to use spectrum more actively. RSPG make definitions and recommendations how collective use of spectrum could be possible. Those rules and instructions are listed in the document ECC Report 205 [4]. The report defines frequency allocation and authorization processes to harmonize the spectrum use in Europe and the report defines:

- individual rights of use
- national authorization

On business point of view the issue is linked to functional architecture, value network and financial model. The value of shared additional spectrum has to be defined. One might guess that local mobile sharing requires a reasonable large subscriber base and well defined network launch and management. More over introduction of growth in business of a MNO has to create new innovative services in creation of additional growth. Performance is still a challenge in spectrum use, because it requires flexibility, capabilities to learn radio environment and control of unpredictable operation in radio environments.

In USA the PCAST report [5] indicates that in the coming years, access to spectrum will be an increasingly important foundation for America's economic growth and technological leadership. In US the study covers the technical requirements, architecture and operational parameters of the proposal Spectrum Access System (SAS) for the 3550–3650 MHz band and not the band 2300–2400 MHz as in Europe. Also to launch the 4G LTE sharing additional technology additional tests will be required. The mobile communication changes the way of behavior and following question could be asked:

- What are spectrum management principles for broadband wireless, content services and applications in sharing?
- What are the technical solutions?
- How the value of shared spectrum could be defined and how it emerges with the mobile broadband in macro and small cell environments?

The rest of this paper is organized as follows. The mobile service provision is presented in Sect. 2. The mobile technology provision in Sect. 3 and the mobile network value provision in Sect. 4. Conclusions are drawn in Sect. 5.

2 Mobile Service Provision

Mobile communication business is characterized by political or governmental interest, cross-border work between countries, operators and services. Mobile communication subscribers can stream audio and video data to the network or load live events from the network. Loading can be done intelligently as the network bandwidth changes, but in real time traffic (like video-on demand, VoD) radio interface capabilities must be continuous. This includes also hand-over (HO) in case a subscriber is moving or is in a bad spectrum field. According to Cisco document [6] real time secondary distribution services requirement for standard definition (SD) video bit rates are 2–4 Mbps and for high definition video (HD) 8–20 Mbps. So the network provider has to manage and ensure the real time service distribution according to service level agreement (SLA). Generally, one could ask what does this mean for mobile telecommunication operators in terms of strategic and network planning. Network infrastructures must be designed for best-effort delivery to meet the exact requirements of next-generation communication services. This includes the real-time video, storage services, servers of internet service providers' networks, which are part of networking (Fig. 1).

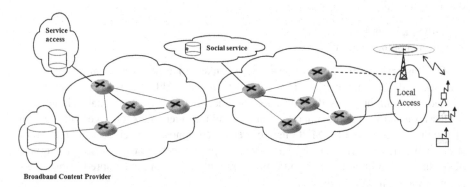

Fig. 1. Communication whenever, where ever: social media, entertainment, cloud computing, banking, Google web etc.

Mobile communication is in front of changes: widespread adoption of new technologies, development of business environment and the way to understand subscribers' behavior in getting new services. In other words it is an opportunity challenge to build new roles for value creation and capturing entrepreneurship [7]. The stakeholders such as spectrum regulators, mobile operators (dominating, incumbent or challenger MNO), subscribers, content-providers and device vendors have different needs in this challenge. Spectrum regulator in a country (National Regulatory Administration, NRA) wants to emphasize innovation and competitive landscape and ensure at the same time equal treatment to all involved stakeholders in spectrum usage cases. Internet players form a source of opportunities, and in some cases internet may be also a threat to nominal pure MNOs. As a whole, content service developers expect MNOs to be operator bit-pipes in information services. To widen MNOs' operations in some cases MNOs are strongly involved in the background of mobile service provisions. The use of radio systems depend on regulation, wireless business and technology development. Ubiquitous communication because of internet is in front of strategy considerations: mobile services, voice and data are challenged by disruptive alternatives of internet. As MNOs take care of the last mile connection new business opportunities are opened in internet world and subscriber requirement with new technologies open new killer applications.

Additional spectrum can bring some benefits for MNOs, but certain regulatory and operational restrictions must be taken into considerations as well as measurements before network launch. As the smart mobile devices and terminals handle internet connectivity in a native way today, the impact of these internet implementations are changing subscribers' behavior. Spectrum management between cellular, additive (cognitive) radio and/or Wi-Fi (see the Fig. 2) networks has to have technical maturity to handle interaction performance between primary and secondary systems and as well has to have a flexible connection to the public internet.

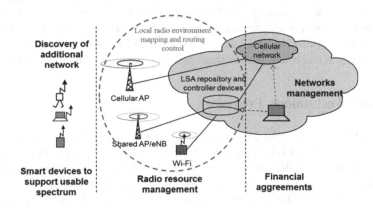

Fig. 2. Shared spectrum management [9]

Communication between networks requires elastic handover processes. In case of connection is from cognitive or Wi-Fi network to internet for capacity reasons, there is no added value of majority of the web traffic to route the data through the operator's core and cellular network. In this case the two networks are in practice totally separate. Management is depicted in the Fig. 2. In modern mobile communication uplink/downlink usage depends on an application. Some of the spectrum has remained unused for the past decade, which means that future candidate applications like terrestrial broadcasting, mobile broadband, mobile supplemental uplink or downlink, etc. application of spectrum requirements are to be defined. Quality requirement of spectrum handover scheme detects link failure and switches the connection to a new spectrum and system. Radio network resource of the MNO network handles access control, load control, power control and hand-over between systems [8].

Changes in mobile communications are sum of widespread adoption of new technologies, development of business environment and understanding how subscribers behave in getting new services. The stakeholders within the use of spectrum mean involvement of spectrum regulator, incumbent spectrum users like dominating MNO and challenger or incumbent MNO and subscribers. Spectrum regulator (NRA) wants to emphasize innovation and competitive landscape and ensure at the same time equal treatment to all involved stakeholders in spectrum usage cases. Internet players form a source of opportunities, and in some cases internet may be also a threat to nominal pure MNOs. As a whole, content service developers expect MNOs to be operator bit-pipes in information services. To widen MNOs' operations in some cases MNOs are strongly involved in the background of mobile service provisions. According to Ofcom report [10] price and speed are driving web-based communication. People at the age of 16–24 are more likely to use their mobile phone than computer in social networking and more and more adults are regular multi-users. Internet browsing is very common activity even when watching television.

The use of radio systems and communication interactors depend on regulation, wireless business and technology development. Ubiquitous communication, because of internet, is in front of strategy considerations: mobile services, voice and data are challenged by disruptive alternatives of internet. As MNOs take care of the last mile connection and networking new business opportunities are opened in internet world. Subscriber requirements and new technologies may open new killer applications.

3 Mobile Technology Provision

LTE FDD has been a mainstream for cellular mobile radio networks. There are references, which show that LTE TDD offers the potential advantages especially for small cell applications. Examples are presented in the documents [11, 12] and according to the documents LTE TDD is well suited to DL/UL traffic asymmetry, using only half of the band compared to FDD. This is the reason why regulators and industry are adopting combination of FDD and small cell TDD to better match the traffic asymmetry of data services and take full advantage of spectrum availability. LTE TDD was specified by the 3GPP already in release 8 for the use of mobile broadband radio access. LTE TDD shares its technical basis with LTE FDD, and LTE TDD is used in many countries already.

Requirement to support local and remote IP access is necessity, which should allow packet data traffic offload via used networks, is it home or corporate network to the public internet. Nowadays internet is a necessity in mobile value provision it is to tackle to the questions - What are the technical solutions – the ITU specification M.1225 [13] defines the combination of technical choices, concepts and a layered structure of radio interface: multiple access technology, modulation technology, channel coding and interleaving, RF-channel parameters such as bandwidth, allocation and channel spacing, duplexing technology, frame structure and physical channel structure and multiplexing.

The performance of shared spectrum is very challenging job for MNOs, device vendors and even local NRAs as regulating body. The interworking requires convincing use of certain services, the broad technical characteristics that may impact the economics and performance of the system. The sharing receiver should have knowledge of the spectrum availability and usability and what kind of communication needs are (as seen in the Fig. 3). Software is currently large portion of the network and device technical usability. With the increased intelligence by Nielsen [14] internet is a future playground. In OSI model [15] different communication technologies with similar functions are grouped into different logical layers of this model. Quality of software engineering product standards is ISO/IEC 9126 [16], where the usability measures are effectiveness, efficiency and satisfaction. Effectivity, efficiency, safety, utility, learnability and memorability are usability goals of interactions by Preece et al. [17].

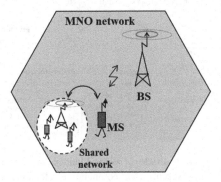

Fig. 3. Communication transfer between MNO macro network and a cognitive small cell

4   Mobile Network Value Provision

Mobile stakeholders have different operational concepts in business activities and in usability of radio network productivity. Productivity concept by Saari [18] defines relation to profitability, economic growth, efficiency, surplus value, quality, performance, partial productivity, need, etc. Model has objectives to exploit a business opportunity and to create value for the telecommunication stakeholders and to fulfill different stakeholders' needs and to create surplus [19].

   As internet connection is a necessity in mobile value provision, one could ask: "How the value of shared spectrum could be defined and how it emerges with the mobile broadband in macro and small cell environments"? This approach contributes a more positive perspective for further developments in the mobile communication markets. MNOs and service providers can increase their profits significantly, if they have lucrative killer applications with which the whole market potential will be realized. The competitive advantages and the business models of the key ecosystem players have to count how those emerge in the mobile broadband business. According to Ballon [20] existing mobile business models have to be reconsidered with regard to:

- *value proposition,*
- *revenue model, and*
- *architecture for value provisioning*

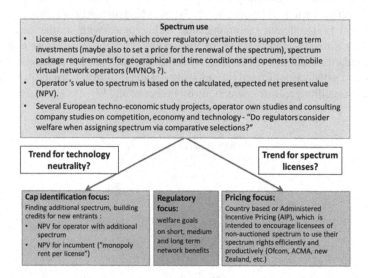

Fig. 4. Spectrum use: ideas from article of Gary Madden and Thien Tran: "Do regulators consider welfare when assigning spectrum via comparative selection?" [21].

Radio spectrum is a valuable and scarce resource, which makes a major contribution to economic and social development, and is necessary in ensuring national and civil security [21]. One view of spectrum use is seen in Fig. 4.

Broadband studies [22] show that economic impact is stronger in the regions of higher level of penetration. The economic goal of the radio spectrum is to maximize the net benefits to society. Spectrum values can also help to get significant revenues for the government. Spectrum value is defined by auctions, spectrum trading or leasing or by administrative means and spectrum management costs are based on authority or regulators rules of a country. Radio spectrum and broadband technology have been found to contribute to economic and business growth at several levels [23]. More efficient business processes like outsourcing services, virtual call centrums, adding virtual working methods, accelerating innovative service solutions and application of new commerce and financial services adopt spectrum efficiency. Mobile broadband telecommunication can be viewed as a methodology, which enables subscribers, society and companies to change their business processes and supply chains in introducing new products and services.

A. Network Sharing, Mobile Virtual Operation (MVNO) and Roaming

Proposals for sharing have been discussed for a long time and the report [24] lists management of sharing cases:

- *Sharing of sites and passive elements*
- *Sharing of antennas*
- *Sharing of base stations*

The passive network element sharing, site sharing and backhaul network of the leasing operator is a joint venture between two mobile operators.

If the MNO has spare capacity, MVNO existence at the markets is possible. The virtual network sharing has effect on capacity at wholesale level. The network capacity is determined on the basis of the MNO's frequency spectrum and the number of sites (capacity/area, subscriber grouping).

The international roaming is typical and supported by the majority of MNOs. The Body of European Regulators for Electronic Communications has launched a public set of regulation proposals, which will bring fundamental change to the structure of the European roaming market. The regulation would require European mobile network operators (MNOs) to open their networks to providers of voice and data roaming services acting as MVNOs, starting in July 2014 [25]. On business point of view is this threat to European MNOs' roaming revenues e.g. will new companies enter the market with compelling prices, brands and service propositions that can compete effectively with European operators? On European level there are guidelines which define some provisions for inadvertent roaming, addressing customer protection measures that operators can consider in roaming cases. In Europe BEREC's proposal for guidelines on roaming regulation is described in [26]. The new European digital market strategy concept is defied in the document [27].

B. Cellular Networks with Femto- and Macro cells

Femto cell is a small cellular base station (BS) designed to be located inside a building and using either DSL or cellular connection to backhaul traffic. The indoor environment is probably the most difficult in which to propagate radio signals. One-third of all mobile voice traffic is generated in the home or office [28]. Femto cells offer network carriers the opportunity to offload a lot of the traffic from their network assets to subscriber home-based cells that are backhauled through the IP core. A small cell base station (BS) is a typically low cost cellular BS with backhaul provided typically by broadband access network. Small cellular cells are offered to subscribers to allow the cellular home operations to improve indoor service coverage with small additional cost to subscribers. Interference management and capacity requirements associate challenges for small cells. As macro cells BS are operator-owned and maintained, small cells may be customer-bought. If there are several small cells in some area with coverage zone of the operator macro cells the operator has to address optimal resource allocation between macro and small cells. Such a deployment may make interference scenarios complicated. The MNO needs coordination between operator's own macro cells and surrounding small cells. In some cases self-configuration can be utilized to avoid severe interferences to maintain the SLA (mobile service level agreement) at adequate level to the small cell subscribers [29, 30].

The introduction of small cells creates a new architecture for mobile operators. The small cell architecture is one component in the networks and operators are looking solutions for addressing the fast-growing wireless data usage demands to provide higher data rates and better quality of experience to the end-users [31]. According to Qualcom unlicensed LTE can give advances in spectrum efficiency and it provides better range than carrier Wi-Fi [32]. Even though LTE is expected to be the biggest driver for future small cells to deploy for coverage and capacity in high traffic areas, mobile network operators seek tighter integration between cellular and non-cellular.

Multifunction subscriber devices support also other radio systems, like Wi-Fi etc. The load of cellular spectrum environments is freed and home networks can widen with help of DHCP (Dynamic Host Configuration Protocol), where TCP/IP networking parameters are automatically distributed from the DHCP server to computers or smart devices. A network administrator needs are reduced, and user network configurations are set. In home network address translation (NAT, network address translation) provides a method to modify network address information and home network has only one IP address.

One example of small cells is the Japanese government aims to license 120 MHz of the 3.5 GHz band for 3 LTE-TDD operators with the 40 MHz block for each successful bidder with the requirement of commercial network plan in 2016 [33].

C. Cognitive Spectrum use

The MNO can use an additional cognitive spectrum for capacity reasons either constantly or for timely basis most probably in dense urban environments. In both of the cases the MNO has to negotiate with local NRA to get permission for the extra use of spectrum and find the proper incumbent and spectrum gap to start sharing joint venture discussions. For the purpose the MNO has to have reasonable subscriber base to make this additional cognitive radio lucrative. Another thing is, are there any other obligations to cover.

In Europe additive spectrum discussions covers the 2.3–2.4 GHz band. The rules and instructions are listed in the ECC Report 205 [4], where frequency allocation and authorization processes are defined. As there are several users in different European countries the interference free use requires high cooperation and time. This is an additional radio spectrum and subscriber has to have this spectrum hole supporting devices. The MNO has to have a repository system (see Fig. 2) to control the traffic balancing and control HO cases. In heavy load use subscriber's device finds an additional spectrum and recognizes spectrum opportunities and channel selection decisions are made. This sharing spectrum usage has to learn how subscribers of the MNO are exploiting the MNO spectrum, and then MNO can exploit the opportunity of sharing. Discovery of an empty local additive (cognitive) radio spectrum block with no additional spectrum incumbent users adds the MNO spectrum capacity. In US the additional spectrum study covers the technical requirements, architecture and operational parameters of the proposal Spectrum Access System (SAS) for the 3550–3650 MHz band [5].

Shared additional spectrum use is now based on network operators, MNO and incumbents, measured spectrum data. From potential users point of view it would be important to characterize how long shared communication channel blocks would be available. This means definitions of call durations and thresholds for changes. In case of increased activity of shared channel subscribers, the systems have to measure and estimate probabilities for a new channel block. Possibilities are either new free own primary (MNO) resource block, and if those are assumed to be crowded, to discover a new spectrum block of shared access. The situation is more complex as behavior of PUs and SUs are independent random variables and how are usable resource blocks at shared spectrum available? If shared spectrum usage is based on measured shared channel data and expected behavior of PUs and SUs, the MNO and incumbent must or could make suitable connection algorithms for the acceptable use of the shared spectrum, which is sometimes settled case by case. The parameters needed are used broadband bandwidth, type of communication (RT or NRT), various power levels, modulation used, possible neighboring channel blocks, HO procedures etc. Shared channel activities and complexity of communication depend on call durations, which may be based on traffic load distributions and MNO and incumbent network owner statistic and measurements.

5 Conclusions

Mobile telecommunication service architecture requires interfaces between different radio networks in the value-added chains. The modern radio networks form bit-pipes for added value services. For stakeholders additional spectrum mean technology environment, economic environment and content wish environment. Firstly mobile operators need lucrative additional spectrum possibilities, secondly regulators have to have clear procedures for spectrum sharing and thirdly future technologies have to support the additional spectrum sharing. For mobile network operator there are mathematic modelling tools to calculate net presenting values. The main value of this business reasoning is that it requires reasonable good subscriber base to be profitable. Spectrum sharing need also radio environment mapping and routing control to manage network hand-overs and continuous mobile communication.

The discussions of the shared mobile communication form a question can additional spectrum provide significant business opportunities? On business point of view the issue is linked to network functional architecture, value networks and finance models. Performance is still a challenge in spectrum sharing and this requires flexibility, capabilities to learn radio environments and control of unpredictable occasions in the radio environment. Possible use of additional spectrum requires support of wireless devices and a network provider must combine and manage last mile connection and meet transport technologies to serve intended service level agreement needs. Mobile broadband will take a significant telecommunication market share and assumption is that the IT industry's growth, cloud technology, big data handling, social technologies using mobile are changing customer behavior.

References

1. Digital Europe: Digital Europe position paper on licensed shared access (LSA) common understanding, status and next steps, February 2013. http://www.digitaleurope.org/
2. ITU Document SMIS/07. www.itu.org. Accessed 10 January 2007

3. Mölleryd, B.G., Markendahl, J., Mäkitalo, Ö.: Spectrum valuation derived from network deployment and strategic positioning with different levels of spectrum in 800 MHz, May 2010. http://www.wireless.kth.se/
4. ECC report 205, Licensed Shared Access (LSA), February 2014
5. The president's council of advisors on science and technology (PCAST) report, Executive Office of the President President's Council of Advisors on Science and Technology, July 2012
6. Cisco White paper: IP/MPLS network optimise video transport for service provider (2011). www.cisco.com/
7. Pagani, Margherita, Fine, Charles H.: Value network dynamics in 3G-4G wireless communication: a system thinking approach to strategic value assessment. J. Bus. Res. **61**, 1102–1112 (2008)
8. Holma, H., Toskala, A.: WCDMA for UMTS. Wiley, New York (2000). ISBN 0471720518
9. Luttinen, E., Matinmikko, M., Ahokangas, P., Katz, M., Yrjölä, S.: Feasibility assessment of licensed shared access (LSA) concept – case of a finnish mobile network operator (MNO). In: 1st International Conference on 5G for Ubiquitous Connectivity, Levi, Finland (2014)
10. Ofcom: Communications market report, 1 August 2013
11. Accelleran: White Paper, the essential importance of LTE TDD for small cell deployments, July 2013. www.acceleran.com/sites/default/files/AcceleranWP101_0.pdf
12. Informa Telecoms & Media: Report on small cell market status, February 2013
13. Rec. ITU-R M.1225: Guidelines for evaluation of radio transmission technologies for IMT-2000 (1997)
14. Nielsen, J.: Progress in usability: fast or slow? "Over the past decade, usability improved by 6 % per year. This is a faster rate than most other fields, but much slower than technology advances might have predicted". http://www.nngroup.com/articles/progress-in-usability-fast-or-slow/. Accessed 22 February 2010
15. The Open Systems Interconnection model (OSI model). https://en.wikipedia.org/wiki/OSI_model
16. ISO/IEC 9126. http://www.iso.org/iso/catalogue_detail.htm?csnumber=22749
17. Preece, J., Rogers, Y., Sharp, H.: Interaction Design: Beyond Human-Computer Interaction. Wiley, New York (2002)
18. Saari, S.: Productivity theory and measurement in business. In: Tuottavuus. Teoria ja mittaaminen liiketoiminnassa, Tuottavuuden käsikirja. MIDO OY. 172 s. (2006)
19. Zott, C., Amit, R.: Business model design: an activity system perspective. Long Range Plan. **43**, 216–226 (2010). https://mgmt.wharton.upenn.edu/files/
20. Ballon, P.: Control and value in mobile communications: a political economy of the reconfiguration of business models in the European mobile industry. http://papers.ssrn.com/sol3/papers.cfm?abstract_id=1331439
21. Madden, Gary, Tran, Thien: Do regulators consider welfare when assigning spectrum via comparative selections. Appl. Econ. Lett. **20**, 852–856 (2013)
22. Katz, R.L., Avila, J.G.: The impact of broadband policy on the economy. In: Proceedings of the 4th ACORN-REDECOM Conference, Brasilia, 14–15 May 2010. http://www.acorn-redecom.org/papers/acornredecom2010katz.pdf
23. RSPG: The Radio Spectrum Policy Group is a high-level advisory group. http://rspg-spectrum.eu/
24. IST-2000-25172 Tonic, Deliverable 11, Final report on seamless mobile IP service provisions economics, 31 October 2002

25. Lambert, P.: Senior Analyst at Informa Telecoms & Media, comments on the proposed changes to European roaming regulations European operators need to develop a coherent strategy to prepare for the arrival of roaming MVNOs in 2014, pp. 1–2. Mobile communication Europe, Strategic intelligence on mobile operators & markets, Issue 584, May 21, 2013

26. Body of European Regulators for Electronic Communications, BEREC: International roaming regulation, BEREC guidelines on roaming regulation (EC) no 531/2012, March 2013. http://berec.europa.eu/eng/document_register/subject_matter/berec/regulatory_best_practices/guidelines/1188-berec-guidelines-on-roaming-regulation-ec-no-5312012-third-roaming-regulationexcluding-articles-3-4-and-5-on-wholesale-access-and-separate-sale-of-services

27. Communication from the commission to the European parliament, the council, the European economic and social committee and the committee of regions. A Digital Market Strategy for Europe, SWD (2015) 100 Final, Brussels, 6 May 2015

28. Hoppi, P., Martinac, I.: Indoor climate and air quality review of current and future topics in the field of ISB study group 10. Int. J. Biometeorol. **42**, 1 (1998)

29. Macaluso, I., Forde, T.K., DaSilva, L., Doyle, L.: Impact of cognitive radio, recognition and informed exploitation of gray spectrum opportunities. IEEE Veh. Technol. Mag. **7**, 85–90 (2012)

30. Shi, Y., MacKenzie, A.B., DaSilva, L.A., Ghaboosi, K., Latva-aho, M.: On resource reuse of cellular networks with femto- and macrocell coexistence. In: IEEE Communication Society 2010 Proceedings

31. 4G Americas: 4G mobile broadband evolution: release 10, release 11 - HSPA + SAE/LTE and LTE advanced, pp. 41–42. www.4gamericas.org. Accessed October 2012

32. Qualcom: Extending the benefits of LTE advanced to unlicensed spectrum (2013)

33. Global Telecom Business, 02 September 2014

Alarm Prioritization and Diagnosis for Cellular Networks

Gabriela F. Ciocarlie[1][✉], Eric Yeh[1], Christopher Connolly[1], Cherita Corbett[1],
Ulf Lindqvist[1], Henning Sanneck[2], Kimmo Hatonen[3], Szabolcs Nováczki[4],
Muhammad Naseer-Ul-Islam[2], and Borislava Gajic[2]

[1] SRI International, Menlo Park, CA, USA
{gabriela.ciocarlie,eric.yeh,christopher.connolly,
cherita.corbett,ulf.lindqvist}@sri.com
[2] Nokia Networks Research, Munich, Germany
{henning.sanneck,muhammad.naseer-ul-islam,borislava.gajic}@nokia.com
[3] Nokia Networks Research, Espoo, Finland
kimmo.hatonen@nokia.com
[4] Nokia Networks Research, Budapest, Hungary
szabolcs.novaczki@nokia.com

Abstract. Alarm events occurring in telecommunication networks can be an invaluable tool for network operators. However, given the size and complexity of today's networks, handling of alarm events represents a challenge in itself, due to two key aspects: high volume and lack of descriptiveness. The latter derives from the fact that not all alarm events report the actual source of failure. A failure in a higher-level managed object could result in alarm events observed on its controlled objects. In addition, alarm events may not be indicative of network distress, as many devices have automatic fallback solutions that may permit normal network operation to continue. Indeed, given the amount of equipment in a network, there can be a "normal" amount of failure that occurs on a regular basis; if each alarm is treated with equal attention, the volume can quickly become untenable. To address these shortcomings, we propose a novel framework that prioritizes and diagnoses alarm events. We rely on a priori information about the managed network structure, relationships, and fault management practices, and use a probabilistic logic engine that allows evidence and rules to be encoded as sentences in first order logic. Our work, tested using real cellular network data, achieves a significant reduction in the amount of analyzed objects in the network by combining alarms into sub-graphs and prioritizing them, and offers the most probable diagnosis outcome.

Keywords: Network automation · Self-organized networks (SON) · Alarm events · Anomaly detection · Diagnosis · Prioritization

1 Introduction

One of the key challenges faced by telecommunication network operators is the management of alarm events issued by managed objects in the network.

© Institute for Computer Sciences, Social Informatics and Telecommunications Engineering 2015
R. Agüero et al. (Eds.): MONAMI 2015, LNICST 158, pp. 28–42, 2015.
DOI: 10.1007/978-3-319-26925-2_3

As network failures can lead to a loss of revenue for the network operator, being able to identify and rectify these failures in a timely fashion is clearly a priority. However, alarm management faces two challenges: volume and descriptiveness. First, the number of discrete alarm events can easily reach tens of thousands per day. This high volume of events makes responding to every alarm a difficult, or more likely, impossible task for most operators. This is also compounded by the fact that there is commonly a level of alarm activity that occurs regularly within a network, and not all of it is indicative of actual network distress. Second, alarms themselves frequently do not describe the actual cause for a failure. For example, alarms may be a result of topological masking, where failures in a high-level or otherwise related component can result in alarms on downstream objects [5]. A failure in a basestation could result in a failure on a cell managed by that basestation, resulting in an alarm event on that cell. Attempting to rectify the problem at that cell would be pointless, as the true cause lies at the basestation level. To make matter worse, these alarms could be reflections of events outside of the network itself. For example, a third-party leased line connecting a set of basestations on the network could unexpectedly break down. The drop in connectivity between these basestations would trigger alarm events indicating failure to connect to each other. However, as the network data model does not describe the leased line, the alarms taken individually would not be able to identify that as the true cause of the failure.

This paper addresses these core needs of organizing and prioritizing alarm events in a network. Current techniques to perform this form of alarm correlation have fallen into two separate bins: data-driven [5,10] and rule-based [10] methods. The former are adaptable to networks, and are intended to facilitate discovery of causes of failure, whether they are repeating patterns of events or a possible point of failure. However, they offer little in the way of concrete diagnostic or prioritization capabilities, as they operate solely on derived statistics and do not incorporate knowledge about the network itself. Rule-based methods offer strong diagnostic capabilities as they do leverage background knowledge about a given network, but are inflexible to new networks or updates to the underlying network itself. Accommodating these changes requires an expert to construct new rules, which historically has proven to be an expensive task. What is needed is a mix of both: a method that can flexibly adapt to new networks while retaining as much background knowledge, and diagnostic capability, as well.

Contributions. This paper proposes novel techniques for determining how anomalous or fault effects are observed through the network using a priori information about the managed network structure, relationships, and fault management practices. The aim is to alleviate operator load by organizing and prioritizing alarm events in a mobile broadband network, and to produce diagnostics when relevant. Main contributions include:

– automatically generating alarm sub-graphs, based on correlated network objects using alarm event temporal windows, FM event data, and managed object and adjacency,

– featurizing the sub-graphs themselves for determining both prioritization and diagnostic information,
– using Markov Logic Networks to easily incorporation background knowledge, in the form of first order logic, into a probabilistic reasoning system.

2   Alarm Prioritization and Diagnosis

We rely on a priori information about the managed network structure, relationships, and fault management practices to determine how the effects of faults are observed through the network. We also alleviate operator load by organizing and prioritizing alarm events, and produce diagnostics when relevant. We model the network as a graph based on hierarchical and adjacency relationships. Unlike prior work that also derived graphs solely from managed object hierarchy information [1], we extract features from alarm sub-graphs, which are network objects correlated together based on managed objects, adjacency information and temporal occurrences of alarms.

2.1   Overall Framework

Figure 1 illustrates the overall approach. Network graph data (1) and alarm event data (2) are both collected by the target broadband network. Our Alarm Sub-graph Generation component (3) performs alarm correlation, incorporating network graph data as well as temporal alarm information to create alarm sub-graphs (4). Sub-graphs are interconnected network objects exhibiting overlapping alarm events.

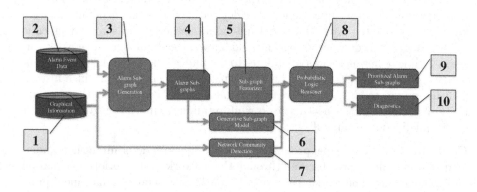

Fig. 1. Overall approach of the alarm prioritization and diagnosis approach. Raw data is depicted in grey, processed data in blue and methods in green.

These alarm sub-graphs are passed to a sub-graph featurizer (5), a novel component that assesses each sub-graph and produces features, i.e. weighted predicates describing characteristics of that alarm sub-graph. Features are derived from a variety of sources, such as the distribution of object types in the sub-graph, as well as characterizations obtained using probabilistic measures derived over the data, such the rarity of a sub-graph. Additionally, we construct a probabilistic generative model of the alarm sub-graphs (6) to characterize their rarity, and use community detection algorithms (7) to identify clusters of objects that may have a stronger influence on each other. To the best of our knowledge, both of these are novel in their application in the network communications domain.

The components above are used as inputs to a probabilistic logic engine that allows evidence and rules to be encoded as sentences in first order logic (8). Using Markov Logic Networks (MLN) [13] as probabilistic logic engines allows us to incorporate this type of background knowledge more readily than purely statistics-driven approaches. MLN rules are encoded in first order logic, allowing experts to more easily express this knowledge. As MLNs perform probabilistic inference, we can accommodate uncertainty and inconsistencies that plague prior rule-based systems [10]. Rules and observations are assigned weights, and probabilistic inference allows the system to determine marginal probabilities associated with hypotheses of interest (where the marginal probability of a hypothesis is the probability of being true irrespective of the other hypotheses). This enables background knowledge to be merged with evidence in a probabilistic fashion, allowing for incomplete and uncertain observations. The set of rules that operates over the alarm sub-graph evidence is used to derive a probabilistically-motivated ranking of sub-graphs by priority (9), as well as diagnostic information (10) when applicable. While output in the form of prioritized alarm sub-graphs and diagnosis information relates to the state of the art, the processes of generating both the prioritization and diagnosis information are novel.

2.2   Alarm Sub-Graph Formulation and Featurizer

The basis for our alarm correlation and diagnostic system consists of alarm sub-graphs, which are groups of network objects connected by network graph relationships that have exhibited alarm events. Network graph relationships encompass both hierarchical relationships (e.g., between a basestation and its constituent cells) and planned adjacencies. To identify the set of sub-graphs from a graph of a given network and the alarm events within a given time span, we first identify edges between objects that have had at least one temporally overlapping alarm event. We then extract sub-graphs by finding constellations of objects that are not connected to each other.

For each sub-graph, we generate a set of features that characterize that sub-graph. Features are propositions that describe some characteristic of the sub-graph. Example features determined based on sub-graph statistics include:

- All objects are of one type (e.g., basestation, .cell);
- The majority of objects (determined as the maximum count per object type) are of a certain type (e.g., basestations, cells);
- The sub-graph is a singleton, containing only one object;
- In the case of singletons, the type of the object;

- The sub-graph is heavily connected, or exhibits a large number of edges (determined by the standard deviation from the mean) between its objects;
- The sub-graph is large, medium, or small, determined by the size distribution over the dataset;
- The sub-graph is rare or frequent, as determined by a probabilistic alarm sub-graph generation model.

2.3   Data-Derived Generative Probabilistic Model

In prior studies, networks have been shown to exhibit a certain background level of alarm activity. However, the alarm background may not necessarily be indicative of a major event. Although every alarm should be resolved, in practice, operators' attention is a limited resource and therefore some alarms have greater priority than others, particularly those that are unusual or rare. To account for this, we construct a probabilistic graphical model that uses statistics from a given dataset to arrive at a score for a given alarm sub-graph, computed as a quantitative measure of priority or likelihood of indicating a root cause. We use this score to rank sub-graphs as frequent versus unusual, with the latter category given higher priority. We formulate a given alarm sub-graph as a Markov model, with the likelihood of observing that sub-graph as:

$$P(O, M, N) = \prod_o \prod_m P(o'|o, m)P(m|o)P(o|N)P(N) \tag{1}$$

where o represents the type of managed object (e.g., basestation, cell) in the graph, m represents the edge degree of the node, O and M represent the vector of object type assignments and edge degrees for all of the managed objects in the graph, N represents the number of objects in this sub-graph, $P(o'|o, m)$ represents the probability of observing an edge starting with an object with type o and ending with an object type o' (conditioned on the edge degree of the starting object), $P(m|o)$ represents the edge degree for the given object type, and $P(o|N)$ represents the probability of seeing a node with the given object type given the size of the sub-graph.

To simplify the model, we make additional independence assumptions:

- The probability of an edge occurring is independent of the node's degree as well as the number of nodes in the graph, or $P(o'|o, m) = P(o'|o)$, $P(o'|o, N) = P(o'|o)$;
- Edges from node o are determined independently of each other, and are also independent of the number of nodes in the graph, or $P(o'|o) = \prod_{o'} P(o'|o)$, $P(o'|o, N) = P(o'|o)$;
- The node types are determined independently of all the other nodes, or $P(O|N) = \prod_o P(o|N)$.

Note that this formulation would double count edges, as we currently do not consider directionality in the model. However, this is unlikely to have negative effects given that our goal is to obtain a ranking between alarm sub-graphs.

To account for possible sparsity, we apply Laplacian noise modeling. Furthermore, if a background corpus of alarm information was available from another network, it can be incorporated via Dirichlet smoothing. In this formulation, the probability estimate is reframed as:

$$P(o'|o) = \frac{I(o'|o) + \mu P(o'_c|o_c)}{E + \mu}$$ (2)

where $I(o'|o)$ represents the frequency of edge transition o to o', E is the number of edges, $P(o'_c|o_c)$ representing the probability derived from the background corpus and μ represents a weighting factor, with larger values giving more weight to the background corpus.

Note that an inherent property of this model is that the more objects there are, the lower the likelihood of observing the graph. We view this as a desirable property, as larger alarm sub-graphs would be considered rarer events compared with other sub-graphs, and thus could very well be indicative of network distress.

2.4   Network Community Generation

One of the key techniques in graph analysis is the identification of communities [2], i.e. groups of objects that are more interconnected with each other than one would expect. Objects that are connected would be more likely to "influence" each other, or, in other words, to exhibit any anomalies or faults together, due to underlying phenomena such as topological masking. In our case, we wish to identify groups of nodes that are more likely to influence each other, given their proximity in the influence network. To identify these communities, we apply two methods: modularity analysis and force-directed layout. Modularity analysis generates a "hard" clustering, and assigns nodes to discrete communities based upon how much more strongly they are connected with each other than if edges were assigned by chance. Force-directed layouts are a way to project the relationships between nodes and edges into a lower dimensional space, and are most often used to make tightly connected nodes more apparent in visualizations. This class of algorithms assigns spatial locations for nodes based on an attraction and repulsion algorithm. Specifically, all nodes exhibit mutual repulsion; those with edges between them have an attractive force. A node layout solution that minimizes the overall energy resulting from these forces generally results in strongly connected communities being closer to each other to produce an intuitively understandable visual layout.

The modularity score of a graph, Q, measures how many more edges appear in a community than if the edges were assigned by chance. Q is given by:

$$Q = \frac{1}{2m} \sum_{v,w} [A_{v,w} - \frac{k_v k_w}{2m}] \delta(c_v c_w)$$ (3)

where m is the number of edges in the graph, the values v and w are node indices, A_{vw} indicates the actual number of edges between nodes v and w, k_v and k_w are their edge degrees, and c_v and c_w their modularity class assignments. The term $\delta(c_v c_w)$ is an indicator variable, set to 1 if the modularity assignment for node v is equal to the one for node w. The term $\dfrac{k_v k_w}{2m}$ corresponds to the expected number of edges between the two nodes, if edges were assigned at random while respecting the original node degrees. As there are $2m$ possible edge assignments, the Q score represents the difference between the fraction of edges occurring within the assigned communities and the fraction that would have been expected in that group. Community assignments c that have an unusually large number of edges between their nodes would thus increase the Q score.

Both the assignments and the number of classes considered are determined by an iterative procedure until the modularity score meets a predetermined threshold, or until no more communities can be added without degrading the score. For our analyses, we used the default setting of 1.0.

For the force directed layout, we used the ForceAtlas2 algorithm [8], which was originally implemented in order to address deficiencies in existing force layout algorithms. Here, the attraction between two connected nodes, $F_a(n_1, n_2)$, is linearly correlated with their distance in the visualization:

$$F_a(n_1, n_2) = d(n_1, n_2) \tag{4}$$

Repulsion between two nodes, $F_r(n_1, n_2)$, is inversely proportional to their distance and directly proportional to the product of their degrees:

$$F_r(n_1, n_2) = \frac{(deg(n_1) + 1)(deg(n_2) + 1)}{d(n_1, n_2)} \tag{5}$$

The intent here is to allow leaves and other poorly connected nodes to move closer to hubs, which have a higher edge degree.

2.5 Markov-Logic Networks for Prioritization and Diagnostics from Alarm Sub-Graphs

Given an alarm sub-graph and a set of constituent features, we combine these against a backdrop of rules and heuristics to obtain prioritization and diagnostic information. Markov Logic Networks (MLN) [13] provide a formalism that allows rules to be expressed in first order logic, but with probabilistic inference. In contrast to approaches like Bayesian Networks [7] or Markov Random Fields [14], the use of first order logic allows a greater degree of flexibility, describing relationships in terms of variables over sets, instead of the instances themselves. Unlike existing rule-based systems, probabilistic inference grants the ability to tolerate noise and uncertainty. These rules are weighted, giving authors the ability to weigh them against each other. This also allows an existing ruleset with different levels of generality to derive hypotheses over a new network. Inference here is conducted using a Monte Carlo sampling algorithm with Boolean satisfiability solving techniques.

To obtain prioritization and diagnostic information from a set of sub-graphs, we first add their features as observations to the MLN inference engine (for our experiments we used the Probabilistic Consistency Engine (PCE) [12]). We then query the system to obtain the probability of occurrence for the set of observations. For prioritization, these probabilities are used to rank sub-graphs for receiving human attention. For diagnostics, they quantify whether a given diagnostic has a higher likelihood of explaining the observations than random chance.

The PCE input language, which is used to express MLNs, consists of the following elements:

1. Definition of types (also called "sorts"). In the alarm sub-graph case, these correspond to alarm sub-graphs.
2. Enumeration of the sets corresponding to each type. In this case, these are the observed sub-graphs.
3. Declarations of the predicates to be used, and the types of each argument. Here, a predicate would be $prioritize(sub-graph)$, which indicates the given alarm sub-graph should be prioritized.
4. A set of weighted clauses comprising the probabilistic knowledge base. An example would be $abnormal(sub-graph) \rightarrow prioritize(sub-graph)2.0$, meaning that if a sub-graph was deemed abnormal by an analysis component, its priority is raised by the given weight.
5. Assertions (predicate forms that express information that is known to be true). Here, these would be the set of observed alarm sub-graphs, along with any other derived observations generated by our analysis tools.

Each clause is an expression in first-order logic. MLNs search for the most likely explanation for the knowledge base in terms of the assignments of variables to predicate arguments. MLNs accumulate the probabilities that each clause is true, given a particular variable assignment. One can also query the knowledge base and ask for the probability that a specific predicate is true under a specific variable assignment or ask how often a predicate is true in general. MLN solvers generally approach the problem by using a Monte Carlo sampling algorithm with satisfiability (SAT) solving techniques.

3   Experimental Evaluation

This section analyzes our framework applied to a real network dataset. The experimental corpus consists of alarm-event data for approximately 3,300 cells, collected from 11/25/2013 to 12/15/2013. The network elements in this dataset are represented as managed objects, for which relationships with the neighboring elements are given, and which are grouped into managed object classes. The managed object classes were tracked through a hierarchy of elements.

Using the 496 available hourly timeslices in our dataset, we automatically identified the alarmed sub-graphs using one-hour windows and generated a PCE [12] ruleset for each of these timeslices. We then ran inference over each of these timeslices, and queried both the priorities that should be assigned to each alarm sub-graph, and the diagnostic information, if available.

3.1   Alarm Sub-Graphs for Diagnostics and Prioritization

Using our network-wide graph-based visualization tool, we identified several interesting timeslices to analyze, based on the size and number of alarm events. One such interesting timeslice is the one for Dec 1st 2013, from 1700–1800 CET. Within this hour there were 673 alarms; after applying our sub-graph analysis we arrived at 28 alarm sub-graphs, providing a significant reduction in data that a human operator would need to investigate. 16 of these sub-graphs were singletons (only one network object), and the remaining were sub-graphs consisting of multiple objects. Figure 2 illustrates the overall network state when viewed from the topologically motivated point of view. An alternative view is

Fig. 2. Graph-level visualization of a portion of the network state at Dec 1st, 1700–1800 CET. Red objects correspond to alarmed objects in the network. Alarmed sub-graphs are highlighted by the red edges between their objects. Purple indicates the object exhibited a high probability of an anomaly. Green indicates a configuration management change was applied, with size indicating the number of changes applied in that window.

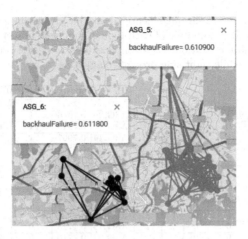

Fig. 3. Graph-level visualization of a portion of the network state at Dec 1st, 1700–1800 CET. The graph-level analysis was overlaid using the lat/long coordinates of the object's multi-radio basestation (MRBTS). Circles correspond to objects that had one or more alarm events within that time window, and edge objects indicate that these belonged to the same alarm sub-graph. As visualization is at the MRBTS level, edges represent planned adjacencies between the MRBTS objects themselves or their objects further down the control hierarchy.

provided by Fig. 3, which illustrates the latitude/longitude coordinates of the alarmed objects. Here, we show a subset of the network state, along with the alarmed objects. As lat/longs were only available for objects at the basestation level, edges are drawn only between basestations or controlled objects that have planned adjacencies with each other.

Table 1 lists the 28 identified alarm sub-graphs with the distribution of managed object types, ranked by priority, which was generated based on the rules presented in Fig. 4. The top five prioritized sub-graphs consisted entirely of base stations (BTS), with multiple alarm events on each node. Of these, the top three were large sub-graphs containing 11–26 objects (note that the likelihood scores are determined based on more features than the number of objects). When querying for possible causes, each of these indicated backhaul failure as a stronger explanation (Fig. 3), given the set of rules that we proposed for diagnosis (Fig. 4).

The second tier of prioritized sub-graphs consisted mainly of clusters of alarmed cells belonging to separate basestations, but connected by planned adjacencies. A more likely possible cause, drawn from the test inventory, was a form of radio interference event. This was derived from the supplementary information field in the alarm data, which contained information such as "Configuration error: Invalid frequency channel for the BTS HW" or "Commissioning error: Invalid Configuration file". The last tier of sub-graphs consisted of singletons; these were prioritized by their position in the control hierarchy.

As severe as alarmed groups of base stations may seem, these alarms occurred frequently enough, when compared with other sub-graphs in the data. An example

Table 1. List of alarm sub-graphs identified in the given timeslice, sorted by the PCE derived priority. The numbers of each type of managed object are also presented (MRBTS=multi-radio basestation; BTS=basestation). Left side presents graphs with more than one node, while right side presents singletons.

ID	Priority	MRBTS	BTS	Cell	Total
ASG_6	0.9560	0	11	0	11
ASG_5	0.9558	0	26	0	26
ASG_0	0.9554	0	13	0	13
ASG_11	0.9027	0	4	0	4
ASG_8	0.9002	0	4	0	4
ASG_2	0.8920	0	0	3	3
ASG_9	0.8911	0	0	3	3
ASG_1	0.8904	0	0	3	3
ASG_10	0.8903	0	0	3	3
ASG_7	0.8767	0	0	2	2
ASG_4	0.8742	0	0	2	2
ASG_3	0.8579	0	1	3	4

ID	Priority	MRBTS	BTS	Cell	Total
ASG_25	0.7948	1	0	0	1
ASG_20	0.7916	1	0	0	1
ASG_12	0.7915	1	0	0	1
ASG_14	0.7907	1	0	0	1
ASG_21	0.7802	0	1	0	1
ASG_22	0.7798	0	1	0	1
ASG_19	0.7786	0	1	0	1
ASG_18	0.7775	0	0	1	1
ASG_23	0.7760	0	1	0	1
ASG_17	0.7754	0	0	1	1
ASG_15	0.7728	0	0	1	1
ASG_13	0.7723	0	0	1	1
ASG_24	0.7710	0	0	1	1
ASG_16	0.7706	0	0	1	1
ASG_27	0.7704	0	0	1	1
ASG_26	0.7700	0	0	1	1

of a rare alarm sub-graph occurred at Dec 13th from 1300–1400 CET. This event consisted of 24 alarmed basestations; the event was considered rare, given the size of the sub-graph. Inspection of the prioritization in that timeslice showed that the rare sub-graph was indeed assigned the highest priority of all identified sub-graphs. In Fig. 5, the graph-level analysis was overlaid using the lat/long coordinates of objects' basestations. We noticed that the basestations were in geographic proximity, indicating high chance of a significant impact in the area.

In addition, we conducted a preliminary evaluation of how well the sub-graph likelihood from the generative model can prioritize sub-graphs with significant network degradation. Using our Key-Performance-Indicator-based topic model [4], we identified 43 events for which cell performance degraded significantly and cells were objects in the sub-graphs. We then summed up the number of this type of events, considering the ones with sub-graph likelihood scores less than or equal to a given threshold, in essence retaining less-likely sub-graphs. Figure 6 presents the percentages of significant degradation events, alarm events, and sub-graphs against the threshold. Although there was a relatively small number of degradation events, the majority of these (39 out of 43) occurred on 25 % of the rare sub-graphs, indicating that prioritization based on likelihood is a viable strategy.

3.2   Computational Performance

Sub-graphs are formed by assessing which objects in the topological graph have an alarm in that time period. We then use a simple iterative agglomerative clustering scheme to group connected objects until no more connections can be made. For a number of alarms A and a total number of distinct objects N, we have a worst case of $O(AN)$ steps for determining which objects have alarms

```
add [x] isAllLNBTS(x) => backhaulFailure(x) 100.0;
add [x] isAllLNCEL(x) => radioInterferenceEvent(x) 100.0;
add [x] isAllLNCEL(x) => interfaceFailure(x) 0.5;
add [x] isLNBTS_LNCEL(x) => basestationBlocked(x) 1.2;
add [x] isMRBTS_LNBTS_LNCEL(x) => issueAtMRBTS(x) 1.1;

# Prioritization strategies
add [x] isRare(x) => priority(x) 10.0;
add [x] isFrequent(x) => priority(x) 1.2;
add [x] isAllMRBTS(x) => priority(x) 4.0;
add [x] isAllLNBTS(x) => priority(x) 2.0;
add [x] isAllLNCEL(x) => priority(x) 1.0;
add [x] isSingleton(x) => priority(x) 0.05;
add [x] ~isSingleton(x) => priority(x) 1.0;

add[x] isHeavilyConnected(x) => priority(x) 1.0;
add[x] ~isHeavilyConnected(x) => priority(x) 0.5;
add[x] isSingleMRBTS(x) => priority(x) 0.4;
add[x] isSingleLNBTS(x) => priority(x) 0.2;
add[x] isSingleLNCEL(x) => priority(x) 0.1;

add [x] isLarge(x) => priority(x) 4.0;
add [x] isMedium(x) => priority(x) 1.0;
add [x] isSmall(x) => priority(x) 0.1;
```

Fig. 4. Example MLN rules applied to each timeslice. The top rules are used for diagnosis, while the rest are intended for prioritization.

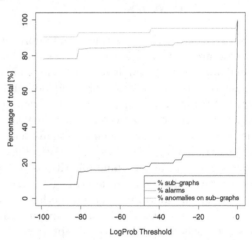

Fig. 5. An example of a rare alarm sub-graph, occurring on Dec 13th from 1300–1400 CET. The graph level analysis was overlaid using the lat/long coordinates of the objects' basestations. Red circles correspond to objects that had one or more alarm events within that time window, and edges objects indicate these belonged to the same alarm sub-graph.

Fig. 6. Percentages of significant degradation events, alarm events, and sub-graphs against the threshold.

when using a strictly naïve analysis without indexing the alarm occurrences. In our case, each iteration in the clustering scheme is $O(A^2)$. Feature computation is strictly $O(FN)$, with F as the number of featurizers in the system. Each featurizer can be considered to run in constant time, due to its templated nature.

PCE uses a Markov Chain Monte Carlo approach for inference, relying on sampling to estimate the probabilities of different indirect predicates in the system. Despite the theoretical worst-case complexity of MLN inference, the MCMC approach has distinct advantages for practical application. The worst-case complexity of MLN inference is dominated by the predicates with the largest number of arguments. Inference is exponential in the number of arguments of these predicates, since the search space grows exponentially. However, careful design of the rule set can alleviate this problem. For our graph-analysis diagnosis, this growth has not presented a problem. Inference running times grow much more slowly in the number of observations (e.g., number of alarm sub-graphs), usually somewhere between linear and quadratic in the number of observation assertions.

4   Related Work

Alarm correlation utilizes rule-based approaches [10], statistical methods [5,10], and hierarchical and adjacency information between network objects [3,9]. Rule-based approaches, though accurate and explainable, tend to be brittle: generated rules are specific to a network and domain, and usually not generalizable to new networks. These approaches thus require a high degree of maintenance to adjust rules in order to accommodate network updates and changes. The formal methods used by these systems also have a difficult time incorporating uncertain and contradictory information. Statistical methods deal with this uncertainty by design, and can use learning algorithms to adapt to new networks, but cannot incorporate valuable rules describing background knowledge about the network.

Among the alarm correlation methods, one body of work does make use of what we have deemed network graph information [3,6,9]. These dependency-based models are similar to our approach in the use of observations of alarms between objects on the network as graphs. However, some of these methods [3,9] make an implicit assumption that faults originate within objects on the network itself, and much of their effort focuses on identifying a minimal set of objects deemed to be responsible for the observed alarms. However, experience shows that it is entirely possible for faults to be triggered by exogenous causes, and oftentimes information useful for diagnostic purposes must be drawn from background knowledge. Along these lines, Hatonen and Klemettinen [6] explore different adjacencies in the network and use different distance metrics between domain objects to reduce the amount of correlating alarm type combinations. Furthermore, prior work in the dependency-based and statistical methods offer limited capabilities for distinguishing between rare and frequent alarm events, or prioritizing between correlated groups of alarms.

One of the more popular methods for alarm correlation in telecommunication networks is the use of Bayesian networks [11]. This class of techniques has been shown to be effective for reasoning under uncertainty. However, these methods require probabilities for each of the possible conditions a network must reason about. These must be derived either from data, or in the frequent case that not enough data is available, must be generated from a human expert. The latter case can become a problematic knowledge engineering task, especially in complex scenarios, where a large number of outcomes must be assigned a valid probability value and assessed against each other. Furthermore, standard Bayesian networks are inherently propositional; thus, reasoning about generalizations is difficult.

Finally, most of the available alarm correlation techniques focus on discovering commonly repeating patterns, for the purposes of identifying persistent faults in the network. As a consequence, there has been little attention paid to prioritizing rare groups of alarm events, in particular methods for deriving this from network data. Given equipment in networks can fail on a regular basis, an argument could be made that many of these cases may generally be known and resolvable by automated measures. Thus alarm events that are unusual or novel would be more likely to represent an unaccounted-for failure, and thus would be likelier to require operator intervention.

5 Conclusions

This paper proposed a novel framework for prioritizing and diagnosing faults in broadband networks based on a priori information about the managed network structure, relationships, and fault management practices. Our system reduces the amount of analyzed objects by combining the alarming objects into subgraphs and prioritizing them, and can also derive the most probable cause for the observed alarms. The design was tested on a dataset collected from a real cellular network. We are planning to test our framework in a realtime setting and to adapt it to highly dynamic environments. We are also planning to expand our framework to more SON use cases and to identify other types of data that can be used in the diagnosis process, including configuration management information.

Acknowledgment. We thank Lauri Oksanen, Kari Aaltonen, and Kenneth Nitz for their contributions.

References

1. Bandh, T., Carle, G., Sanneck, H.: Graph coloring based physical-cell-ID assignment for LTE networks. In: International Conference on Wireless Communications and Mobile Computing: Connecting the World Wirelessly. ACM (2009)
2. Blondel, V.D., Guillaume, J., Lambiotte, R., Lefebvre, E.: Fast unfolding of communities in large networks. J. Stat. Mech. Theor. Exp. **2008**, October 2008
3. Bouillard, A., Junier, A., Ronot, B.: Alarms correlation in telecommunication networks. [Research Report] RR-8321, p. 17 (2013)

4. Ciocarlie, G.F., Connolly, C., Cheng, C.-C., Lindqvist, U., Nováczki, S., Sanneck, H., Naseer-ul-Islam, M.: Anomaly detection and diagnosis for automatic radio network verification. In: Agüero, R., Zinner, T., Goleva, R., Timm-Giel, A., Tran-Gia, P. (eds.) MONAMI 2014. LNICST, vol. 141, pp. 163–176. Springer, Heidelberg (2015)
5. Hatonen, K.: Data mining for telecommunications network log analysis. PhD thesis, University of Helsinki (2009)
6. Hätönen, K., Klemettinen, M.: Domain structures in filtering irrelevant frequent patterns. In: Meo, R., Lanzi, P.L., Klemettinen, M. (eds.) Database Support for Data Mining Applications. LNCS (LNAI), vol. 2682, pp. 289–305. Springer, Heidelberg (2004)
7. Heckerman, D.: A tutorial on learning with Bayesian networks. In: Jordan, M. (ed.) Learning in Graphical Models. MIT Press, Cambridge (1999)
8. Jacomy, M., Venturini, T., Heymann, S., Bastian, M.: ForceAtlas2, a Continuous Graph Layout Algorithm for Handy Network Visualization Designed for the Gephi Software. PloS one (2014)
9. Katzela, I., Schwartz, M.: Schemes for fault identification in communication networks. IEEE/ACM Trans. Netw. 3(6), 753–764 (1995)
10. Martin-Flatin, J.P., Jakobson, G., Lewis, L.: Event correlation in integrated management: lessons learned and outlook. J. Netw. Syst. Manage. 15(4), 481–502 (2007)
11. Meira, D.M.: A Model for Alarm Correlation in Telecommunications Networks. PhD dissertation, Federal University of Minas Gerais, Belo Horizonte, Brazil (1997)
12. Probabilistic Consistency Engine. https://pal.sri.com/Plone/framework/Components/learning-applications/probabilistic-consistency-engine-jw
13. Richardson, M., Domingos, P.: Markov logic networks. Mach. Learn. 62(1–2), 107–136 (2006)
14. Wu, C.-H., Doerschuk, P.C.: Cluster expansions for the deterministic computation of Bayesian estimators based on Markov random fields. IEEE Trans. Pattern Anal. Mach. Intell. 17(3), 275–293 (1995)

Exposure Assessment in Heterogeneous Networks Accounting for up- and Downlinks

Daniel Sebastião[✉], B.W. Martijn Kuipers, and Luis M. Correia

IST/INOV-INESC, University of Lisbon, Lisbon, Portugal
{daniel.sebastiao,martijn.kuipers,
luis.correia}@inov.pt

Abstract. EMF exposure of people induced by both base station antennas and mobile terminal devices, in a heterogeneous network environment, in a given area, is addressed in this paper. The Specific Absorption Rate (SAR) and the Exposure Index (EI) are used to evaluate exposure, which takes multiple systems, users, postures, and usage profiles into account, among other aspects. One analyses the exposure in heterogeneous networks, consisting of GSM, UTMS, LTE and WLAN systems, for multiple usage scenarios. By using full systems simulations and exposure models, one estimates the EI for several conditions. The use of power control has a major impact on the SAR a person is exposed to. It is verified that, for the scenario under analysis, the uplink power of users' own terminal contributes to more than 90% to the overall SAR.

Keywords: EMF population exposure · Exposure Index · Simulation · Heterogeneous networks · Up- and downlinks

1 Introduction

Exposure induced by electromagnetic fields (EMF) emitted by wireless telecommunication systems is limited by threshold reference values recommended by international bodies, as ICNIRP [1]. Existing metrics to evaluate EMF exposure are well adapted to check the compliance with limits, but not at all to evaluate a global exposure of a population. Previous studies on this matter usually only look into a specific system, or to a specific mechanism that allows one to reduce exposure [2, 3]. Other studies analyse heterogeneous networks, but usually looking at the effect of adding small cells [4], or by using different allocation or routing strategies [5]. In the context of concern about possible health effects of EMF, the LEXNET project [6] (co-funded by the European Commission, under Framework Programme 7), started in November 2012 in response to this demand.

The strategic goal of LEXNET is to take the public concern on EMF possible health effects into account, and to improve the acceptability of existing and future wireless systems, through low exposure systems, without compromising the user's perceived Quality of Experience. One of the objectives of LEXNET was to define a new metric to evaluate the exposure of a population induced by a given wireless telecommunication network. The so-called Exposure Index (EI) [7] evaluates simultaneously the contributions of personal devices (e.g., mobile phones) and of networks' infrastructures (e.g., base station antennas) to the global exposure of users.

© Institute for Computer Sciences, Social Informatics and Telecommunications Engineering 2015
R. Agüero et al. (Eds.): MONAMI 2015, LNICST 158, pp. 43–54, 2015.
DOI: 10.1007/978-3-319-26925-2_4

To the best of our knowledge, this is the first paper to address and quantify this exposure from heterogeneous wireless communication systems using LEXNET's EI model. By using this approach, initial simulations were made to estimate global exposure on heterogeneous networks (GSM, UTMS, LTE and IEEE 802.11 g-WiFi systems), considering different scenarios, varying usage, mobility, number of users, etc. Afterwards, the EI was estimated for the considered systems and given scenarios. This enabled to have a better understanding of the overall exposure in heterogeneous networks, allowing one to know the exposure impact of the different considered systems, and for different users' behaviours.

Following this introduction, the EI model of the LEXNET project is described in Sect. 2. The simulation scenario is detailed in Sect. 3, followed by the analysis of simulation results in Sect. 4. Conclusions are drawn in Sect. 5.

2 Exposure Index Model

The model proposed to evaluate the EI of users in a given area with several communication systems is based on the work carried out in the LEXNET project [7–10] and is summarised here for clarity. The model divides the EI into down- and uplink components:

$$EI = EI^{\mathrm{DL}} + EI^{\mathrm{UL}} \quad [\mathrm{J/kg}] \tag{1}$$

where:

- EI^{DL} is the total downlink EI for all communication systems,
- EI^{UL} is the total uplink EI, coming from the devices in the proximity of the user.

The downlink EI exists independent of whether the user has an active connection, or even carries a communication system, i.e., it merely exists due to the presence of base stations. The total downlink EI is the sum of the EI components for each system, each one depending on the distance of the user to the base station, and the duration of the stay of the user inside the scenario.

The downlink EI_s^{DL} for a single system is given by

$$EI_S^{DL}(r_s, t, f_s) = P_{\mathrm{tx}} G_{\mathrm{tx}} \left(\frac{4\pi r_s f_s}{c} \right) t d_{f_s}^{DL} \tag{2}$$

where:

- P_{tx} is the transmission power [W],
- G_{tx} is the antenna gain,
- c is the speed of light in vacuum [m/s];
- r_s is the distance to the base station of system s [m];
- f_s is the carrier frequency of the used communication system s [Hz];
- t is the duration of the connection [s];
- $d_{f_s}^{DL}$ is the normalised Specific Absorption Rate (SAR) for the downlink [kg^{-1}].

Power control is not considered for the downlink. Since a single user cannot control the total downlink power of the base station, a worst case transmission power is assumed. The used frequencies for the various communication systems are given in Table 1. Although these communications systems can operate in a variety of frequency bands, the listed frequencies were used, because they coincide with the studied normalised SAR values within LEXNET. The normalised SAR for the downlink is given in Table 2.

Table 1. Frequency, maximum transmission power and antenna gain for the simulated systems.

	f_s [MHz]	P_{tx} [W]	G_{tx} [dBi]
GSM	1 800	40.0	0
UMTS	1 940	40.0	14
LTE	2 600	40.0	14
WLAN	2 400	00.1	0

Table 2. Normalised SAR for the different communication systems.

	Normalised SAR [kg^{-1}]	
	Downlink	Uplink
GSM (1 800 MHz)	0.0043	0.0053
UMTS (1 940 MHz)	0.0043	0.0053
LTE (2 600 MHz)	0.0039	0.0053
WLAN (2 400 MHz)	0.0053	

The total downlink EI, for a total of S systems, is then given by:

$$EI^{DL}(t) = \sum_{s=1}^{S} EI^{DL}_{S_n}(r_s, t, f_s) \qquad (3)$$

where:

- $EI^{DL}_{S_n}(\ldots)$ is the downlink EI for system n.

Unlike the downlink, the EI of the uplink depends solely on the active connections of the user with system S. The distance to the communication device is taken into account by the normalised SAR value. The uplink EI for a given system, EI^{UL}_s, is given by

$$EI^{UL}_s(t) = P_{tx} A_{s,u} d^{UL}_{fs} c \qquad (4)$$

where:

- $A_{s,u}$ is the activity factor, depending on the users' activity and the used system, assumed to be 1 in here.
- d^{UL}_{fs} is the uplink normalised SAR [kg^{-1}] for the different frequencies, given in Table 2.

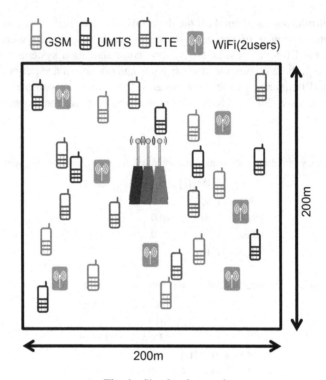

Fig. 1. Simulated scenario

3   Simulations and Scenarios

The scenarios were simulated using Riverbed Modeler [11], and show a macro-cell approach [12], with a 200 m side square area, where there are GSM, UMTS and LTE base-stations collocated at the centre of the cell, see Fig. 1. Power control is considered only for GSM and UMTS. The GSM base station is omni-directorial, whereas, the UMTS and LTE ones are tri-sectorised. The cell also contains a number of WLAN access points, randomly positioned within the cell. Users are also randomly positioned within the cell. The receive power values at the user terminal is used for downlink simulations. For uplink measurements, the transmit power is measured at 5 cm distance from the terminal, which roughly corresponds to the distance of a phone to a person. All users are outdoors, and only a single cell, albeit sectorised, is considered.

The considered reference scenario is composed of the four considered systems, with 7 users per cellular system, and 7 APs with 2 users each. As for the service, GSM users are using voice, while the rest of the users from the other systems are using P2P. It was decided to focus on the worst-case approach when designing and configuring the scenario: although the area under study is small, it is considered to be a macro-cell (thus, larger BS transmission power), the used propagation model being free space loss only.

Based on the reference scenario, several variations were defined to analyse specific scenarios:

- user's movement (pedestrian speed, without leaving the area under study);
- different types of traffic (FTP, P2P with heavier load, video conferencing) for all users except GSM ones who are always just doing voice;
- clustering of the cellular users with different distances to the bases stations (10, 50, 100, 200, and 500 m);
- increase the number of users of the cellular systems (to the double, triple, and quadruple of the reference situation).

The LEXNET *EI*-model was implemented in Octave, using reference values from the aforementioned simulations.

4 Simulation Results

This section evaluates the results of various scenarios and simulations. First the transmission powers of both down- and uplink are analysed, since the position of a user with respect to the base station and other users' has a direct impact to the EI. Secondly, the distribution of the EI of the different systems is evaluated, to give insights into the impact of these distances to the EI. Lastly, the EI of a single user is simulated for 1 h periods, to quantify the exposure a user can expect.

4.1 Received Power Simulations

The EI is highly dependent on the transmission powers, see Eqs. (2) and (4), therefore these values were obtained first. The results are the power values for both the down- and uplinks for each of the users, in each of the systems. In Table 3, the results from the reference scenario are presented, including the standard deviation. The results from all the users of a given system are averaged so that one can compare the "average exposure" among systems in both links.

Table 3. Received power for the different communication systems.

	Received power			
	Downlink		Uplink	
	Mean [dBm]	StdDev [dB]	Mean [dBm]	StdDev [dB]
GSM	−25.4	0.00	9.3	0.00
UMTS	−96.2	0.54	−48.4	0.59
LTE	−37.3	0.87	12.9	2.18
WLAN	−54.9	5.22	−40.1	23.35

As it can be seen, UMTS has much lower exposure values compared to other cellular systems. This is easily explained, since in our simulations UMTS uses advanced power control in the uplink, and there is a reduced number of users/load in the considered reference scenario. For LTE and GSM, the values are several orders of magnitude higher, but nevertheless, the power values are quite low, due to the relative small scenario, thus, all users being at a relatively short distance from the base stations. As for WLAN, power values are quite low in both up- and downlinks.

As for the cellular systems, the standard deviation is quite low as expected: there is no movement on the reference scenario, and thus, the transmitted power variation is also quite low. The standard deviation of WLAN is quite high, which can be explained by the reduced number of terminals (2 per AP) used in the simulations for WLAN users, thus, leading to higher variability between results.

There was also a variation on the type of service being considered, and it was seen that independently of the type of service used as a traffic load, the received powers do not show any appreciable variation, as it can be seen in Fig. 2. This indicates that the type of service does not yield a great influence on the received powers.

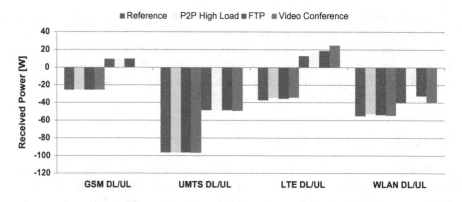

Fig. 2. Comparison of the received signal powers for different services.

The next step was to look at the impact of clustering, and of the distance from the users to the base station, the results being presented in Fig. 3. Simulations were performed with users clustered at distances of 10, 50, 100, 200 and 500 m from the base stations. There are no big changes in the results, but one can see the effects of power control (or lack thereof) on the received and transmitted power of the various systems under consideration.

In Fig. 4, the results are shown for the received powers when the number of users (or the load) increases. This was done with an increase by a factor of 2, 3 and 4 on the number of users, compared to the reference scenario.

UMTS power values, as expected, are very dependent on the load, but even so, it continues to be the system with the lower exposure values. As for the other systems, the variation is negligible among the different scenarios.

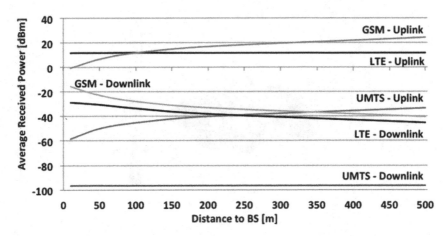

Fig. 3. Comparison of the received signal powers at the users' location of the systems for different distances to the BS

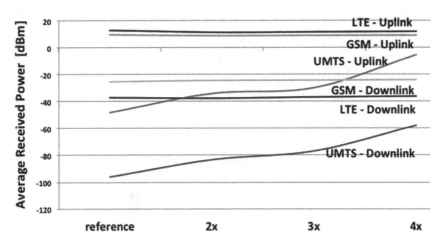

Fig. 4. Received signal powers at the users' location for user densities

4.2 SAR Distribution Simulations

In this section, the SAR was simulated for the down- and uplinks of each simulated systems, for the same considered scenario. The results for all systems combined are shown in Fig. 5. The SAR values from the downlink transmission are given in Fig. 5a, the SAR values from the uplink transmissions in Fig. 5b, and the combined down- and uplink SAR values in Fig. 5c.

For UMTS, LTE and GSM, an exclusion zone of 10 m around the base-station is considered. The closest distance to the communication device of any system is 10 cm. Both up- and downlinks of WLAN are considered with a 10 cm exclusion zone. These exclusion zones are just for representation purposes, and do not interfere with the

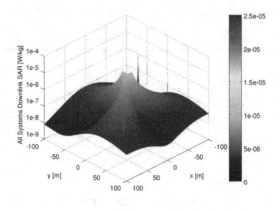

a) Downlink SAR.

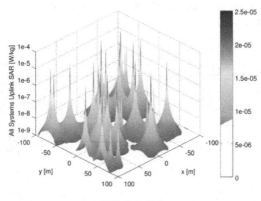

b) Uplink SAR.

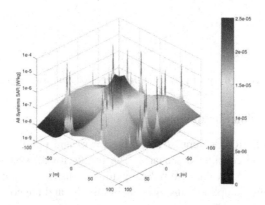

c) Combined Downlink and Uplink SAR.

Fig. 5. Combined UMTS, LTE, GSM and WLAN SAR Distribution in a single cell

results. The effect of the exclusion zones around the base-stations can be recognised by flattened peaks of the SAR around the base-station, i.e., at coordinates (0, 0).

Each WLAN AP has 2 active users in its vicinity as it has been considered on the system level simulations, and this is easily recognisable in Fig. 5c, as there are some clusters of three peaks closely together.

In all simulations, the results are well below the limit of 2 W/kg (head) and the maximum average of 0.8 W/kg (complete body) as defined by ICNIRP's recommendations [1].

4.3   Exposure Index Simulations

The total cumulative SAR for a single user without mobile terminal is simulated and averaged over 1000 runs for a cell with four communication systems, with the same transmission characteristics as presented in Table 1. Three different traffic levels are simulated, i.e., low, medium and high. The low traffic level is the same level as the standard scenario, i.e., 7 active users for UMTS, 7 active users for LTE, 7 active users for GSM and 2 APs with 7 active users each. In the medium traffic scenario, the number of active users is increased to 14 for each of the cellular systems, and in the high traffic scenario the number is increased to 28.

The user follows a random-walk with a constant speed of 4 m/s. The user is bounced back from the outer areas of the cell and keeps on moving during the entire simulation. The user position is evaluated every second for a period of 1 h. The results for these simulations are given in Table 4. Due to the fast-decay of the transmitted powers with distance; the increase in active users does not have a significant impact in the observed cumulative SAR.

Table 4. Exposure index simulations for different user densities for a user without a mobile terminal.

	Exposure index [mJ/kg/h]		
	Mean	Max	StdDev
Low (7 active users)	0.76	5.17	0.83
Medium (14 active users)	0.81	5.44	0.84
High (28 active users)	0.76	5.35	0.76

The results from Table 5 do not include the radiation from the users' own mobile terminal. Assuming a sufficient number of active users in the cell, such that the radiation of the users' mobile is independent of the exposure from all other radiators, the component of the radiation perceived from the own terminal can simply be added to the already obtained values.

Also, the calculations were done considering perfect power control for all systems and using a noise margin for the receiver of -120 dBm and a receiver margin of 30 dB. Both LTE and UMTS use directional base station antennas with a maximum gain of

Table 5. Exposure index of the different systems.

	Exposure index [mJ/kg/h]		
	Mean	Max	StdDev
GSM	29.12	62.47	11.16
UMTS	07.77	35.90	06.08
LTE	13.56	64.48	10.92

14 dB and no antenna gain at the mobile terminal. The results in Table 5 are the average value, maximum and standard deviation for 1 000 random walk patterns. Since the added value is purely dependent of the users' mobile, the number of active users in the cell does not have any influence.

It is worth noting that although the maximum values are a factor of 3 to 5 times higher than the average value, they are still well below the legal limits. UMTS shows the lowest EI, followed by LTE and then GSM. WLAN was not considered, as it is not reasonable to expect WLAN coverage over the entire cell-range, which would lead to underestimated results.

In Table 6, the total Exposure Index (down- and uplinks) is given for the different systems, as well as the relative components for the down- and the uplinks.

Table 6. Absolute and relative exposure index of the different systems.

	Exposure index		
	Total [mJ/kg/h]	Downlink [%]	Uplink [%]
GSM	29.88	2.5	97.5
UMTS	08.53	8.9	91.1
LTE	13.56	5.3	94.7

As expected, the radiating power from ones' own mobile terminal is responsible for over 90 % of the SAR on the human body.

5   Conclusions

The goal of the LEXNET project is to take into account the public concern on possible health effects of electromagnetic fields and to improve the acceptability of existing and future wireless systems through low exposure systems without compromising the user's perceived quality. Under this flag, this paper investigates the Exposure Index for the down- and uplinks, as experienced by users in a single cell.

The scenario under evaluation is a single macro-cellular scenario, with GSM, UMTS, LTE and WLAN systems. GSM, UMTS and LTE BSs are co-located at the centre of the cell, where UMTS and LTE are tri-sectorised. Simulations, using Riverbed Modeler, were made for different mobility patterns, services, users and user clustering. The base scenario (no mobility, 7 users for each system in a 200×200 m^2 area) shows that UMTS has a much lower exposure value, compared to the other systems. Increasing the number of users shows the largest impact in UMTS, as it is based on Code Division Multiple Access. The type of service does not have a large impact on the results, as in all cases the system has a decent traffic load.

Exposure Index simulations, implemented in Octave, show the SAR distribution for each system in the down- and uplinks, and a combined SAR distribution for all systems. From these figures one can extract that the peaks for the SAR follow the user distribution.

Simulations showed that power control has a major impact on the cumulative SAR a person is exposed to. More interestingly, simulations have also shown that the uplink from the users' terminal is responsible for over 90 % of the exposed SAR, when the user is making a call or using a data connection. Also, the user has little control over the downlink contribution to the SAR, as it depends on all the users in the cell. Future communications systems need to optimise the uplink power, as it is the main component of the SAR exposure of users. Denser networks can lead to a decrease in SAR, as the user is closer to the base station, needing less power to transmit.

Although many simulations have been run, the scenario (200×200 m^2) does not vary. It would be interesting to analyse the EI for more realistic scenarios and path-loss models. More recent releases of LTE have added power control, and this may have a severe (positive) impact on the LTE results. Future work will also include the received powers of base stations in neighbouring cells and of multiple operators to better match a realistic environment.

Acknowledgment. The research leading to these results has received funding from the European Commission's Seventh Framework Program project entitled "Low EMF Exposure Networks" (LEXNET Project, Grant No. 318273).

References

1. Rüdiger, M., et al.: International commission on non-ionising radiation protection (ICNIRP), "Guidelines for limiting exposure to time-varying electric, magnetic, and electromagnetic fields (up to 300 GHz). Health Phys. **4**, 494–522 (1998)
2. Pedersen, K.I., Wang, Y., Strzyz, S., Frederiksen, F.: Enhanced inter-cell interference coordination in co-channel multi-layer LTE-advanced networks. IEEE Wireless Commun. **20**(3), 120–127 (2013)
3. Plets, D., Wout, J., Vanhecke, K., Martens, L.: Exposure optimisation in indoor wireless networks by heuristic network planning. Prog. Electromagn. Res. **139**, 445–478 (2013)
4. Stephan, J., Brau, M., Corre, Y., Lostanlen, Y.: Joint analysis of small-cell network performance and urban electromagnetic field exposure. In: Proceedings of 8th European Conference on Antennas and Propagation (EuCAP2014), The Hague, Netherlands (April 2014)

5. El Abdellaouy, H., Pelov, A., Toutain, L., Bernard, D.: Mitigation of electromagnetic radiation in heterogeneous home network using routing algorithm. In: Proceedings of 12th International Symposium on Modelling and Optimisation in Mobile, Ad Hoc, and Wireless Networks (WiOpt), Hammamet, Tunisia (May 2014)
6. LEXNET project. http://lexnet-project.eu
7. Conil, E. (ed.): D2.4 Global wireless exposure metric definition v1, LEXNET project deliverable (2013). http://www.lexnet.fr/ fileadmin/user/Deliverables_P1/LEXNET_WP2_ D24_Global_wireless_exposure_metric_def_v2.pdf
8. Vermeeren, G. (ed.): D2.1 current metrics for EMF exposure evaluation, LEXNET project deliverable (April 2013). http://www.lexnet.fr/fileadmin/user/Deliverables_P1/LEXNET_ WP2_D2_1_Current_exposure_metrics_v4.0.pdf
9. Wiedemann, P.M., Freudenstein, F.: D2.2 risk and exposure perception LEXNET project deliverable (July 2013). http://www.lexnet.fr/fileadmin/user/Deliverables_P1/LEXNET_ WP2_D22_Risk_and_exposure_perception_v1.pdf
10. Popović, M. (ed.): D5.1 smart low-EMF architectures: novel technologies overview, LEXNET project deliverable (October 2014). http://www.lexnet.fr/fileadmin/user/ Deliverables_P2/LEXNET_WP5_D51_Smart_low-EMF_architectures_novel_ technologies_overview_v6.1.pdf
11. Riverbed Modeler (March 2015). http://riverbed.com/
12. Vermeeren, G. (ed.): D2.3 scenarios, LEXNET project deliverable (November 2013). http:// www.lexnet.fr/fileadmin/user/Deliverables_P2/LEXNET_WP2_D23_Scenarios_v2.pdf

A Predictive Model for Minimising Power Usage in Radio Access Networks

Emmett Carolan[✉], Seamus C. McLoone, and Ronan Farrell

Department of Electronic Engineering,
Maynooth University, Maynooth, County Kildare, Ireland
{ecarolan, seamus.mcloone}@eeng.nuim.ie,
ronan.farrell@nuim.ie

Abstract. In radio access networks traffic load varies greatly both spatially and temporally. However, resource usage of Base Stations (BSs) does not solely depend on the traffic load; auxiliary devices contribute to resource usage in a load invariant manner. Consequently, BSs suffer from a large underutilisation of resources throughout most of the day due to their optimisation for peak traffic hours. In this paper an energy saving scheme is proposed with the use of an Artificial Neural Network (ANN) predictive model to make switching decisions ahead of time. The optimum set of BS to turn off while maintaining Quality Of Service (QoS) is formulated as a binary integer programming problem. We validated our model and found large potential savings using an extensive data set spanning all network usage for three months and over one thousand BSs covering the entirety of Dublin city and county.

Keywords: Cellular usage · Traffic prediction · Cellular networks · Temporal dynamics · Spectrum sharing · Green networks

1 Introduction

In the past two decades mobile phones and devices utilising the mobile phone network have become ubiquitous in modern society. Mobile phone penetration has approached and in some nations exceeded 100 % [1]. Cellular networks are undergoing, and will continue to experience, a large and sustained increase in demand for network resources [2]. Demand is particularly acute at the radio access level where service is constrained by the availability of valuable licensed spectrum [3]. Concomitant with the growth of cellular usage there has been a large increase in the energy used by cellular networks [4]. It is estimated that cellular networks account for approximately 10 % of the total carbon emitted by the Information and Communication Technology (ICT) sector with this expected to increase further in the future [5]. In addition to the environmental concerns there are real economic benefits for network operators to minimise power consumption [6].

It is currently estimated that 80 % of the overall infrastructure power consumption takes places in the Radio Access Network (RAN), particularly Base Stations (BSs) [7]. Despite significant temporal and spatial variations in demand [8–10], networks are currently optimised for peak throughput at peak demand. As shown in [3] large

© Institute for Computer Sciences, Social Informatics and Telecommunications Engineering 2015
R. Agüero et al. (Eds.): MONAMI 2015, LNICST 158, pp. 55–67, 2015.
DOI: 10.1007/978-3-319-26925-2_5

underutilisation of RAN resources are present and particularly pronounced at the cell level. Unfortunately, the infrastructure of currently deployed networks is largely load invariant meaning largely underutilised cells stay active despite a lack of demand. This is a costly inefficiency in terms of power consumption but it also underutilises valuable licensed spectrum which could be made available for secondary usage [3].

Accurate short and medium term predictive models of load (primary usage) at the local level (cell, BS, local grid etc.) are critical if Self-Organising Networks (SON) are to ameliorate the network's inefficient usage of power and spectrum. For example, if it can be predicted that traffic in a particular cell or group of cells falls below a certain threshold at certain times then SON algorithms can use this information to alter the network to save energy [11–13]. Also, if low demand by primary users of valuable licensed spectrum can be predicted in certain cells/areas at for example off-peak times this can provide opportunities for secondary usage in these bands [14].

Much work has gone into algorithms and techniques to dynamically switch on/off cells or BSs [11–13]. However, most work in the area simply uses historical static load profiles or assumes that switching decisions can be made instantaneously. However, real world measurement results such as presented in [15] show that switching can take up to 30 min due to the heating systems. Thus, predictions of the need to perform a switch ahead of time are important.

2 Background

The infrastructure of the 3G network is comprised of two main parts: the RAN and the Core Network (CN). The RAN is comprised of the User Equipment (UE), the Radio Network Controller (RNC), and the BS which can be further subdivided into cells. Each RNC manages many BSs which are split into cells and service subscribers through their air interface with the UE [16] (Fig. 1).

There are two primary subsystems: the communications subsystem and the support subsystem. The communications subsystem is comprised of the Remote Radio Unit (RRU), the Feeder, and the Base Band Unit (BBU). The RRU provides the radio hardware for each sector of the base station. Each BS may have several RRUs near the antennas to allow for varying coverage and capacity [15]. The BBU is responsible for all the other communication functions such as control, Iub interfaces to the RNC, base band, scrambling, link quality measurements, soft handovers etc. [16]. Each BS may also have several BBUs. The feeder is a fiber optic pair cable connecting the RRUs to the BBUs. The supporting subsystem is comprised of the cooling subsystem and supporting devices. The cooling subsystem maintains an appropriate operating temperature at the BS.

The cooling subsystem coupled with some of the transmission modules are responsible for the consumption of a significant amount of the power in a BS (over 50 % [15]) but are load invariant i.e. their power consumption does not proportionately scale down with low demand. Thus, the RAN can conserve large amounts of power by powering down certain BSs under low load conditions.

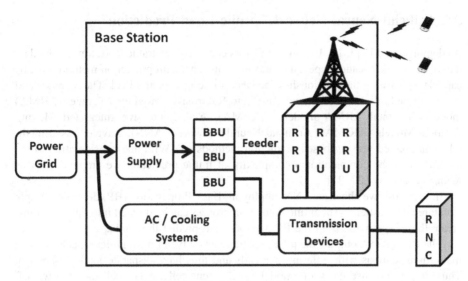

Fig. 1. A typical BS in a 3G Network

For base stations we employ the power consumption models outlined in [15, 17] where the total power consumption P at a given BS is given by:

$$P = P_{tx} + P_{misc} \qquad (1)$$

where P_{tx} accounts for the power used to provide network access to subscribers UE. This includes power consumed by the RRUs, the BBUs, the feeder, and the RNC transmissions. P_{misc} is the power consumed by cooling, monitoring and the auxiliary power supply.

P_{tx} can be linearly approximated as:

$$P_{tx}(L) = P_{\alpha} \cdot L + P_{\beta} \qquad (2)$$

where L is the traffic load factor on a BS. P_{tx} varies as a result of both the RRU and BBU. For example, during periods of high traffic the RRU consumes more power servicing more active links. Thus, the power consumption varies with traffic load. Conversely, the BBU carries out base band processing for all frequencies used by the BS. Its power consumption is mainly determined by the number of frequency carriers and not the number of active links. Also, other operations such as such as signaling over control channels use energy even under low loads. The coefficient P_{α} depends on the transmission distance of the base station as greater power is consumed communicating over a greater distance.

P_{misc} as outlined in [15] is mainly a function of external conditions such as temperature. It is largely invariant with load and thus we assume that the supporting subsystem power consumption stays constant in this work.

3   Artificial Neural Network Traffic Load Prediction

As demonstrated in [3, 18, 19] several factors can affect the traffic load: time of the day, day of the week, location, special events etc. Thus, a useful prediction method must be capable of learning the relationships between these factors and load. There are several possible methods available such as Auto-Regressive Moving Average (ARMA) models, Seasonal ARMA models (SARMA), Auto-Regressive Integrated Moving Average Models (ARIMA), Artificial Neural Networks (ANN), wavelet based methods, compressed sensing based prediction methods etc. With due consideration to the accuracy and the computational complexity of traffic prediction we employ ANN as recommended by [20, 21].

In this work we chose an ANN employing Back Propagation (BP) due to its simple structure and plasticity. The traffic prediction process can be divided into three sections: create the BP network, train the BP network, and predict the traffic.

The BP network outputs the predicted traffic at a given time t. Different cells service many diverse areas with differing demands and thus have disparate load profiles [3]. Thus, we do not use the same model for different cells; every cell has its own BP network model. We chose day of the week (D), time of the day (t), and past traffic which is relevant to the predicted value as input parameters. As in [21] the relativity R_τ between $\rho_m(t\text{-}\tau)$ and $\rho_m(t)$ is measured by:

$$R_\tau = \frac{\sum_{t=1}^{T}\left(\rho_m(t) - \bar{\rho}_{m,1}\right)\left(\rho_m(t - \tau) - \bar{\rho}_{m,2}\right)}{\sqrt{\sum_{t=1}^{T}\left(\rho_m(t) - \bar{\rho}_{m,1}\right)^2}\sqrt{\sum_{t=1}^{T}\left(\rho_m(t - \tau) - \bar{\rho}_{m,2}\right)^2}} \tag{3}$$

where T is the total number of points in time, $\bar{\rho}_{m,1}$ and $\bar{\rho}_{m,2}$ are the mean values of $\rho_m(t)$ and $\rho_m(t\text{-}\tau)$ respectively. If the load at time $t\text{-}\tau$ (denoted $\rho_m(t\text{-}\tau)$) has a $R_\tau > 0.8$ it is considered to be strongly related to time $\rho_m(t)$; the number of related past time points $\rho_m(t\text{-}\tau)$ is denoted M.

The number of hidden layers and neurons is application dependent; output sensitivity is used to estimate the effect of each input or neuron to ensure efficiency. We denote an input or a neuron as θ, the output sensitivity of θ at t is defined as

$$S_\theta(t) = \frac{\delta\rho_m(t)}{\delta\theta} \tag{4}$$

the variance of sensitivity can be estimated by:

$$\sigma_{s_\theta}^2 = \frac{\sum_{t=1}^{T}\left(S_\theta(t) - \bar{S}_\theta\right)^2}{T - 1} \tag{5}$$

where $\bar{S}_\theta$ is the mean value of $S_\theta(t)$. Based on the variance of S_θ, v_{S_θ} describes the availability of θ and

$$v_{s_\theta} = \frac{(T - 1)\sigma_{s_\theta}^2}{\sigma_0^2} \tag{6}$$

where σ_0 is a regularization parameter; increasing σ_0 leads to more θ being discarded and a simpler network architecture. However, a network architecture that is too simplistic may also lead to a poorer predictive performance. Assuming zero variance, $v_{s_\theta} \approx \chi^2(T-1)$, a critical value v_c can be found in the χ^2 distribution table:

$$v_c = \chi^2_{T-1,(1-\alpha/2)} \tag{7}$$

where α denotes the significance level which we set to 0.05. Values of $v_{s_\theta} < v_c$, result in a θ being abandoned. This procedure is carried out for each input parameter and neuron to build a network with a simple but effective structure.

The BP network is trained with the Levenberg-Marquardt (LM) algorithm [21, 22]; training is a cyclical process where t, D and traffic from t-M to t-1 are provided to the BP network at the start of each iteration. The difference between the predicted traffic $\rho^p_m(t)$ and real traffic $\rho_m(t)$ is:

$$\xi(w) = \frac{1}{T}\sum_{t=1}^{T}\left(\rho^p_m(t) - \rho_m(t)\right)^2 \tag{8}$$

which can be rewritten as:

$$\xi(w) = \frac{1}{T}\sum_{t=1}^{T}\left(f(\omega, t) - \rho_m(t)\right)^2 \tag{9}$$

where the output $\rho^p_m(t)$ is expressed as a function of the weights ω and t represented by $f(\omega,t)$. The weights ω are adjusted as:

$$\omega = \omega_{last} + \Delta\omega \tag{10}$$

with,

$$\Delta\omega = -\frac{d}{H + e^\beta I} \tag{11}$$

where ω_{last} is initially randomly chosen and thereafter the weight from the previous iteration. $\Delta\omega$ is the change in ω between iterations, I is the identity matrix, β is used to maintain stability and adjusted in each iteration [21], and H is the Hessian matrix which provides the learning rate. H can be obtained by taking the second derivative of ξ with respect to all weights. The sum of the gradient is denoted by d and is equal to:

$$\mathbf{d} = \frac{\delta\xi}{\delta\omega} = \sum_{t=1}^{T}\frac{\delta\xi}{\delta\rho_m(t)}\frac{\delta\rho_m(t)}{\delta\omega} \tag{12}$$

The algorithm continues until the prediction error is acceptable or the maximum number of iterations is reached; each network is only trained once.

4 Traffic Prediction Based Energy Savings Scheme

In a typical network many BSs are vastly underutilised for most of the day as demonstrated in [3]. As discussed in Sect. 1, this underutilisation is wasteful of both power and valuable licensed spectrum which could be used by unlicensed secondary usage. As shown in [3], the coverage areas of many BSs overlap to reliably service demand during the short and predictable hours of peak demand. A reduction in the underutilisation of network resources can thus be achieved by putting redundant BSs to sleep at off-peak times. Once redundant BSs are put to sleep, the active BSs can take advantage of modern techniques such as beamforming to cover the spaces left by inactive BSs [23]. When the traffic increases above a certain threshold the inactive BSs are switched on again. However, real world measurements [15] show that the switching process is not instantaneous. Thus, predicting the load ahead of time is important to the smooth operation of such a system.

To tackle the problem we first divide the coverage area of each base station into equal sized squares. As the coverage area of each BS is generally small in the areas of most interest (dense urban [3]) we assume that the traffic load of each BS is evenly distributed between its squares. We then map all the BSs and squares as the vertices of an undirected graph $G = (V,E)$. BS i and square k form and edge $e_{i,k} \in E$ if the entire area of the square falls within the maximum transmission range of the BS. Thus, we want to form a graph with the minimum number of edges while ensuring that: every square is covered by one BS, and every BS is not connected to more squares than it can reasonably service. Thus the problem can be formulated as:

$$
\begin{aligned}
min &\sum_{i=1}^{n} sgn\left(\sum_{e_{i,k} \in E} I_{e_{i,k}}\right) \\
s.t. &\sum_{e_{i,k} \in E} V_{e_{i,k}} \times I_{e_{i,k}} \le C_i, \qquad \forall i \in 1 \ldots n \\
&\sum_{e_{i,k} \in E} I_{e_{i,k}} \ge 1, \qquad\qquad \forall k \\
&I_{e_{i,k}} \in \{0,1\} \qquad\qquad \forall e_{i,k} \in E
\end{aligned}
\tag{13}
$$

where $e_{i,k}$ is the edge between BS i and square k; $V_{ei,k}$ denotes the traffic load in square k. If $I_{e_{i,k}} = 1$ then $e_{i,k}$ is included in the optimal solution while $I_{e_{i,k}} = 0$ means it is not. C_i is the capacity threshold of BS i [24]. The first constraint prohibits the distribution of a traffic load to any BS that exceeds the BS's capacity. The second constraint guarantees that every square is covered by a BS.

The above solution allows for adjustments to be made to the coverage areas of BS. However, it does not take into account that (as discussed in Sect. 2) a certain amount of the power consumption is proportional to transmission distances and load. To that end the edge weight $P_{ei,k}$ is introduced to the graph $G = (V,E)$ and denotes the power required by BS i to service the traffic load in square k. The magnitude of $P_{ei,k}$ depends on the load, and the distance between BS i and square k. $P_{ei,k}$ is analogous to P_{tx}, the transmit power discussed in Sect. 2. Following on from the power model in Sect. 2 we incorporate $P_{constant}$ which represents the constant power usage of the BS independent of load and transmission distance. Thus the objective function in (13) is extended to include power consumption:

$$\min \sum_{e_{i,k} \in E} P_{ei,k} \times I_{e_{i,k}} + \sum_{i=1}^{n} P_{i,constant} \times sgn\left(\sum_{e_{i,k} \in E} I_{e_{i,k}}\right) \qquad (14)$$

Equation (14) can be transformed into a more manageable form as in [24]:

$$\min \sum_{e_{i,k} \in E} P_{ei,k} \times I_{e_{i,k}} + \sum_{i=1}^{n} P_{i,constant} \times I_{s_i}$$
$$s.t. \sum_{e_{i,k} \in E} V_{e_{i,k}} \times I_{e_{i,k}} \le C_i, \qquad \forall i \in 1 \ldots n$$
$$\sum_{e_{i,k} \in E} I_{e_{i,k}} \ge 1, \qquad \forall k \qquad (15)$$
$$\sum_{e_{i,k} \in E} I_{e_{i,k}} - I_{s_i} \times N_{s_i} \le 0, \qquad \forall i \in 1 \ldots$$
$$I_{e_{i,k}} \in \{0,1\} \qquad \forall e_{i,k} \in E$$
$$I_{s_i} \in \{0,1\} \qquad \forall i \in 1 \ldots n$$

If $I_{si} = 1$ then BS i will be active in the final energy saving scheme while $I_{si} = 0$ means it will be inactive. N_{si} denotes the number of edges connected to BS i. The new constraint in (15) ensures that if BS i is selected to be inactive ($I_{si} = 0$) it does not need to service any of the squares. (15) is a binary integer programming problem which can be approximated by the branch and bound plus primal and dual algorithms [25].

5   Evalulation and Results

To evaluate the performance of our prediction algorithm and energy savings scheme we use three months of real world traffic data taken from 1145 BSs covering the four administrative counties comprising county Dublin in Ireland (Dublin City, Dún Laoghaire-Rathdown, Fingal and South Dublin)[1].

The data set includes information on all calls, SMS and cellular data usage for each of the network's users over the time period. Where appropriate, both voice calls and SMS are treated as an equivalent data service expressed in bytes and added to cellular data to get the Total Equivalent Data (TED). Voice is encoded in mobile phone networks using adaptive multirate (AMR) codecs. In GSM and wCDMA, a narrow-band AMR scheme is used with a typical data rate of 12.2 kbps. A higher quality wideband AMR is used in LTE and offers superior quality at a data rate of 12.5 kbps [26, 27]. Higher and lower data rates are possible, but for this paper a rate of 12.5 kbps will be used in converting voice channels to an equivalent data session. Text messages will be treated as a 200 byte message with 1 s duration.

---

[1] The boundary files used to define the four administrative counties can be obtained from the Irish Central Statistics Office. (2011, 01/02/2015). *Census 2011 Boundary Files*. Available: http://www. cso.ie/en/census/census2011boundaryfiles/.

The privacy of individual subscribers is paramount, thus all personal information in the dataset is anonymised and cannot be used to identify individual customers. No information was provided relating to the content of any call, SMS or data session.

5.1   Performance of Traffic Load Prediction

To evaluate the performance of our traffic load prediction algorithm we divide the dataset into three sets: 50 % training, 25 % test, and 25 % validation.

In [28] the authors suggest the use of scaled error metrics as an alternative to percentage error techniques when working with data on different scales. They propose the scaling of errors based on the training MAE from a "*naïve*" forecasting method. In the non-seasonal case using the naive method, we compute one-period-ahead forecasts from each data point in the training sample. Thus, a scaled error is defined as:

$$q_j = \frac{e_t}{\frac{1}{T-1}\sum_{t=2}^{T}|y_t - y_{t-1}|} \tag{16}$$

where we denote y_t as the observation of the load y at time t; $\hat{y}_t$ denotes a forecast of y_t T is the number of steps; the forecast error is defined as $e_t = y_t - t$.

As both the numerator and denominator include values on the scale of the original data, the result is independent of the data's scale. A scaled error of less than one results when the forecast is better than the mean naive forecast of the training data. A value greater than one indicates that the forecast was worse than the naive forecast calculated from the training set. As discussed in [3] network load exhibits a strong diurnal i.e. seasonal pattern which must be accounted for in our naive forecast component.

In the case of seasonal data we define the scaled error by employing a seasonal naive forecast:

$$q_j = \frac{e_t}{\frac{1}{T-m}\sum_{t=m+1}^{T}|y_t - y_{t-m}|} \tag{17}$$

where m is the seasonality component of the data. For example, setting m = 24 uses the value of the load 24 h ago as a naïve forecast of the load now.

The Mean Absolute Scaled Error (MASE) is thus defined as:

$$MASE = mean(|q_j|) \tag{18}$$

We calculate q_j from (17) for all the BSs, and we then get the MASE of all these results as in (18). We plot the MASE for one representative day for over 1000 BSs.

Figure 2 shows that the MASE value for the ANN prediction is usually less than 0.4 and hence a significant improvement on the naive method. As well as presenting the results for our ANN method we also plot results obtained from a Seasonal Auto Regressive Moving Average (SARMA) method presented in [3]. We see that the SARMA model again outperforms the naive method but is at all times, on average less accurate than our ANN method.

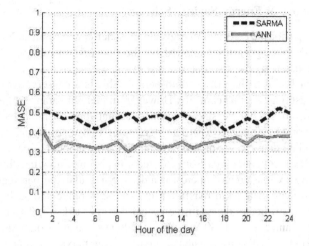

Fig. 2. The MASE over the course of one representative day for both SARMA and ANN.

Figure 3 illustrates the performance of the ANN load prediction method on one representative BS over a 24 h period. Generally the load prediction algorithm is stable under different load conditions; it consistently outperforms the naive and SARMA methods. We will now use it as a basis to perform predictions about the traffic load in our energy savings scheme.

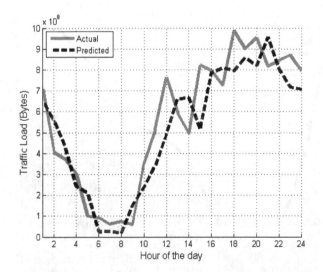

Fig. 3. Performance of the ANN traffic load prediction: Predicted value for one representative BS versus actual value over 24 h.

5.2   Performance of Energy Savings Scheme

To evaluate the performance of our energy saving scheme we inatalise the 1145 BSs to
their real world coverage grids (supplied by the network operators). The following
parameters are used: (i) the maximum capacity of each BS is set to the peak load
observed in that BS over the three month period. This is a conservative estimate and
probably underestimates actual capacity. However, in picking parameters we feel that it
is more realistic to err on the side of caution as network operators will invariably
overprovision for QoS reasons. (ii) The maximum transmission range depends on
population/building density. We previously calculated the amount of people working or
living in each BS's coverage area from call records [19] and now use these figures as
proxy for density. As our area of interest is a densely populated urban region we use a
conservative estimate of a 2 km maximum transmission range and scale down to the
order of hundreds of meters depending on local density [15]. (iii) The power models
$P_{tx} = 6L + 600$ W and P_{misc} = 1500 W are used at lower transmission ranges; the power
model $P_{tx} = 12L + 600$ W is used when approaching the maximum transmission range
[15_ENREF_15].

To quantify our results we calculate the power saving ratio which is defined as the
power consumption of the optimised network divided by the original unoptimised
power consumption of the network. Figure 4 shows the power saving ratio for Dublin's
1145 BSs over 24 h and the corresponding traffic load. We see that throughout the
entire day there is great scope to conserve energy in the network, particularly at times
of low load. For instance, over 70 % of the networks power consumption can be saved
during the early morning hours. Even during peak times energy savings of over 35 %
are possible.

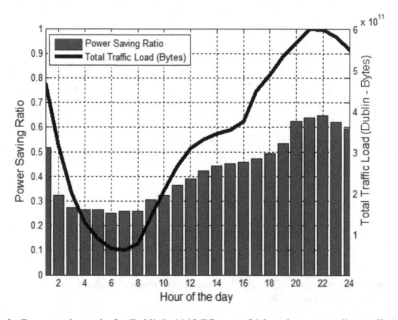

Fig. 4. Power saving ratio for Dublin's 1145 BSs over 24 h and corresponding traffic load.

6 Conclusion and Future Work

In this paper we have shown the potential for large resource savings by switching off underutilised BSs. Unlike other works in the area we use an ANN based predictive model of usage to make the switching decision ahead of time. The optimum set of BSs to turn off while maintaining QoS is formulated as a binary integer programming problem. We verified our results by using an extensive data set spanning all network usage over three months and 1145 BS covering all of Dublin city and county; we used actual BS locations and real world coverage zones provided by a network operator. Although our results are very promising, network operators may be reluctant to turn off BS for fear of degrading QoS. To assuage these fears in future work we hope to improve our prediction algorithm to provide robust prediction intervals based on long term traffic data. We also feel that it would be beneficial to examine the potential for improvements in resource usage at a more fine grained level. For example, dense city center v sparser suburban neighborhood, etc.

In this work we mainly focused on energy savings. However, in future work we wish to focus on identifying spectrum that is being underutilised by primary users. To that end we wish to reformat our optimisation routine to focus on maximising the considerable amount of underutilised spectrum in the network. This valuable licensed spectrum could be made available for secondary usage, particularly at off-peak times.

Acknowledgments. This work was supported through the Science Foundation Ireland Centre for Telecommunications Research (SFI-CE-I1853). The authors would like to thank the anonymous reviewers for their valuable comments and suggestions.

References

1. Chuang, Y.F.: Pull-and-suck effects in Taiwan mobile phone subscribers switching intentions. Telecommun. Policy **35**, 128–140 (2011)
2. Cisco.: Cisco Visual Networking Index: Global Mobile Data Traffic Forecast Update, 2011–2016. http://www.cisco.com/en/US/solutions/collateral/ns341/ns525/ns537/ns705/ns827/white_paper_c11–520862.html2012
3. Carolan, E., McLoone, S.C., Farrell, R.: Predictive modelling of cellular load. In: Proceedings of the Irish Signals & Systems Conference 2015 (26th IET), IT Carlow (2015)
4. C.M.R. Institute.: C-RAN: Road Towards Green Radio Access Network, Technical report (2010)
5. Hakim Ghazzai, E.Y., Alouini, M.-S., Adnan, A.-D., Ghazzai, Hakim: Smart grid energy procurement for green LTE cellular networks. In: Khan, S., Mauri, J.L. (eds.) Green Networking and Communications: ICT for Sustainability. CRC Press, Boca Raton (2013)
6. Reviriego, P., Maestro, J.A., Hernández, J.A., Larrabeiti, D.: Study of the potential energy savings in ethernet by combining energy efficient ethernet and adaptive link rate. Trans. Emerg. Telecommun. Technol. **23**, 227–233 (2012)
7. Fettweis, G., Zimmermann, E.: ICT energy consumption-trends and challenges. In: Proceedings of the 11th International Symposium on Wireless Personal Multimedia Communications, p. 6 (2008)

8. Carolan, E., McLoone, S., Farrell, R.: Characterising spatial relationships in base station resource usage. In: Proceedings of the 17th Research Colloquium on Communications and Radio Science into the 21st Century (2014)

9. Carolan, E., McLoone, S.C., Farrell, R.: Exploring spatial relationships and identifying influential nodes in cellular networks. In: Proceedings of the Irish Signals and Systems Conference 2014 and 2014 China-Ireland International Conference on Information and Communications Technologies (ISSC 2014/CIICT 2014), 25th IET, pp. 245–250 (2014)

10. Farrell, R., Carolan, E., McLoone, S.C., McLoone, S.F.: Towards a quantitative model of mobile phone usage ireland – a preliminary study. In: Proceedings of the Irish Signals and Systems Conference 2012 (IET), NUI Maynooth, Ireland (2012)

11. Oh, E., Son, K., Krishnamachari, B.: Dynamic base station switching-on/off strategies for green cellular networks. IEEE Trans. Wirel. Commun. 12, 2126–2136 (2013)

12. Saker, L., Elayoubi, S.-E., Chahed, T.: Minimizing energy consumption via sleep mode in green base station. In: IEEE 2010 Wireless Communications and Networking Conference (WCNC), pp. 1-6 (2010)

13. Hasan, Z., Boostanimehr, H., Bhargava, V.K.: Green cellular networks: A survey, some research issues and challenges. IEEE Commun. Surv. Tutorials 13, 524–540 (2011)

14. Willkomm, D., Machiraju, S., Bolot, J., Wolisz, A.: Primary users in cellular networks: a large-scale measurement study, pp. 1-11 (2008)

15. Peng, C., Lee, S.B., Lu, S., Luo, H., Li, H.: Traffic-driven power saving in operational 3G cellular networks, pp. 121-132 (2011)

16. Sauter, M.: From GSM To LTE: An Introduction to Mobile Networks and Mobile Broadband. Wiley Publisher, New York (2011)

17. Son, K., Kim, H., Yi, Y., Krishnamachari, B.: Base station operation and user association mechanisms for energy-delay tradeoffs in green cellular networks. IEEE J. Sel. Areas Commun. 29, 1525–1536 (2011)

18. Carolan, E., McLoone, S.C., Farrell, R.: Comparing and contrasting smartphone and non-smartphone usage. In: Proceedings of the Irish Signals and Systems Conference 2014 (IET), LYIT (2013)

19. Carolan, E., McLoone, S., McLoone, S., Farrell, R.: Analysing Ireland's interurban communication network using call data records. In: Proceedings of the Irish Signals and Systems Conference 2012 (IET), NUI Maynooth (2012)

20. Feng, H., Shu, Y.: Study on network traffic prediction techniques. In: Proceedings of 2005 International Conference on Wireless Communications, Networking and Mobile Computing, pp. 1041-1044 (2005)

21. Wang, G., Guo, C., Wang, S., Feng, C.: A traffic prediction based sleeping mechanism with low complexity in femtocell networks. In: 2013 IEEE International Conference on Communications Workshops (ICC), pp. 560-565 (2013)

22. Samarasinghe, S.: Neural Networks For Applied Sciences and Engineering: From Fundamentals to Complex Pattern Recognition. CRC Press, Boca Raton (2006)

23. Niu, Z., Wu, Y., Gong, J., Yang, Z.: Cell zooming for cost-efficient green cellular networks. IEEE Commun. Mag. 48, 74–79 (2010)

24. Li, R., Zhao, Z., Wei, Y., Zhou, X., Zhang, H.: GM-PAB: a grid-based energy saving scheme with predicted traffic load guidance for cellular networks. In: 2012 IEEE International Conference on Communications (ICC), pp. 1160–1164 (2012)

25. Bradley, S.P., Hax, A.C., Magnanti, T.L.: Applied Mathematical Programming. Addison Wesley, Reading (2007)

26. Bessette, B., Salami, R., Lefebvre, R., Jelinek, M., Rotola-Pukkila, J., Vainio, J., Mikkola, H., Jarvinen, K.: The adaptive multi-rate wideband speech codec (AMR-WB). IEEE Trans. Speech Audio Proc. **10**, 620–636 (2002)

27. Taddei, H., Varga, I., Gros, L., Quinquis, C., Monfort, J.Y., Mertz, F., Clevorn, T.: Evaluation of AMR-NB and AMR-WB in packet switched conversational communications. In: 2004 IEEE International Conference on Multimedia and Expo ICME 2004, pp. 2003-2006 (2004)

28. Hyndman, R.J., Koehler, A.B.: Another look at measures of forecast accuracy. Int. J. Forecast. **22**, 679–688 (2006)

A Framework for Cell-Association Auto Configuration of Network Functions in Cellular Networks

Stephen S. Mwanje[1]([⊠]), Janne Ali Tolppa[1], and Tsvetko Tsvetkov[2]

[1] Nokia, Munich, Germany
{stephen.mwanje,janne.ali-tolppa}@nokia.com
[2] Department of Computer Science, Technische Universität München,
Munich, Germany
tsvetko.tsvetkov@in.tum.de

Abstract. Self-Organizing Networks (SONs) introduce automation in Network Management (NM). Herein, SON functions automate the traditional NM tasks in the network. For some of these tasks, several cells must be associated together in order to achieve the intended objectives. As such, part of the process of configuring SON function is the configuration or selection of the required cell associations. For end-to-end automated NM, it is necessary that this task is also automated, especially in an environment with many SON functions.

This paper proposes an applicable auto configuration solution, called Cell Association Auto-Configuration (CAAC). First, we justify the need for the solution and describe the design of its component parts. Then, we evaluate the application of components of the approach to a real LTE network. The results, based on real network data, prove that CAAC is able to select the most appropriate associations for the SON functions, reducing the potential for run-time conflicts among the functions.

1 Introduction

Self-Organizing Networks (SONs) is an approach in managing mobile networks, which introduces automation in the typical NM tasks [1]. A set of autonomous SON functions undertake the traditionally manual NM tasks, i.e. Configuration Management (CM), network optimization or Performance Management (PM), Fault Management (FM), as well as failure detection and recovery. Each SON function is a closed control loop, which adjusts a set of Network Configuration Parameters in order to optimize a set of Key Performance Indicator (KPIs). Typical SON functions include network level function like Energy Saving (ES), Mobility Load Balancing (MLB) and others defined e.g., in [1]. In this paper, however, we use the term SON function (SF) to refer not only to the traditional SON functions but also to the other multi-cell features like Carrier Aggregation (CA) or Coordinated Multi-point Transmission (Comp), whose requirements for multi-cell operation are similar to the ones for typical SON functions.

© Institute for Computer Sciences, Social Informatics and Telecommunications Engineering 2015
R. Agüero et al. (Eds.): MONAMI 2015, LNICST 158, pp. 68–80, 2015.
DOI: 10.1007/978-3-319-26925-2_6

The behavior of each function can be configured by means of CM parameters, so that, depending on the CM parameter values, the function's behavior may differ at two different time or spatial instances. Consequently, we explicitly use the term "instance" for the function instances, and always use "SON function" to refer to the function type.

For many SON functions, several cells must cooperate to achieve the intended objective. For example, consider that cell 2 in Fig. 1 is to be deactivated for ES. It is necessary to ensure that another cell (e.g., cell 4) is able to guarantee coverage for the areas initially served by the deactivated cell. Similarly, before cells 1 and 2 are grouped together for CA, it needs to be confirmed that both cells support CA and if so the frequencies that are supported. For such use cases, cells must be configured to associate for the respective functions.

Generating the cell associations involves two prerequisite processes - determination of adequate overlap and detection of the requisite capabilities. In the first case, usually the coverage area of the cells must overlap in a suitable way. For example, two cells are associated for CA, when a sufficient number of users receive good coverage from both cells. Then, besides appropriate overlap, the cells must have the required capabilities which must also be communicated amongst the cells. For instance, CA requires that the supported frequencies are determined and communicated.

Moreover, it is also necessary to ensure that the selected cell associations do not conflict with each other. Consider the conflict in Fig. 1 where cell 2 is associated with cell 1 for CA but also associated with cell 4 for ES. Although cell 4 will compensate for coverage in case cell 2 is deactivated, an unexpected behavior may result for CA between cells 1 and 2 if cell 2 is deactivated without

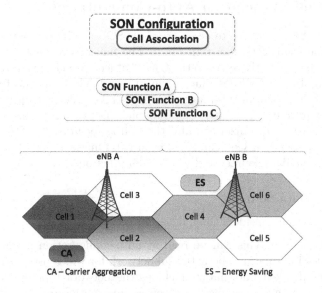

Fig. 1. Configuration of Cell Association for SON functions

consideration of this effect on CA. In that case, the cell associations need to be configured in such a way that these conflicts are eliminated or at least minimized.

It is imaginable that conflicts can be managed through runtime SON coordination and verification that have been widely studied, e.g. in [2–12]. The challenge is that as the number and complexity of SON functions increases, so does the complexity of runtime coordination. In the extreme case, this can be exponential, since the Coordinator must account for all possible combinations of the SON functions. A highly complex set of conflicting SON functions can lead to too much SON coordination and verification, which would make it difficult to undertake the necessary optimizations, as the system is in a constant state of conflict resolution. SON configuration should therefore minimize the reliance on SON coordination and verification, improving the end-to-end system performance; in effect by complementing the two processes.

In this paper, we propose a framework for the auto-configuration of cell associations. The framework implements four components that aim to automate:

1. the computation of overlap among cells
2. the detection of cell capabilities for the SON functions
3. the detection of conflicts among cell associations
4. the resolution of detected conflicts

The rest of the paper is structured as follows: Sect. 2 describes the solution and how it achieves the objectives of autonomous association of cells for SON and optimizing the associations to minimize conflicts. Then, in Sect. 3, we present results of applying the proposed approach to a real network scenario. Finally, we conclude with a summary and outlook to our expected future work in Sect. 4.

2   SON Cell Association Auto-Configuration

For the SON CAAC expected to be a part of the SON configuration task (Fig. 1), we propose the framework shown in Fig. 2. The function consists of two major components which directly relate to the CAAC objectives: (1) a Cell Association Constructor and (2) a Cell Association Optimizer. Each of the two functions is composed of two sequential sub-functions: the Cell Association Constructor having Cell Overlap Detection and the Cell Capability Detection sub-functions while the Cell Association Optimizer contains the Cell Association Conflict Detection and the Cell Association Conflict Resolution sub-functions. The following sections describe the data sources and CAAC sub-functions.

2.1   CAAC Data Sources

The CAAC function considers three data sources:

1. Network CM data: This can be read at auto-configuration execution time, and includes information about the subnetwork for which associations are to be configured. Such information includes the network topology, cells characteristics (e.g., macro or pico), as well as information on any existing cell associations.

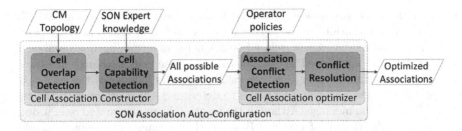

Fig. 2. Structure of the SON CAAC framework

2. SON expert knowledge: This is expected to be provided as part of the SON solution by its vendor and mainly defines two elements. First, it must define the association pre-requisites for the SON function, which are typically different for each SON function and may be different for any two vendors. In the case of CA for example, besides defining the supported frequencies, the vendor should define which particular inter-band CA combinations are supported. Secondly, expert knowledge for a given SON function should define the rules for assessing the function's likelihood and severity of runtime conflicts with other SON functions. For instance, ES is expected to conflict with CA, but its likelihood and severity, when compared say to the conflict between ES and MLB, needs to be defined.
3. Network operator's policies and targets: Defined as part of the network planning process, these are intended to optimize the conflicting objectives of the SON functions depending on the operating environment. Most critical here are priorities given to the different SON functions and the conflict threshold, which defines the acceptable level of runtime conflict (That is expected to be managed by the SON coordinator). Both the priorities and threshold may be set differently for different environments. For example, ES may be prioritized higher than CA in a rural setting and vice versa in a city business district.

2.2 Cell Overlap Detection

For two or more cells to be associated for a certain SON function, their coverage area must overlap in a suitable way. For example, two cells are associated for CA when a sufficient number of users receive good coverage from both cells. The required overlap may not be the same for all SON functions but overlap must either way be quantified. The overlap quality contains requirements on:

1. the percentage of overlap for each of the neighbor cells
2. the nature of the overlap either as intra- or inter-frequency
3. the type of the cells (e.g., macro or small cell)
4. the multiplicity defined in terms of the number of cells that overlap with the selected cell

Cell overlaps can be calculated based on the combination of radio propagation models and network planning data such as antenna coordinates, direction, angle, beam width and transmission power. Such data does not, however, necessarily reflect the real situation in the active network and so a real-time-data based solution is required. A closely related solution for determining if a number of cells overlap was introduced in [13]. In this case, the cells exchange messages, whose content relates to the user terminals within the vicinity of the cells. The concerned cell then uses the list of UEs to determine if it overlaps with the cell that originated the message. Although the solution is an automated one, it does not quantify the degree of overlap. Besides, the exchange of messages would, in a highly dynamic environment, place an extra constraint on the signaling resources.

Our proposal is an improved approach based on User Equipment (UE) measurements that are translated into an interference matrix. We note here that the cell overlap detection component aims at determining whether the concerned cells have a region of overlapping radio coverage and if this region has a sufficient number of users that the two cells should be associated for the said SON function. For example, if a cell A is a full underlay cell of another cell B (A's coverage area is a subset of B's area), the two can be associated for ES, since the smaller cell can be deactivated for ES. Alternatively, the two cells can be associated for CA.

Consider a primary cell p and an intra-frequency secondary cell s as shown in Fig. 3. The degree of overlap between p and s defines the proportion of the users served by p that lie within a region where they could also be served by s. The overlap detection component evaluates the interference C/I that users in p receive from s. This interference is defined as:

$$(C/I)_s = RSRP_s - RSRP_p, \tag{1}$$

where $RSRP_s$ and $RSRP_p$ are respectively the Reference Signal Received Power (RSRP) from cells s and p as measured by the reporting user device.

For cell p, the overlap is the proportion of users that have significant interference from s. As shown in Fig. 3, a user is considered to have "significant interference" if:

1. The neighbor cell RSRP is above a threshold ThMIN_RSRP, which represents the lowest possible RSRP at which a cell is able to serve a user.
2. C/I is below a threshold ThMAX_IF. This condition is optional and may be neglected by relying on the handover procedure to set the highest acceptable interference. The assumption in that case is that if interference from the neighbor becomes too high, then the user will initiate handover to the neighbor cell.

For the cell p and in a given time frame, we track a counter TotalUserCount that counts all users that have been served by p. Then for each neighbor s, we track another counter HighIFUsers that counts the number of users with significant interference from s. The degree of overlap between p and s is, therefore, the ratio of HighIFUsers to TotalUserCount. Note that what we quantify here is the proportion of users in the overlapping region as opposed to the percentage of geographical overlap. For many SON use cases, this overlap of users is

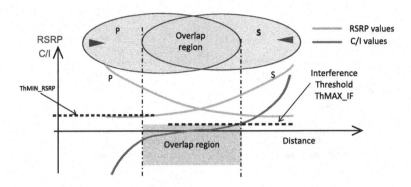

Fig. 3. Overlap detection thresholds

more important than the geographical overlap since the metrics rely on user experience counter statistics.

The approach as described above is also applicable for inter-frequency overlap detection. Therein, C/I is not the degree of interference between p and s but the cell coupling between the two cells. To achieve it, UEs must report RSRP measurements for the inter-frequency neighbors, which is possible when inter-frequency Automatic Neighbor Relation (ANR) [1] is activated. Meanwhile, this need for RSRP measurement (in both inter and intra-frequency scenarios) implies that the solution is only applicable during network operations. Where it may be needed to configure associations at network commissioning, planning data would have to be used as seed and the associations re-optimized on starting normal operations.

2.3 Cell Capability Detection

For a set of cells to be associated for some SON function(s), the cells or their eNBs must have the required capabilities and prerequisites for the particular SON function(s). This includes having the required features installed and enabled or disabled. Given the observed overlaps among a set of cells, the capability detection determines what each of the cells is capable of. Matching the overlapping pairs with the capabilities, it generates a list of all possible associations among the given set of cells. It then gives a score for each association depending on how well the association is suited for the particular SON function. This score defines the quality of the association and would be used, for example, if choice had to be made on retaining one of two conflicting associations.

The set of all possible associations can be represented by a cell association graph that shows the interrelations among the different cells. Consider a network topology like the example in Fig. 4a with a set of cells and a set of SON functions available to each cell. The corresponding association graph is Fig. 4b. It should be noted that capability detection is SON function and vendor specific. It heavily depends on expert knowledge as supplied by the vendor's SON experts.

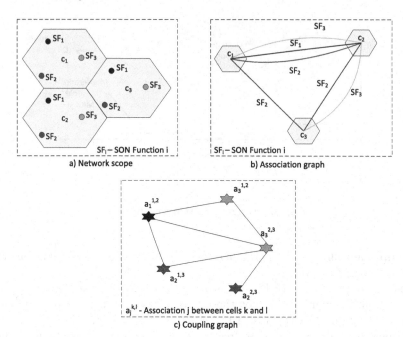

Fig. 4. Cell Association example

Consequently, CAAC only defines an interface for the capability detection to which a plug-in implementation needs to be attached for each function to be supported by the CAAC.

2.4 Cell Association Conflict Detection

For each function, an "impact area" can be defined as the spatial scope within which the function instance modifies CM parameters, takes measurements, affects metrics after taking action or in general the set of cells it affects. Cells or functions can be considered coupled if their impact areas overlap.

The conflict detection component looks for the potentially conflicting cell associations for the considered functions and network scope. Each pair of coupled cells i.e., cells where the associations have an overlapping impact area, is given a coupling score which quantifies the expected effect of the conflict between these associations. The score is based on:

1. The likelihood and severity of a runtime conflict among the particular functions, as defined by the applicable expert knowledge.
2. The respective priorities of conflicting function instances as defined in the operator policy.
3. The quality of the respective cell association instances as determined by the capability detection.

Consider that an association $a_k^{i,j}$ is configured between cells i and j for a SON function instance k. Then, if the set of all possible cell associations is A, consider that association $a_k^{i,j}$ is coupled with another association $a_l^{m,n}$ (the association between cells m and n for SON function instance l). We define a coupling score for the effect of $a_k^{i,j}$ on $a_l^{m,n}$ as $C(a_k^{i,j}, a_l^{m,n})$ or simply $C(k,l) \in [0; 100]$ for brevity. $C(k,l)$ defines the coupling score accorded to $a_k^{i,j}$ for its effect on $a_l^{m,n}$ as:

$$C(k,l) = P(k,l) \cdot imp(k,l) \cdot [w \cdot prio(l) + (1 - w) \cdot q(l)] \qquad (2)$$

$P(k,l)$ and $imp(k,l)$ both in the range [0-1] and defined by the SON expert knowledge, respectively give the probability of occurrence and the impact of a runtime conflict between k and l. $prio(l) \in [0\text{-}100]$ is the operator-defined priority of the SON function in instance l. Such priorities can be configured to different values per sub-network or maintenance region to ensure that different SON functions are executed as priority in different parts of the network. One example could be to prefer CA in urban areas for increased capacity and ES in rural areas for reduced energy consumption. Meanwhile, $q(l) \in [0 - 100]$ is the quality of cell association $a_l^{m,n}$, in principle the outcome of the cell association construction. The relative significance of $prio(l)$ and $q(l)$ is controlled by the weighing factor $w \in [0 - 1]$. Two critical properties of $C(k,l)$ should also be noted:

1. only the priority and quality of l are considered in evaluating $C(k,l)$ since the aim is to measure the impact of association instance k on instance l.
2. $C(k,l)$ is not commutative i.e. $C(k,l) \neq C(l,k)$.

Given the definitions, any Cell association pair (k,l) for which $C(k,l) > 0$ is a potential conflict since its SON functions are coupled.

2.5   Cell Association Conflict Resolution

The Conflict-Resolution component attempts to reduce the degree of coupling, and consequently the need for run-time coordination, by eliminating those cell associations with the most coupling effects. The degree of conflict is modeled by a coupling graph that is derived from the cell association graph. Such a coupling graph is given in Fig. 4c for the network presented in Fig. 4a. In the coupling graph, each cell association is modeled as a vertex, whereas an edge is added connecting each pair of coupled associations, i.e. those for which $C(k,l) > 0$. The intention of Conflict-Resolution therefore is to decouple the graph in the best possible way (as controlled by the operator's policy).

For each function instance k (and its corresponding association), a conflict score, $S_k \in [0 - 100]$, is calculated as the normalized sum of $C(k,l), \forall a_l \in A$, $l \neq k$, i.e. the sum of the coupling scores of the association between k with all the other cell associations. The normalization is relative to the maximum cardinality of the set of all the SON functions, i.e.:

$$S_k = \frac{\sum\limits_{\forall l \in A, l \neq k} C(k,l)}{\max\limits_{a \in A}(|A_a|)} \qquad (3)$$

where A is the set of all associations and $|A|$ is the cardinality of set A.

The operator policy sets a conflict threshold, Th_Max_S $\in [0 - 100]$ which defines the acceptable degree of coupling within the system, i.e. it defines the conflicts which would be coordinated at runtime. The Cell Association Conflict Resolution component then implements a simple Constraint Satisfaction Problem (CSP) solver which removes the most conflicting cell associations for which $S_k >$ Th_Max_S. By using this threshold, the operator can control the compromise between having as many SON functions running in the network as possible and reducing the required runtime coordination. For instance, setting Th_Max_S $= 0$ would mean that all coupled cell associations are removed. This will greatly reduce the need for runtime coordination, but at the same time will deactivate a high number of SON functions. Conversely, setting Th_Max_S $= 100$ would allow all the possible cell associations at the cost of significant runtime conflicts.

The removal of the most coupled cell associations is undertaken by removing one association at a time starting with the one having the highest S_k value. After each removal, S_k is recalculated for all k and removal continues to the next association for which $k = argmax\{S_k\}$. Once the process is finished, CAAC notifies the relevant SON functions of the changed cell associations. The SON functions then translate the associations into concrete network changes or reconfigurations of the centralized SON system.

3   Conceptual Results

In this section, we describe our results for the proposed solution when applied to data from a real LTE network topology as shown in Fig. 5. We assume that only two SON functions (ES and CA) are implemented in the SON-CAAC. The considered use case is the addition of a new cell to the network (cell 50), i.e. we assume that cell 50 has been added to the network and that associations for the two SON functions must be configured for this cell.

As described in Sect. 2.2, overlap detection requires actual UE measurements. As such, a planning-data based overlap calculation has been implemented in the experimental system to calculate the overlaps, which are used as basis for the association quality scores. We therefore do not show any results for overlap detection, and instead mainly focus on the conflict detection and resolution. We, however, pair cells for association using planning data, i.e., when cell 50 is introduced, the overlap detection component calculates the cell's overlap with all neighboring cells. These neighboring cells are also defined using planning data as opposed to being detected by the ANR SON use case.

Evaluations begin with an initially high conflict threshold, set such that all possible new associations are included. This is then later lowered to evaluate the effects of different policies. In particular, we evaluate the three scenarios:

Scenario (1) Default scenario with SON functions equally prioritized (prio=50) and the default threshold, Th_Max_S $= 20$.

Scenario (2) ES priority scenario which applies the default conflict threshold, but prioritizes ES higher than CA (i.e. prio(ES)=80,
prio(CA)=10).

Scenario (3) Low conflict scenario where ES is again prioritized, but with a
lowered conflict threshold, Th_Max_S = 10.

We assume a simple capability detection feature that assumes that all cells
are capable of ES and CA and that the applicable prerequisites can be met in all
circumstances. The overlap information is provided to the capability detection
components created for CA and ES. For each SON function, based on the amount
of overlap (and its directionality) between cell 50 and any neighboring cell c, the
respective plug-in calculates the quality $q(l)$ of that cell association. This is
then applied in computing the coupling score as defined in Eq. 2. Meanwhile, we
assume also that the quality and priority of the SON functions are equally as
important in calculating the coupling score, i.e. $w = 0.5$ in Eq. 2.

The result of this process, when applied to scenario 1, is the set of all the
possible associations between cell 50 and the other existing cells for the ES and
CA SON functions. This is depicted in Fig. 5a. Each node in the figure is a cell
with the lines indicating the possible associations between the different cells.
The meanings of the colour coding scheme is as follows:

- pink and green - respectively for CA and ES
- solid and dotted - respectively for existing and new asociations
- bold red - for the conflicting associations, i.e. those for which $S_k >$ Th_Max_S

The coupling graph for the associations in Fig. 5a is the graph in Fig. 5b, which
highlights all the conflicts in Fig. 5a and their corresponding coupling scores.

As seen in Fig. 5b, the ES associations between the new cell (cell 50) and
cell 86 are the most conflicting and are, therefore, the recommended ones to
be removed. Applying the conflict resolution removes these assoiations with the
result being Fig. 5c where there is no more conclict between CA and ES.

Meanwhile, we expect that the associations selected to be removed and consequently the reduction in conflict will depend on the applied threshold. To
evaluate the effect of the threshold, the association graph is regenerated for the
two other scenarios where ES is prioritized, i.e. $prio(ES) = 80, prio(AC) = 10$.
The conflict threshold Th_Max_S is maintained at 20 in the first scenario, but
reduced to 10 in the second. The resulting association graphs are Figs. 6 and 7
respectively.

Compared to Fig. 5a, we observe in Fig. 6a that the most conflicting SON
function ceases to be ES and becomes CA. This is because the priority of ES
has been raised, implying that other SON functions (CA in this case) are now
penalized more for conflicting with instances of ES. The corresponding conflict
resolution result is Fig. 6b, where the high conflict CA association is removed
and both ES associations retained.

When Th_Max_S is, however, reduced as is the case in scenario 3 (in Fig. 7a),
more associations are expected to exceed the threshold. From Fig. 7a, besides
the CA association, the coupling scores of the two ES associations also exceed

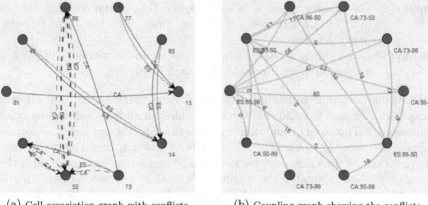

(a) Cell association graph with conflicts   (b) Coupling graph showing the conflicts

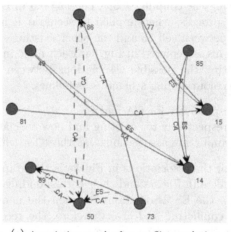

(c) Association graph after conflict resolution

Fig. 5. Conflicts resolution between ES and CA function instances

the threshold (i.e. S_{ES} >Th_Max_S), adding the two ES associations to the list
of removal candidates. The ES associations are nevertheless maintained after
conflict resolution, a result of the one-by-one removal process. Since the conflict
scores are recalculated after removing the most conflicting association, the ES
scores cease to exceed the threshold. It is then no longer necessary to remove
the ES associations. Noted that with the lower conflict threshold (Fig. 7a), one
of the existing CA cell associations also exceeds the threshold. This is however
not removed because by default CAAC does not optimize existing associations.

These results show that given appropriate overlap detection, the CAAC is not
only able to generate a set of cell associations for a given set of SON functions
in consideration of the operator's objectives, but also minimizes the conflicts
among the selected associations.

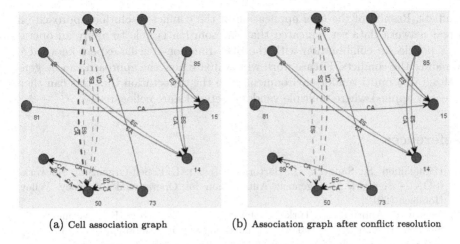

(a) Cell association graph   (b) Association graph after conflict resolution

Fig. 6. Conflict resolution with priority for ES

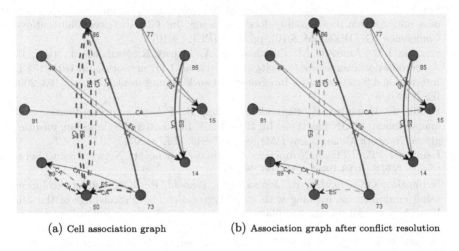

(a) Cell association graph   (b) Association graph after conflict resolution

Fig. 7. Conflict resolution with priority for ES and a reduced conflict threshold

4 Conclusion

Based on the observation that cells need to associate with one another for some traditional Self-Organizing Network functions as well as for multi-cell network features, this paper has proposed a framework for auto-configuration of such associations. We have justified the need for the Cell Association Auto Configuration (CAAC) solution and, proposed requirements and designs for its constituent components. We proposed automated solutions for detecting the overlap among cells with the intention of associating the cells for the SON functions. We then described a conflict detection and resolution solution through which we are able to minimize the coupling among cell associations thereby reducing their run time

conflicts. Results of the trial application of the conflict resolution approach on
a real network data set indicated that the solution is able to apply an operator's policies in combination with the SON-function-specific expert knowledge
to reduce the conflicts. Future work will evaluate how the approach can be gen-
eralized in a multi-vendor environment with the expectation that this can then
be easily applied where multiple vendors' networks are collocated.

References

1. Hämäläinen, S., Sanneck, H., Sartori, C. (eds.): LTE Self-Organising Networks
   (SON) - Network Management Automation for Operational Efficiency. Wiley,
   Hoboken (2012)
2. Jansen, T., Amirijoo, M., Turke, U., Jorguseski, L., Zetterberg, K., Nascimento, R.,
   Schmelz, L.C., Turk, J., Balan, I.: Embedding multiple self-organisation functionalities in future radio access networks. In: 69th Vehicular Technology Conference,
   2009. VTC Spring 2009, pp. 1–5. IEEE (2009)
3. Liu, Z., Hong, P., Xue, K., Peng, M.: Conflict avoidance between mobility robust-
   ness optimization and mobility load balancing. In: Global Telecommunications
   Conference (GLOBECOM 2010), pp. 1–5. IEEE (2010)
4. Schmelz, L.C., Amirijoo, M., Eisenblaetter, A., Litjens, R., Neuland, M., Turk, J.:
   A coordination framework for self-organisation in LTE networks. In: IFIP/IEEE
   International Symposium on Integrated Network Management (IM), pp. 193–200.
   IEEE (2011)
5. Bandh, T., Romeikat, R., Sanneck, H., Tang, H.: Policy-based coordination and
   management of SON functions. In: IFIP/IEEE International Symposium on Integrated Network Management (IM), pp. 827–840. IEEE (2011)
6. Kemptner, T.: LTE SON-function coordination concept. Netw. Archit. Serv.
   (NET) **NET-2013-08-1**, 101–106 (2013)
7. Iacoboaiea, O.C., Sayrac, B., Jemaa, S.B., Bianchi, P.: SON conflict resolution
   using reinforcement learning with state aggregation. In: Proceedings of the 4th
   Workshop on All Things Cellular: Operations, Applications, & Challenges, pp.
   15–20. ACM (2014)
8. Mwanje, S.S., Mitschele-Thiel, A.: Minimizing handover performance degradation
   due to LTE self organized mobility load balancing. In: 77th Vehicular Technology
   Conference (VTC Spring), pp. 1–5. IEEE (2013)
9. Mwanje, S.S., Mitschele-Thiel, A.: STS: space-time scheduling for coordinating self-
   organization network functions in LTE. In: IFIP/IEEE International Symposium
   on Integrated Network Management (IM 2015), Ottawa, Canada (2015)
10. Zia, N., Mwanje, S.S., Mitschele-Thiel, A.: A policy based conflict resolution mechanism for MLB and MRO in LTE self-optimizing networks. In: IEEE Symposium
   on Computers and Communication (ISCC), pp. 1–6. IEEE (2014)
11. Mwanje, S.S., Mitschele-Thiel, A.: Concurrent cooperative games for coordinating
   SON functions in cognitive cellular networks. In: IFIP/IEEE International Symposium on Integrated Network Management (IM 2015), Ottawa, Canada (2015)
12. Vlacheas, P., Thomatos, E., Tsagkaris, K., Demestichas, P.: Operator-governed
   SON Coordination in downlink LTE Networks. In: Future Network & Mobile Summit (FutureNetw), pp. 1–9. IEEE (2012)
13. Ericsson Telefon Ab L M: Method of discovering overlapping cells (2010)

Radio Resource Management in LTE and 5G Networks

On the Performance of Indoor Ultra-Dense Networks for Millimetre-Wave Cellular Systems

Saray Renilla Lamas$^{(\boxtimes)}$, David González G., and Jyri Hämäläinen

Department of Communications and Networking,
Aalto University School of Electrical Engineering, Espoo, Finland
{saray.renillalamas,david.gonzalezgonzalez,
jyri.hamalainen}@aalto.fi

Abstract. The combination of Ultra-Dense Networks (UDN) and millimetre Waves (mmW) communications has recently been recognized by the industry and research community as a promising solution to cope with the evolving requirements of the fifth generation (5G) of cellular networks. Indeed, the problem of capacity provisioning has drawn the attention to mmW due to the spectrum scarcity at lower frequency bands. Additionally, the densification process has already started with the introduction of the well-known Heterogeneous Networks (HetNets).Thus the use of UDN is another natural approach for increasing the overall network capacity, especially in such indoor environments where high data rates and service demand are expected. In this paper, the combination of the previous paradigms is analysed by means of comprehensive system-level simulations. Unfortunately, the particularities of indoor deployments make radio propagation difficult to predict and limit the macro-cell coverage, hence these simulations have been evaluated using advanced Ray Tracing (RT) techniques. Results confirm the superior system performance of the mmW and UDN tandem with respect to current operating bands.

Keywords: Millimetre waves · mmW · Ultra-dense networks · UDN · Energy efficiency · System-level simulations · 5G · Indoor planning

1 Introduction

During the last decade, cellular networks have witnessed the rapid penetration of smart-devices. This tendency has recently been fuelled by the evolution of these devices into the so-called *smarter* smart-phones and the irruption of a new wide range of wireless devices, including tablets, wearable sensors, and smart-watches [1]. Our society can be referred as the *Networked Society* [2]; in fact, we will be more *networked* than ever in coming years since it is expected that the total number of mobile subscriptions keeps exponentially growing year-by-year, and the amount of wirelessly connected devices will increase by 40 % at the beginning of 2020 [3,4]. As a result of this unprecedented revolution, the fifth generation (5G) of cellular systems will target significantly increased network

© Institute for Computer Sciences, Social Informatics and Telecommunications Engineering 2015
R. Agüero et al. (Eds.): MONAMI 2015, LNICST 158, pp. 83–94, 2015.
DOI: 10.1007/978-3-319-26925-2_7

capacity and better spectral efficiency to answer the rapidly increasing cellular traffic demand [5]. For instance, it is expected that 5G networks will need to support peak data rates of 10 Gbps for downlink, 1000 times higher mobile data volume per area, and up to 100 times higher number of mobile devices [6]. Moreover, operators will also have to face the challenge that a significant portion of this traffic will be generated in indoor locations, accounting for up to 90 % of the total network load [7].

Given this, both the industry and standardization bodies have joined efforts to make current networks meet future user's requirements; however, these are not likely to suffice. It is obvious that radio spectrum is scarce at current operation bands due to the growing service demand, and that liberating bandwidths up to 100 MHz in the existing licensed bands would be at a considerable expense in both economic and technological aspects [8]. Moreover, according to the International Telecommunication Union (ITU), the estimated spectrum bandwidth requirements will be between 1340 MHz and 1960 MHz by 2020 [9]. To that end, millimetre Waves (mmW) communications have emerged as the key enabler of such networks due to the vast amounts of contiguous available spectrum within this frequency range [10].

Without any doubt, mmW communications will boost network capacity by increasing the available spectrum. Nevertheless, due to the propagation characteristics at these frequencies, and particularly, in indoor environments, they also bring the possibility of further exploiting network densification in order to provide better coverage. Precisely, Ultra-Dense Networks (UDN) are also considered a key paradigm for future 5G scenarios since they aim at improving the overall network areal spectral efficiency by increasing the total number of access points [11].

It is this combination, the tandem constituted by mmW and UDN, the one that has been envisioned as a promising solution in order to solve the challenge of indoor service provisioning in the next generation of cellular systems [12,13]. Existing network planning methods have mainly been conceived to ensure outdoor coverage; however, due to the strong outdoor-to-indoor penetration loss, indoor areas suffer from poor Signal-to-Interference-plus-Noise Ratio (SINR), and hence, the indoor service demand becomes very expensive in terms of resources for the already congested macro-cells [14]. Thus, there is an urge to investigate the impact both paradigms in the context of 5G networks. Previous studies on the mmW side have mainly been focused on their propagation characteristics [15–18]. In [19,20], coverage and capacity provisioning of mmW have been studied in the context of outdoor communications. Likewise in [21], coverage probability and cell throughput have been compared for microwave networks.

Similarly, on the UDN side, a mathematical model and performance characterization of dense heterogeneous networks have been proposed in [22]. Energy Efficiency (EE) is another *hot topic* in this field, and examples can be found in [23,24]. However, the research focused on mmW and UDN for indoor cellular deployments is still in its infancy, and therefore, few publications can be found

Table 1. Summary of related work.

Ref.	mmW	Test case	Method	Main aspect
[27]	×	Indoor	Measurements	Channel modeling
[28]	×	Outdoor	Simulations	Interference manag
[17]	✓	Outdoor	Simulations	Channel modeling
[18]	✓	Outdoor	Analytical	Downlink coverage
[29]	✓	Outdoor	Measurements	Network capacity
[14]	✓	Indoor	Measurements	Outdoor-indoor cov
[16]	✓	Indoor	Measurements	Channel modeling
[30]	✓	Outdoor	Simulations	Network Capacity
[31]	×	Outdoor	Simulations	Scheduling

that investigate it. Table 1 provides a comparative perspective of several related contributions in both areas.

To the best of the authors' knowledge, only very recent publications [25] have contributed with system-level performance evaluations of UDN and mmW, although realistic scenarios were not considered. In our previous work [26], we presented a novel framework for cellular indoor planning and deployment optimization of indoor UDN operating at mmW based on Multiobjective Optimization (MO) and Ray Tracing (RT) techniques. By means of the statistical method presented therein, it was shown that effective network planning and topology/layout adaptation [32] provide significant improvements in terms of system capacity, cell-edge performance, and energy efficiency. In this paper, we continue the research in that line and further analyze the proposed framework by means of system-level simulations. Thus, the contribution of this paper is a detailed performance assessment and a comparative analysis of different ultra-dense topologies at both low and high frequencies. The results show that, besides the clear gain associated to the allocation of more bandwidth operating at mmW, several other benefits including better energy efficiency and cell-edge performance exist.

The rest of the document is organized as follows: First, the system model and performance metrics are described in the next section. Section 3 describes the evaluation settings and the analysis of the results. Finally, conclusions are drawn in Sect. 4.

2 Methodology

This section is divided in three parts that provide a detailed description of the experiments and the adopted methodology.

2.1 Simulation Scenario

The simulated scenario is a realistic indoor dense deployment covering a specific area of the School of Electrical Engineering of Aalto University as Fig. 1a illustrates.

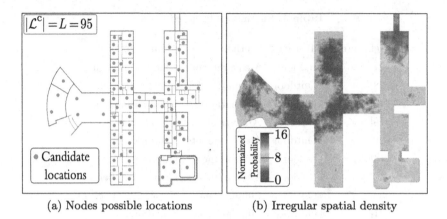

(a) Nodes possible locations   (b) Irregular spatial density

Fig. 1. Simulation environment

As mentioned, mmW propagation models are still immature [33]. Indeed, results show that the accuracy of these models are highly dependent on the environment and simulation characteristics. Thus, in order to have a precise radio characterization of the indoor environment, the propagation has been simulated by means of RT techniques [34]. RT is a deterministic propagation model that allows for accurate radio propagation prediction in indoor layouts at different frequency ranges [35].

The evaluation area corresponds to an indoor sub-area of the building of 92×84 m^2 with a pixel resolution of $1/7 \times 1/7$ m^2. In order to create a highly densified environment, an average Inter-Site Distance (ISD) of 3–4 m was set between each access point. The possible locations of all possible nodes are also shown in Fig. 1a. Antennas were placed on the ceiling (at a distance of 2.4 m from the floor) and the height of the users was set to 1.5 m, according to [36]. For evaluation purposes, 140 users are distributed within the area of interest following a given traffic distribution. In this work, only an irregular service demand is considered (see Fig. 1b).

2.2 System Model

This study focuses on the system level evaluation within the LTE-Advanced framework [36], an extended statistical analysis of the proposed system model can be found in [26]. The downlink of an Orthogonal Frequency Division Multiple Access (OFDMA) cellular network is considered herein. A frequency reuse factor of one (full reuse scheme) has been selected among all active access points. In terms of resource allocation, a Round Robin (RR) scheduler is considered and all available resources in a cell are assigned at a given time. That is

$$m_i = \frac{m_C}{m_U}, \tag{1}$$

where m_i is the number of Physical Resource Blocks (PRBs) assigned to the user i, m_C is the total number of PRBs assigned to each cell, and m_U is the total number of users attached to the node. We note that, as the focus is on

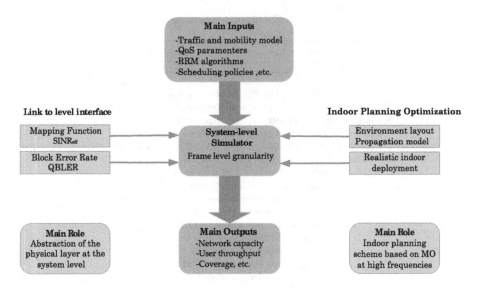

Fig. 2. System-level simulations framework

the comparison among network topologies and operating bands, the selection of an arbitrary scheduling discipline does not affect the conclusions. The same applies to the size of the operating band size.

The implementation of the semi-static system-level simulations have been developed in a MATLAB environment, and based on Monte Carlo experiments (a schematic of the simulator is illustrated in Fig. 2). The SINR to link throughput mapping has been carried out by the guidelines provided in [37]. In total, results compiled statistics taken from 3000 independent experiments or user drops. Table 2 summarizes the simulation parameters based on 3GPP specifications [38]. Precisely, the system considers a 20 MHz of bandwidth ($B_{\text{eff}} = 18$ MHz) thus the total number PRBs available for users is 100, each simulated drop corresponds to a Transmission Time Interval (TTI), that is 1 ms.

2.3 Performance Metrics

Performance metrics were selected according to 3GPP recommendations [39]. For instance, to evaluate and illustrate the network performance, Cumulative Distribution Functions (CDFs) of user's throughput were computed. Additionally, numeric results were documented for the 50th-tile and 5th-tile representing the in-cell and cell-edge users, respectively. Finally, three additional aspects have been investigated: the network energy efficiency as defined in [26], the impact of user density on the end-to-end performance, and the system fairness by means of the Jain's index (Υ) defined as follows:

$$\Upsilon(T_1, T_2, \cdots, T_m) = \frac{\left(\sum_{i=1}^{m} T_i\right)^2}{m \cdot \sum_{i=1}^{m} T_i^2}, \tag{2}$$

Table 2. Simulation parameters

Parameter Value	Parameter Value
System parameters	
Nodes $L \in [10, 95]$	Inter-site distance 3-4 m
Pixels resolution $1/7 \times 1/7 \, \text{m}^2$	Number of pixels 391510
Sys. bandwidth (B) 18 MHz	Number of PRBs 100
Sub-carriers power -17.8 dBm	Interference margin 4.0 dB
Shadowing STD 7.0 dB	Rx. noise figure 7.0 dB
Thermal noise -174 dBm/Hz	Receiver height 1.5 m
Min. SINR -10.0 dB	Sensitivity $(P_{\min})$ -126 dBm
Carrier Frequencies: 2.6 GHz and 28 GHz	
Antenna Sectorization: No	
Power Allocation: Homogeneous	
Propagation Model: Ray Tracing / Deterministic	
Highest MSC: 64-QAM, R = 9/10	
Scheduler: Round Robin	
Simulation Type: Monte Carlo	
User Drops: 3000	
Min. UEs per drop: 140	
Coverage outage threshold (κ_{COV}): 97.5%	
Transmitter parameters	
Antenna height 2.4 m	Power (P_T) 13 dBm
Antenna pattern: omnidirectional	
Antenna gains: 3 dBi @2.6 GHz and 12 dBi @28 GHz	

where T_i is the throughput of the ith user. The ideal fairness case is achieved when the index Υ is equal to 1.

3   Simulation Results and Discussion

This section is divided into two main parts. The first part explains the evaluation scenarios. The second part presents the results obtained for the experiments previously described in each of the considered scenario.

3.1   Simulation Setup

In this study, two different frequencies (see Table 2) were considered. The particular topologies ($L \in \{10, 20, 40, 65, 95\}$) were the obtained from the statistical optimization process presented in [26]. For completeness, our baseline scenario, where node locations are not optimal, has been also included in the evaluation. Specifically performance metrics were evaluated in 10 independent scenarios.

3.2   Impact on Signal Quality

This section evaluates the degradation of the signal quality (in terms of the downlink SINR) when selected topologies move from sparse to denser ones. In LTE

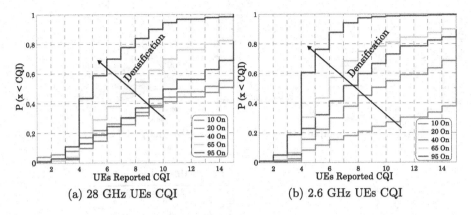

(a) 28 GHz UEs CQI   (b) 2.6 GHz UEs CQI

Fig. 3. Reported UEs CQI

systems, users report the status of their radio channel using the Channel Quality Indicator (CQI); as the reported CQI gets better, a higher modulation scheme is selected [37]. Figure 3 depicts the results at frequencies previously described. From the figure, it is clear that the degradation ratio is more critical at lower frequencies where Inter-Cell Interference (ICI) increases together with network densification. At higher frequencies, ICI effects are reduced as a result of the natural and better isolation of the indoor cells. Thus, the high penetration loss of mmW can be exploited constructively in indoor environments. For instance, the network densification can be increased by a factor of 4 and still user's reported CQI distribution is comparable with sparse scenarios (see Fig. 3b).

3.3 Impact on User Throughput and Energy Efficiency

In the following, the average user's throughput, network EE, and cell-edge performance are analysed at the proposed scenarios. Due to the amount of independent experiments, previous metrics are represented by means of surface plots which indicate average values (see Fig. 4). Looking at Fig. 4a, results confirm the observed behaviour in [26]: 1) an indoor-planning aware network will provide substantial gains in terms of user's throughput at both frequencies, and 2) if we compare the performance of both frequencies, we can observe that mmW communications will provide considerable gains (up to 54 %) with respect to the operation at 2.6 GHz. Regarding the EE, defined as the sum-rate to energy consumption ratio, Fig. 4b shows the EE for each simulation. In this manner, the conclusions and observations drawn from our previous work, have also been verified through a more realistic, yet highly complicated, system-level simulations, where the effect of many network functionalities such as Channel State Information (CSI) feedback, realistic link adaptation, and scheduling cannot be captured without losing mathematical tractability. In addition, mmW will also improve the EE providing gains of 39 % over the 2.6 GHz band. Similar results can be observed in Fig. 4c where 5th-tile gains can increase up to 18 % operating at higher frequencies.

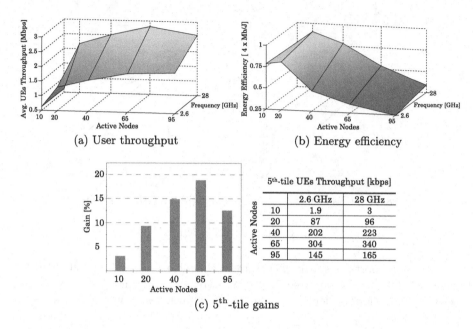

(a) User throughput

(b) Energy efficiency

5th-tile UEs Throughput [kbps]

Active Nodes	2.6 GHz	28 GHz
10	1.9	3
20	87	96
40	202	223
65	304	340
95	145	165

(c) 5th-tile gains

Fig. 4. Results on user's throughput, EE, and cell-edge

3.4 Impact on System Fairness

Figure 5 depicts the results corresponding to the evaluation of the system fairness at two different frequency values for the proposed network topologies. Particularly, Fig. 5a represents the CDF of Jain's fairness index of the users in the whole system for a selected number of topologies. Looking comparatively at both frequencies, results show that similar fairness improvements are noticed at 28 GHz and at 2.6 GHz. In fact, it is clear that the sparsest topology, with 10 active nodes, may even result in a deterioration of the system fairness. On the other hand, the greater the value of active nodes, the better fairness performance can be achieved (up to 37.5 % gains). For the sake of clarity, system fairness of all topologies has also been represented in Fig. 5b by means of surface plots. From the figure, it can be seen that previous behaviour is confirmed, and even expected, since activating more nodes in a given area will increase the number of available resources per user. However, one common aspect at both frequencies is that, for a given network densification value, system fairness does not change significantly.

3.5 Impact of Service Demand Volume

It is also interesting to consider the effect of changing user density at both frequencies and at different network topologies. To that end, the initial number of users ($\nu = 140$) has initially been doubled, and finally, increased by a factor of 4. Figure 6 presents the system performance of two separate network deployments

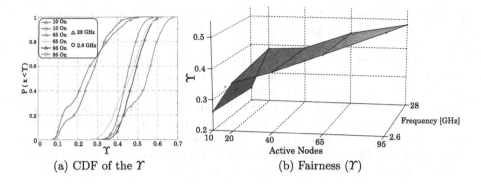

(a) CDF of the Υ (b) Fairness (Υ)

Fig. 5. System fairness for different scenarios

with 10 and 65 active nodes, respectively. From the figure, it can be observed how the increment of the total amount of users present on the network can rapidly deteriorate the performance in terms of end-to-end throughput. However, results clearly show how dense networks operating at higher frequencies can mitigate this degradation, outperforming those cases where 2.6 GHz and sparse topologies are considered (see Fig. 6b), which makes sense because more nodes can be activated to support the user density increment without noticing the negative impact of the ICI.

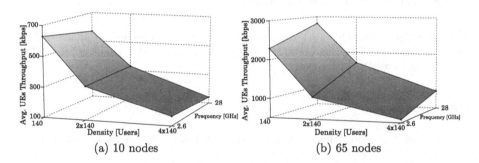

(a) 10 nodes   (b) 65 nodes

Fig. 6. UEs volume densification

4 Conclusions and Future Work

Ultra-dense networks based on millimeter-wave communications have been identified as part of the key enablers of future 5G cellular systems. Consequently, the main objective of the work presented in this document was to investigate the feasibility and effectiveness of the novel network planning framework for indoor cellular environments proposed in [26]. Indeed, by means of system-level simulations, this study has verified the compatibility of the analysis, the statistical optimization process, and the obtained outputs presented in our previous work. The main conclusions can be summarized as follows:

- First, the performance of dense environments operating at 28 GHz have been evaluated in terms of user throughput, cell-edge performance, and network energy efficiency. The results clearly validate the already investigated advantages of such environments, including the possibility of having more energy efficient topologies, that at the same time, provide more capacity (compared with lower carrier frequencies) and better cell-edge performance.
- Second, Radio Resource Management (RRM) challenges related to resource allocation and scheduling were analyzed. It was shown that throughput fairness can by significantly increased in network topologies much denser than the existing ones.
- Third, an additional aspect has been investigated: the impact of the volume of users within the selected topologies. Results have shown that vast volume of users mitigate the overall network performance, although its effect is less harmful when both mmW and UDN are considered.

The natural continuation of this work relies on the evaluation of the proposed framework considering additional RRM functions, load balancing techniques, and the further extension of the simulator to compute traffic-aware system-level simulations. Additionally, future work includes the analysis of RRM mechanisms and indoor networks in the context of Machine-to-Machine (M2M) communications focusing on traffic profiling methods.

Acknowledgments. This work was supported in part by Academy of Finland under grant 284811 and by EIT (European Institute for Innovation and Technology) and ICT Labs through the EXAM project.

References

1. Ericsson, A.B.: More than 50 billion connected devices. In: Ericsson White Paper, February 2011. www.ericsson.com
2. Ericsson A,B.: Networked society essentials (2014). www.ericsson.com/thinkingahead/
3. Cisco Systems Inc.: Cisco visual networking index: global mobile data traffic forecast update, 2014–2019. In: Cisco White Paper, February 2015. www.cisco.com
4. GSMA Intelligence: The mobile economy 2015. In: GSMA Reports (2015). www.gsmaintelligence.com
5. Nokia Solutions and Networks Oy.: Ten key rules of 5G deployment. In: Nokia White Paper (2015). http://networks.nokia.com/innovation/5g
6. The METIS 2020 Project: Mobile and wireless communications enablers for the twenty-twenty information society. In: Deliverable D6.5, Report on Simulation Results and Evaluations, March 2015. www.metis2020.com
7. Chen, S., Zhao, J.: The requirements, challenges, and technologies for 5g of terrestrial mobile telecommunication. IEEE Commun. Mag. **52**(5), 36–43 (2014)

8. Nikolikj, V., Janevski, T.: Profitability and comparative cost-capacity analysis of 5G millimeter-wave systems. In: 22nd IEEE Telecommunications Forum (2014)
9. Radiocommunication Sector of ITU: Future spectrum requirements estimate for terrestial IMT. In: International Telecommunication Union (ITU), M.2290-0 (2014)
10. Andrews, J., Buzzi, S., Choi, W., Hanly, S., Lozano, A., Soong, A., Zhang, J.: What will 5G be? IEEE J. Sel. Areas Commun. **32**(6), 1065–1082 (2014)
11. Osseiran, A., et al.: Scenarios for 5G mobile and wireless communications: the vision of the METIS project. IEEE Commun. Mag. **52**(5), 26–35 (2014)
12. Boccardi, F., Heath Jr., R.W., Lozano, A., Marzetta, T.L., Popovski, P.: Five disruptive technology directions for 5G. IEEE Commun. Mag. **52**(2), 74–80 (2014)
13. Wei, L., Hu, R.Q., Qian, Y., Wu, G.: Key elements to enable millimeter wave communications for 5G wireless systems. IEEE Wirel. Commun. **21**(6), 136–143 (2014)
14. Larsson, C., Harrysson, F., Olsson, B.-E., Berg, J.-E.: An outdoor-to-Indoor Propagation Scenario at 28 GHz. In: 8th European Conference on Antennas and Propagation (EuCAP 2014), April 2014
15. Anderson, C., Rappaport, T., Bae, K., Verstak, A., Ramakrishnan, N., Tranter, W., Shaffer, C., Watson, L.: In-building wideband multipath characteristics at 2.5 and 60 GHz. In: 56th IEEE Vehicular Technology Conference 2002 (VTC 2002F) (2002)
16. Baykas, T., Materum, L., Kato, S.: Performance evaluation of mmwave single carrier systems with a novel NLOS channel model. In: 24th IEEE International Symposium on Personal Indoor and Mobile Radio Communications (PIMRC), September 2013
17. Larew, S., Thomas, T., Cudak, M., Ghosh, A.: Air interface design and ray tracing study for 5G millimeter wave communications. In: 2013 IEEE Global Communications Conference Workshops, December 2013
18. Bai, T., Heath, R.: Coverage analysis for millimeter wave cellular networks with blockage effects. In: 2013 IEEE Global Conference on Signal and Information Processing (GlobalSIP), December 2013
19. Kulkarni, M.-N., Thomas, T.-A., Vook, F.-W., Ghosh, A., Visotsky, E.: Coverage and rate trends in moderate and high bandwidth 5G networks. In: 2014 IEEE Globecom Workshop, Mobile Communications in Higher Frequency Bands (2014)
20. Bai, T., Heath, R.: Coverage analysis for millimeter-wave cellular networks. IEEE Trans. Wirel. Commun. **14**(2), 1100–1114 (2015)
21. Bai, T., Desai, V., Heath, R.: Millimiter wave cellular channel models for system evaluation. In: 2014 IEEE International Conference on Computing, Networking and Communications (2014)
22. Galinina, O., Pyattaev, A., Andreev, S., Dohler, M., Koucheryavy, Y.: 5G multi-RAT LTE-WiFi ultra-dense small cells: performance dynamics, architecture, and trends. IEEE J. Sel. Areas Commun. (2015)
23. Zhou, C., Bulakci, O.: Stability-aware and energy efficient cell management in ultra dense networks. In: 2014 IEEE 80th Vehicular Technology Conference (VTC Fall), September 2014
24. Koudouridis, G.-P.: On the capacity and energy efficiency of network scheduling in future ultra-dense networks. In: 2014 IEEE Symposium on Computers and Communications (ISCC), June 2014
25. Baldemair, R., Irnich, T., Balachandran, K., Dahlman, E., Mildh, G., Selén, Y., Parkvall, S., Meyer, M., Osseiran, A.: Ultra-dense networks in millimeter-wave frequencies. IEEE Commun. Mag. **53**, 202–208 (2015)

26. Lamas, S.R., González G.D., Hämäläinen, J.: Indoor planning optimization of ultra-dense cellular networks at high carrier frequencies. In: 2015 IEEE Wireless Communications and Networking Conference (WCNC) Workshops, March 2015

27. Chuang, M., Chen, M., Sun, Y.S.: Resource management issues in 5G ultra dense smallcell networks. In: 2015 International Conference on Information Networking (ICOIN), January 2015

28. Jiming, C., Peng, W., Jie, Z.: Adaptive soft frequency reuse schemefor in-building dense femtocell networks. Chin. Commun. 10(1), 44–55 (2013)

29. Akdeniz, M., Liu, Y., Samimi, M., Sun, S., Rangan, S., Rappaport, T., Erkip, E.: Millimeter wave channel modeling and cellular capacity evaluation. IEEE J. Sel. Areas Commun. 32(6), 1164–1179 (2014)

30. Nassar, A.-T. et al.: Achievable RF coverage and system capacity using millimeter wave cellular technologies in 5G networks. In: 2014 IEEE 27th Canadian Conference on Electrical and Computer Engineering (CCECE), pp. 1–6, May 2014

31. Gomez, K., Goratti, L., Granelli, F., Rasheed, T.: A comparative study of scheduling disciplines in 5g systems for emergency communications. In: 2014 1st International Conference on 5G for Ubiquitous Connectivity (5GU), pp. 40–45 (2014)

32. González, G.D., Yanikomeroglu, H., Garcia-Lozano, M., Boque, S.R.: A novel multiobjective framework for cell switch-off in dense cellular networks. In: 2014 IEEE International Conference on Communications (ICC), pp. 2641–2647, June 2014

33. Rangan, S., et al.: Millimeter-wave cellular wireless networks: potentials and challenges. IEEE Proc. 102(3), 366–385 (2014)

34. Trueman, C., Paknys, R., Zhao, J., Davis, D., Segal, B.: Ray tracing algorithm for indoor propagation. In: 16th Annual Review of Progress in Applied Computational Electromagnetics (2000)

35. Remley, K., Anderson, H., Weisshar, A.: Improving the accuracy of ray-tracing techniques for indoor propagation modeling. IEEE Trans. Veh. Technol. 49(6), 2350–2358 (2000)

36. Group Radio Access Network: Small cell enhancements for E-UTRA and E-UTRAN. In: 3rd Generation Partnership Project (3GPP) Technical report (TR) 36.872 v12.1.0, Release 12, December 2013

37. Ikuno, J.-C., Wrulich, M., Rupp, M.: System level simulation of LTE networks. In: IEEE Transactions on Vehicular Technology, May 2010

38. Group Radio Access Network: Evolved Universal Terrestrial Radio Access (E-UTRA); Radio Frequency (RF) system scenarios. In: 3rd Generation Partnership Project (3GPP) Technical report (TR) 36.942 v12.0.0, Release 12, September 2014

39. Group Radio Access Network: Further Advancements for E-UTRA, Physical Layer Aspects. In: 3rd Generation Partnership Project (3GPP) Technical report (TR) 36.814, Release 9, March 2010

Optimal Uplink Scheduling for Device-to-Device Communication with Mode Selection

Raphael Elsner[✉], John-Torben Reimers, Maciej Mühleisen,
and Andreas Timm-Giel

Institute of Communication Networks (ComNets),
Hamburg University of Technology, Hamburg, Germany
{raphael.elsner,john.reimers,maciej.muehleisen,timm-giel}@tuhh.de

Abstract. Device-to-Device communication is discussed for future mobile communication systems. In this work, an upper bound capacity limit is determined for a mobile communication system consisting of Device-to-Device and cellular users is determined. Therefore, we formulate the problem as a linear program and solve it optimally. The potential of Device-to-Device communication is evaluated using a distance based mode selection scheme. It is shown that the amount of traditional cellular users is influencing the optimal distance for using Device-to-Device communication instead of traditional cellular transmission. The optimisation potential is then analysed for a different amount of users and cell sizes.

Keywords: Device-to-Device · Mode selection · LTE-Advanced · 5G · Linear programming

1 Introduction

Device-to-Device communication (D2D) in mobile communication systems is intended in future 5th generation mobile communication systems (5G) to reach the requirements of high data rates and low latencies. In traditional mobile communication systems, user terminals only transmit data to base stations. This is even done in the case of close proximity of users wanting to exchange data, where a direct communication would be possible. With D2D communication, mobile terminals can communicate directly with each other without transmitting the data through the base station. Thus, this approach is especially beneficial for users in close proximity. If users are communicating directly, they can use lower transmission power, and therefore radio resources can be reused within the cell without or with little interference. Thus, Device-to-Device communication is a promising approach to increase the Cell Spectral Efficiency (CSE) of the system.

An open question with respect to D2D communication is when to use it and when to prefer cellular transmission. This decision making is referred to as mode selection. It is the process of deciding whether D2D communication is performed or whether the demand is served using "traditional" transmissions via the base station.

© Institute for Computer Sciences, Social Informatics and Telecommunications Engineering 2015
R. Agüero et al. (Eds.): MONAMI 2015, LNICST 158, pp. 95–106, 2015.
DOI: 10.1007/978-3-319-26925-2_8

In this paper mode selection and optimising D2D communication is investigated. We consider a simple mode selection scheme based on the distance and therefore on the received signal strength of the users. A factor is introduced to weight the distance between the users with respect to the base station. In this work the optimal value of this weighting factor is determined.

When designing and evaluating a new communication system, it is always desirable to have an upper bound capacity limit as reference. This paper evaluates this capacity limit of a system including users demanding data exchange in close proximity. Furthermore, the influence of the amount of traditional cellular users and D2D users on the capacity of the system is evaluated. This goal is formulated as a linear program and optimally solved with regard to maximum CSE. It is shown that optimising the transmission schedule of D2D and cellular users increases the system throughput, and the optimal threshold for mode selection based on the distance is determined.

1.1   Related Work

Device-to-Device (D2D) communication is a research area receiving increased attention over the past years. D2D communication in LTE [1] is considered by the 3rd Generation Partnership Project as proximity services in [2]. An extensive survey on current research and the benefits of D2D communication is given in [3]. It provides a state of the art overview together with a taxonomy on the topic. Following the classification of this survey, our paper is investigating D2D communication for inband underlay spectrum usage. A number of key aspects which have to be considered when designing D2D communication systems are presented in [4] and in a more detailed way in [5]. There, the architectural requirements are analysed and the authors describe mode selection, peer discovery techniques, and interference management as major issues when designing D2D communication systems. When dealing with inband underlay, a key challenge is to avoid and mitigate interference between cellular and D2D users. Interference avoidance between cellular and D2D users has been investigated under different aspects and different methods, as e.g. in [6–8]. In [8], the authors present the signaling traffic changes for D2D communication and propose interference avoidance mechanisms. Those methods are used to mitigate interference in the uplink and downlink of a time division duplex system. Their proposed mechanism is limiting the maximum transmit power for interference avoidance. In [6], the authors present an algorithm to minimise interference among D2D users and cellular users by means of graph theory. They evaluate their proposed scheme and compare it with a greedy and an optimal resource assignment scheme. Their proposed scheme improves the network performance, and they state that the near optimal resource assignment solution can be obtained at the base station. Resource allocation in D2D communication underlaying LTE was investigated in [9]. The problem is formulated as an integer linear program, and it is stated that it is infeasible to solve. Instead, heuristic distributed algorithms are presented and evaluated. Contrary to that work, we introduce several simplifications to be able to solve the scheduling problem optimally. In [7], the authors propose an interference-aware jointly optimised resource allocation for D2D and cellular users. They consider uplink and downlink in a time division duplex system. Multi-user diversity gain is exploited resulting in an overall system performance improvement.

Based on these contributions, the present work investigates the upper bound capacity limit of a mobile communication system with D2D and cellular users with a distance-based mode selection criterion.

The paper is organised as follows: First, the problem of D2D communication and cellular transmission in an inband underlay model is described. A description of the used system model is presented. The optimisation problem is then described mathematically and solved by linear programming. Afterwards, the additionally investigated mode selection problem is described. The simulation results are described and analysed. Finally, a conclusion and outlook on further research directions is given.

2   Problem Description and System Model

In this section, the problem of joint scheduling of Device-to-Device and cellular users is introduced.

2.1   Problem Description

This paper analyses the resource allocation for an inband underlay system for D2D communication. In this system D2D users are transmitting on the same frequencies as the cellular users, whenever appropriate. In this paper the full uplink frequency spectrum is reused for D2D communication. This is depicted in Fig. 1. Thus, the D2D users interfere with the cellular users at the base station when transmitting simultaneously. Time domain scheduling is applied to avoid interference. Therefore, users can transmit consecutively, but this often requires more time to serve all demands. Then, the optimal scheduling decision has to be determined between accepting interference and consecutive transmission. In the following, our system model is presented.

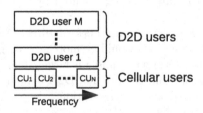

Fig. 1. Schematic representation of frequency reuse for D2D communication

2.2 System Model

In this contribution, we evaluate the potential of D2D and therefore introduce a simplified model for which we can determine the optimal solution serving as upper limit for system throughput.

User terminals are placed uniform randomly as stated in the ITU and 3GPP evaluation guidelines [2,10], respectively within a circular area. The set of n users $U = \{u_1, u_2, ...u_n\}$ is placed randomly for each simulation run. Simulations are repeated to obtain reliable results, which is evaluated using confidence intervals. In order to limit the complexity, we consider single cell scenarios with one base station only.

We do not consider user mobility, and no small scale fading model is applied. As the aim of this work is to evaluate an upper bound, both mobility and small scale fading are neglected. Estimating D2D channels is an open research area [11,12] which is not the focus of this work. User mobility introduces a change in large scale fading with large coherence time. The serving channel can be estimated with common methods using pilot tones. Yet, it remains an open question how to estimate interfering channels. Small scale fading introduces further difficulties in channel estimation, resulting in packet losses if the channel is overestimated. On the other hand, it enables multi antenna transmission systems, and hence it provides gains in the Signal-to-Interference-and-Noise-Ratio (SINR) [13]. Both is not considered here for complexity reasons. We expect channel estimation to be even more difficult in D2D scenarios and higher experience performance degradation due to estimation errors than in purely cellular scenarios.

Traffic demands $d_{i,j}$ from user i towards user j serve as input to the system, describing the amount of data user i wants to send to user j. Demands can either be directed to another user in the same cell or towards the Internet. A demand in direction of the Internet has to be served by the base station. To simplify the evaluation, each user has exactly one demand on a link towards a data sink, which can be either another user or the base station. It is randomly determined towards which user or base station this demand is addressed to. The traffic destination is determined randomly with 0 % to 75 % probability of having a demand in the direction of the base station i.e. the Internet. The demands on the link from a node i to j are then represented by matrix entries $d_{i,j}$ of the demand matrix D.

This demand matrix is adapted to not perform direct D2D communication in cases where cellular communication would be more advantageous. If the distance between both involved user terminals i and j is larger than the distance between each of them to the base station, the original D2D demand is transformed to a "traditional" one and served via the base station.

In the next step, the possible feasible network states are determined. Following the definition of [14], a feasible network state is a set of demands which can be served at the same time. Feasible network states have to fulfill the following restrictions:

- User terminals can only send to one destination at the same time
- User terminals can only receive from one source at the same time
- User terminals are not able to receive and transmit at the same time

Simultaneous transmissions cause mutual interference. The goal is to select the states minimising the transmission time for serving all demands. Therefore an optimal tradeoff between serving many demands in parallel with high interference and consecutive transmissions without interference has to be found. An example for different network states is given in Fig. 2. In this example either network state 1 has to be used to serve all demands from user terminal UT_1 to UT_3 and UT_2 to UT_4, or the network states 2 and 3 have to be used consecutively. The consecutive transmissions are always possible as a solution without interference and therefore called "trivial states" in the following.

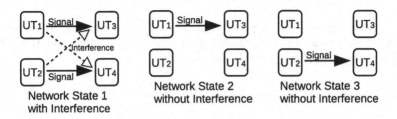

Fig. 2. Three possible network states for two transmissions from user terminal UT_1 to UT_3 and from UT_2 to UT_4.

Calculation of the mutual interference and the SINR of each user receiving a demand, is performed for all feasible network states. Hence, each network state results in a throughput for each user being served in that state. As simplification and therefore worst case scenario, we do not consider power control. For interference calculation, the set of interfering users consists of all users transmitting on any part of the jointly used frequency spectrum. Accordingly, in Fig. 1 the cellular users are not interfering with each other but with all D2D users transmitting at the same time. For simplification, no partial interference on parts of the spectrum is taken into account but always full interference.

The cellular users radio resource allocation is done in a resource fair manner as depicted in Eq. (1). Thus, all cellular users get the same amount of resources.

The $SINR_{i,j}$ at user j when serving the link between user i and j is calculated as follows:

$$SINR_{i,j} = \frac{P_i h_{i,j}}{N + \sum_{\forall u \in I} P_u h_{u,j}} \qquad (1)$$

Here, I is the set of all nodes interfering with user i. P is the transmit power experiencing path loss represented by channel attenuation h. As path loss model we take the indoor-hotspot non-line-of-sight model as described in [10]. The SINR is mapped to an achievable rate $r_{i,j}$ of this link serving the demand using a table of minimal SINR values for LTE modulation and coding schemes from [15].

The rates $r_{i,j}$ of all links of network state s are represented by matrix entries of the rate matrix R_s. Let S be the set of all network states, then for all network states $s \in S$ this rate matrix has to be calculated.

Mathematical Model: To maximise the overall system throughput, the transmission time T to serve all demands has to be minimised. The following linear program describes this optimisation problem:

$$\text{Minimise } T = \sum_{k=1}^{|S|} t_k \tag{2}$$

$$\text{subject to } \sum_{k=1}^{s} t_k \cdot R_k \geq D \tag{3}$$

$$\text{with } t_k \geq 0. \tag{4}$$

The optimised transmission schedule leads to the minimal time needed to serve all demands. From the minimised transmission time and the initial demands the system throughput is calculated as

$$\text{System throughput} = \frac{\sum_{i=1}^{n} \sum_{j=1}^{n} d_{i,j}}{\sum_{k=1}^{|S|} t_k}. \tag{5}$$

Two baseline results are considered as references. The first one assumes a transmission of all users at the same time leading to high interference. Furthermore, it includes non-feasible states where users can receive from and transmit to multiple nodes at the same time. This baseline is violating the previously mentioned requirements for feasible network states, but is useful for evaluating an interference dominated scenario. For the second baseline, we assume that all users transmit consecutively one after another to avoid interference, i.e. the "trivial states" as transmission schedule. As the "trivial states" are a subset of the feasible states, this baseline is a possible solution and lower bound for our optimisation process. Hence, the optimised solution must be at least as good as this baseline.

Mode Selection: As described above, D2D communication is not always performed. Mode selection is performed on the basis of the distance between the users that want to exchange data and their distance to the base station. Therefore, each distance between the two D2D users and the base station is compared to the direct distance between the users. For users i and j and base station BS, D2D communication is performed only if distance$(i, j) < \alpha \cdot$ distance(i, BS) or distance$(i, j) < \alpha \cdot$distance(j, BS). If the distance of both involved user terminals to the base station is below the distance between the users, no D2D communication is selected. Thus, the demand is served in the "traditional" way by sending the data via the base station. The factor α is adapted from zero to two. Zero prohibits D2D communication, and hence all D2D demands are served using direct communication. The highest possible distance between the two involved user terminals can be at most twice the distance of the node which is further away from the base station and therefore $\alpha = 2$ is the upper bound and equals to the situation of all D2D demands served using direct communication. We evaluate how the overall system throughput changes with an increasing weighting factor α, and the optimal value of α for different scenarios is determined. As cellular transmissions has the disadvantage of additional processing time in the base station compared to direct transmission, we take a slightly higher factor α than the optimal value to prefer D2D and implicitly consider a penalty for cellular transmissions.

3   Results

In this section, simulation results are evaluated. Simulation parameters have been varied with respect to cell radius, amount of user terminals, and mode selection weighting factor α. First, the optimal value α is determined. In the following simulations, the factor α is chosen slightly higher than the optimal value to account for the additional processing time in the base station. Afterwards, the optimisation of the transmission schedule is evaluated with an increasing number of user terminals. Finally, the optimisation potential is evaluated with respect to increasing cell radius.

As described in Sect. 2.2, it has been analysed which distance multiplicator α is most favourable for highest system throughput of D2D and cellular users. Figure 3 shows the overall system throughput over increasing factor α. Each subfigure in Fig. 3 shows the throughput for a different amount of additional cellular users which have a demand in direction of the Internet. The error bars indicate the 95 % confidence intervals.

From Fig. 3 (a)-(d), the amount of users having a demand to the Internet is increasing. Therefore, the influence of α is decreasing as this factor is only relevant for users having a D2D demand. Furthermore, the highest possible throughput is decreasing as less resources are reused. The influence of α is especially visible in Fig. 3 (a)-(c). For lower values of α, less D2D communication is allowed, and therefore the advantage of using D2D transmissions can not be fully exploited. For higher values of α, more demands are served using D2D, but due to the higher distances of the communication partners, the throughput decreases. Furthermore, the interference due to resource reuse is increasing and degrading the throughput.

For all scenarios, the optimal value for α is between 1.1 and 1.3, and increases with increasing number of Internet users. This results from the fact that the less D2D demands exist, the more they should be favoured. Likewise, the more D2D demands exist the more they interfere and must eventually be served via the base station.

In all graphs, it is visible that mode selection has a large impact on the overall system throughput. Generally allowing D2D communication with our frequency reuse scheme even degrades throughput compared to no D2D communication. Thus, it is vital to perform intelligent mode selection to optimally exploit the opportunities of D2D communication. Furthermore, it is beneficial to have an estimate of the ratio of D2D demands versus demands towards the Internet for determining an approriate value for mode selection.

In the following simulations, the probability of having a demand in direction of the Internet was chosen to be 25 %. The optimal weighting factor for mode selection as determined above (Fig. 3 (b)) is $\alpha \approx 1.1$. As described before, we chose $\alpha = 1.3$ for all following simulations to pay contribute to base station processing cost.

In the following, it is evaluated whether the optimisation potential is changing with the amount of users within the cell. Therefore, we increase the amount of users while keeping the percentage of D2D demands constant. In Fig. 4, the Cell Spectral Efficiency (CSE) is depicted over an increasing amount of users. It is visible that the baseline 1 (all links active at the same time) is drastically decreasing with an increasing number of base stations. This is due to the higher interference with many D2D user terminals active in one cell. In contrast to that, the baseline 2 (consecutive transmissions only) is only slightly decreasing

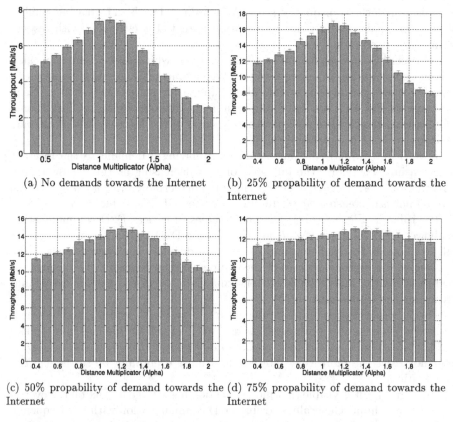

(a) No demands towards the Internet

(b) 25% propability of demand towards the Internet

(c) 50% propability of demand towards the Internet

(d) 75% propability of demand towards the Internet

Fig. 3. Overall system throughput over increasing factor α for different amount of additional cellular users with traffic demands towards the Internet.

and in the end almost remaining constant. Thus, with an increasing number of users consecutive transmissions become more favourable. If all users transmit at the same time, interference is limiting the possible throughput. If, on the other hand, data is to be tranmitted consecutively, it takes a longer time to serve all demands. However, proportional to that, more data is transmitted in the same time.

The optimised transmission schedule makes use of both transmission schemes, parallel and consecutive transmissions. Hence, reusing some resources –and meanwhile accepting interference– leads to a higher throughput (Fig. 4). Our optimisation process of the schedule (described in Sect. 2.2) mitigates the negative effects of the first baseline. It is visible that the CSE is increased compared to baseline 2 as well. With more users, more possibilities of simultaneous transmissions exist. Thus, more possiblities of parallel, but only little interfering transmissions exist. Hence, the optimisation potential is increased and the CSE is increasing with more users.

In Fig. 5, the potential of D2D communication compared to traditional "cellular" transmissions is evaluated. The overall system throughput is compared for two scenarios. In the first scenario all demands are served using the base station. In the second scenario D2D communication is enabled and demands towards users in the same cell are served directly when allowed by the mode selection. It is visible that D2D communication always improves the system throughput. The more user terminals are within a cell the more gain in throughput can be achieved by enabling D2D communication. Thus, it is always recommended to enable D2D communication, especially with more users per cell.

In all following simulation scenarios the number of users is chosen to be 14. As the computing time for the optimisation is increasing exponentially with the

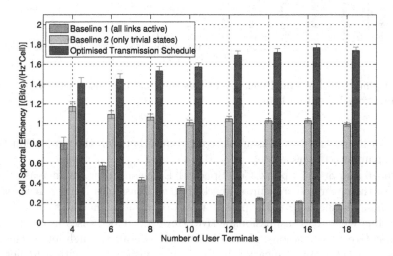

Fig. 4. Uplink Cell Spectral Efficiency per user of baselines and optimised scheduling versus numbers of user terminals

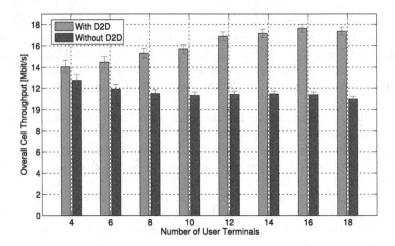

Fig. 5. Comparison of throughput for simulations with and without D2D communication versus different numbers of user terminals

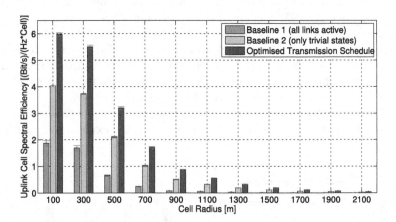

Fig. 6. Uplink Cell Spectral Efficiency of baselines and optimised scheduling versus cell radius from 100 m to 2.1 km

number of users, this is a reasonable compromise between the simulation time and the number of users.

Figure 6 shows the uplink Cell Spectral Efficiency over an increasing cell radius for the optimised transmission schedule and baselines 1 and 2. It is visible that with increasing cell size the potential for optimisation increases compared to the baseline with all transmissions active. However, it decreases in comparison to consecutive transmissions. If we observe the overall throughput of enabled and disabled D2D communication in Fig. 7, it is visible that with a higher cell size the throughput as well as the achievable gain obtained by our optimisation is decreasing. Large cell sizes with more than 1.3 km radius have such a low

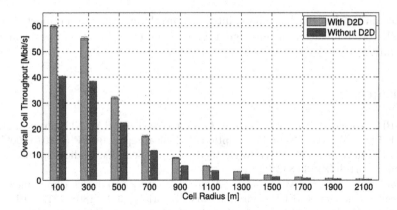

Fig. 7. Comparison of throughput for simulations with and without D2D communication versus cell radius from 100 m to 2.1 km

cell throughput that the scenario is noise limited. Hence, it almost makes no difference whether D2D is used or not. As a result, in larger the cells consecutive transmissions and traditional cellular transmissions are more favourable due to the impact of lower mutual interference.

4   Conclusion and Outlook

In this work the upper capacity bound of a mobile communication system with cellular and D2D users is determined via an optimised transmission schedule. The optimisation problem is fomulated as a linear program and solved optimally. The calculated transmission schedule is evaluated using different simulation scenarios and compared against two baselines. It is shown that an increase in throughput can be achieved for all considered scenarios. Our capacity bound shows that using D2D communication especially increases the throughput for larger numbers of users in medium size cells.

It can be assumed that, especially in large scenarios, D2D communication offers the potential for higher throughput. In this case however, the users still need to be in close proximity. In our scenario, the amount of users remains constant with an increasing cell size. Therefore, the average distance increases with increasing cell size, and thus the path loss also increases. In future work larger scenarios with non-uniform distributed user locations should be considered.

Furthermore, the usage of D2D users is compared to scenarios of "traditional" cellular communication only. Mode selection is performed based on distance. The influence of a weighting factor of the inter-user distance relative to the base station is analysed. It is shown that this value is depending on the amount of additional base station users.

In this work, only uplink transmission is taken into account. A next step is to include an appropriate model for downlink transmission. Furthermore, more sophisticated mode selection mechanisms can be analysed. Another open topic is given by multi cell scenarios. There, inter-cell interference plays an important role and D2D communication of cell-edge users may increase the system performance drastically.

References

1. 3GPP, Evolved Universal Terrestrial Radio Access (E-UTRA); LTE physical layer; LTE Physical layer; General description, Technical report 3GPP 36.201 (2009)
2. 3GPP, Study on LTE Device to Device Proximity Services; Radio Aspects; Technical report 3GPP 36.843 (2014)
3. Asadi, A., Wang, Q., Mancuso, V.: A survey on device-to-device communications in cellular networks. IEEE Commun. Surv. Tutorials **16**(4), 1801–1819 (2014)
4. Doppler, K., Rinne, M.P., Janis, P., Ribeiro, C., Hugl, K.: Device-to-device communications; functional prospects for LTE-Advanced networks. In: Proceedings of IEEE ICC Workshops, pp. 1–6 (2009)
5. Fodor, G., Dahlman, E., Mildh, G., Parkvall, S., Reider, N., Miklós, G., Turányi, Z.: Design aspects of network assisted device-to-device communications. IEEE Commun. Mag. **50**(3), 170–177 (2012)
6. Zhang, R., Cheng, X., Yang, L., Jiao, B.: Interference-aware graph based resource sharing for device-to-device communications underlaying cellular networks. In: Proceedings of IEEE WCNC, pp. 140–145 (2013)
7. Janis, P., Koivunen, V., Ribeiro, C., Korhonen, J., Doppler, K., Hugl, K.: Interference-aware resource allocation for device-to-device radio underlaying cellular networks. In: IEEE 69th Vehicular Technology Conference, pp. 1–5 (2009)
8. Doppler, K., Rinne, M., Wijting, C., Ribeiro, C., Hugl, K.: Device-to-device communication as an underlay to LTE-Advanced networks. IEEE Commun. Mag. **47**(12), 42–49 (2009)
9. Zulhasnine, M., Changcheng H., Srinivasan, A.: Efficient resource allocation for device-to-device communication underlaying LTE network. In: IEEE 6th International Conference on Wireless and Mobile Computing, Networking and Communications (WiMob), pp. 368–375, Niagara Falls (2010)
10. ITU, ITU-R M.2135 Guidelines for evaluating of radio interface technologies for IMTAdvanced, Technical report (2009)
11. Tang, H., Ding, Z., Levy, B.C.: Enabling D2D communications through neighbor discovery in LTE cellular networks. IEEE Trans. Signal Process. **62**(19), 5157–5170 (2014)
12. Lee, K., Kang, W., Choi, H.-J.: A practical channel estimation and feedback method for device-to-device communication in 3GPP LTE system. In: 8th International Conference on Ubiquitous Information Management and Communication, pp. 17–20 (2014)
13. Muehleisen, M.: VoIP Performance of LTE Networks - VoLTE versus OTT, Verlag Mainz, ABMT, vol. 74. RWTH Aachen University (2015)
14. Toumpis, S., Goldsmith, A.J.: Capacity regions for wireless ad hoc networks. IEEE Trans. Wireless Commun. **2**(4), 736–748 (2003)
15. Mühleisen, M., Bültmann, D., Schoenen, R.: Analytical validation of an IMT-Advanced compliant LTE system level simulator. In: 11th European Wireless Conference 2011 - Sustainable Wireless Technologies (European Wireless), pp. 1–5, Wien (2011)

Making HeNB More Secure with Improved Secure Access Protocol and Analyzing It

Fariba Ghasemi Najm[1(✉)], Ali Payandeh[2], and Hashem Habibi[3]

[1] Informatics Services Corporation (ISC), Network Support Building,
Tehran, Iran
F_Ghasemi@ISC.CO.IR
[2] Faculty of Information, Communication and Security Technology, Malek
Ashtar University of Technology (MUT), Tehran, Iran
[3] Faculty of Computer Engineering, Sharif University of Technology,
Tehran, Iran

Abstract. The 3rd Generation Partnership Project (3GPP) defined a new architecture, called Home eNode B (HeNB). HeNB is able to provide new services with higher data rate in a low cost. Security is a critical aspect of HeNB. In order to have HeNB secure access to core network, 3GPP defines an authentication protocol based on IKEv2. A number of security vulnerabilities such as HeNB masquerading have not been addressed and solved by 3GPP technical specification yet. In this paper an improved HeNB authentication protocol is introduced which does not allow an attacker to connect unauthorized network users using a mask. Finally, we evaluate our protocol performance and verify it by Automated Validation of Internet Security Protocols and Applications (AVISPA). Through our security analysis, we conclude that not only the proposed protocol prevents the various security threats but also it has no significant effect on authentication delay and cost.

Keywords: LTE · HeNB · Protocol · Authentication · Security · IPSec

1 Introduction

LTE (Long Term Evolution) was investigated by 3GPP in 2004. LTE general structure has two parts; access network (E-UTRAN) [21, 22] and core network (CN) [1, 19]. One of elements of E-UTRAN is HeNB that is introduced by 3GPP in release 9.

HeNB is located on the customer premises and connected to the core network via unsafe links such as broadband lines [1]. Some vulnerabilities are emerged by introducing HeNB. 3GPP specifies threats, requirements, and corresponding solution of HeNB security in [4, 16]. 3GPP points that the following authentications are necessary for HeNB authentication:

- Mutual authentication between HeNB device and the operator's network
- Authentication of the Hosting Party (HP) by the operator's network

Among several authentication issues, combined device and HP authentication is an important security mechanism; it guarantees that HeNB device can access Core

© Institute for Computer Sciences, Social Informatics and Telecommunications Engineering 2015
R. Agüero et al. (Eds.): MONAMI 2015, LNICST 158, pp. 107–120, 2015.
DOI: 10.1007/978-3-319-26925-2_9

Network safely. To achieve this aim, 3GPP has proposed a method that combines certificate and Extensible Authentication Protocol [8] for Authentication and Key Agreement (EAP-AKA [9]) –based authentication running within Internet Key Exchange (IKEv2) protocol [3, 14] between HeNB and security gateway (SeGW) for mutual authentication of HeNB and CN.

To reduce the communication costs of authentication protocol introduced by 3GPP, a low-cost re-authentication protocol [10, 15] is proposed in [5]. HeNB can't access CN via these two protocols (EAP-AKA and the proposed protocol in [5]) safely yet; the threats that make HeNB access unsafe via these two protocols, are explained in [6]. One of these threats is HeNB masquerading attack in which HeNB uses other HeNB's ID during UE connection that that ID differs from the one used during its mutual authentication with SeGW.

In this paper, we propose a method that solves the problems disregarded by available protocols; this aim is done by adding a digital signature of HeNB's identity information that is sent to the CN. Therefore, HeNB masquerading attack and derived attacks such as denial of service, billing issues and user privacy issues [17] are avoided.

The remainder of the paper is organized as follows. A brief explanation of HeNB architecture in LTE is provided in Sect. 2. We specify initial and re-authentication protocol between HeNB and SeGW and their analyzing in Sects. 3 and 4. In Sects. 5 and 6, the proposed improved HeNB secure access protocol and its security analyzing are presented. Finally, conclusions are offered in Sect. 7.

2 LTE Structure with HeNBs

HeNB is introduced to provide mobile communication coverage and allows users to have a local and public access. HeNB architecture in LTE is shown in Fig. 1; some of its elements are described below.

Home eNode B: HeNB is introduced by 3GPP in release 9 and known as a femtocell [2]. HeNB is a base station that makes small cellular communication possible. It is designed for using in small business or residential environments [5].

Security Gateway (SeGW): SeGW is an entrance gateway for all traffics routed to the network and is located on the border of core network. HeNB connects to core network via an IPSec tunnel [12, 13] that is created after mutual authentication of HeNB and SeGW [5, 20].

Backhaul link: The link between HeNB and SeGW that carries S1 and routed management traffic is called backhaul link. Because of extension of backhaul link across the public internet, this link is unsafe; therefore, many of HeNB threats are related to this unsafe link [1].

HeNB Management System (HeMS) or operation, administration and maintenance (OAM): HeMS or OAM is responsible for the management of the HeNB [2]. Depending on the operator's decision, this element may be located within the operator core network or accessible directly on the public Internet [1].

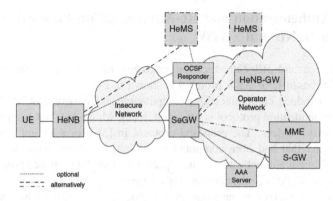

Fig. 1. Structure of HeNB access to the core network [1].

Authentication, Authorization and Accounting (AAA) server and Home Subscriber Server (HSS): HSS stores the compromised, signed, and authenticated data of the HeNBs. When hosting party authentication is required, AAA server authenticates the hosting party based on the authentication information retrieved from HSS [5].

Figure 2 describes the system architecture of HeNB. A HeNB needs to be configured and authorized by the OAM or HeMS. In Fig. 2, UE-A and UE-B belong to the LTE core network-1 and core network-2, respectively. OAM supports both HeNB-A and HeNB-B and allows them to operate. CN has a contractual relationship with limited number of OAMs [18]. In this circumstance, UE must confirm whether the specified HeNB belongs to one of the contracted OAM or not; for example, UE-A cannot connect to its CN via the HeNB-C because its CN does not have any contract with the HeNB-C's OAM while UE-B can do [7].

TR 33.820 defines the security requirements for the support of HeNB; one of these requirements is mutual authentication between HeNB and SeGW for HeNB secure access.

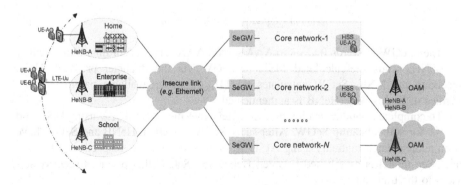

Fig. 2. HeNB system architecture [7].

3   Initial Authentication and Re-Authentication Protocol Between HeNB and SeGW

Combined device and HP authentication including mutual authentication between HeNB and CN based EAP-AKA protocol is shown in Fig. 3.

In order to reduce communication, computation and energy cost, a simple and low-cost re-authentication protocol is proposed in [5], which does not compromise the provided security services. The proposed protocol in [5] uses a Master Session Key (MSK) parameter that had been computed in the initial authentication, and does not require the full initial authentication to be repeated. In fact the proposed protocol in [5] does not modify 3GPP infrastructure and is applied to the HeNB system.

For implementation of re-authentication protocol, it is required to apply minor changes to the initial authentication protocol. In Fig. 3, Step 10, when AAA server received AVs from HSS, it computes an MSK as

$$MSK = prf(CK|| \ IK \ ||Identity). \tag{1}$$

Where prf is a pseudo-random function, "$||$" denotes concatenation, CK is the encryption key, IK is the integrity key, and Identity belongs to HeNB. In initial authentication, MSK is used in AUTH calculation. In addition MSK is an authentication parameter in re-authentication protocol.

Then AAA server stores the calculated MSK and creates a list that binds the identity of HeNB with corresponding MSK. Similarly, HeNB computes an MSK using formula (1) and stores it. The proposed re-authentication protocol is shown in Fig. 4.

We present a brief description of Fig. 4 in the following. At first, HeNB and SeGW shares their security association [11], nonce and Diffie-Hellman value (details are available in [3]). After establishment of first phase of IKEv2 or IKE_SA, HeNB sends its ID, nonce, and $AUTH_{HeNB}$ (*i.e.* a MAC value computed over the first IKEv2 message using the stored MSK and its N_{HeNB}) to the SeGW.

$$AUTH_{HeNB} = prf(MSK||N_{HeNB}). \tag{2}$$

Then SeGW forwards ID_{HeNB} to AAA server. AAA server according to the identity of HeNB, sends pre-calculated MSK to SeGW via the diameter protocol. Upon receiving the MSK, SeGW calculates $AUTH_{HeNB}$ using available parameters and verifies it. In this way, HeNB is authenticated.

To complete re-authentication protocol, HeNB verifies $AUTH_{SeGW}$ using MSK and N_{SeGW} for authenticating SeGW. After successful verification, HeNB and SeGW have been authenticated mutually using $AUTH_{HeNB}$ and $AUTH_{SeGW}$, respectively. Finally, an IPSec tunnel is established between HeNB and SeGW that provides security services to the transmitted data [5].

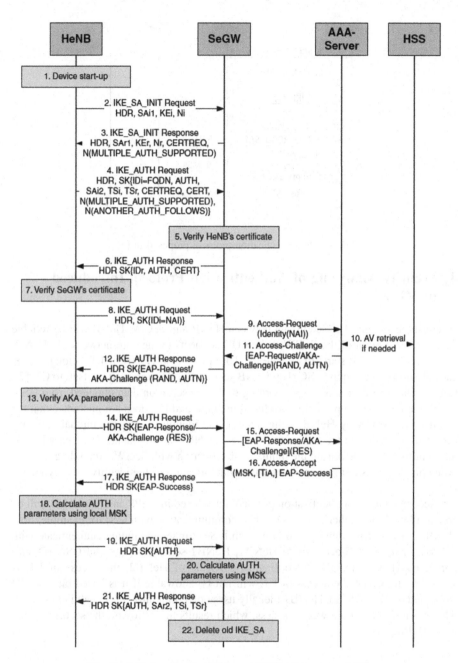

Fig. 3. Initial authentication based EAP-AKA protocol [1].

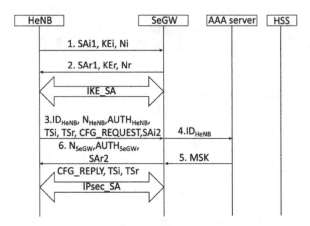

Fig. 4. Re-authentication protocol proposed in [5].

4   Security Analyzing of Authentication Protocol Introduced in 3GPP

After establishment of IPSec tunnel between HeNB and SeGW, HeNB will be reliable from the view point of the SeGW. When UE connects to the core network via HeNB, access control on UE starts to operate. As UE connects to HeNB, if UE belongs to the Closed Subscriber Group (CSG) list, HeNB sends CSG ID supported by itself to CN [2]. CN specifies UE access license according to the subscription data obtained from HSS.

The authentication protocol introduced in 3GPP and [5], does not guarantee that the identity sent to CN by HeNB is the same as the identity during the mutual authentication with SeGW. In fact, in a lot of scenes, HeNB uses the identity in CN, which is different from the one during the mutual authentication with SeGW. According to these protocols SeGW is not responsible for the authentication of the identity used by HeNB in CN.

According to the authentication protocol introduced in 3GPP and [5], HeNB will be able to illegally use other's user IDs when communicating with CN; for example, first, HeNB1 uses the true identity to establish an IPSec tunnel and mutual authenticate with SeGW; when the UE accesses to HeNB1, HeNB1 sends ID_{HeNB2} and CSG ID supported by HeNB2 to CN. According to CSG ID of HeNB2, the access of UE is allowable; however, the access of UE will not be allowable if it is based on CSG ID supported by HeNB1. So, HeNB1 illegally uses other's identity, thus enabling the user, who is originally not allowed to access, which results in destroying the security of the network [6].

5   Improved HeNB Secure Access Protocol

According to the current problem of the introduced protocol in 3GPP and [5], SeGW should send valid information of HeNB used in establishment of IPSec tunnel to the CN; so one interface is added between SeGW and CN which carries HeNB characteristics and forwards it to the CN. Note that in order to design an improved protocol, the selected network element by SeGW (for sending characteristics of HeNB) and the selected network element by HeNB (for connecting to CN) must be the same.

Improved HeNB authentication protocol is shown in Fig. 5 (some of payloads are ignored) and operates as follows.

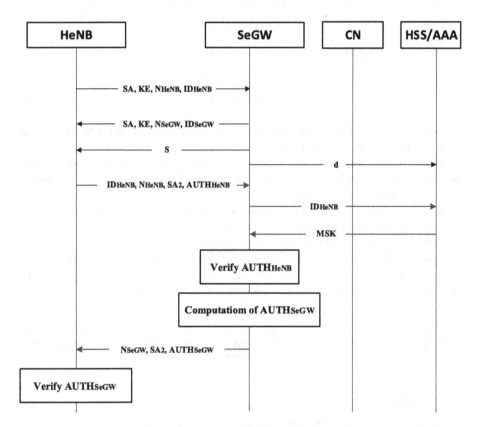

Fig. 5. Improved protocol to authenticate HeNB by SeGW (some of payloads are ignored).

Step 1. At first, IKE phase I exchanges are done as HeNB authentication; this step is explained in Sect. 3.

Step 2. After IKE phase I exchange, SeGW obtains HeNB identity and performs as below.

$$X = \text{hash}(\text{ID}_{\text{HeNB}}|\text{IP}_{\text{HeNB}}). \tag{3}$$

Hash function algorithm is MD5 in this protocol.

Then, SeGW signs X using RSA algorithm. To do this, SeGW selects two large primitive numbers p, q and computes $\gamma(n)$ as

$$\gamma(n) = \text{lcm}(p - 1, q - 1). \tag{4}$$

Then it selects integers e and d that holds following conditions respectively,

$$\gcd(e, \gamma(n)) = 1,$$
$$e \times d = 1 \bmod \gamma(n). \tag{5}$$

d is private key. Digital signature is calculated as

$$S = (X)^d \bmod n . \tag{6}$$

SeGW sends S to the HeNB and stores d in HSS and creates a list that binds the identity of HeNB with corresponding d.

Step 3. In this step, for creating IPSec SA, IKE phase II exchanges are done as explained in Sect. 3. In fact, for designing of improved HeNB secure access protocol, the re-authentication protocol is used.

Now, UE wants to connect to the network. Exchanges related to UE connection is shown in Fig. 6 (some of payloads are ignored).

Step 1. UE sends attachment request to HeNB.

Step 2. HeNB forwards UE's request to CN which checks whether HeNB can connect to the network or not; if not, CN sends failure message to HeNB. In this step, CN stores HeNB information such as ID_{HeNB}, IP_{HeNB} and digital signature S.

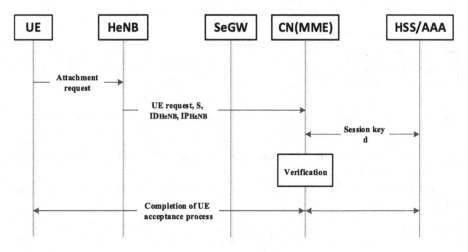

Fig. 6. UE connection to the network in improved HeNB secure access protocol (some of payloads are ignored).

Step 3. CN sends ID_{HeNB} to HSS. Then, HSS sends CSG ID supported by HeNB and digital signature key (d) that had been stored in HSS by SeGW, to CN.

After that, CN verifies the digital signature using d,

$$X' = \text{hash}(ID_{HeNB}|IP_{HeNB}), \quad Y = (X')^d \text{mod } n. \tag{7}$$

If $Y = S$, then the signature is verified. After verification, remaining procedure for attachment request or routing area is done. This procedure is out of our discussion.

In this protocol, HeNB cannot access to the network by another's ID except provided ID in IPSec protocol (authentication between HeNB and SeGW). The only drawback of this protocol is that obtaining HeNB identity can only be triggered by IPSec message to send to SeGW.

6   Evaluation of the Improved HeNB Secure Access Protocol

6.1   Security Evaluation

This improved protocol satisfies the following basic features of IKEv2.
Confidentiality
Integrity
Anonymity protection
Perfect forward secrecy
Protection against traffic analysis
Authentication of HeNB
MSK security: The ways that an attacker can discover MSK are:

1. retrieving the MSK from $AUTH_{HeNB}$ or $AUTH_{SeGW}$;
2. compromising the security of the entities stored MSK (i.e., the HeNB device and the AAA server);

For first case, the adversary may get physical access to the channel and obtain $AUTH_{HeNB}$ or $AUTH_{SeGW}$. Then, it tries to retrieve MSK using $AUTH_{HeNB}$ or $AUTH_{SeGW}$. However, the intruder is not able to do this, since he should invert one-way hash functions used for generation of $AUTH_{HeNB}$ or $AUTH_{SeGW}$ that it is inapplicable.

Second attack targets are HeNB device and AAA server. The adversary may attempt to retrieve the stored MSK either from HeNB device or AAA server. To defeat such attacks, MSK must be stored in an encrypted form. Moreover, AAA server must be secured using firewalls [5].

Replay attack: Due to the parameter N_{HeNB} and N_{SeGW} included in $AUTH_{HeNB}$ and $AUTH_{SeGW}$ respectively, in each authentication protocol, N_{HeNB} and N_{SeGW} are different. Even if an attacker gains N_{HeNB} and N_{SeGW}, he cannot be able to retrieve $AUTH_{HeNB}$ and $AUTH_{SeGW}$ by reusing the nonce in the new authentication protocol.

Now, security of proposed protocol against related attacks on HeNB specified in 3GPP, is presented.

Compromise of HeNB authentication token by a brute force attack via a weak authentication algorithm: The authentication parameter in this protocol is MSK. According to the aforementioned description of MSK security, this attack is not applicable.

Moreover, some threats included *compromise of HeNB authentication token by local physical intrusion, inserting valid authentication token into a manipulated HeNB* and *user cloning HeNB authentication token* are inapplicable due to the same reason mentioned above.

Man-in-the-Middle (MitM) attacks on HeNB first network access: Due to the establishment of IKEv2 protocol between HeNB and SeGW, and diameter protocol between SeGW and AAA server, the tunnel between HeNB and AAA server is completely safe; hence implementation of MitM attack in the improved protocol is impossible.

Denial of service attacks (DOS): In DOS attacks, adversary tries to flood SeGW. In order to make SeGW more secure against DOS attack, unauthorized traffic should be filtered out on the links between the SeGW and HeNB by introducing appropriate policies in IPSec that are out of the scope of proposed protocol security. In addition, IKEv2 protocol used in authentication procedures can also resist DOS attacks.

HeNB Masquerading: Probably after establishing IPSec tunnel and authenticating HeNB, HeNB uses other's ID for connecting an unauthorized user to the core network, such that this ID differs from used HeNB ID in authentication process. Due to the proposed protocol, since SeGW signs HeNB identity and also HeNB forwards it to CN during UE connection, even if HeNB wants to connect to the network using another ID, it will not be authenticated by CN.

6.2   Cost Analysis

Due to the added exchanges in a new modified HeNB secure access protocol with the purpose of preventing from HeNB attacks, we decided to show that these added exchanges have no significant effect on authentication delay and cost.

Communication Cost Analysis. According to [23], we assume that the transmission cost of a message between HeNB and AAA server is one unit, between HeNB and SeGW is $a(<1)$ unit and between SeGW and AAA server is $b(<1)$ unit. In the improved HeNB secure access protocol that is shown in Fig. 5, it involves the exchange of four messages between HeNB and SeGW, and three messages between SeGW and AAA server. Thus, $C_{improved}$ is computed as formula (8), where $C_{improved}$ is transmission cost for the improved HeNB secure access protocol. According to the computed C_{re} in Ref. [5], degradation (d) of the communication cost of proposed protocol over the re-authentication protocol in [5], is:

$$C_{improved} = 4a + 3b, d = \frac{C_{improved} - C_{re}}{C_{re}} = \frac{b}{4a + 2b}. \tag{8}$$

In order to facilitate analysis, we suppose that a and b are equal and set a = 0.5, b = 0.5. Therefore, the degradation parameter becomes mostly 16 %; it means that the added exchanges in our protocol do not mostly affect communication cost of re-authentication protocol.

Computational Cost Analysis. We further compare the computational cost of re-authentication and our improved protocol. First, the elapsed time of primitive cryptography operations has been measured using C/C++ OPENSSL library [24] tested on a Celeron 1.1GHZ processor as an HeNB and Dual-Core 2.6GHZ as an SeGW [5] in Table 1. Table 2 shows the duration of authentication time.

The experimental results show that added exchanges in new improved protocol does not affect computational cost of HeNB; also its effect on computational cost of SeGW is negligible.

Table 1. Time costs of the primitive cryptography operations (1024 bits) [5].

	T_E^1	T_H^2	T_{RV}^3	T_{PM}^4
HeNB	1.698 ms	0.0356 ms	0.957 ms	1.537 ms
SeGW	0.525 ms	0.0121 ms	0.301 ms	0.475 ms

[1]T_E: modular exponentiation
[2]T_H: hash
[3]T_{RV}: RSA verification
[4]T_{PM}: point multiplication

Table 2. Comparison of computational cost.

	Re-authentication protocol	Improved protocol
T_{HeNB}^1	$T_E + 2T_H + T_{PM} = 3.947$ ms	$T_E + 2T_H + T_{PM} = 3.947$ ms
T_{SeGW}^2	$T_E + 2\,T_H + T_{PM} = 1.0242$ ms	$T_E + 2\,T_H + T_{PM} + T_{RV} = 1.3252$ ms

[1]T_{HeNB}: the total operation time of HeNB.
[2]T_{SeGW}: the total operation time of SeGW.
Note: It is assumed that time cost of RSA signing and RSA verification are same.

6.3   Formal Analysis

As mentioned before, we tried to prevent HeNB masquerading attack in this new protocol. The goal of this protocol is first, mutual authentication between HeNB and SeGW using EAP-AKA protocol based on IKEv2. This goal is achieved in previous protocols. The second goal of our improved protocol and in fact, the only aim that makes this new protocol special among other protocols is re-authentication of HeNB by

CN during UE connection in order to prevent HeNB of false claim. The next goal is secrecy of dynamic key d generated by SeGW. To insure that our protocol provides these goals, we test it using formal security verification tool known as AVISPA [25]. AVISPA provides both automatic security analysis and verification back-end servers like "On-the-Fly Model-Checker" (OFMC), "Constraint-Logic based Attack Searcher" (Cl-AtSe), and SAT-based Model-Checker (SATMC). Protocols must be written in "High Level Protocol Specifications Language" (HLPSL) before verification in AVISPA. We use OFMC and Cl-AtSe to test our improved protocol.

Table 3 shows the specified goals in our test. Figures 7 and 8 show the output of OFMC and Cl-AtSe back-end, respectively. We can see that OFMC and Cl.AtSe found no attacks. In other words, the stated security goals were satisfied for a bounded number of sessions as specified in environment role. According to these figures, we conclude that this new protocol meets all of these goals and it can resist those malicious attacks such as replay attacks, MitM attacks, HeNB masquerading attack, and secrecy attacks under the test of AVISPA.

Table 3. Specified goals in the test.

goals	description
secrecy_of d	Survey of d security
authentication_on sk1	SeGW authentication by HeNB
authentication_on sk2	HeNB authentication by SeGW
authentication_on si	HeNB authentication by CN during UE connection

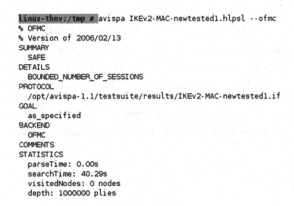

Fig. 7. Results reported by OFMC.

```
Linux-thnv:/tmp # avispa IKEv2-MAC-newtested1.hlpsl --cl-atse

SUMMARY
  SAFE

DETAILS
  BOUNDED_NUMBER_OF_SESSIONS
  TYPED_MODEL

PROTOCOL
  /opt/avispa-1.1/testsuite/results/IKEv2-MAC-newtested1.if

GOAL
  As Specified

BACKEND
  CL-AtSe

STATISTICS

  Analysed    : 4476 states
  Reachable   : 1840 states
  Translation: 0.01 seconds
  Computation: 0.62 seconds
```

Fig. 8. Results reported by Cl-AtSe.

7 Conclusion

In this paper, description and security analyzing of HeNB authentication protocol introduced in 3GPP and re-authentication protocol proposed in [5] is provided. These protocols are yet unsafe against some applicable attacks on HeNB; such as HeNB masquerading. Vulnerability of these protocols allows HeNB to connect to the network using other user's ID that differs from the ID used during IPSec tunnel establishment. Therefore, the new improved HeNB secure access protocol is introduced, in which, SeGW signs HeNB identity provided by HeNB during initial authentication, and sends it to CN via HeNB during UE connection. In this way, even if HeNB wants to connect to CN with another ID, it will not be verified by CN, and unauthorized users connection becomes impossible. Security analyzing and verification of our protocol in AVISPA shows that it is robust against applicable threats on HeNB and solves the present security problems of previous protocols. Moreover, according to the experimental results, it has no significant effect on communication and computational cost.

References

1. Forsberg, D., Horn, G., Moeller, W., Niemi, V.: LTE Security. Wiley Publishing, New York (2010)
2. Ali-Yahiya, T.: Understanding LTE and its Performance. Springer, Berlin (2011)
3. Doraswamy, N., Harkins, D.: IPSec: The New Security Standard for the Internet, Intranets, and Virtual Private Networks, 2nd edn. Prentice Hall PTR, Upper Saddle River (2003)
4. 3rd Generation Partnership Project: Technical Specification Group Services and System Aspects; Security of H(e)NB (Rel. 8). 3GPP TR 33.820 v1.3.0 (January 2009)

5. Chengzhe, L., Hui, L., Yueyu, Z., Jin, C.: Simple and Low-cost re-authentication protocol for HeNB. IEEE J. Mag. Chin. Commun. **10**, 105–115 (2013)
6. Zong, Z., Zhou, X., Zhu, L.: HNB or HeNB security access method and system and core network element. U.S. Patent No. 355, 299, Shenzhen City (2014)
7. Han, C.K., Choi, H.K., Kim, I.H.: Building femtocell more secure with improved proxy signature. In: Global Telecommunications Conference, pp. 1–6 (2009)
8. Aboba, B., Blunk, L., Vollbrecht, J., Carlson, J., Levkowetz, H.: Extensible authentication protocol (EAP). RFC3748 (2004)
9. Arkko, J., Haverinen, H.: Authentication and key agreement (EAP-AKA). RFC4187 (2006)
10. Narayanan, V., Dondeti, L.: EAP extensions for EAP re-authentication protocol (ERP). RFC5296 (2008)
11. Kent, S., Atkinson, R.: Security architecture for the internet protocol. RFC2401 (1998)
12. Kent, S., Atkinson, R.: IP authentication header. RFC2402 (1998)
13. Kent, S., Atkinson, R.: IP encapsulating security payload (ESP). RFC2406 (1998)
14. Piper, D.: The internet IP security domain of interpretation for ISAKMP. RFC2407 (1998)
15. Clancy, T., Nakhjiri, M., Narayanan, V., Dondeti, L.: Handover key management and re-authentication problem statement. RFC5169 (2008)
16. 3rd generation partnership project: technical specification group services and system aspects; 3GPP system architecture evolution (SAE); security architecture (Release 10). 3GPP TS 33.401 V10.2.0 (September 2011)
17. 3rd generation partnership project: technical specification group services and system aspects; rationale and track of security decisions in long term evolved (LTE) RAN/3GPP System Architecture Evolution (SAE) (Release 8). 3GPP TR 33.821 V8.0.0 (March 2009)
18. Han, C.K.: Security analysis and enhancements in LTE-advanced networks. Ph.D. Thesis, Sungkyunkwan University (2011)
19. Cao, J., Ma, M., Li, H., Zhang, Y., Luo, Z.: A survey on security aspects for LTE and LTE-A networks. IEEE J. Mag. Commun. Surv. Tutorials **16**, 283–302 (2014)
20. Smaoui, S., Zarai, F., Kamoun, L.: IPSec tunnel establishment for 3GPP-WLAN interworking. In: 8th International Conference on Informatics and Systems (INFOS), pp 74–80 (2012)
21. Raza, H.: A brief survey of radio access network backhaul evolution, Part I. IEEE J. Mag. Commun. Mag. **49**, 164–171 (2011)
22. Raza, H.: A brief survey of radio access network backhaul evolution, Part II. IEEE J. Mag. Commun. Mag. **51**, 170–177 (2013)
23. Ntantogian, C., Xenakis, C.: One-pass EAP-AKA authentication in 3G-WLAN integrated networks. Wireless Pers. Commu. **48**, 569–584 (2009)
24. OPENSSL[EB/OL] (2012). http://www.openssl.org/
25. AVISPA—Automated Validation of Internet Security Protocols [EB/OL] (2012). http://www.avispa-project.org

Radio-Aware Service-Level Scheduling to Minimize Downlink Traffic Delay Through Mobile Edge Computing

Jose Oscar Fajardo$^{(\boxtimes)}$, Ianire Taboada, and Fidel Liberal

University of the Basque Country (UPV/EHU), ETSI Bilbao, 48013 Bizkaia, Spain
{joseoscar.fajardo,ianire.taboada,fidel.liberal}@ehu.eus
http://det.bi.ehu.es/NQAS

Abstract. One of the most challenging problems in mobile broadband networks is how to assign the available radio resources among the different mobile users. Traditionally, research proposals are either specific to some type of traffic or deal with computationally intensive algorithms aimed at optimizing the delivery of general purpose traffic. Consequently, commercial networks do not incorporate these mechanisms due to the limited hardware resources at the mobile edge. Emerging 5G architectures introduce cloud computing principles to add flexible computational resources to Radio Access Networks. This paper makes use of the Mobile Edge Computing concepts to introduce a new element, denoted as Mobile Edge Scheduler, aimed at minimizing the mean delay of general traffic flows in the LTE downlink. This element runs close to the eNodeB element and implements a novel flow-aware and channel-aware scheduling policy in order to accommodate the transmissions to the available channel quality of end users.

Keywords: Mobile networks · Flow scheduling · Mobile edge computing · 5G

1 Introduction

Complex future content centric Internet and the 5G paradigm, including Network Function Virtualization (NFV) and Software Defined Networking (SDN), suggest the introduction of intelligent network nodes that will enable more powerful adaptation and prioritization frameworks over the whole transmission chain, and especially at the edge of mobile network segments [1].

The classical issue in current Radio Access Networks (RAN), including 4th Generation (4G) Long Term Evolution (LTE), is related to the problem of how to handle the assignment of shared radio resources among multiple mobile users in order to maximize the overall service experience. Many research proposals have dealt with the problem, aimed at optimizing the provision of certain services and traffic patterns [2]. Most of these works are based on the introduction of

© Institute for Computer Sciences, Social Informatics and Telecommunications Engineering 2015
R. Agüero et al. (Eds.): MONAMI 2015, LNICST 158, pp. 121–134, 2015.
DOI: 10.1007/978-3-319-26925-2_10

service and channel awareness in the scheduling function of the eNodeB, considering channel awareness as fine-grain Channel Quality Indicator (CQI) feedbacks provided by mobile devices.

Unfortunately, most of these types of scheduling functions are based on ideal channel awareness and are driven by complex mathematical logic. The associated complexity prevents its implementation into real-world eNodeBs, which need to determine the multi-user traffic assignments at Transmission Time Interval (TTI) slots (i.e., 1 ms in LTE).

In the framework of future 5G mobile networks, different proposals are emerging aimed at overcoming the capacity limitations of current Radio Access Networks (RAN). Cloud computing principles are being proposed to design the future RAN, in order to create Cloud Radio Access Networks (C-RAN) with increased flexible capacity [3], and to deploy service instances within the C-RAN enabling increased adaptability to mobile users' context.

One of the emerging technologies to cope with more personalized and user-centric service provisioning is the novel Mobile Edge Computing (MEC) industry initiative [4], a promising approach to solve these types of problems from an operator-supported approach. This initiative proposes that mobile network operators would provide an API to third-party partners, offering them access to critical features such as location awareness and network context information. This information may be exploited to deploy proximity-enabled services with close-to-zero latency characteristics, in order to optimize the management of future mobile networks.

Figure 1 illustrates different alternatives for the centralization of RAN functions. On one hand, fully centralized RAN entails that all the processing is deployed in centralized data centers. In 3GPP terminology, the BaseBand Unit (BBU) would perform all the required functions including the Radio Resource Management (RRM), while the Remote Radio Header (RRH) would only transmit the generated radio signals. This architecture enables a full virtualization of RAN functions, but requires reliable high speed connections in the fronthaul. Other alternatives, as discussed in [5], allow the centralization of specific RAN functions. As shown in Fig. 1, the RRM functions may still run at the eNodeB specific hardware in order to guarantee accurate channel state information. Meanwhile, other functions are more feasible for centralization/virtualization, usually associated to the higher layers.

Regardless the adopted architecture, MEC-driven service instances must be deployed over the cloud resources available at the RAN. Thus, the degree of coupling between service-level instances and RRM functions may differ.

This paper focuses on the network-assisted optimization of downlink traffic flows in the latter scenarios, as a solution to introduce network intelligence in partially centralized RAN deployments. Rather than applying complex scheduling logic at the eNodeB hardware, this paper explores the possibility to deploy user-aware service instances within the C-RAN in order to optimize the delivery of traffic flows based on close-to-the-user channel awareness.

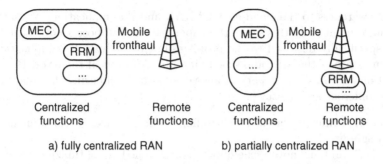

Fig. 1. Fully centralized vs. partially centralized RAN.

1.1 Contributions and Schedule of the Paper

In this paper, we analyze the possibility of extracting the intelligent scheduling logic out of the eNodeB specific hardware to the cloud-enabled RAN. This novel approach emerges as a non-optimal but implementable solution, bringing service optimization close to mobile end users while reducing the complexity required by radio hardware elements.

The main contributions of this paper are:

- A novel service delivery architecture, based on the principles of C-RAN and MEC, which allows deploying intelligent scheduling logic at the mobile edge without requiring high computational resources at the eNodeB hardware.
- The study of the resulting two-round channel-aware scheduling process, comprising a first traffic conformance deployed as a MEC instance and a latter RRM at the eNodeB hardware.
- The analysis of some preliminary results for the proposed solution obtained through simulations, which incorporates authors previous results in the field of intelligent scheduling and experimental LTE channel measurements.

Section 2 describes the proposed architecture, where a novel flow- and channel-aware scheduling policy is located at the mobile edge just before the eNodeB scheduling function. The new scheduler is aimed at implementing context-aware traffic shaping to minimize the average delay of traffic flows; meanwhile, eNodeB scheduling is driven by a classical implementable scheduling policy [6]. Section 2 also discusses some technological issues that determine the achievable performance in this kind of multi-user mobile service provisioning, such as the partially observable channel problem.

Section 3 focuses on the scheduling policy proposed to drive the cloud-enabled traffic shaping. The proposed scheduling policy is based on [7], where authors define a near-optimal index policy named Attained Service dependent Potential Improvement (ASPI). ASPI solves the opportunistic scheduling problem for general file size distributions and multiple channel states, restricted to i.i.d. channels and single user transmissions. In this paper, we apply ASPI to multi-user simultaneous transmissions leading to Multi-user Attained Service Potential Improvement (MASPI). Additionally, we analyze the problem of moving the channel awareness to the cloud-enabled RAN and the implications of using non i.i.d. radio channels. In this sense, the paper does not propose a novel scheduling policy specifically designed to the problem, but it analyzes the implications of deploying state of the art radio scheduling functions out of the eNodeB.

Section 4 focuses on the performance evaluation, comparing the delay results of three different architectures:

- eNodeB running classical scheduling policy aimed at maximizing cell throughput.
- eNodeB running novel scheduling policy aimed at optimizing mean flow delays.
- MEC function running novel scheduling policy aimed at optimizing mean flow delays together with eNodeB running classical scheduling policy aimed at maximizing cell throughput.

As derived from the performance evaluation and discussed in Sect. 5, the proposed novel architecture allows improving the overall performance of the mobile services without increasing the computational requirements of eNodeB elements.

2   MEC-assisted Traffic Scheduling

The proposed novel service element to be deployed within the C-RAN is intended to incorporate novel concepts of complex radio scheduling logic through software-based Mobile Edge Computing instances. This way, the new service element provides the required user awareness to deploy optimized service delivery over current eNodeB scheduling functions.

Figure 2 illustrates the overall network architecture of the resulting solution.

A number of Internet traffic sources deliver traffic flows towards the mobile end users following arbitrary flow distributions. These flows traverse the Internet segments and the mobile backhaul before arriving at the RAN.

In current 4G mobile network architectures the scheduling logic is run at the eNodeB elements, which also implement the radio air interface. Therefore, these eNodeB elements are the unique network nodes endowed with user-reported channel awareness. Channel awareness is indeed implemented by means of CQI reporting from mobile devices to the eNodeB, based on the configured CQI Reporting Rate (CRR). Although perfect channel awareness is not possible, CRR is usually configured to a low value (e.g., 5 ms) in order to avoid imprecise scheduling decisions.

In emerging C-RAN architectures, Internet applications would be able to gather users' channel feedbacks to some extent in order to optimize their traffic delivery to mobile users. As illustrated in Fig. 2, the key element in the MEC industry initiative is the MEC Server, which is integrated into the mobile operators' RAN in order to provide value-added capabilities to third party developers [4]. In the case of LTE, the MEC Server is directly integrated into the

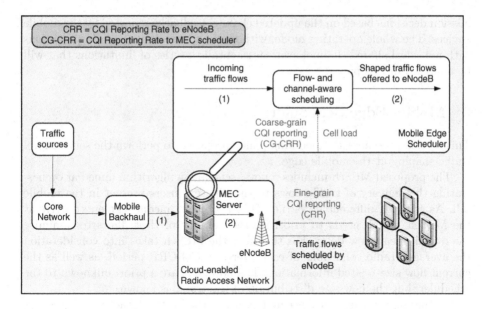

Fig. 2. Proposed MEC-assisted flow scheduling architecture.

eNodeB. The MEC Server is based on cloud computing principles to run third-party applications over a common hardware infrastructure. These applications may range from lightweight monitoring instances, which would provide relevant RAN-related information to optimize external OTT servers, to more complex applications, intended to handle and modify the traffic to/from the mobile users at RAN level.

Upon this MEC Server element, we propose to deploy the Mobile Edge Scheduler (MESch) as an intelligent node aimed at optimizing the traffic delivery to multiple mobile users. MESch is included in the service provisioning chain, enabling the required flow awareness concepts. At the same time, MESch interacts with the MEC Server in order to retrieve cell and user context information, such as the cell load or per-user radio performance statistics.

The MEC API is the designated interface for retrieving cell statistics and individual channel quality information. In multi-user scenarios, the CQI feedback granularity would entail a high load and traffic volume in the interface between MEC Server and MESch. Thus, a coarse-grain feedback statistic is defined in Fig. 2 as CG-CRR. Besides, MESch implements the flow- and channel-aware scheduling policy in order to maximize the service experience. This module combines flow awareness, user context awareness and cell status awareness, in order to run the required intelligent logic that will be detailed in the following section.

The output of MESch can be seen as a series of decomposed traffic flows, properly segmented in chunks according to the optimization logic and being forwarded to the eNodeB for its delivery to the end users. Consequently, the eNodeB will run a more basic scheduling logic at TTI level and making transmission decisions based on the updated channel feedbacks reported by the mobile devices. The whole operating mode, with two concatenated scheduling functions with non-ideal shared channel awareness, entails a series of limitations that will be analyzed in this paper.

3 Mobile Edge Scheduler

This section presents the scheduling policy proposed to perform the service-level traffic shaping at the mobile edge.

The proposed MESch includes a novel scheduling algorithm aimed at orchestrating the delivery of traffic flows to the different users present in the mobile cell. As a result, different flows (i.e., HTTP objects, media segments) arrive at the MESch, which needs to prioritize the delivery of these flows to minimize the overall mean flow delay. For this aim, the MESch takes into consideration the averaged radio conditions of each user in a CG-CRR period, as well as the current flow size-related information. The flow sizes are a priori unknown to the scheduler, but the flow size distribution of the traffic is known.

In the next subsections, we first analyze the state of the art of relevant scheduling policies and discuss the adopted alternatives. Later, the proposed scheduling policy is detailed.

3.1 Background on Flow Scheduling for Wireless Systems

Over the years the literature on performance evaluation and optimal scheduling of traffic flows in time-varying wireless channels has grown tremendously. Undoubtedly, the most studied resource allocation problems aim at minimizing the mean transfer delay of user flows. Although several channel-aware strategies exist with the objective of minimizing the mean flow delay, Best CQI and Proportional Fair [6] among the most popular ones, the achievement of the optimal solution for time-varying scheduling optimization problems is computationally and analytically unfeasible. To cope with this problem, flow-level channel-aware opportunistic scheduling in time-varying systems has been analyzed by approximate techniques [8,9] in order to design simple, tractable and implementable well-performing heuristic priority scheduling rules [7,9,10].

On the other hand, classical results show that prioritizing short flows minimizes the overall mean delay [11,12]. However, this is only applicable if there is a priori knowledge of flow sizes, which is not generally the case in current IP networks. For this reason, non-anticipating size-based scheduling disciplines make use of flow attained service, i.e. the bits that have been transferred of a flow, for making scheduling decisions. In this context, Gittins proposes an index rule that, based on the attained service of jobs, minimizes the mean delay when channel capacity is constant [13].

Therefore, an approach that combines both flow size awareness and channel awareness seems promising [8]. Our previous work in [7] proposes a simple, analytically founded, tractable and well-performing scheduling index rule that combines non-anticipating size awareness and channel awareness. The obtained priority-based discipline is called ASPI rule, which was derived by using Whittle approach [14]. However, this work assumes that a single user transmits in each transmission time interval, while modern cellular networks entail simultaneous transmission of multiple flows.Therefore, in the following subsection we propose a scheduler based on ASPI that overcomes the lack of the simultaneous transmission of flows.

3.2 MASPI Scheduling Algorithm

The ASPI index rule is our previous solution for solving an attained service-dependent and channel-aware Markov Decision Process by Whittle methodology [7]. To achieve this non-anticipating size-based and channel-aware solution, we first formulated the mean delay minimizing scheduling problem in the framework of Markovian decision processes. Then, since obtaining the optimal solution of this analytical model unachievable, we derived ASPI by using methodologies based on Whittle approach.

The Whittle method [14] consists in obtaining a metric per flow state that measures the dynamic transmission priority of a single flow. In this way, a simple scheduling index rule appears: at every slot, select for transmission the K flows with the highest current Whittle index value. With that aim, the non-anticipating size-based and channel-aware scheduling problem aimed at minimizing the mean delay can be relaxed by requiring to serve K jobs per slot on average, and further approached by Lagrangian methods [14]. As a result, a single-job price-based parametrized optimization problem is achieved, where the Lagrangian parameter can be interpreted as the per-slot cost of transmitting. Thus, the Whittle index is the break-even value of the Lagrangian parameter. For our case study, it measures the expected efficiency of transmitting a flow in each attained service and channel condition state. Note that the opportunistic and non-anticipating size-aware ASPI index was derived for an uncorrelated channel model and for the significant class of size distributions with Decreasing Hazard Rate (DHR).

The so-called ASPI index rule gives priority to users that are in their best channel conditions. The index value for users that are not in their maximum achievable channel condition equals the ratio between the instantaneous transmission completion probability and the expected potential improvement of the instantaneous transmission completion probability.

Thus, the ASPI scheduling discipline consists in, at every decision slot:

- choosing to transmit a flow from a user that is in the best channel condition with the highest value of $c\mu_{(a,N)}$;
- and if there is no user in the best channel condition, choosing the flow with the highest value of $\dfrac{c\mu_{(a,n)}}{\sum\limits_{m>n} q_m\left(\mu_{(a,m)}-\mu_{(a,n)}\right)}$.

Where q_m is the probability of being in channel state m, $\mu_{a,n}$ the flow transmission completion probability ($P(a < X \le a + r_n | X > a)$), being X the flow size, a the instantaneous attained service and r_n the bits transmitted in channel condition n (being N the best channel condition that a user can achieve), and c the holding cost per slot while the flow transmission is not completed (when the objective is minimizing the mean delay the value of c is 1). Note that if the flow size distribution belongs to the DHR class, $\mu_{a,n}$ also decreases with attained service [10].

Nevertheless, the performance of this Whittle-based policy has only been validated considering the transmission of a single flow in each TTI, this is, assigning all the available network resources to the same flow, which is not realistic in current and future wireless networks. However, a Whittle-based policy allows the simultaneous transmission of multiple flows. In such situation, we extend ASPI proposal to a multi-user approach. We propose an enhanced ASPI scheduler, denoted as Multi-user ASPI or MASPI, which considers the transmission of multiple user traffic flows per TTI.

In this way, the MASPI discipline consists in: at every decision slot, having K network resources to assign:

- choosing to transmit K flows from users that are in their best channel condition with the highest value of $c\mu_{(a,N)}$;
- and if there are less than K user flows in their best channel condition, being K' flows in the best channel conditions, choosing to transmit the $K - K'$ flows with the highest value of $\dfrac{c\mu_{(a,n)}}{\sum\limits_{m>n} q_m\left(\mu_{(a,m)} - \mu_{(a,n)}\right)}$.

4   Performance Evaluation

In this section, we analyze the performance of the proposed MEC-assisted scheduling. For that purpose, we compare the achieved performance in terms of mean delay of the following different approaches:

- Classical eNodeB scheduler (eNodeB(BC)): eNodeB running Best CQI (BC) discipline. This discipline gives priority to those users with higher reported CQI values.
- Near-optimal eNodeB scheduler (eNodeB(MASPI)): eNodeB running MASPI scheduler. This discipline aims at prioritizing those flows with lower expected time to finish.
- The proposed two-stage proposal (MESch-eNodeB(BC)): MASPI running at MESch and classical BC policy at eNodeB.

As can be observed, all these schemes are channel-aware. Based on the CQI values, eNodeB applies Adaptive Modulation and Coding (AMC) to select the most suitable Modulation and Coding Scheme (MCS) for each UE. Similarly, MASPI incorporates the coarse-grain channel awareness for decision making. Additionally, MASPI takes into account the monitored Block Error Rate (BLER) and would apply conservative MCS assignations when required in order to mitigate the effect of radio retransmissions under highly variable radio channel conditions.

For performance evaluation, we simulate the behavior of an LTE network configured with 20 MHz of bandwidth. Consequently, the eNodeB scheduling function arranges the transmissions of multi-user traffic at every TTI of 1ms, optimally allocating the set of the available 100 Resource Blocks (RBs). For simplicity, we assume that all the UEs are LTE Category 4 using LTE MIMO, with up to 150 Mbps of downlink peak rate.

In order to capture the effects of real-world radio channels, we employ actual CQI traces from live LTE networks as reported in [15]. Therefore, we use our own system-level simulation environment implemented in MATLAB. This implementation allows us to simulate the radio channel at CQI level, and to apply the required RRM functions. BLER is generated based on the difference between the last reported CQI and the actual CQI.

Table 1 illustrates the channel state probabilities of the experimental CQI traces captured for mobile users and used for performance evaluation. In our set up, CQI traces at eNodeB provide a granularity of 5 ms, while CQI traces available at MESch are generated from averaging these experimental traces with 1 s granularity. The average CQI value is 9.47 and, consequently, the average data rate individually achievable is 67.326 Mbps.

Table 1. Channel state probabilities for different CQIs.

CQI	0	1	2	3	4	5	6	7	8	9	10	11	12	13	14	15
q_n	0	0	0	0.00046	0.024	0.078	0.0047	0.015	0.1918	0.13	0.202	0.19	0.0842	0.056	0.0173	0.00132

Regarding traffic demands, we consider Pareto distributed flow sizes that belong to DHR class. It is known that Internet traffic flows are properly modeled by means of Pareto distributions [16]. In this case, we assume a mean flow size of 5 Mbit and a shape parameter of 1.3. These flows arrive according to a Poisson process, whose rate determines the network load. We consider six network states: low load ($\rho = 0.25, 0.375$), medium load ($\rho = 0.5, 0.75$) and high load ($\rho = 0.9, 0.95$).

4.1   Results

Now we analyze the performance in terms of delay for the aforedescribed wireless scenario, considering delay as the total time since the reception of a flow until its complete transmission to the mobile user. For that aim, we will show the mean delay results of the three schemes under study for the considered network loads. In addition to the mean value, the 95 % confidence intervals are included.

Figure 3 collects the mean delay results of the analyzed LTE settings. As can be observed, on the one hand, our two-phase scheduling proposal behaves notably better than a classical scheduler at the eNodeB such as BC. On the other hand, MESch-eNodeB(BC) provides worse results than a near-optimal eNodeB scheduling solution such as MASPI with BLER awareness. Moreover, it is worth to mention that both the difference in mean delay among schedulers and the confidence intervals increase with the network load value.

Therefore, the average delays achieved with our proposal enhance those obtained with eNodeB(BC), while not requiring high computing capabilities in the eNodeB hardware. These results are in the same scale as those achieved by the one-phase MASPI solution at the eNodeB, even if MESch-eNodeB(BC) makes use of more uncertain channel information due to the CG-CRR parameter.

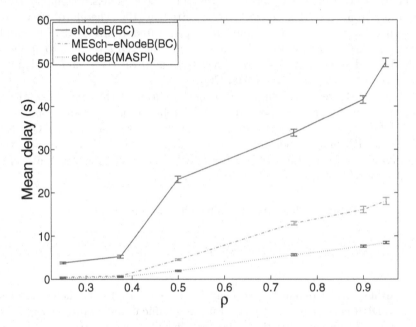

Fig. 3. Mean delay results.

Tables 2, 3, 4 show the detailed results for three representative test points, corresponding to low, medium and high radio network loads. Three parameters are shown for each test scenario: the ratio of completed flows in the simulation time, the average BLER through the whole simulation and the average flow delay experienced due to the additional MESch node. Logically, the latter value is only significant for the MESch-eNodeB(BC) case.

As can be observed, the ratio of flows completely transmitted to the UE follows the same behaviour than the average delays. For all the considered network loads, eNodeB(MASPI) and eNodeB(BC) provide the lowest and highest values respectively. The proposed MESch-eNodeB(BC) scheme achieves intermediate results.

Similarly, we can observe that experienced BLER is higher for eNodeB(BC), while eNodeB(MASPI) reduces the BLER significantly. The enhancement achieved in the proposed MESch-eNodeB(BC) scheme is considerable at low network loads, and converges to eNodeB(BC) at high loads.

Finally, it is remarkable that the average flow delay due to the added MESch scheduling phase also increases with the network load, reaching up to 1.5 s at high network load conditions.

As a result, we can state that the proposed MESch-eNodeB(BC) provides accurate performance outcomes, exhibiting average flow delays that are closer to the near-optimal eNodeB(MASPI) scheduling policy than to the classical eNodeB(BC) policy. At the same time, the complexity of the radio head is reduced to BC scheme and the complex logic is deployed at the cloud facilities of the RAN.

Table 2. Detailed results for $\rho = 0.25$.

	Finished flows	BLER	MESch delay
eNodeB(BC)	0.9805	0.2186	-
MESch-eNodeB(BC)	0.9991	0.1467	0.2061
eNodeB(MASPI)	0.9994	0.0932	-

Table 3. Detailed results for $\rho = 0.75$.

	Finished flows	BLER	MESch delay
eNodeB(BC)	0.9531	0.3019	-
MESch-eNodeB(BC)	0.9755	0.1709	0.6731
eNodeB(MASPI)	0.9896	0.1029	-

Table 4. Detailed results for $\rho = 0.95$.

	Finished flows	BLER	MESch delay
eNodeB(BC)	0.9299	0.3047	-
MESch-eNodeB(BC)	0.9549	0.3072	1.4491
eNodeB(MASPI)	0.9892	0.1176	-

5   Conclusions

This paper deals with the inclusion of complex scheduling algorithms in the context of emerging mobile broadband networks. The scenario analyzed includes a multi-user LTE network, where mobile users wander through the LTE cell experiencing realistic variable channel conditions. Since the paper focuses on the optimization of mean flow delays in general-purpose conditions, the traffic profile is assumed to be a Pareto distribution.

Taking into account several recent research results, flow- and channel-aware scheduling policies provide near-optimal results in these types of dynamic wireless scenarios. However, even the most efficient of those algorithms entail high computational requirements preventing their application in real-world eNodeB scheduling functions.

This paper proposes an alternative way of running this complex scheduling logic within the mobile edge but out of the eNodeB hardware element. This solution is based on the concepts of Mobile Edge Computing, which specifies the architecture to run personalized services close to the end mobile users and defines an interface to provide radio channel feedbacks to these service instances.

As a result, we propose a two-stage scheduling process. First, the Mobile Edge Scheduling -MESch- algorithm is aimed at shaping the traffic according to the actual flow and coarse-grain channel conditions. Second, the eNodeB runs its lightweight scheduling function with fine-grain channel information.

In this context, we compare the performance results obtained for (i) an eNodeB running the near-optimal MASPI scheduling policy, (ii) an eNodeB running the classical Best CQI scheduling policy, and (iii) the proposed solution with a double MESch-eNodeB scheduling.

As expected, eNodeB(MASPI) provides the lowest mean delays for the complete set of traffic flows. While the proposed architecture provides higher mean delays compared to eNodeB(MASPI), it significantly improves the results of the simple eNodeB(BC) approach. The total transmission delays in the proposed architecture are the combination of the scheduling function at MESch and the scheduling function at eNodeB. The first contribution provides slightly higher delay values than eNodeB(MASPI). Although the scheduling logic is the same, the results of MESch cannot capture the effects of radio retransmissions due to the variability of radio channels. The second contribution provides significantly lower average delay values compared to eNodeB(BC). MESch decomposes the Pareto traffic into a new train of flow segments according to the actual flow and channel characteristics. Thus, for example, heavy flows associated to users in good channel conditions may be delayed by MESch preventing higher delays for other flows with higher probability to finish.

MASPI is only based on the flow size distribution and the attained service of each flow. This characteristic allows implementing this kind of logic without the constraint of requiring the complete reception of flows to capture flow sizes. As a result, we show how this kind of intelligent scheduling logic may be implemented in emerging cloud-enabled multi-user mobile networks, relaxing the computing requirements of the eNodeB scheduling functions.

5.1 Future Work

The presented preliminary performance results anticipate the benefits of the proposed two-stage channel-aware scheduling architecture. Anyway, a more comprehensive performance analysis is required in order to identify the specific sources of delay and possible ways of improvement. This study would likely lead to a further enhancement of the MESch algorithm, in order to get closer to the optimal solution. Additionally, the computational and energy requirements in the different elements of the architecture should be thoroughly analyzed.

Possible malfunction of the MESch shall also be analyzed. Since the MESch element is introduced as an add-on to the service chain, the effect of disabling this new function would result in falling back to the default situation, where only the eNodeB RRM is performed. However, the effect of highly variable CQI could lead to unstable situations where MESch applies inaccurate scheduling decisions leading to performance degradations.

In the current implementation of the MESch algorithm, the coarse-grain CQI values reported by the MEC Server are used during the whole CG-CRR period. In highly variable radio channels, this assumption may introduce further performance degradations due to inaccurate channel estimations. Therefore, the inclusion of partially observable channel models could enhance the performance of the proposed MESch in those scenarios.

Acknowledgments. The research leading to these results has received funding from the European Union's H2020 Research and Innovation Project SESAME, under the Grant Agreement H2020-ICT-671596, and from the Spanish Ministerio de Economia y Competitividad (MINECO) under grant TEC2013-46766-R: QoEverage - QoE - aware optimization mechanisms for next generation networks and services.

References

1. Soldani, D., Manzalini, A.: Horizon 2020 and beyond: on the 5G operating system for a true digital society. IEEE Veh. Technol. Mag. **10**(1), 32–42 (2015)
2. Fouziya Sulthana, S., Nakkeeran, R.: Study of downlink scheduling algorithms in LTE networks. J. Netw. **9**(12), 3381–3391 (2014)
3. Wu, J., Zhang, Z., Hong, Y., Wen, Y.: Cloud radio access network (C-RAN): a primer. IEEE Netw. **29**(1), 35–41 (2015)
4. Patel, M., et al.: Mobile-Edge Computing Introductory Technical White Paper. White Paper, Mobile-edge Computing (MEC) industry initiative (2014)
5. Small Cell Forum, Small cell virtualization functional splits and use cases, Document 159.05.1.01 (2015)
6. Aalto S., Lassila P.: Flow-level stability and performance of channel-aware priority-based schedulers. In: Proceeding of NGI 2010 (6th EURO-NF Conference on Next Generation Internet) (2010)
7. Taboada, I., Liberal, F., Jacko, P.: An opportunistic and non-anticipating size-aware scheduling proposal for mean holding cost minimization in time-varying channels. Perform. Eval. **79**, 90–103 (2014)
8. Aalto S., Penttinen A., Lassila P., Osti P.: On the optimal trade-off between SRPT and opportunistic scheduling. In: Proceedings of ACM Sigmetrics, pp. 185–196 (2011)
9. Ayesta, U., Erausquin, M., Jacko, P.: A modeling framework for optimizing the flow-level scheduling with time-varying channels. Perform. Eval. **67**, 1014–1029 (2010)

10. Taboada I., Jacko P., Ayesta U., Liberal F.: Opportunistic scheduling of flows with general size distribution in wireless time-varying channels. In: 26th IEEE International Teletraffic Congress (ITC), pp. 1–9 (2014)
11. Kleinrock, L.: Queueing Systems, Volume 2: Computer Applications. Wiley, New York (1976)
12. Avrachenkovt, K., Ayesta, U., Brown, P., Nyberg, E.: Differentiation between short and long TCP flows: predictability of the response time. In: IEEE Computer and Communications Societies, INFOCOM 2004, vol. 2, pp. 762–773 (2004)
13. Gittins, J., Glazebrook, K., Weber, R.: Multi-armed Bandit Allocation Indice. Wiley, New York (2011)
14. Nino-Mora, J.: Dynamic priority allocation via restless bandit marginal productivity indices. TOP **15**(2), 161–198 (2007)
15. Fajardo, J.O., Taboada, I., Liberal, F.: Analysis of CQI traces from LTE MIMO deployments and impact on classical schedulers. In: Aguayo-Torres, M.C., Gómez, G., Poncela, J. (eds.) WWIC 2015. LNCS, vol. 9071, pp. 60–73. Springer, Heidelberg (2015)
16. Thompson, K., Miller, G.J., Wilder, R.: Wide-area Internet traffic patterns and characteristics. IEEE Netw. **11**(6), 10–23 (1997)

Techniques and Algorithms
for Wireless Networks

A Context-Aware Method Decoupled from Protocol for Adapting Routing Process in DTN

Cinara Menegazzo[1,2], Eduardo Spinosa[2], and Luiz Carlos P. Albini[2]([⊠])

[1] Santa Catarina State University, Joinville, Santa Catarina, Brazil
cinara.menegazzo@udesc.br
[2] Federal University of Parana, Curitiba, Brazil
{spinosa,albini}@inf.ufpr.br

Abstract. Several routing protocols for Delay-Tolerant Networks (DTNs) can be found in the literature. All these protocols have strengths and weaknesses depending on the usage scenario. Nevertheless, in DTNs, messages are forwarded hop-by-hop autonomously, without an on-line path connecting the source and the destination. This unique characteristic of DTNs allows the routing protocol to be changed on-the-fly while a message traverses the network. The only limitation is that each pair of nodes must share the same routing protocol. If each node is able to choose the best routing protocol based on its context and on the available routing protocols, it is possible to minimize the weaknesses of the chosen protocols. In this way, this article proposes an on-the-fly context-aware routing adaptation method. Each node, independently, chooses the routing protocol to forward a message, based on its own context information and on the routing protocols available at the possible next hops. Thus, in order to explore the strengths of all protocols and reduce their weaknesses, every message can be forwarded from the source to the destination through several different routing protocols, one for each hop if necessary. The feasibility and the efficiency of the proposed method are evaluated through simulations, and the results demonstrate that it is possible to increase the delivery ratio and reduce the delay with a small increase on the overhead.

Keywords: DTN · Routing · Performance analysis · Network parameters

1 Introduction

Delay Tolerant Networks (DTNs) are opportunistic networks mainly composed by mobile nodes without a persistent connection between them. Routing represents a challenge for DTNs since the communication path from a source to a destination is intermittently connected; the message delivery relies on a predicted sequence of communication opportunities, which is defined as a **contact**. Thus, routing protocols should be able to forward, store, and deliver messages

© Institute for Computer Sciences, Social Informatics and Telecommunications Engineering 2015
R. Agüero et al. (Eds.): MONAMI 2015, LNICST 158, pp. 137–149, 2015.
DOI: 10.1007/978-3-319-26925-2_11

without any contact guarantee, aiming at maximizing data delivery and minimizing delay. A key factor for routing protocols in DTNs is the selection of the best candidate node to store and carry messages towards the destination.

Traditional routing protocols for DTNs, such as *Epidemic* [19], *Spray-And-Wait* (SPW) [17], and *Probabilistic Routing using History of Encounters and Transitivity* (PRoPHET) [10], consider contact history or the amount of messages in the network as parameters to choose the best next hop to forward each message. While these context information is not sufficient to achieve a satisfactory view of the network, forwarding messages without considering the node's willingness to contribute in the delivery process may waste network resources with unnecessary overhead. Moreover, all these protocols focus on achieving good performance under specific scenarios/contexts and may behave below expectations on different ones. On the other hand, context-aware routing protocols [3] consider that network context information, as geographic position and link quality, may impact on routing performance. Such information is used in order to choose the best next hop candidate to forward the messages. Several approaches such as [9,13,14,16] have shown that a context provides consistent and optimized information for routing protocols, adapting critical values according to a certain threshold, thus reflecting the importance of context information into a decision making.

In DTNs, messages are forwarded hop-by-hop autonomously, without an online path connecting the source and the destination. This unique characteristic of DTNs allows the routing protocol to be changed on-the-fly while a message traverses the network, i.e. each hop can forward the message using a different routing protocol, decoupling the source-destination path from the routing protocol. If each node is able to choose the best routing protocol based on its context and on the available routing protocols, it is possible to minimize the weaknesses of the chosen protocols. Thus, this paper proposes the first on-the-fly Context-Aware Routing Protocol Adaptation (CARPA) Method for DTNs. It aims at optimizing the network resources while ensuring specific routing metrics. At each contact opportunity, CARPA determines the "best" suitable routing protocol based on the current network state vision of the node, expressed as a context. This process is run at each hop transmission of each message, adapting the routing protocol and its parameters to the actual network context, searching the "best" suitable values at every moment. This is the first work applying multiple routing protocols into a trajectory of a single message in DTNs, without altering the routing protocol.

Simulation results show that CARPA significantly achieves a good performance trade-off among several metrics. It outperforms protocols such as Epidemic and PRoPHET on delivery, delay and overhead ratio and SPW about delay, mainly at sparse networks. Moreover, these results are achieved using only these three protocols for CARPA to choose.

This paper is organized as follows: Sect. 2 reviews the context-aware routing protocols for DTNs; the system model, assumptions, and the proposed method are described in Sect. 3; Sect. 4 evaluates the impact of different contexts over routing protocols in DTN; the experimental results about the feasibility of the proposed method are shown in Sect. 5; finally, conclusions and future work are presented in Sect. 6.

2   Context-Aware Routing Protocols for DTN

The first context-aware routing protocols consider only one context to adapt the routing method. All of them modify the routing protocol, proposing a new one which must be used for the entire network. The RAPID protocol [2] treats the routing as a resource allocation problem, based on utility. It calculates the replication effect on the routing metric while accounting for resource constraints. However, only one metric can be satisfied at a time. In the HiBOp protocol [4], context is a collection of information which describes the user's community and social relationship. Nodes share information to learn the context, resulting on a qualitative classification about the accuracy of the attribute class. However, routing data in HiBOp depends on widely available context information in the network. The Context-Aware Routing Protocol for Opportunistic Network (CARTOON) [13] switches dissemination between Epidemic and PRoPHET protocols based on three parameters: density, contact time and the available buffer size for each node. Nevertheless, CARTOON requires high processing at nodes, being indicated for unlimited resources networks, and low mobility. The Opportunistic Routing with Window-Aware Replication (ORWAR) [16] considers the average message transmission rate and contact window size to adapt routing. Although the ORWAR is concerned about network resources including energy and bandwidth, it may loose the opportunity to replay messages due to the use of fixed number of message copies. The Context-Aware Routing (CAR) protocol [11] periodically measures some information about the nodes to determine the best forwarding node. Without previous acknowledgment about routes, the replication is proportional to the frequency and the time of nodes' contacts. CAR deals exclusively with unicast, though the definition and management of context information is not addressed. The context is only exploited to evaluate probabilities for the destinations that the node is aware of.

Different solutions were proposed to adapt the routing to multiple contexts in DTN. In [3], the definition and implementation of a middleware that collects and provides information on the context and the social interaction of users is explored. The context is defined by two functions: utility and cost. The middleware is integrated to the Haggle platform [12], and become able to share context information with all the interested components independent of the services and protocols. However, this middleware only supplies the interested services with network information; it neither analyzes nor decides which routing protocol is the best for the current context. A similar approach is proposed in [15]. It uses a passive adaptation context through a framework called Context-Aware Network Coding (CANC). It implements an adaptation portal to a context agent which collects and processes context information to reconfigure the router behavior. The context agent is independent of any routing protocol, however, CANC behavior can cause overhead due to sharing network view by epidemic protocols.

Related work analysis shows that current solutions are composed by protocols or a mechanism to provide a context for routing in DTN, based on different context information, such as density, energy, bandwidth, social relationships, contact time, and buffer size. However, most of the proposals consider only a few context information or just supply context information for other layers, leaving the decision of which protocol is the best suited for the current context an open issue. The CANC [15] is an exception: it aims to integrate context information with router module, but only for coding networks. On the other hand, the method proposed in this paper explores the ability of nodes to decide which protocol to use according to the interested context and current network conditions. Thus, multiple network information is exploited to identify the node's context, and then apply it to choose the most suitable protocol to the current context.

3   The On-the-fly Context-Aware Routing Protocol Adaptation Method for DTN

This section details the CARPA, the first on-the-fly Context-Aware Routing Protocol Adaptation Method. The identification of a context requires specific rules to detect and analyze the network status information in order to enable decision making. The context is composed by a set of attribute-value pair of information which may impact on routing performance. A context is formally defined as a vector c of attributes $c = (c_1, \ldots, c_n)$, where $c_1 \in C_i$ and $C = C_1 \times \cdots \times C_n$ representing the potential search space values. In DTN, context may consider several attributes as buffer size, density, remaining energy, network bandwidth, etc.

The context C_i is composed by two parts, α which is the message attributes and β which is the current locally collected network context. α is defined by the source of each message, and it represents the attributes that this message should perceive, for example, message m must be forwarded with the smallest delay possible. On the other hand, β represents the actual node context, such as bandwidth, size of the buffer, etc.

In this paper, DTN is modeled as a graph $G_t(V, E)$, composed by a finite set V of nodes $N = |V|$ and a dynamic set E of connections (contacts) between these nodes during time t. Nb_n represents the neighbor set of node n. Nodes are heterogeneous, and they have a finite buffer. Transmissions occur whenever a node is in the transmission range of another node. Any node $n \in V$ stores a set of messages $M_n = \{m_1, \ldots, m_k\}$, such that $k \in [1, m_k]$.

CARPA evaluates the network context during the routing process. It receives as input the actual context of the current node, and the summarized context of the estimated next hop. Then it evaluates them, and suggests the most appropriate available routing protocol. Note that, the information about the next hop includes the routing protocols it understands. Moreover the chosen protocol must be known by the both nodes as messages are processed according to the policy of the used routing protocol policy. This decision is taken on every node before

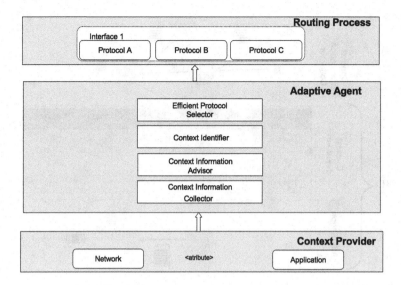

Fig. 1. CARPA Overview.

forwarding a message. Figure 1 illustrates the proposed context-aware model. It is composed by three processes: *context provider*, *adaptive agent*, and *routing process*. The *context provider* is responsible for feeding the *adaptive agent* (AA) with the actual context of the node. The context provider may gather any type of information from the network interfaces, users and/or applications, depending on the user allowance. The AA is in charge of acquiring and selecting network attributes, defining the context type, and making the decision to select the "best" available routing protocol. The *routing process* is a set of standard routing protocols, which are not altered by CARPA. The routing process receives the decision from the method and sets this protocol as active. The message is then forwarded using this routing protocol.

The *context provider* process analyses and defines certain thresholds, for example the minimal delivery ratio, maximum delay or limits on the resource consumption. These parameters are defined based on the actual network configuration and on the available routing protocols, as each protocol has distinct thresholds about different network attributes. The output of the context definition process is β.

The AA processes derives an heuristic (H), which guides the selection of attributes to form a context, as an utility function over the attributes. Figure 2 summarizes the AA process. The heuristic returns the "best" suitable routing protocol for the context requirements, as the trade-off between performance and constraint. Every DTN node constructs its own context by using instantaneous attributes collected by the *context provider* process. The heuristic used in this paper is a simple one, it is based on the results provided on Sect. 4. The best protocol for each simulated context is set as the "best" protocol for this context on CARPA. Future work consists in creating a swarm intelligence based heuristic to implement the AA process.

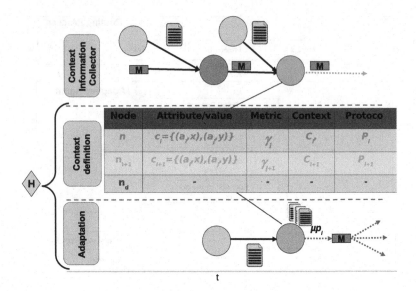

Fig. 2. CARPA - Adaptive Agent.

4   Impact of Different Contexts over Standard Routing Protocols in DTN

This section demonstrates the impact of different contexts on three standard routing protocols in DTN: Epidemic, PRoPHET and SPW. The analysis of these protocols has two implications: i to demonstrate each protocol outperforms the other in specific scenarios; and ii to create the heuristic which is used in the CARPA demonstration.

All routing protocols are implemented and simulated on the ONE simulator [7], according to parameters shown on Table 1. The network is composed by mobile nodes equipped with a WiFi 802.11 network interface with the transmission speed of 1375 Kbps and transmission ranges of 50 m and 150 m. Two movement models are used in the simulations: the *Shortest Path Map-Based Movement* (SP) [6] model, which uses the shortest path algorithm to move the nodes on the Helsinki city map, and the *Random Waypoint* (RW) model, in which nodes randomly move to the given destination along a zig-zag path. Sources are randomly selected and they generate messages in an interval from 1 to 10 s until the amount of 11914 is reached. Messages size range from 1 KB to 200 KB. All results are the average of 24 different simulation runs.

The protocols are evaluated using three metrics: message delivery ratio, average delay and overhead ratio. Delivery ratio is defined as the ratio of the successfully received packets at the destination divided by the total packets generated at the sources [1], average delay denotes the average end-to-end delay for all successfully received packets at the destination, and overhead ratio is calculated as the number of messages introduced in the network by the protocol in order to deliver the messages [2]. Messages are discarded when they reach their TTL deadline.

Table 1. Scenarios parameters.

Parameters	Values
Area $(m \times m)$	$800 \times 800, 1000 \times 1000, 1500 \times 1500, 2000 \times 2000, 5000 \times 5000$
Duration (sec)	2115, 43200, 86400, 172800
Host	30, 70, 90, 120
Buffer Size(MB)	1, 2.5, 5, 10, 20
Message Size(KB)	1, 100, 200
TTL (min)	10, 100, 1000

Delivery ratio

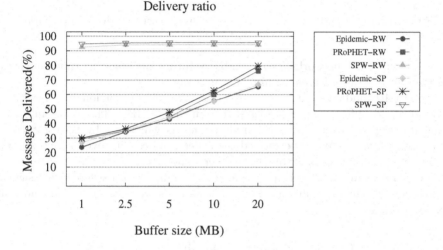

Buffer size (MB)

Fig. 3. Protocols performance for delivery ratio over different scenarios.

4.1   Scenario A: Buffer Size Effect

Figure 3 presents the delivery ratio for each protocol varying the movement model and buffer size from 1 MB to 20 MB. Due to page limitation, only the results for 80 nodes with communication range of 50 m spread over a 800m × 800m network area are shown. However, the results for other parameters follow the same pattern. SPW limits the number of copies (L) in 8.

It is possible to notice that the performance of Epidemic and PRoPHET suffers from the buffer size limitation. Their delivery ratio is directly proportional to the buffer size. Moreover, the performance of Epidemic for this context is worse than PRoPHET due to the fact that Epidemic retransmits messages to all neighbors, leading to a buffer exhaustion. Nevertheless, SPW is not affected and provides a delivery ratio higher than the others.

Figure 4(a) shows the delay for the scenario. The delay of Epidemic and PRoPHET varies with the buffer size. This follows the delivery ratio variation, with limited buffer. These protocols deliver fewer messages but faster.

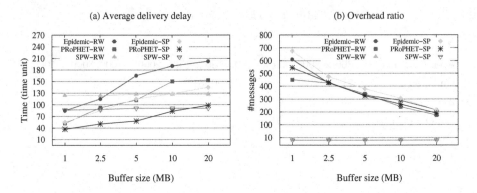

Fig. 4. Protocols performance for message delivery cost over different scenarios.

However, in sparse networks it can be observed that the buffering time increases as the delivery ratio decreases, implying in delay.

Figure 4(b) indicates that the overhead is inversely proportional to the delivery ratio and buffer size for the Epidemic and PRoPHET. This is because the more messages delivered, the less redundancy is generated by the protocols. As observed, the SPW outperformed the other protocols in several contexts, in terms of consumption of resources, delivery and delay ratio. This behavior is due to its dynamic mechanism for limiting the number of forwarded messages. However, SPW has several variations [5, 8, 18, 20] as its performance depends on the network scenario.

4.2   Scenario B: The Influence of Density

This scenario is used to demonstrate the influence of node density on the Epidemic, PRoPHET and SPW protocols. The simulation area is then varied in order to examine its impact on the effectiveness of the protocols. In the first scenario settings, considered as dense, the area is set to 2 km × 2 km, while the sparse scenario, the second one, is composed by a 5 km × 5 km area. The transmission range is fixed in 50m.

As reported in Fig. 5, the performance of all protocols shows that they have poor efficiency in very disconnected areas. In this case, a few copies are spread out. As a result, it may take a long time for a message to traverse the network and reach the destination or it may never meet it. Thus, the sparser the scenario, the lower the delivery ratio is.

The evaluation of the simulation results indicates that all protocols have similar behavior for sparse networks, the delivery ratio decreases and the delay increases following the connectivity. Also, the buffer size represents a sensitive attribute for the protocols, which increases their delivery ratio in accordance with its size.

Delivery over area (km x km)

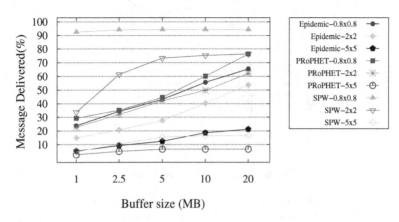

Buffer size (MB)

Fig. 5. Delivery from density.

5   CARPA Performance Evaluation

By definition, most of the DTNs are expected to operate in sparse and stressed environments. Nevertheless, in many situations the network designer or the application itself might impose certain performance requirements to the routing protocols (e.g. maximum delivery, maximum delay, minimum throughput, etc.). For example, a message sending over a DTN, notifying a number of peers about a catastrophe, would obviously be of no use if it arrived after the disaster time. Despite a large number of existing proposals, there is no routing protocol that outperform the others in all scenarios.

To assess the feasibility of the proposed method and demonstrate that the best option is an on-the-fly combination of routing protocols to achieve the desired performance in a specific scenario, simulations are performed using an extended version of the ONE simulator. In this version, each node runs CARPA, and before forwarding messages, nodes share their network attributes with their own one hop neighbors.

CARPA's decisions are based on the node's own instantaneous context information, the message context and the routing protocols available. The CARPA heuristic was defined based on the results presented in 4.1 and 4.2. Table 2 summarizes the heuristic. Note that heuristic can be changed without altering the rest of CARPA.

This analysis considers the context information regarding the number of messages, free buffer size, and density degree, and it focuses on achieving the highest message delivery ratio with the smallest delay. Thus, CARPA is examined under two network scenarios: dense and sparse networks. The first scenario is evaluated using the scenario 4.1 with a few modifications: there are 200 nodes with infinite buffer, moving according to the RW movement model in an 800 m × 800m network area. The transmission range is switched among 50 m, 100 m and 150 m.

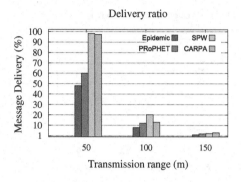

Fig. 6. Delivery for dense scenario.

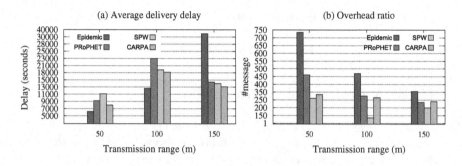

Fig. 7. Delay and cost for dense scenario.

The second scenario exploits limited resources and a sparse network. For this, 200 nodes randomly move in three different network areas: 5 km × 5 km, 10 km × 10 km and 20 km × 20 km. In both scenarios, messages are generated every five seconds.

All results presented here consist of four data: (*i*) using the standard Epidemic protocol during all messages routing; (*ii*) using standard PRoPHET to route all messages; (*iii*) using Spray-and-Wait to route all messages; (*iv*) using CARPA on all nodes, at each hop CARPA chooses the "best" suitable routing protocol for the context (among Epidemic, PRoPHET and SPW) and uses this protocol for this hop transmission.

Figures 6 and 7 show the performance evaluation of the protocols under different transmission ranges. In these dense scenarios, as the density and the traffic load are high, the available bandwidth decreases and the buffer occupancy increases proportionally, which reduces the performance of all protocols, especially for the Epidemic and PRoPHET. The Epidemic produces the largest delay and requires a higher number of transmissions compared to all the other schemes. The PRoPHET produces a high overhead. CARPA achieves the same delivery ratio as SPW with a lower delay for less density, but higher overhead.

Figure 8 shows that under sparse scenario, CARPA can achieve a higher delivery ratio than the Epidemic and PRoPHET. Note that even with infinite

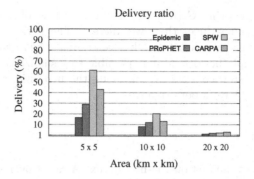

Fig. 8. Delivery ratio for sparse scenario.

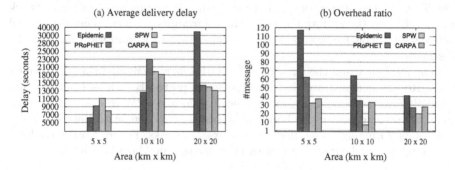

Fig. 9. Delay and cost for sparse scenario.

Table 2. Relation between context information and protocols.

C_i	Range	Protocol
Degree density	$1 = |Nb_n|$	Epidemic
	$2 \leq |Nb_n| \geq 10$	SPW
	$|Nb_n| < 10$	PRoPHET
Number of messages	$|M_n| < 20$	SPW
Free buffer size	$\tilde{B}_{free} \geq 90\%$	PRoPHET

buffer the delivery ratio is low due to the very sparse network. Also, Fig. 9(a) and 9(b) show that the delay and overhead ratio are proportionally improved. The two metrics are better observed in the 5 km × 5km network area, while the delivery ratio of CARPA is about 45 % better than Epidemic and PRoPHET. Even though its delay is greater then the Epidemic, it is much smaller than the PRoPHET and SPW. Likewise, the overhead ratio obtained by CARPA is 70 % less than the Epidemic, about 45 % less than the PRoPHET and 35 % smaller than SPW. On the other hand, the results show that the SPW outperforms the proposed method for the overhead and delivery, except over a 20 km × 20 km network area in which CARPA's performance is better.

The results suggest that CARPA takes full advantage of the strengths of the routing protocols and reduces their weaknesses. The performance of CARPA highly depends on the snapshot network. Even though the method in this article is composed by simple heuristics, it is possible to visualize the effectiveness of CARPA. The next step consists in improving the heuristic, which will have a direct impact on CARPA's performance.

6   Conclusion

This paper presented the first on-the-fly Context-Aware Routing Protocol Adaptation method (CARPA) for DTN. The method evaluates the network context before each hop transmission and chooses the "best" suitable routing protocol to use. The purpose of the context is to evaluate the requirements of the network which influence the performance of protocols towards a metric. Thereby, several different protocols can compose the message trajectory from the source to the destination.

The feasibility and the efficiency of CARPA were evaluated through simulations. Results demonstrate that it outperforms protocols such as Epidemic and PRoPHET in delivery, delay and overhead ratio and SPW in delay, using only these three protocols for the hop transmissions. This demonstration shows significant performance gains, mainly at sparse networks. Future work includes a swarm intelligent heuristic to improve the decision making of CARPA.

Acknowledgments. This work was partially supported by CNPq and by FAPESC (Human Resources Program 01/2012).

References

1. Abdulla, M., Simon, R.: The impact of the mobility model on delay tolerant networking performance analysis. In: 40th Annual Simulation Symposium, ANSS 2007, pp. 177–184, March 2007
2. Balasubramanian, A., Levine, B., Venkataramani, A.: Dtn routing as a resource allocation problem. ACM SIGCOMM Comput. Commun. Rev. **37**(4), 373–384 (2007)
3. Boldrini, C., Conti, M.: Context-and social-aware middleware for opportunistic networks. J. Netw. Comput. Appl. **33**(5), 525–541 (2010)
4. Boldrini, C., Conti, M., Jacopini, J., Passarella, A.: Hibop: a history based routing protocol for opportunistic networks. In: IEEE International Symposium on a World of Wireless, Mobile and Multimedia Networks (WOWMOM), pp. 1–12 (2007)
5. Huang, W., Zhang, S., Zhou, W.: Spray and wait routing based on position prediction in opportunistic networks. In: 2011 3rd International Conference on Computer Research and Development (ICCRD), vol. 2, pp. 232–236, March 2011
6. Karvo, J., Ott, J.: Time scales and delay-tolerant routing protocols. In: Proceedings of the Third ACM Workshop on Challenged Networks (CHANTS), pp. 33–40 (2008)

7. Keränen, A., Ott, J., Kärkkäinen, T.: The ONE simulator for DTN protocol evaluation. In: Proceedings of the 2nd International Conference on Simulation Tools and Techniques (SIMUTools) (2009)

8. Kim, Y.-P., Koo, J.-I., Jung, E., Nakano, K., Sengoku, M., Park, Y.-J.: Composite methods for improving spray and wait routing protocol in delay tolerant networks. In 2010 International Symposium on Communications and Information Technologies (ISCIT), pp. 1229–1234, October 2010

9. Lakkakorpi, J., Pitkänen, M., Ott, J.: Adaptive routing in mobile opportunistic networks. In: Proceedings of the 13th ACM International Conference on Modeling, Analysis, and Simulation of Wireless and Mobile Systems (MSWIM), pp. 101–109 (2010)

10. Lindgren, A., Doria, A., Schelén, O.: Probabilistic routing in intermittently connected networks. ACM SIGMOBILE Mob. Comput. Commun. Rev. **7**(3), 19–20 (2003)

11. Musolesi, M., Mascolo, C.: Car: Context-aware adaptive routing for delay-tolerant mobile networks. IEEE Trans. Mob. Comput. **8**(2), 246–260 (2009)

12. Nordström, E., Rohner, C., Gunningberg, P.: Haggle: Opportunistic mobile content sharing using search. Comput. Commun. **48**, 121–132 (2014)

13. Oliveira, E.C.R., Albuquerque, C.V.N.: Roteamento adaptativo a contextos para redes tolerantes a atrasos e desconexões. In: Proceedings of the XXX Brazilian Symposium of Computer Networks / XXX Simpósio Brasileiro de Redes de Computadores e Sistemas Distribuídos (SBRC), pp. 872–885 (2012)

14. Pelusi, L., Passarella, A., Conti, M.: Opportunistic networking: data forwarding in disconnected mobile ad hoc networks. IEEE Commun. Magazine **44**(11), 134–141 (2006)

15. Petz, A., Hennessy, A., Walker, B., Fok, C.-L., Julien, C.: An architecture for context-aware adaptation of routing in delay-tolerant networks. In: Proceedings of the 4th Extreme Conference on Communication (ExtremeCom) (2012)

16. Sandulescu, G., Nadjm-Tehrani, S.: Opportunistic dtn routing with window-aware adaptive replication. In: Proceedings of the 4th Asian Conference on Internet Engineering (AINTEC), pp. 103–112 (2008)

17. Spyropoulos, T., Psounis, K., Raghavendra, C.S.: Spray and wait: an efficient routing scheme for intermittently connected mobile networks. In: Proceedings of the 2005 ACM SIGCOMM Workshop on Delay-Tolerant Networking (WDTN), pp. 252–259 (2005)

18. Tournoux, P., Leguay, J., Benbadis, F., Conan, V., Dias de Amorim, M., Whitbeck, J.: The accordion phenomenon: analysis, characterization, and impact on dtn routing. In: INFOCOM 2009, pp. 1116–1124. IEEE, April 2009

19. Vahdat, A., Becker, D.: Epidemic routing for partially connected ad hoc networks. Technical report, CS-200006, Duke University (2000)

20. Wang, G., Wang, B., Gao, Y.: Dynamic spray and wait routing algorithm with quality of node in delay tolerant network. In: 2010 International Conference on Communications and Mobile Computing (CMC), vol. 3, pp. 452–456, April 2010

Algorithms for Theoretical Investigation of Fairness in Multipath Transport

Amanpreet Singh[1], Andreas Könsgen[1]([⊠]), Hakim Adhari[2], Carmelita Görg[1], and Erwin P. Rathgeb[2]

[1] University of Bremen, Bremen, Germany
{aps,ajk,cg}@comnets.uni-bremen.de
[2] University of Duisburg-Essen, Essen, Germany
{hakim.adhari,rathgeb}@uni-due.de

Abstract. With the onset of multipath transport protocols such as MPTCP and multihomed mobile devices, fairness considerations which have been widely analyzed for legacy TCP need to be re-investigated. A practical realization of fairness amongst different participants is known to be difficult but even the theoretical calculation of the resource capacity and its allocation is not a trivial task. Therefore in this work, resource allocation algorithms are presented to thoroughly evaluate the impact of the fairness definitions. For a rigorous analysis, existing fairness definitions are identified according to the resources (bottleneck or network) and the competing participants (flow, tariff or user). Tariff as the participant, provides a realistic option to comply with the service level agreement between the operator and the user where as flow as the participant leads to TCP-compatible allocation. From the obtained results, it can be seen that if fairness is applied at the bottleneck then it is absolutely fair to the individual participants w.r.t. the bottleneck. On the other hand, fairness mechanisms considering the whole network as a single resource exploit the freedom of resource allocation (due to multipath flows) to achieve an overall similar allocation for the different participants (irrespective if the participant is composed of singlepath or multipath flows) but are still restricted by the topological constraints and might even result in a lower overall network throughput (This work has been funded by the German Research Foundation (Deutsche Forschungsgemeinschaft – DFG)).

1 Introduction

The Internet of today is dominated by singlepath TCP flows [1] and therefore it is considered as fair not to push away TCP flows, also termed as TCP friendliness [2] i. e. if n TCP sessions share the same bottleneck link, each should get $1/n$ of the bottleneck link capacity. Thus, a transport layer protocol is fair if it displaces no more TCP traffic than a TCP stream itself would displace i. e. it is TCP-compatible and defined by RFC 2309 [3].

Mechanisms that protocols commonly use to meet the TCP-friendly requirement use some form of *additive increase multiplicative decrease* (AIMD) congestion window management or compute a transmission rate based on equations

© Institute for Computer Sciences, Social Informatics and Telecommunications Engineering 2015
R. Agüero et al. (Eds.): MONAMI 2015, LNICST 158, pp. 150–163, 2015.
DOI: 10.1007/978-3-319-26925-2_12

derived from an AIMD model [4]. Therefore, the TCP-friendly or -compatible view basically controls the rates of the flows in such a way that during congestion the bottleneck link capacity (resource) is shared equally by the competing flows (participants). This fairness view can also be called *flow rate fairness* [5] or *bottleneck flow fair (BFF)* [6]. RFC 6077 [7] outlines fairness issues as part of the open research issues in the Internet congestion control without favoring any particular fairness definition.

With the emergence of multipath transport protocols like CMT-SCTP [8] and MPTCP [9], a flow can have several (k) subflows (which are comparable to singlepath flows) to increase its overall throughput by utilizing the multihoming capability of the endpoints and at the same time make the network more efficient. With this new terminology, a singlepath flow can be seen as a flow composed of a single subflow. If any of the standard TCP congestion control methods (e.g., NewReno) is used for multipath transport then every subflow will behave as an individual TCP connection. Hence the realized fairness mechanism is called *bottleneck subflow fair (BSfF)* i. e., it considers *subflows* as the participant and *bottlenecks* as the resource that should be shared.

The multipath transport standardization group at the IETF felt that since the current Internet is based on the principle of "do no harm" to existing singlepath flows, any multipath transport protocol design should satisfy this goal [10]. Bottleneck subflow fairness is deemed too aggressive on a bottleneck link, if two or more subflows of a flow share the same bottleneck link, therefore bottleneck flow fairness is the desired mechanism. In order to have bottleneck flow fairness, all subflows of a multipath flow sharing the same bottleneck should not get a combined share more than that of a singlepath flow [11].

Since a flow can have several subflows using different paths, the overall throughput is not limited by a single bottleneck link anymore. In addition, different subflows will observe different degrees of congestion on their respective paths. The idea of *Resource Pooling (RP)* that makes network resources behave like a single pooled resource, exploits this feature of the multipath transport to *balance congestion* [11–13] in the network. RP aims at shifting traffic from more to less congested paths and thereby decreasing the overall congestion in the network and increasing the performance. Thus, RP brings in a new fairness perspective by considering the whole network as a resource while the participants are still the flows. This new fairness view is denoted as *network flow fair (NFF)*.

The flow rate fairness approach means that it is considered fair that two flows from the same application or endpoint can get double share of the bottleneck link capacity at the expense of another flow from another endpoint (Fig. 1(a)), but it is deemed unfair if a multipath flow with two subflows gets a double share (Fig. 1(b)). In previous work [6,14,15], issues related with the current fairness methods proposed for multipath transport have been highlighted. In order to deal with this limited scope of *(bottleneck/network) flow fairness*, alternative methods w. r. t. the additional participants that still tackle fairness at the transport layer but also consider the higher layer aspects, the end user as well as the network are discussed in Sect. 3.

Independent of the way where/how fairness methods can be deployed, a comprehensive analysis is required to determine their impact. In addition it has been shown in [6] that even for simple topologies, neither the theoretical allocation of the resources nor the calculation of the resource capacity is an obvious task. This work presents resource assignment algorithms for the discussed fairness methods as a first step towards such an analysis.

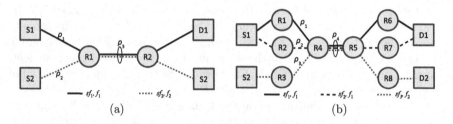

Fig. 1. Issue with fairness definition for multipath

This paper is structured as follows: in Sect. 2 the important terms which are essential for the fairness discussion are defined in an abstracted form. The definition of the alternative fairness mechanisms follows in Sect. 3. In Sect. 4 resource allocation algorithms that determine the theoretical share of the participants are presented and the corresponding impact analysis of the fairness definitions as well as the validation of the algorithms is discussed in Sect. 5 with the help of an example scenario. Finally, Sect. 6 concludes this paper with a summary and a short outlook.

2   Terminology

For a better overview and systematic analysis, the different fairness methods discussed in this work are categorized based on the choice of the resource and participant. Therefore, a formal abstraction of the different networking resources and participants is given in this section.

Network: A *network* $\Gamma := (L, N, C)$ can be abstracted as:

- L – a finite locator set,
- $N \subseteq \mathfrak{P}(L)$ – a node set, $\mathfrak{P}(L)$ is the powerset of L,
- $C \subseteq L \times L$ – a connectivity set.

Locator: A locator $l \in L$ is a network interface where L defines a finite set of unique locators. The connectivity among the locators is described by the connectivity set C which also describes the individual link capacity ρ.

User: A user u_q is defined as an entity which can simultaneously use more than one terminal node for its applications/connections.

Source: A source $n_{sr} \in N_{sr}$ is the source node in a communication e. g., it represents a computer or mobile device. N_{sr} and N_{ds} are the set of source and destination nodes, respectively used to define the demand matrix $D := N_{sr} \times N_{ds}$.

Tariff: A tariff t is defined by the access network with which the user has a contract. There can also be a shared-tariff model where the subscription is shared amongst several locators by a user e.g., a mobile operator also provides a WLAN hotspot or partner cards under a common tariff.

Flow: A flow f_x between two nodes $n_{sr} \in N_{sr}$ and $n_{ds} \in N_{ds}$ is composed of all Protocol Data Units (PDU) belonging to the same communication (e.g. an individual file transfer between n_{sr} and n_{ds}) irrespective of whether it is connection-oriented or connection-less and using a path set P_x. The bandwidth allocated to a flow $f_{q,x}$ of user u_q is denoted as $b_{q,x}$.

Subflow: A subflow $s_{q,x}^a$ denotes the subset of PDUs belonging to $f_{q,x}$ initiated by user u_q and using a specific path $p_{q,x}^a \in P$. The bandwidth allocated to this subflow is denoted by $b_{q,x}^a$.

Bottleneck: Let $\langle i, j \rangle$ be a link in Γ with the bandwidth $\rho\langle i, j \rangle$. The set of subflows crossing this link builds the subflow set $S\langle i, j \rangle$. A link is considered to be bottlenecked if no spare capacity is left after allocation of the subflow capacities that share this link i. e.,

$$\sum_{s_{q,x}^a \in S\langle i,j \rangle} b_{q,x}^a = \rho\langle i, j \rangle$$

3   Alternative Fairness Definitions

To design a fair multipath transport protocol, the standardization community has decided to remain with the notion of TCP-compatible flows even if a flow as known from a singlepath environment is different from the new kinds of flows used by the multipath protocols [10]. With the use of RP, the decision was taken to couple all subflows belonging to a single multipath flow. However, in multiple situations, multipath flows appear to be penalized to the advantage of singlepath flows [14,16,17]. In order to deal with these issues, in this section alternative ways to define the set of subflows that should be coupled together are presented.

For multipath subflows it is highly likely that not all the subflows have the same end locator. A simple case is to share the resource amongst the different locators fairly. Thus, for *network locator fairness (NLF)* all the (sub)flows initiated from the same locator are coupled together and for *bottleneck locator fairness (BLF)* all (sub)flows that share the same bottleneck and locator are coupled together.

A user may use multiple tariffs, e. g. one for LTE and one for WLAN. In this case, it is fair if the source node/user gets a share of the bottleneck/network capacity w. r. t. its tariff. Thus, for *network tariff fairness (NTF)* all the (sub)flows initiated from the same tariff and being part of the same network are coupled together while for *bottleneck tariff fairness (BTF)* all (sub)flows that share the same bottleneck and tariff are coupled together.

There are various tariff models which grant different guarantees e. g. different capacities in the access link. In order to reflect this property of tariffs in fairness methods, weighting factors could be used. Each tariff, whether inside the scope of bottleneck or network fairness, is then assigned a capacity share proportional to the weighting factor. An important aspect of weighted fairness is the mapping between the tariff plan and the weighting factor. In addition, a weighting factor could be adopted by other participants as well e. g. by flows to prioritize different types of applications or subflows to prioritize an interface.

Defining the source node as the participant leads to *network source fairness (NSrF)* or *bottleneck source fairness (BSrF)* where for the former, all subflows and flows initiated from the same source node are coupled together and for the latter, subflows and flows sharing the same bottleneck as well as the same source node are coupled together. Since a user may use multiple devices simultaneously the fairness can be taken to even a higher participant level wherein all the (sub)flows initiated by a user should be coupled depending on which resource they are sharing – a bottleneck (*bottleneck user fairness (BUF)*) or the network (*network user fairness (NUF)*).

4   Algorithms for the Considered Fairness Views

Different fairness types can be realized practically by applying various methods of coupled congestion control. But these realizations have imperfect knowledge of the network conditions and are limited by their respective protocol design [16,17]. Therefore to determine the theoretical optimum share of the participants, resource allocation algorithms are presented in this section. In addition the results from these algorithms can be used to thoroughly evaluate the impact of the different fairness methods introduced in Sects. 1 and 3 on both the network and the user. Thus these algorithms enable a systematic comparison of the various fairness mechanisms but do not have any influence on the practical realization in form of coupled congestion control variants.

4.1   Bottleneck Scope

This section describes the means to achieve the theoretical allocation of subflow capacities within the network at a given time with respect to the different fairness definitions that share the bottleneck as a resource. The subflow capacities are obtained in an iterative process to consider the bottlenecks and spare capacity within the network. Due to elastic traffic, subflow capacity is bounded by the minimum share with respect to the links on its path i. e. , other non bottlenecked links of its path will have spare capacity left. Therefore *fair plus spare* share allocation considers the spare capacity made available by the participants that are bottlenecked by other links on their respective paths. Hence in the algorithm, multiple iterations are needed to identify all bottlenecked flows. In each iteration, bottlenecked subflows are identified by searching for links that are fully utilized by their respective fair share constraint. In each iteration a new set of links and corresponding subflows becomes bottlenecked. Once all the subflows are bottlenecked, the final allocation of subflow capacities is obtained.

A user may initiate multiple flows which in turn might consist of several subflows. Thus, a bottleneck link may be shared by multiple flows or subflows from a single user. By definition of the *Bottleneck user fair*, all flows or subflows belonging to a single user should get a combined share equal to that of other sharing users. Since the subflow is the smallest entity, its capacity share is calculated dependent on the fairness policy with multiple iterations based on which subflows get bottlenecked first.

The link that will bottleneck an unbottlenecked subflow has to be identified which not only depends on the user share of the link but also the number of subflows that share the bottleneck link. To obtain the unbottlenecked subflow capacity, first a fair share of the respective user on each link of the subflow's path is calculated. Therefore, the remaining bandwidth of link $\langle i,j \rangle$ is determined by considering the link-specific bottlenecked users $\Upsilon\langle i,j \rangle_{\mathrm{b}}$ (i.e., all the flows of the user on the link are bottlenecked) and then shared amongst non-bottlenecked user's $\Upsilon\langle i,j \rangle_{\mathrm{ub}}$ to provide the fair+spare user share of the link. The fair share of user v_q on link $\langle i,j \rangle$ is denoted by $ub_q\langle i,j \rangle$ and can be futher apportioned equally amongst its unbottlenecked subflows and single-path flows or first at the level of flows $(b_{q,x}\langle i,j \rangle)$ and then subflows $(b_{q,x}^a\langle i,j \rangle)$. In this way, the subflow capacity share over each link of its path is obtained. Finally, the subflow capacity which is the minimum capacity over all links that constitutes its path is determined.

Once the capacity of all the subflows is obtained, the bottleneck link(s) can be identified i.e., a link which does not have any spare bandwidth is bottlenecked and all the subflows that share this link have reached their maximum capacity. The bottlenecked subflows are now made part of the bottlenecked subflows set over all users S_{b} as well as the bottleneck subflow set $S_{q,x}\langle i,j \rangle_{\mathrm{b}}$ for a particular user and flow on link $\langle i,j \rangle$. If all the subflows of a flow $f_{q,x}$ on link $\langle i,j \rangle$ are bottlenecked then the flow becomes part of the user-specific bottlenecked flow set $F_q\langle i,j \rangle_{\mathrm{b}}$ over link $\langle i,j \rangle$. Similarly, the link-specific bottlenecked user set $\Upsilon\langle i,j \rangle_{\mathrm{b}}$ is also updated. The capacity of the remaining unbottlenecked subflows needs to be determined again with the extended set of bottlenecked subflows, flows and users until all the subflows are bottlenecked.

For multipath flows, different subflows might use different tariffs and therefore there is an inter-dependency between the different tariffs that might even go across multiple source nodes/users depending on the shared tariffs. For tariff as the participant, only the network that is affected by the tariffs is considered i.e., a subset $\Gamma'_{child} = (L', N', C')$ of the whole network $\Gamma = (L, N, C)$. Outside the tariff-specific network, the complete network could be seen as a hierarchical graph where inside Γ also a weighting factor is associated to Γ_{child}. Based on this weighting factor, the resources associated to the sum of all subflows going out of Γ_{child} and crossing for example a bottleneck in Γ is determined. Amongst

Algorithm 1. Bottleneck weighted user fair allocation algorithm

- Input: network $\Gamma := (L, N, C)$, demand matrix $D := N_{sr} \times N_{ds}$, user set Υ, flow set F, user-specific flow sets F_q, non-bottlenecked subflow set S_{ub}, bottlenecked subflow set S_b, user and flow specific subflow sets $S_{q,x}$ and path set P.
- Output: user (weighted) share ub_q, flow (weighted) share $b_{q,x}$ and subflow (weighted) share $b_{q,x}^a$.
- Initialization: $ub_q := 0 \ \forall \ v_q \in \Upsilon; b_{q,x} := 0 \ \forall \ f_{q,x} \in F; b_{q,x}^a := 0 \ \forall \ s_{q,x}^a \in S$;
$S_{ub} := S; S_b := \emptyset; \Upsilon\langle i,j \rangle := \emptyset \ \forall \ \langle i,j \rangle \in C; F_q\langle i,j \rangle := \emptyset \ \forall \ v_q \in \Upsilon, \langle i,j \rangle \in C$;
$S_{q,x}\langle i,j \rangle := \emptyset \ \forall \ f_{q,x} \in F_q, \langle i,j \rangle \in C$;

foreach $\langle i,j \rangle \in C$ **do**
   foreach v_q *in* Υ **do**
      foreach $f_{q,x}$ *in* F_q **do**
         foreach $s_{q,x}^a$ *in* $S_{q,x}$ **do**
            $\ S_{q,x}\langle i,j \rangle := S_{q,x}\langle i,j \rangle \cup \left\{ s_{q,x}^a \mid \langle i,j \rangle \in p_{q,x}^a, p_{q,x}^a \in P \right\}$
         $F_q\langle i,j \rangle := F_q\langle i,j \rangle \cup \{ f_{q,x} \mid S_{q,x}\langle i,j \rangle \neq \emptyset \}$
      $\Upsilon\langle i,j \rangle := \Upsilon\langle i,j \rangle \cup \{ v_q \mid F_q\langle i,j \rangle \neq \emptyset \}$

$S_{q,x}\langle i,j \rangle_b := \emptyset; S_{q,x}\langle i,j \rangle_{ub} := S_{q,x}\langle i,j \rangle; F_q\langle i,j \rangle_b := \emptyset, F_q\langle i,j \rangle_{ub} := F_q\langle i,j \rangle$
$\Upsilon\langle i,j \rangle_b := \emptyset; \Upsilon\langle i,j \rangle_{ub} := \Upsilon\langle i,j \rangle.$

- Computation: **while** $S_{ub} \neq \emptyset$ **do**
   foreach $s_{q,x}^a$ *in* S_{ub} // for each non-bottlenecked subflow //
   do
      foreach $\langle i,j \rangle \in p_{q,x}^a$ // for each link on the subflow's path //
      do

$$ub_q\langle i,j \rangle := \left[\frac{\left(\rho\langle i,j \rangle - \sum_{(v_r \in [\Upsilon\langle i,j \rangle]_b)} \left(\sum_{f_{r,y} \in F_r\langle i,j \rangle} \left(\sum_{s_{r,y}^d \in S_{r,y}\langle i,j \rangle} b_{r,y}^d \right) \right) \right) \cdot \Xi_q}{\sum_{\Upsilon\langle i,j \rangle_{ub}} \Xi_r} \right]$$

$$b_{q,x}\langle i,j \rangle := \left[\frac{\left(ub_q\langle i,j \rangle - \sum_{f_{q,y} \in F_q\langle i,j \rangle_b} \left(\sum_{s_{q,y}^d \in S_{q,y}\langle i,j \rangle} b_{q,y}^d \right) \right) \cdot \Psi_{q,x}}{\sum_{F_q\langle i,j \rangle_{ub}} \Psi_{q,n}} \right]$$

$$b_{q,x}^a\langle i,j \rangle := \left[\frac{\left(b_{q,x}\langle i,j \rangle - \sum_{s_{q,x}^d \in S_{q,x}\langle i,j \rangle_b} b_{q,x}^d \right) \cdot \psi_{q,x}^a}{\sum_{S_{q,x}\langle i,j \rangle_{ub}} \psi_{q,x}^d} \right]$$

      where,
      Ξ_q is the weight of user $\mathbf{U}_q$, $\Psi_{q,x}$ is the weight of flow $f_{q,x}$ that belongs to user q and $\psi_{q,x}^a$ is the weight of subflow $s_{q,x}^a$ that belongs to flow $f_{q,x}$.
   $b_{q,x}^a = \min_{\langle i,j \rangle \in p_{q,x}^a} \left(b_{q,x}^a\langle i,j \rangle \right)$ // intermediate subflow capacity //

// update the respective non-/bottlenecked sets //
$S_b := \left\{ s_{q,x}^a \in S \mid \exists \langle i,j \rangle \in p_{q,x}^a, \sum_{s_{q,x}^a \in S\langle i,j \rangle} \left(b_{q,x}^a \right) = \rho\langle i,j \rangle \right\}, S_{ub} := S \setminus S_b$
foreach $\langle i,j \rangle \in C$ **do**
   foreach v_q *in* Υ **do**
      foreach $f_{q,x}$ *in* F_q **do**
         $S_{q,x}\langle i,j \rangle_b := S_b \cap S_{q,x}\langle i,j \rangle$
         $S_{q,x}\langle i,j \rangle_{ub} := S_{q,x}\langle i,j \rangle \setminus S_{q,x}\langle i,j \rangle_b$
         $F_q\langle i,j \rangle_b := F_q\langle i,j \rangle_b \cup \{ f_{q,x} \mid S_{q,x}\langle i,j \rangle_b = S_{q,x}\langle i,j \rangle \}$
      $F_q\langle i,j \rangle_{ub} := F_q\langle i,j \rangle \setminus F_q\langle i,j \rangle_b$
      $\Upsilon\langle i,j \rangle_b := \Upsilon\langle i,j \rangle_b \cup \{ v_q \mid F_q\langle i,j \rangle_b = F_q\langle i,j \rangle \}$
   $\Upsilon\langle i,j \rangle_{ub} := \Upsilon\langle i,j \rangle \setminus \Upsilon\langle i,j \rangle_b$

the subflows belonging to Γ_{child}, the Γ_{child} weighting factors are still valid even if the bottleneck is outside Γ_{child}.

A user might be interested to use its different interfaces/flows in a particular way and therefore might have different weights attached to it. Similarly a user might have a common tariff over multiple interfaces and hence also have weights depending on the tariff cost. A general algorithm with weights that allows a user to give weights to specific users, flows or interfaces (subflows) is given in Algorithm 1. *Bottleneck source fair, bottleneck flow fair, bottleneck locator fair* and *bottleneck subflow fair* mechanisms share the bottleneck link capacity fairly amongst the participants: source node, flow, locator and subflow, respectively. Thus, this is either a subset of the algorithm presented in Algorithm 1 or can be derived from it.

4.2   Network Scope

In this section the network is seen as a single resource which can be shared by different participants. The dependency between the calculation of the network capacity ρ^n and subflow capacity $b_{u,f}^{sf}$ can be solved by forming a linear set of equations. The linear equation system can be classified into two parts:

- Bottleneck bound: the subflows that are bounded by the bottleneck link capacity,
- Fairness bound: the participants (i.e. flows/users) that should get a fair share.

If the number of equations fits the number of variables, there is exactly one solution. If the number of equations is less (the system is underdetermined), there are multiple solutions, i. e. in the network, distributing capacities to different subflows is arbitrary within a specific range dependent on the network topology and bottleneck link capacities.

In some cases a perfectly fair solution may not be possible due to the unavailability of sufficient capacity corresponding to a flow that cannot get a fair share. An iterative method is then applied which systematically performs allocations to flows that are restricted due to the limited bottleneck capacity and identifies its dependencies on the other flows. Any allocation update of a flow share may introduce new dependencies. Once all the dependencies are taken care of then a final allocation of subflow capacities is obtained. For complex and large networks such an iterative method might become too difficult to handle and therefore, an alternative method of mixed integer (non-)linear programming may be used to identify the network fair allocation of flow capacity. In this method, the fairness requirement is represented in the form of constraints while the optimum solution is obtained by the objective function. Here multiple objectives can be defined such as maximizing the network throughput while at the same time minimizing the difference between the share of the participants.

Due to the fact that subflows may share different bottlenecks, it is highly unlikely that all the subflows can get an equal share. Since a flow is defined as a set of subflows, a *network flow fair* solution is feasible wherein the allocation of the different subflows corresponding to a flow can be tuned. To obtain a *network locator fair*, *network tariff fair*, *network source fair* or *network user fair* solution, the *fairness bound* equations have to be formulated with respect to locator, tariff, source node or user, respectively. The bottleneck bound equations are always applied at the subflow level.

5   Validation of the Algorithms and Analysis of Fairness Mechanisms

To validate the algorithms implemented in MATLAB as well as highlight the advantage of considering tariff as the participant, an example scenario shown in Fig. 2 is used. For better overview, the notation used in this scenario differs from the one used in the algorithm previously described e.g., subflow $sf_k, 1 \leq k \leq 7$. The scenario consists of two users where user u_1 has two source nodes sr_1 and sr_2 while user u_2 has a single source node sr_3. Source node sr_1 initiates two multipath flows, each composed of two subflows initiated from two different locators (l_1 and l_2) under different tariffs (t_1 and t_2). The different tariffs are shown with different colors while subflows of the same flow have the same line style. Source node sr_2 is also under tariff t_2 and initiates a singlepath flow. Source node sr_3 initiates a multipath flow also composed of two subflows via two different locators (l_4 and l_5) having independent tariffs (t_3 and t_4). In the scenario's topology, there are three bottleneck links where ρ_1, ρ_2 and ρ_3 are defined as the capacities of these bottleneck links.

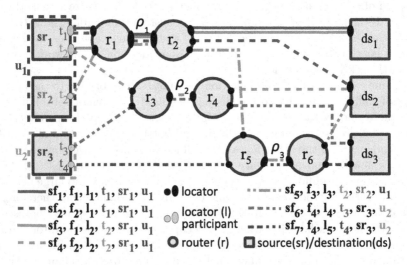

Fig. 2. Example scenario for fairness methods analysis
(participants - sf: subflow, f: flow, l: locator, t: tariff, sr: source, u: user)

Table 1 depicts the results obtained from the bottleneck and network resource allocation algorithms (introduced in Sect. 4) for the scenario shown in Fig. 2 with

Table 1. Capacity share in Mbit/s for scenario in Fig. 2, (N: Network, B: Bottleneck, Sf: Subflow, F: Flow, L: Locator, T: Tariff, Sr: Source and U: User)

sf#	share $b_{u,f}^{sf}$	$\rho_1 = \rho_2 = \rho_3 = 100$										
		BSfF	BFF	BLF	BTF	BSrF	BUF	NFF	NLF	NTF	NSrF	NUF
sf$_1$	$b_{1,1}^1$	25.0	16.67	16.67	25.0	16.67	16.67	25.0	50.0	33.33	12.5	21.5
sf$_2$	$b_{1,2}^1$	25.0	33.33	16.67	25.0	16.67	33.33	00.0	00.0	33.33	00.0	14.0
sf$_3$	$b_{1,1}^2$	25.0	16.67	33.33	25.0	16.67	16.67	25.0	00.0	0.00	12.5	21.5
sf$_4$	$b_{1,2}^2$	50.0	50.00	50.00	50.0	50.00	50.00	75.0	50.0	33.33	50.0	29.0
sf$_5$	$b_{1,3}^1$	25.0	33.33	33.33	25.0	50.00	33.33	50.0	50.0	33.33	75.0	43.0
sf$_6$	$b_{2,1}^1$	50.0	50.00	50.00	50.0	50.00	50.00	25.0	50.0	66.67	50.0	71.0
sf$_7$	$b_{2,1}^2$	75.0	66.67	66.67	75.0	50.00	66.67	50.0	50.0	66.67	25.0	58.0
sum		275.0	266.67	266.67	275.0	250.00	266.67	250.0	250.0	266.67	225.0	258.0
Jain's SfFI		0.823	0.8312	0.8312	0.823	0.8242	0.8312	0.741	0.714	0.7619	0.625	0.778
Jain's FFI		0.776	0.7805	0.8205	0.776	0.8654	0.7805	0.961	0.893	0.7273	0.880	0.750
Jain's TFI		0.917	0.9143	0.8205	0.917	0.7922	0.9143	0.595	0.893	1.0000	0.570	0.850

$\rho_1 = \rho_2 = \rho_3 = 100$. In this scenario, flows 1, 2 and 4 are multipath flows, each composed of two subflows while flow 3 is the only single path flow and part of two bottleneck links ρ_1 and ρ_3. As a metric to compare the different fairness mechanisms, the overall throughput and Jain's fairness index (FI) [18] is used. In order to highlight that fairness can be perceived differently with respect to the different participants, Jain's fairness index is shown for the following participants - subflow (SfFI), flow (FFI) and tariff (TFI).

The *bottleneck subflow fair* allocation algorithm identifies the link between routers r_1 and r_2 to be bottlenecked first as this link has four subflows sharing its capacity $\rho_1 = 100$. Thus, the four subflows sf$_1$, sf$_2$, sf$_3$ and sf$_5$ get bottlenecked with a share of 25 each. Subflows sf$_4$ and sf$_6$ get bottlenecked next on link $\langle r_3, r_4 \rangle$ with limited capacity $\rho_2 = 100$ with a share of 50 each. The third bottleneck link $\langle r_5, r_6 \rangle$ with capacity $\rho_3 = 100$ is shared between subflows sf$_5$ and sf$_7$ but since sf$_5$ is already bottlenecked with a share of $b_{1,3}^1 = 25$, the remaining capacity of the link is allocated to subflow $s_{2,1}^2$ i.e., $b_{2,1}^2 = 75$.

The *bottleneck flow fair* allocation shares the available bottleneck link capacity between flows and subflows. Therefore, $\rho_1 = 100$ capacity is shared between 3 flows (not 4 subflows) giving a share of 33.33 to each of the three flows (f_1, f_2 and f_3) initiated from the same user u_1. Since both the subflows of flow f_1 are part of this bottleneck, the flow allocation is shared equally between the two subflows sf$_1$ and sf$_3$. The higher-level participants such as locator or tariff share their respective allocations equally amongst their flows and then the flow share is shared equally between its respective subflows (hierarchical equal share policy). For example, the *bottleneck tariff fair* allocation first shares the bottleneck link capacity $\rho_1 = 100$ equally between the two tariffs (t_1 and t_2). Both the tariffs t_1 and t_2 have two subflows of different flows over this bottleneck link and therefore they further share the tariff allocations equally. Even though flow f_1 has two subflows over this bottleneck, each subflow gets a share equal to the share of the single subflows belonging to other flows by the virtue of being part of two different tariffs.

The hierarchical equal share policy used by the bottleneck resource allocation algorithm is not trivial for the network resource because all the participants and their inter-dependency have to be considered. For example, a flow can allocate its share equally between its two subflows only if they are part of the same bottleneck and participant. In the investigated scenario (Fig. 2) both subflows of flow f1 share the same bottleneck link and for participants such as flow (Eq. nf5), source (Eq. nsr5) and user (Eq. nu3) the two subflows can have equal allocation. If a subflow is part of more than one bottleneck then the network capacity ρ^n is not just the sum of the bottleneck link capacities. Therefore, the network capacity is defined to be the sum of all subflow capacities in the network (Eq. n1) where $b_{q,x}^a$ is the capacity assigned to the subflow $s_{q,x}^a$ of flow $f_{q,x}$ that is initiated by user u_q. The linear equation system representation of the scenario considered in Fig. 2 implemented in MATLAB is as follows.

– Network capacity equation:
$$\rho^n = b_{1,1}^1 + b_{1,1}^2 + b_{1,2}^1 + b_{1,2}^2 + b_{1,3}^1 + b_{2,1}^1 + b_{2,1}^2 \,(\text{n1}).$$
– Bottleneck bounded set of equations:
$$b_{1,1}^1 + b_{1,1}^2 + b_{1,2}^1 + b_{1,3}^1 = \rho_1 \,(\text{b1}); \quad b_{1,2}^2 + b_{2,1}^1 = \rho_2 \,(\text{b2}); \quad b_{1,3}^1 + b_{2,1}^1 = \rho_3 \,(\text{b3}).$$

Depending on the participant i.e., flow (nf1-nf5), tariff (nt1-nt4), etc. different set of fairness equations are used to obtain the respective allocation of subflow capacities.

– Fairness bounded set of equations for network flow fair (NFF):
$$b_{1,1}^1 + b_{1,1}^2 = \rho^n/4 \,(\text{nf1}); \quad b_{1,2}^1 + b_{1,2}^2 = \rho^n/4 \,(\text{nf2}); \quad b_{1,3}^1 = \rho^n/4 \,(\text{nf3});$$
$$b_{2,1}^1 + b_{2,1}^2 = \rho^n/4 \,(\text{nf4}); \quad b_{1,1}^1 - b_{1,1}^2 = 0 \,(\text{nf5}).$$
– Fairness bounded set of equations for network locator fair (NLF):
$$b_{1,1}^1 + b_{1,2}^1 = \rho^n/5 \,(\text{nl1}); \quad b_{1,1}^2 + b_{1,2}^2 = \rho^n/5 \,(\text{nl2}); \quad b_{1,3}^1 = \rho^n/5 \,(\text{nl3});$$
$$b_{2,1}^1 = \rho^n/5 \,(\text{nl4}); \qquad b_{2,1}^2 = \rho^n/5 \,(\text{nl5}).$$
– Fairness bounded set of equations for network tariff fair (NTF):
$$b_{1,1}^1 + b_{1,2}^1 = \rho^n/4 \,(\text{nt1}); \quad b_{1,1}^2 + b_{1,2}^2 + b_{1,3}^1 = \rho^n/4 \,(\text{nt2}); \quad b_{2,1}^1 = \rho^n/4 \,(\text{nt3});$$
$$b_{2,1}^2 = \rho^n/4 \,(\text{nt4}).$$
– Fairness bounded set of equations for network source fair (NSrF):
$$b_{1,1}^1 + b_{1,1}^2 + b_{1,2}^1 + b_{1,2}^2 = \rho^n/3 \,(\text{nsr1}); \quad b_{1,3}^1 = \rho^n/3 \,(\text{nsr2});$$
$$b_{2,1}^1 + b_{2,1}^2 = \rho^n/3 \,(\text{nsr3}); \quad b_{1,1}^1 - b_{1,1}^1 = 0 \,(\text{nsr4}); \quad b_{1,1}^1 - b_{1,1}^1 = 0 \,(\text{nsr5}).$$
– Fairness bounded set of equations for network user fair (NUF):
$$b_{1,1}^1 + b_{1,1}^2 + b_{1,2}^1 + b_{1,2}^2 + b_{1,3}^1 = \rho^n/2 \,(\text{nu1}); \quad b_{2,1}^1 + b_{2,1}^2 = \rho^n/2 \,(\text{nu2});$$
$$b_{1,1}^1 - b_{1,1}^2 = 0 \,(\text{nu3}).$$

The *network flow fair* allocation based on the linear set of equations n1, b1-b3 and nf1-nf5, as desired, results in an equal allocation of 60 to the competing four flows within the network. But in order to do so, it gave an allocation of -20 and 80 to subflows $s_{1,2}^1$ and $s_{1,2}^2$ respectively of flow $f_{1,2}$. A negative allocation implies that the competing flows on the bottleneck link have got an overall larger share than the bottleneck link capacity. Thus, with the help of a simple corrective algorithm the additional share is reduced equally from the competing flows $f_{1,1}$ and $f_{1,3}$. Thus a maximum possible allocation of 50 for the two flows due to topological restriction is obtained. A reduced set of linear equations related to the remaining network capacity and unallocated participants is solved to obtain an equal share of 75 between flows $f_{1,2}$ and $f_{2,1}$. The *network tariff fair* allocation results in each tariff getting an equal share of 66.66. Due to topological constraints i.e., tariff t_1 only shares the bottleneck link with capacity $\rho_1 = 100$, the tariff t_2 can only get a share of 33.33 on this link. Thus, the tariff t_2 cannot be shared equally amongst its three flows i. e., an equal share of 22.22. In addition, priority is given for a further fair share amongst flows leading to an allocation of 33.33 to flow $f_{1,3}$ and nothing to subflow $s_{1,1}^2$ as the other subflow $s_{1,1}^1$ of flow $f_{1,1}$ gets a share of 33.33 from tariff t_1. A similar allocation discrepancy due to the topological limitation is observed for the *network source fair* allocation where all the three source nodes get an equal share of 75 each, but due to flow $f_{1,3}$ share of 75 from source sr_2, flow $f_{1,1}$ can be allocated only 25 (limited by ρ_1) from the share of source sr_1. The *network user fair* allocation can achieve an equal share of the user u_1 allocation amongst its 3 flows, each getting a share of 43.

From the obtained results it can be seen that if fairness is applied at the bottleneck then it is absolutely fair to the individual participants w. r. t. the bottleneck. Fairness mechanisms considering the whole network as a single resource is restricted by the topological constraints and might even result in a lower overall network throughput when a flow is part of multiple bottleneck links (Fig. 2). Flows can be chosen as participants if TCP compatible fairness is preferred while tariffs combine the individual flows and couple their share together w.r.t. economical aspects thereby allowing for a better implementation of service level agreements between the user and the service provider. The network flow fair solution for the investigated scenario leads to a highly unfair distribution of network capacity between the four different tariffs, which highlights the issue in selecting the flow as a participant for resource allocation.

6   Conclusion and Outlook

In this work, the investigated fairness mechanisms are not limited to universally accepted TCP-friendly notions but defined w. r. t. available resources (e. g. bottleneck and network) and competing participants (e. g. subflow, flow, locator, tariff, source and user). The discussed alternative fairness mechanisms extend the scope of fairness beyond a transport flow to include the higher layer aspects, the end user as well as the network. Furthermore, theoretical resource (bottleneck/network) allocation algorithms with regard to different fairness goals are presented as a means for a comprehensive analysis of the various fairness definitions. With the help of a carefully chosen scenario, different aspects of fairness in multipath transport are highlighted with the help of results obtained from the introduced theoretical resource assignment algorithms. In addition, the investigated scenario is kept small enough to validate the operation of the proposed algorithms.

To achieve a fair end-to-end solution without the aid of the network, congestion windows of subflows belonging to the same participant can be coupled. Internal weighting of the subflows corresponding to the same participant may be achieved at the end host but for weights to work at the participant level, network elements need to collaborate. Exchange of signaling information between the end host and the network can further enhance the performance of the congestion control mechanisms in achieving the desired goals specified in [10]. Thus, these theoretical allocation algorithms can be used not only to classify but also validate the performance of the multi/single-path congestion control algorithms for complex scenarios.

The theoretical algorithm for bottleneck fair allocation is presented as a flexible method which assumes that due to the elastic traffic, every subflow will be bottlenecked by the network and not restricted by the application. The algorithm can also be extended to include the application limited cases (realtime traffic). The algorithm allocates the fair share to every subflow by utilizing the subflow path mapping information. The functionality of choosing a limited set of subflows out of all the available subflows can also be added, if needed, but will introduce large computational complexity due to the number of possible combinations.

With a linear equation system, a fair share solution might not be obtained if the bottleneck link does not allow a participant to get its fair share. In this case, some of the subflows competing for the bottleneck link capacity will be assigned a negative allocation. In this work, an iterative method is used to overcome this shortcoming by systematically updating the capacity allocations. Also care is taken that no flow gets starved if the participant is a higher level entity such as tariff. In future work, a comprehensive solution which is capable of both fair resource allocation as well as optimum routing will be worked out based on mixed-integer (non-)linear programming.

References

1. Postel, J.B.: Transmission Control Protocol. IETF, Standards Track RFC 793 (1981)
2. Welzl, M.: Network Congestion Control: Managing Internet Traffic. Wiley, New York (2005)
3. Braden, R., Clark, D.D., Crowcroft, J., Davie, B., Deering, S.E., Estrin, D., Floyd, S., Jacobson, V., Minshall, G., Partridge, C., Peterson, L., Ramakrishnan, K.K., Shenker, S., Wroclawski, J., Zhang, L.: Recommendations on Queue Management and Congestion Avoidance in the Internet. IETF, Informational RFC 2309 (1998)
4. Tse, R.H., Jannotti, J.H., Tse, R.H.: TCP fairness in multipath transport protocols, Department of Computer Science, Brown University, Bachelor's thesis (2006)
5. Briscoe, B.: Flow rate fairness: dismantling a religion. ACM SIGCOMM Comput. Commun. Rev. (CCR) **37**, 63–74 (2007)

6. Adhari, H., Rathgeb, E.P., Singh, A., Könsgen, A., Goerg, C.: Transport Layer Fairness Revisited, Submitted (2015)
7. Papadimitriou, D., Welzl, M., Scharf, M., Briscoe, B.: Open Research Issues in Internet Congestion Control. IRTF, RFC 6077 (2011)
8. Dreibholz, T., Becke, M., Adhari, H., Rathgeb, E.P.: On the impact of congestion control for concurrent multipath transfer on the transport layer. In: Proceedings of the 11th IEEE International Conference on Telecommunications (ConTEL) (2011)
9. Ford, A., Raiciu, C., Handley, M., Bonaventure, O.: TCP Extensions for Multipath Operation with Multiple Addresses. IETF, RFC 6824 (2013)
10. Ford, A., Raiciu, C., Handley, M., Barr, S., Iyengar, J.R.: Architectural Guidelines for Multipath TCP Development. IETF, Informational RFC 6182 (2011)
11. Raiciu, C., Handley, M., Wischik, D.: Coupled Congestion Control for Multipath Transport Protocols. IETF, RFC 6356 (2011)
12. Wischik, D., Handley, M., Braun, M.B.: The resource pooling principle. ACM SIGCOMM Comput. Commun. Rev. (CCR) 38(5), 47–52 (2008)
13. Raiciu, C., Wischik, D., Handley, M.: Practical congestion control for multipath transport protocols. University College London, Technical report (2009)
14. Becke, M., Dreibholz, T., Adhari, H., Rathgeb, E.P.: On the fairness of transport protocols in a multi-path environment. In: Proceedings of the IEEE International Conference on Communications (ICC) (2012)
15. Adhari, H., Becke, M., Dreibholz, T.: On the fairness of transport protocols in a multi-path environment. In: Proceedings of the 83rd IETF Meeting (2012)
16. Singh, A., Xiang, M., Könsgen, A., Goerg, C.: Performance and fairness comparison of extensions to dynamic window coupling for multipath TCP. In: 9th International Wireless Communications and Mobile Computing Conference (IWCMC) (2013)
17. Singh, A., Xiang, M., Könsgen, A., Goerg, C., Zaki, Y.: Enhancing fairness and congestion control in multipath TCP. In: 6th Joint IFIP Wireless and Mobile Networking Conference (WMNC) (2013)
18. Jain, R., Chiu, D., Hawe, W.: A quantitative measure of fairness and discrimination for resource allocation in shared computer systems. CoRR, vol. cs.NI/9809099 (1998). http://arxiv.org/abs/cs/9809099

Lightweight Random Linear Coding over Wireless Mesh Networks

Pablo Garrido[1(✉)], David Gómez[1], Jorge Lanza[1], Ramón Agüero[1],
and Joan Serrat[2]

[1] University of Cantabria, Santander, Spain
{pgarrido,dgomez,jlanza,ramon}@tlmat.unican.es
[2] Universitat Politecnica de Catalunya, Barcelona, Spain
serrat@tsc.upc.edu

Abstract. We propose an enhanced version of an *intra-flow* Network
Coding protocol, which was conceived to offer a reliable communication
service, by means of the combination a Random Linear Coding (RLC)
scheme with the UDP protocol. We reduce the overhead that was originally required in the protocol header and we assess, through an extensive
campaign carried out over the `ns-3` framework, the performance gain
that is brought by this enhancement, comparing it to the TCP protocol,
as the mainstream transport-level solution to offer a reliable service. We
study the impact of the various configuration parameters of the solution.
Afterwards, we challenge the proposed scheme over random topologies
(Wireless Mesh Networks or WMNs). The results show a remarkable
gain (approximately 20 times higher) of the performance over an ideal
channel, thanks to the aforementioned overhead reduction.

Keywords: Random linear coding · Network coding · Simulation ·
Wireless mesh networks

1 Introduction

Wireless networks have become the most widespread communication alternative.
The fast roll-out of new technologies, such as LTE, and the strong consolidation
of other alternatives, being WiFi the most outstanding example, together with
the growing presence of advanced end-users devices (smartphones, tablets, etc.),
are some of the main reasons behind this fact.

Despite the evolution that we have witnessed on the access to the Internet,
the most used transport layer protocol, TCP, exhibits a poor performance over
wireless networks. This problem has been tackled by the research community,
which has made a great effort to come up with new approaches to provide a reliable end-to-end transport solution suitable for the hostile conditions of wireless
networks. Several proposals have been made, ranging from modifications of the
legacy TCP protocol to novel transport and cross-layer solutions that address
the problem from different perspectives.

© Institute for Computer Sciences, Social Informatics and Telecommunications Engineering 2015
R. Agüero et al. (Eds.): MONAMI 2015, LNICST 158, pp. 164–178, 2015.
DOI: 10.1007/978-3-319-26925-2_13

Amongst them, *Network Coding* (NC) appears as one of the most promising techniques. Its basic principle is allowing nodes to process and code packets before sending them again, opposed to the classical *store-and-forward* paradigm.

In a previous work [9], we studied the joint operation of a Random Linear Source Coding scheme and the UDP protocol to provide a reliable service over a single wireless link. The main goal of this paper is to extend that initial contribution; first, we propose an enhancement of such scheme, which allows reducing the required overhead, since we minimize the information that needs to be sent for coding and decoding purposes. We analytically study the gain that is brought by this modification and, afterwards, we use an implementation over the ns-3 platform [1] to validate such analysis and to broaden the comparison. The simulation results show that the throughput of the proposed solution is remarkably higher than the one observed with the legacy TCP protocol. In addition, we also assess the performance of the proposed solution over *Wireless Mesh Networks (WMN)*, which lead to random topologies.

This paper is structured as follows: Sect. 2 discusses some related works that address the topics covered herein. Section 3 briefly describes the RLC scheme and details the proposed enhancement; it also depicts the analytical study of the throughput over ideal channels. Afterwards, Sect. 4 discusses the results that were obtained after an extensive simulation campaign carried out over the ns-3 platform to corroborate the previous analysis and to broaden it, considering more complex network deployments. Finally, Sect. 5 concludes the paper, identifying a number of issues that will be tackled in our future research.

2   Related Work

TCP was originally designed with the assumption that packet losses were mostly caused by the congestion of intermediate network routers, which was a sensible belief, since almost all communications happened over wired links. The little attention that was paid to other types of errors leads to a remarkable performance decrease. In particular, this is the case over WMNs [3], which are believed to play an important role in the forthcoming wireless networking realm. Their main limitation comes from the severe impact that wireless communications (due to the appearance of errors and the interference) might have over the performance.

Several works studied the impact that the error-prone characteristic of wireless networks has over the TCP performance [15,18]. In addition, a number of proposals have been made to overcome the limitations exhibited by TCP over wireless networks. One of the most promising techniques amongst them is NC.

The term *Network Coding* was originally coined by Ahlswede *et al.* in [2]. They discussed the suitability of the classic *store-and-forward* paradigm in IP networks, advocating that the integration of some additional functionalities at the intermediate nodes could yield remarkable performance enhancements. Since then, several works have proposed the use of this technique, to get either performance enhancements or more reliable communications.

One of the most relevant contributions is the work presented by Katti *et al.* [12]. They proposed the COPE protocol, where the forwarding nodes code packets that belong to different flows, combining them by means of a simple *XOR* operation. They exploited the broadcast nature of the wireless medium, assuming that the neighboring nodes were able to overhear packets not directly addressed to them; this would eventually reduce the number of transmissions, yielding a significant performance gains. However, it has been shown [8] that when the conditions of the wireless channels are poor, the performance gain of this approach is not so relevant.

Chachulski *et al.* proposed in [5] the protocol *MAC-independent opportunistic routing protocol* (MORE). MORE combines a *Random Linear Coding* (RLC) scheme with opportunistic routing; the source combines (codes) information belonging to the same flow. Besides, the authors also proposed a number of additional mechanisms to avoid unnecessary retransmissions by the relaying nodes. Nodes estimate the quality of each link by means of echo messages and, using this information, they decide whether to forward a packet. However, the authors did not consider the interplay with any transport protocol, and their analysis is mostly focused on the lower layers.

The approach fostered by the MORE protocol can be referred to as an *intra-flow* coding scheme. There are various works that follow a similar approach: for instance, [16] demonstrates that by linearly combining various packets, the maximum capacity bounds for multicast traffic can be assessed. On the other hand, Ho *et al.* [11] demonstrated that the use of random linear coefficients over a finite field was the best solution.

In our previous work [9] we proposed the combined use of RLC and the UDP protocol. We studied the performance over a single wireless link. In this paper we extend that initial contribution, by modifying the protocol specifications, so as to reduce the protocol required overhead, since we avoid transmitting the complete vector of random coefficients, only adding the corresponding (random) *seed* within the header. Using such seed, the destination is able to generate the same random coefficient vector, with which it can decode the original information. We analytically study the additional gain brought about by this enhancement, using an approach similar to that of used by Trullols *et al.* in [17].

This improvement might be rather relevant, since there is an impact of the finite field size over the system performance. Heidi *et al.* [10] showed that the overall complexity and the required overhead increase with the size of the finite field. In [9] we also concluded that the longer the finite field size the less likely is to have linearly dependent combinations, leading to a performance boost. However, there exists a clear trade-off between this improvement and the required overhead, that might even lead to lower throughputs. With the modification proposed in this work we make the overhead independent of the size of the finite field.

A complete different approach is the one by Kim *et al.* in [13], where they proposed a reliable solution that combined TCP and NC, the so-called Network Coded TCP (CTCP). Although they showed that CTPC outperforms the legacy

TCP, the behavior over networks with large Round Trip Time (RTT) was not appropriate. They also proposed sending a seed to alleviate the overhead that would have been otherwise needed for the decoding process, as we propose herewith.

In a more recent work, Krigslund et al. [14] have proposed an integration of COPE and MORE, to exploit the benefits brought by each of them. The intra-flow scheme provides a more reliable communication, reducing the impact of packet losses over the wireless channel. However, the basic principles of both schemes are unaltered.

Last, we should also highlight other works that have focused on the improvement of the traditional routing solutions. These, which are usually based on the shortest route goal, might not lead to the highest performances over wireless networks. One of the most relevant works in this group, carried out by De Couto et al. in [6], proposes the Expected Transmission Count (ETX) metric to estimate the quality of the wireless links, to boost the performance over multi-hop wireless networks.

3   Model and Design

As was already said, in [9] we proposed the combined use of RLC scheme and the UDP protocol to offer a reliable communication service. In this section we introduce an enhancement of such solution, allowing the use of larger Galois Field, $GF(2^q)$, and block sizes. We analytically prove the potential gain that can be achieved with these improvements.

3.1   RLC Protocol

Before depicting the proposed changes we briefly describe the basic operation of the RLC scheme. At the source, an RLC entity, placed between the IP and UDP layers, divides the upper layer information, which is stored in its own RLC *transmission buffer*, into fixed blocks of K packets. It sends linear combinations (we refer to them as coded packets) of these K packets belonging to the same block, which are built according to the following expression $p' = \sum_{i=0}^{K-1} c_i \cdot p_i$, where $c = \{c_0 \ c_1 \ldots c_{K-1}\}$ represents the corresponding coefficient vector. It is worth highlighting that the random coefficients c_i are generated from a finite Galois Field $GF(Q = 2^q)$. The procedure followed by the transmitted is depicted in Fig. 1.

When the destination receives a coded packet, it checks whether the corresponding coefficient vector is linearly independent from the previously received ones, by appending it to the $\mathbf{C}(K \times K)$ matrix and performing a rank calculation operation. In such case, the corresponding coded packet is said to be *innovative* and is stored at the RLC *reception buffer*. When c is linearly dependent, the packet is silently discarded.

Once the destination has received K *innovative* packets, it is able to decode the whole block, obtaining the original information; in addition, it sends an

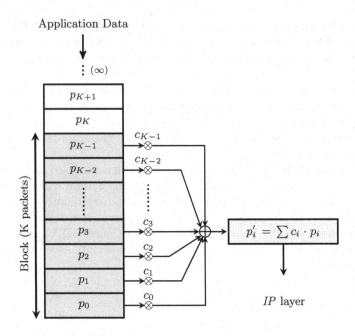

Fig. 1. Codification procedure at the source node

acknowledgment back to the source node, so that it can remove the corresponding block and start with the next one. If the acknowledgment was lost, the source would keep on sending packets of the previous block, which would cause the destination node to retransmit the corresponding acknowledgments, until the source realizes it needs to move forward to the next block.

Figure 2 shows the original RLC header, which is divided into two parts. The first one, with a fixed length of 9-bytes, contains all the information that needs to be exchanged from the source towards the destination. The second part of the header carries the corresponding random coefficients (i.e. **c**), whose length depends on the particular configuration of the coding processes.

- Type of message (1B): This field indicates the packet type: data packet ('0') or an acknowledgment ('1').
- Block Size K (1B): Number of packets per block. The maximum block size is 256, since the latency for larger blocks would be probably too high.
- Galois Field size - $GF(Q)$ (1B): The linear combination coefficients are randomly obtained from the Galois Field $GF(Q)$. In order to carry out the required operations, we have integrated the M4RIE [4] library into the **ns-3** platform; it imposes a limit of $Q = 2^8$.
- Fragment Number (2B): This field identifies the block that is being sent by the source and allows identifying spurious transmissions of an already received block.

- UDP source and destination ports (4B): A flow is identified by the source and destination IP address/UDP port tuples. Since the UDP header is coded, these ports need to be included in the RLC header.
- Coefficient vector, c (1-256B): Each coefficient, c_i, requires q bits and the header must include all the K coefficients.

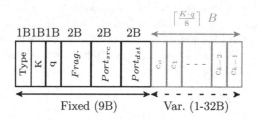

Fixed (9B)   Var. (1-32B)

Fig. 2. Original RLC header

The overall header length in the first version of the protocol was therefore $9 + \lceil \frac{K \cdot q}{8} \rceil$, since all the coefficients need to be transmitted within every coded packet.

In order to avoid such large overhead, we propose keeping track of the *seed* used by the source node to generate the random coefficients by means of a *pseudo random number generator* and to actually send such seed in the RLC header, rather than the complete vector. When the destination node receives a coded packet it uses the seed to generate the same coefficient vector that the one used by the source entity. Taking this into account, we propose a new header, which is depicted in Fig. 3, where we substitute the variable length part of the original header by a fixed 4-byte field that indicates the random seed. The new header has a fixed length (no matter the values of K and q are) of 13 bytes.

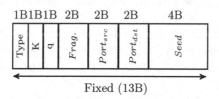

Fixed (13B)

Fig. 3. Enhanced RLC header

3.2 Analytical Model

Following an approach similar to the one we already used in [9] we aim at analytically finding the performance gain brought by the proposed enhancement. We want to obtain the throughput that is perceived at the RLC layer, i.e. the one offered by the UDP protocol, which mostly depends on two main factors: the *spurious* transmissions (linearly dependent coefficient vectors) and the backwards acknowledgments that are sent by the destination.

On the first hand, the *spurious* transmissions are consequence of the transmission of linearly dependent coefficient vectors c, which are silently dropped by the receiver, as was already said. We can establish their impact over the overall performance using the model proposed by Trullols-Cruces *et al.* in [17]. They derived the probability that a block of K packets can be successfully decoded after N receptions, as a function of the Galois Field $GF(Q)$ size, as can be seen in Eq. 1, where $P_{K,Q}(K)$ is the probability of an ideal block transmission, i.e. the destination node got K *innovative packets* after K receptions, Eq. (2), without any spurious transmissions.

$$P_{K,Q}(N > K) = P_{K,Q}(K) \cdot$$ (1)

$$\cdot \left(\begin{bmatrix} N \\ N-K \end{bmatrix}_Q + \sum_{t=1}^{N-K} (-1)^t \binom{N}{t} \begin{bmatrix} N-t \\ N-K-t \end{bmatrix}_Q \right)$$

$$P_{K,Q}(K) = \frac{Q^{K^2}}{(Q^K - 1)^K} \cdot \prod_{j=1}^{K} \left(1 - \frac{1}{Q^j} \right)$$ (2)

Therefore, we can calculate the average number of *spurious* transmissions, as can be seen in Eq. 3 and the ratio between the number of excess packets and the overall transmissions, as is shown in Eq. 4. This ratio, ϵ, is the factor that jeopardizes the performance, being $0 \leq \epsilon \leq 1$.

$$E[N] = \sum_{i=N-K}^{\infty} i \cdot P_{K,Q}(i)$$ (3)

$$\epsilon = \frac{E[N]}{K + E[N]}$$ (4)

As a second factor, the penalization caused by the acknowledgments sent by the destination, ϵ_{ack}, is expressed as the ratio between the time required to send such confirmation packet, τ_{ack}, and the average transmission time of a data packet, τ_{data}, as defined in Eq. (5). Finally, we can model the *goodput*, i.e. the throughput perceived by the application layer, $\overline{Thput_{RLC}}$, as shown in Eq. (6).

$$\epsilon_{ACK} = \frac{\overline{\tau_{ack}}}{(K + \epsilon) \cdot \overline{\tau_{data}} + \overline{\tau_{ack}}}$$ (5)

$$\overline{Thput_{RLC}} = \overline{Thput_{UDP}} \cdot (1 - \epsilon) \cdot (1 - \epsilon_{ack})$$ (6)

Section 4 discusses the results that are obtained applying this model. We will study the influence of both finite field and block sizes, i.e. q and k, over the achieved throughput, both with the original and the enhanced RLC header. This is of outer relevance to better understand the relationship between the system performance and configuration of the RLC scheme (block and Galois Field size), and to assess the gain that is brought by the new proposed coding solution.

Table 1. Simulation parameters

Feature	Value
Physical link	*IEEE 802.11b* (11 *Mbps*)
Error Model	Fixed FER (memoryless)
FER Values	[0:0.1:0.6]
RTX IEEE 802.11	1(RLC), 3(TCP)
Transport Layer	*UDP (NC)/TCP*
Application Data Rate	Fixed (Saturation)
MTU	1500 *Bytes* at *IP* layer

4 Results

In this section we outline the process that was followed to assess the performance of our proposal. Starting from the analytical model presented in Sect. 3, we analyze the potential benefits of using larger field ($Q = 2^q$) and block (K) sizes.

Afterwards, we carry out an extensive simulation campaign over the ns-3 simulator to study the performance over the same scenario, allowing us to validate the analytical model. In addition, we exploit the implementation that was done to evaluate the behavior of the RLC scheme over more complex scenarios (Wireless Mesh Networks), comparing the achieved throughput (measured at the received application) with that of exhibited by the traditional reliable transport protocol, TCP (in particular, using the New Reno [7] version).

Table 1 summarizes the most relevant parameters of the scenario that was used throughout the simulations. The physical and Medium Access Control (MAC) layers follow the IEEE 802.11b recommendation. The retransmission scheme is disabled for the RLC protocol, since it does not provide any additional gain [9], while we fix a maximum of 3 retransmissions when the legacy TCP is used. Regarding the application layer at source nodes, we use a constant transmission rate, ensuring a saturated situation, so that the system bottleneck stays at the wireless channel.

First, we study the impact of the Galois Field and block sizes, q and K, respectively, over the system performance. As was already derived from Eqs. 4 and 5, the higher the K, the lower the performance penalization, while when q gets lower, the probability of having linearly dependent coefficient vectors increases (more spurious transmissions), with the consequent throughput reduction. Figures 4a and b show the evolution of these two penalization factors as a function of both parameters (block and Galois field sizes, K and q, respectively). Figure 4a yields that the use of a higher q greatly reduces the penalization on the performance, regardless of the block size. This stresses the relevance of the proposed enhanced header, since it would allow using a higher Galois Field without requiring an increase of the overhead. On the other hand, Fig. 4b shows that the acknowledgment penalization is mostly affected by the block size (the influence of the finite field is rather negligible), and this again would be solved with the

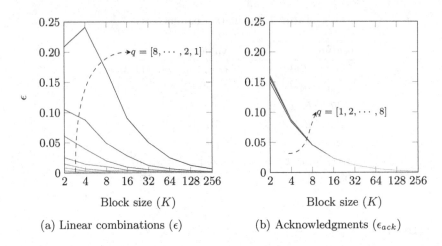

(a) Linear combinations (ϵ)   (b) Acknowledgments (ϵ_{ack})

Fig. 4. *RLC* performance penalization factors

proposed new header, since in the original scheme, a higher block size would lead to an increased overhead and the throughput (as will be seen later) could be even reduced.

In order to complement the previous results, we can analytically establish the region where the use of the new header format would be worthy, if only the overhead, and not the penalization factors, was taken into account. If the previous header had a size of $\lceil 9 + \frac{K \cdot q}{8} \rceil$ bytes, and the new header has a fixed length of 13 bytes, Eq. 7 establishes the condition in which the use the new proposed format would lead to a lighter overhead. Figure 5 graphically represents this region; as can be seen, regardless of the q value, with a block size greater than 32 packets the new header is always beneficial; in addition, by increasing q we broaden the range of K values that are worth using.

$$\left\lceil \frac{K \cdot q}{8} \right\rceil > 4 \tag{7}$$

Once we have assessed the impact of the new header, we carry out an extensive simulation-based analysis to better understand the behavior of various configurations of the RLC scheme. We deploy two nodes and we represent the throughput that was observed when using different combinations of $q = [2, \cdots, 8]$ and $K = [2, \cdots, 256]$. Figures 6 and 7 shows the results that were observed for the original (variable-length) RLC header and for the one proposed in this paper, respectively. For the former case (see Fig. 6), the impact of both penalization factors is clearly seen. For a binary Galois Field ($q = 1$), the performance increases with K; however, when $q > 1$, the overhead required to transmit the corresponding coefficients leads to a performance reduction for large K values. As can be seen, the performance of the RLC scheme surpasses the TCP throughput either when $K > 16$ and $q \leq 1$, or for $K > 4$ and $q > 2$.

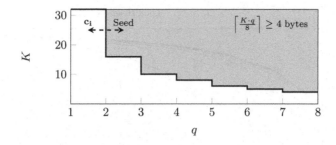

Fig. 5. Region where the use of the new RLC header is worthy

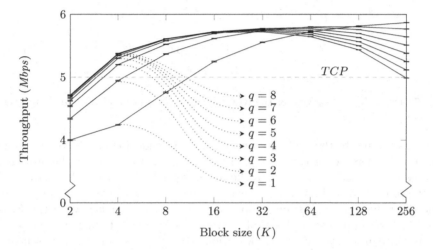

Fig. 6. Throughput observed for the RLC long header over an ideal single hop transmission

Figure 7 shows the throughput that was observed when the new header was used; in order to ease the comparison it also includes the curve corresponding to the original header and $q = 1$. It is worth highlighting that in this case, the new format allows maintaining the performance even for $K > 64$, while the throughput was severely jeopardized in the original solution. Thanks to this enhancement, we can take full advantage of the configuration that reduces the impact of the two aforementioned penalization factors, without increasing the overhead. The throughput gain, compared with the legacy TCP, under ideal conditions and for $K > 128$, is $\approx 18\%$, regardless of the q value.

Figure 8 shows the throughput that was observed when the quality of the wireless link between the source and the destination gets worse[1]. We increase the FER between 0 and 0.6, and we analyze the behavior of two configurations of the proposed scheme: $q = 1, K = 64$ and $q = 6, K = 256$, since the were

---

[1] For the sake of simplicity, we assume that the acknowledgment messages will never get lost in the inverse link.

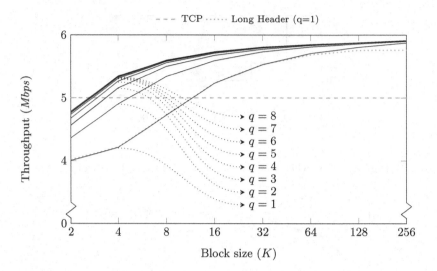

Fig. 7. Throughput observed for the RLC short header over an ideal single hop transmission

the ones leading to the optimum performance over ideal channels for the short and long headers, respectively. We can see that the performance of the proposed scheme is remarkably higher than the one observed when using the traditional TCP protocol, especially when the conditions of the wireless link are worse (the throughput is for instance approximately 10 times higher when the FER is 0.5). The figure also yields that there is not a relevant difference between the performances assessed with the various configurations of the RLC scheme. As can be seen, only the configuration with a slight lower throughput is the one using the original header and the larger Galois Field and block, since the required header length jeopardizes its performance, as was also seen over the ideal channel (see Fig. 6).

After assessing the potential benefits of the combination of RLC and UDP to provide a reliable communication service, and having measured the additional gain that can be achieved by modifying the original coding scheme, we exploit the framework that was integrated into the ns-3 simulator in order to study the performance over wireless mesh networks, which lead to random topologies. In particular, we consider the characteristics that are enumerated below.

- A square area of 100 m × 100 m.
- 32 Nodes randomly deployed throughout the scenario, following a *Poisson Point Process*, i.e. the x and y coordinates are selected with a uniform random variable between 0 and 100.
- We ensure that all network deployments are connected, discarding those whose underlying graph does not fulfill this constraint.
- Each node has a coverage area of 20 m, using the well-known disk radius model.
- We randomly select the source and the destination nodes.

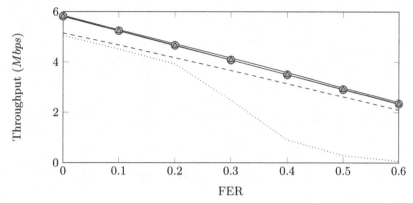

Fig. 8. Throughput observed for various configurations as a function of the wireless link quality

- We set the quality of the existing links (always with an euclidean distance lower than 20 m), by means of a FER randomly selected within the interval $[0.0\ldots0.6]$.
- The route between the source and the destination is established with the *Dijkstra* algorithm, which minimizes the overall cost, based on the ETX metric.
- We carry out a Monte-Carlo process, by randomly generating 1000 scenarios.

We use the following configuration for the RLC: $q = 6$ and $K = 256$. Figure 9 shows the throughput *cumulative distribution function* (cdf). As can be seen, the new header brings a performance gain of $\approx 16\,\%$ as compared with the original format, while the throughput is $\approx 1.7\times$ the one that was observed for the legacy TCP protocol.

It is worth highlighting the bad behavior exhibited by TCP either when the number of hops is increased and when the qualities of the wireless channels get worse. In fact, TCP is able to successfully finalize the connection (throughput greater than 0) in only $\approx 40\,\%$ of the scenarios.

To conclude the analysis, Fig. 10 shows the evolution of the throughput as a function of the number of hops of the route that is found between the source and destination nodes. First of all, we can again see the poor behavior exhibited by TCP when the quality of the wireless channels gets worse; for 1-hop routes, the performance of the RLC scheme is $\approx 3x$ the one observed for the legacy TCP case. On the other hand, the results also yield that the throughput that was measured with the new RLC header always surpasses the one observed for the initial RLC implementation.

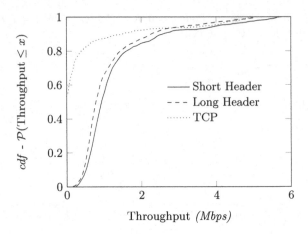

Fig. 9. *cdf* of the throughput observed over random wireless networks

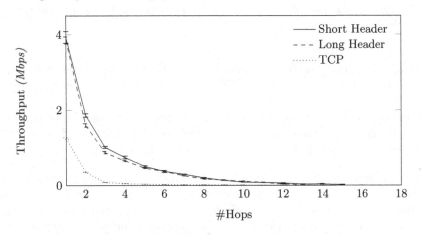

Fig. 10. Throughput vs. the # of hops

5   Conclusions

The use of Network Coding techniques to enhance the performance over wireless networks has received significant attention during the last years. The related research has covered various aspects, ranging from the analysis of the efficiency of coding/decoding procedures to the proposal of novel protocols able to promote these solutions. Some of the existing proposals belong to the so-called *Intra-flow* techniques group, since they are based on performing random linear combinations of packets that belong to the same data flow. Some of these works have discussed the relevance of using large Galois Fields for the coding/decoding purposes.

In a previous work [9], we proposed the combination of a RLC scheme and the UDP protocol to offer reliable communications over wireless links, and now, we propose a modification in the header format to alleviate the required overhead. Instead of sending the full coefficient vector, we include the random seed that was used by the source to generate it; this allows having a fixed-length header and using larger block and Galois Field sizes, K and q, respectively. By means of an analytical model we have evaluated the impact of the performance and the influence of K and q; we also assessed the relevance of using larger field sizes, which is favored by the use of the novel header format.

Afterwards, we have analyzed the performance of the two approaches over a single wireless link, comparing it with that observed with the legacy TCP protocol, which always showed much lower performances. The new header allows keeping the throughput regardless of the block size, while for the initial RLC scheme a strong reduction was observed. Finally, we have also assessed the performance of the RLC scheme over random network topologies (wireless mesh networks). We can highlight the low TCP performance over either low quality links or long routes. The throughput observed for the RLC scheme is, in average, approximately 1.7 times higher.

This work has also opened some new items that will be taken in our future research. Special attention will be paid to the integration of the RLC scheme with opportunistic routing techniques, which have been shown to provide relevant benefits over wireless mesh networks [5,14]. In addition, we will explore the possibilities that are brought about if the forwarding nodes take a more active role, by *re-coding* the packets previously stored previously.

Acknowledgments. This work has been supported by the Spanish Government by its funding through the project **COSAIF**, *"Connectivity as a Service: Access for the Internet of the Future"* (TEC2012-38754-C02-01).

References

1. The ns-3 network simulator. http://www.nsnam.org/
2. Ahlswede, R., Cai, N., Li, S.Y., Yeung, R.: Network information flow. IEEE Trans. Inf. Theory **46**(4), 1204–1216 (2000)
3. Akyildiz, I.F., Wang, X., Wang, W.: Wireless mesh networks: a survey. Comput. Netw. **47**(4), 445–487 (2005). http://www.sciencedirect.com/science/article/pii/S1389128604003457
4. Albrecht, M.R., Bard, G.V., Hart, W.: Efficient multiplication of dense matrices over GF(2). CoRR abs/0811.1714 (2008). http://arxiv.org/abs/0811.1714
5. Chachulski, S., Jennings, M., Katti, S., Katabi, D.: Trading structure for randomness in wireless opportunistic routing. SIGCOMM Comput. Commun. Rev. **37**(4), 169–180 (2007). http://doi.acm.org/10.1145/1282427.1282400
6. De Couto, D.S.J., Aguayo, D., Bicket, J., Morris, R.: A high-throughput path metric for multi-hop wireless routing. Wirel. Netw. **11**(4), 419–434 (2005). http://dx.doi.org/10.1007/s11276-005-1766-z
7. Floyd, S., Gurtov, A., Henderson, T.: The NewReno modification to TCP's fast recovery algorithm (2004)

8. Gomez, D., Hassayoun, S., Herren, A., Aguero, R., Ros, D.: Impact of network coding on TCP performance in wireless mesh networks. In: 2012 IEEE 23rd International Symposium on Personal Indoor and Mobile Radio Communications (PIMRC), pp. 777–782, September 2012

9. Gomez, D., Rodriguez, E., Aguero, R., Munoz, L.: Reliable communications over lossy wireless channels by means of the combination of UDP and random linear coding. In: 2014 IEEE Symposium on Computers and Communication (ISCC), pp. 1–6, June 2014

10. Heide, J., Pedersen, M.V., Fitzek, F.H., Médard, M.: On code parameters and coding vector representation for practical RNLC. In: 2011 IEEE International Conference on Communications (ICC), pp. 1–5. IEEE (2011)

11. Ho, T., Medard, M., Shi, J., Effros, M., Karger, D.R.: On randomized network coding. In: Proceedings of the Annual Allerton Conference on Communication Control and Computing, vol. 41, pp. 11–20. The University 1998 (2003)

12. Katti, S., Rahul, H., Hu, W., Katabi, D., Médard, M., Crowcroft, J.: XORs in the air: practical wireless network coding. SIGCOMM Comput. Commun. Rev. 36(4), 243–254 (2006). http://doi.acm.org/10.1145/1151659.1159942

13. Kim, M., Cloud, J., ParandehGheibi, A., Urbina, L., Fouli, K., Leith, D., Médard, M.: Network coded TCP (CTCP) (2012). arXiv preprint arXiv:1212.2291

14. Krigslund, J., Hansen, J., Hundeboll, M., Lucani, D., Fitzek, F.: CORE: COPE with MORE in wireless meshed networks. In: 2013 IEEE 77th Vehicular Technology Conference (VTC Spring), pp. 1–6, June 2013

15. Lefevre, F., Vivier, G.: Understanding TCP's behavior over wireless links. In: 2000 Symposium on Communications and Vehicular Technology, SCVT-2000, pp. 123–130 (2000)

16. Li, S.Y., Yeung, R.W., Cai, N.: Linear network coding. IEEE Trans. Inf. Theory 49(2), 371–381 (2003)

17. Trullols-Cruces, O., Barcelo-Ordinas, J., Fiore, M.: Exact decoding probability under random linear network coding. IEEE Commun. Lett. 15(1), 67–69 (2011)

18. Zorzi, M., Chockalingam, A., Rao, R.: Throughput analysis of TCP on channels with memory. IEEE J. Sel. Areas Commun. 18(7), 1289–1300 (2000)

Video Streaming over Wireless Networks

Energy Considerations for WiFi Offloading
of Video Streaming

Valentin Burger[1][(✉)], Fabian Kaup[2], Michael Seufert[1], Matthias Wichtlhuber[2],
David Hausheer[2], and Phuoc Tran-Gia[1]

[1] Insitute of Computer Science, University of Würzburg, Würzburg, Germany
{burger,seufert,trangia}@informatik.uni-wuerzburg.de
[2] Peer-to-Peer Systems Engineering Lab, TU Darmstadt, Darmstadt, Germany
{fabian.kaup,mwichtlh,hausheer}@ps.tu-darmstadt.de

Abstract. The load on cellular networks is constantly increasing. Especially video streaming applications, whose demands and requirements keep growing, put high loads on cellular networks. A solution to mitigate the cellular load in urban environments is offloading mobile connections to WiFi access points, which is followed by many providers recently. Because of the large number of mobile users and devices there is also a high potential to save energy by WiFi offloading. In this work, we develop a model to assess the energy consumption of mobile devices during video sessions. We evaluate the potential of WiFi offloading in an urban environment and the implications of offloading connections on energy consumption of mobile devices. Our results show that, although WiFi is more energy efficient than 3G and 4G for equal data rates, the energy consumption increases with the amount of connections offloaded to WiFi, due to poor data rates obtained for WiFi in the streets. This suggests further deployment of WiFi access points or WiFi sharing incentives to increase data rates for WiFi and energy efficiency of mobile access.

Keywords: WiFi offloading · Energy efficiency · Cellular networks · Mobile access · Video on demand · Modelling · Performance evaluation

1 Introduction

Cellular networks are facing an ever-increasing growth of data traffic combined with immense demands for service and quality. Especially video streaming, being a popular, data-intensive, and quality-sensitive service, contributes to this load as it accounts for 55 % (1.38 exabytes) of all mobile traffic by the end of 2014. As the number of mobile devices is increasing, also mobile traffic is expected to grow. The demanding video streaming will reinforce its position and its share is expected to rise up to 72 % (17.45 exabytes) in 2019. [8]

A new trend to handle these huge demands of mobile users and to reduce the load on cellular networks is WiFi offloading [29]. Thereby, users connect to WiFi access points instead of cellular base stations. Thus, the traffic flows through well-dimensioned fixed networks, which is more efficient for providers both in terms of

© Institute for Computer Sciences, Social Informatics and Telecommunications Engineering 2015
R. Agüero et al. (Eds.): MONAMI 2015, LNICST 158, pp. 181–195, 2015.
DOI: 10.1007/978-3-319-26925-2_14

cost and energy. In addition, end users can benefit from higher throughput and avoid exceeding their data plan. Due to the growing WiFi infrastructure (e.g., in cities like Berlin [3], London [1], or Singapore [4]) and independently operated free public WiFi hotspots (e.g., provided by cafes, shops, libraries), which can be found in hotspot databases like WeFi[1], offloading is increasingly available. In 2014, already 45 % of the total mobile data was offloaded onto the fixed network through WiFi or small-cells, and this ratio is expected to increase up to 54 % in 2019 [8].

In this work, we investigate the energy efficiency of WiFi offloading for video streaming, which is among the most popular and demanding Internet services. We present a framework for the simulative evaluation of video streaming energy consumption for mobile users. The simulation framework is based on citywide connectivity measurements and uses a simple streaming model, which allows for an assessment of the resulting data transmission bursts. We evaluate the energy consumption of these bursts for WiFi offloading based on different WiFi sharing percentages, i.e., percentage of accessible WiFi hotspots, and different cellular technologies. Thus, we are able to assess in which cases the energy consumption of video streaming can be improved by WiFi offloading or not.

Our results show that for equal data rates WiFi connections consume less energy, than cellular connections. Independent of the access technology the energy consumption decreases exponentially with the data rate. As the data rates for WiFi measured in the streets of an urban city center are rather low compared to 3G and 4G, offloading connections for video sessions to WiFi increases the energy consumption of mobile devices. However, minimal energy consumption is obtained for WiFi connections with high throughput. This suggests deploying WiFi access points or providing incentives for WiFi sharing to obtain high data rates while reducing energy consumption of mobile devices.

The paper is structured as follows. Background and research on WiFi offloading and mobile video streaming are outlined in Sect. 2. Section 3 presents the measurement setup, the resulting data set, and the simulation framework. The results, which were obtained through the simulation framework, are described in Sects. 4 and 5 concludes.

2   Background and Related Work

WiFi offloading has been widely adopted in commercial services and is also in the focus of research works. Ubiquitous Internet access via WiFi is offered by specialized WiFi-sharing communities (e.g., Fon[2]) but also by big telecommunication operators (e.g., BT[3]) to provide their users fast access bandwidth and reduce the load on mobile networks. Incentives and algorithms for Internet access sharing are investigated in [18] and many works focus on the deployment of architectures for ubiquitous WiFi access in metropolitan areas [9,24,28]. Systems for

---

[1] http://wefi.com/.

[2] http://www.fon.com.

[3] http://www.btwifi.co.uk/.

sharing WiFi passwords via online social network apps with trusted friends are described in [10,17,25]. Offloading in heterogeneous networks is modeled and analyzed in [26]. [16] presents available features for mobile traffic offloading, and [7,12,19] show that multipath TCP can be utilized for handovers between WiFi and mobile networks. [11] outlines approaches, which enable mobility and multihoming. Finally, WiFi onloading [23] is an opposed concept, which utilizes different peaks in mobile and fixed networks to onload data to the mobile network to support applications on short time scales.

The mobile network quality (WiFi/cellular) must be known to determine the energy consumption of individual connections. A number of studies focuses on analyzing the mobile network performance in terms of RTT and throughput of the user [22,27,30]. The expected performance for different network technologies can be derived from these data.

Energy models for smartphones were derived in a number of publications [5,13,31] for different devices and network technologies. Still, due to the steady progress in hardware development and changes in the network infrastructure and configuration, the transferability of these models is limited. Balasubramanian et al. [5] analyzed the influence of different network interfaces on the energy cost of different data transmissions. Power models for WiFi, 2G, and 3G connections including the connection setup and tear-down cost are analyzed, with the goal of developing an algorithm reducing the energy wasted in ramp and tail states. Zhang et al. [31] describe an approach to reduce the effort for creating power models for smartphones. This is demonstrated on the HTC One (hardware similar to the Nexus One), from which a detailed power model including the 3G power states is derived. Huang et al. [13] present a detailed analysis of the power characteristics of 4G networks in the US. Using the data from a dedicated user study, the different network states, their duration and power consumption are derived. From these models the energy cost of loading different web-pages is derived.

Comparative measurements conducted on the Nexus 5 still show a different picture. The ramp and tail states measured in 2014 are considerably shorter compared to [13]. Also, the measured data rates are considerably higher. Hence, in this work the results of independent measurements are used that were conducted on the Nexus 5, resulting in realistic power models for an operational 4G network in 2014.

3   Measurement and Model

In order to derive locations of mobile users in an urban area and the location and throughput of WiFi access points, we use different data sets and models. In the following the data sets derived by mobile network measurements and existing data sets are described. Further on, the video on demand traffic model and the applied energy model for mobile devices is described.

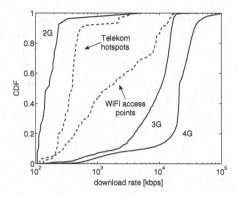

Fig. 1. Throughput of mobile connections for different access technologies.

3.1   Data Sets

To derive the throughput of mobile connections, we use the network performance data set, as described in [6]. The data was gathered in and around Darmstadt, Germany, using the NetworkCoverage App[4] [14]. For details please refer to [6,14]. The measurement consist of 4436 4G connections, 1043 3G, 23 2G, and 173 WiFi connections. The WiFi measurements were conducted mainly outdoors and reflect the variability of WiFi access rates.

Figure 1 shows the cumulative distribution function of the down-link throughput for different mobile access technologies. WiFi access is distinguished between hotspots by a major German provider (i.e., Deutsche Telekom) and other WiFi access points. Less than 10 % of connections with Telekom hotspots achieve a throughput higher than 10^3kbps. Since we investigate the potential of shared WiFi access points, we only consider the throughput of the other WiFi access points, which have a throughput higher than 10^3kbps in 60 % of the cases. 3G and 4G connections have highest throughput, where about half of the 3G connections get more than 10^4kbps and almost 90 % of the 4G connections.

To derive the location of WiFi access points in Darmstadt, a data set is used, consisting of 1527 AP locations measured in the inner city of Darmstadt. The measured APs are a mix of open and private APs, and hence are expected to match common usage patterns. In [20] the locations of the access points were interpolated from the observed WiFi beacons at street level.

In order to determine the location of end-users in the Darmstadt city area a street map of Darmstadt from OpenStreetMap [2] is used. As locations for end-users we use the way points provided in the street map that describe buildings, facilities, local businesses or sights. The way points are interconnected and used to define streets. The way points are all set up by users contributing to the OpenStreetMap platform.

---

[4] https://play.google.com/store/apps/details?id=de.tudarmstadt.networkcoverage accessed: 2015-01-21.

3.2   Video on Demand Traffic Model

To evaluate the energy efficiency of mobile video requests the traffic bursts generated in a video session have to be analyzed. For that purpose the arrivals and volumes of the traffic bursts need to be known. Current video streaming platforms and clients use an algorithm based on thresholds of the playback buffer to stream the video data with HTTP Range requests. This algorithm tries to maintain a certain level of the playback buffer that ensures smooth video playback and prevents the video from stalling, while keeping the amount of downloaded video data low.

To derive the bit rate and duration of videos streamed by mobile devices we use the results from [21] where the video formats in mobile networks were characterized by analysing 2000 videos streamed from the video on demand platform YouTube. The format selected depends on the YouTube player of the terminal used. The authors find that terminals using Android and iOS select format *itag*36 in more than 80 % of the streams. Figure 2 shows the cumulative distribution of video bit rates of the codec and durations for mobile videos in *itag*36. The majority of the videos have a bit rate between 220 and 250 kbps.

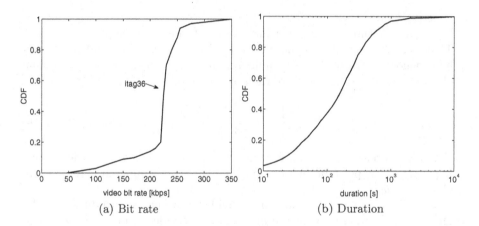

(a) Bit rate   (b) Duration

Fig. 2. Bit rate and duration of youtube videos in *itag*36 format [21].

We generate video requests by a Poisson process with rate λ. For each video request i we determine the duration d_i and mean bit rate b_i according to the empiric cumulative distributions from [21]. The volume of the video equals $v_i = d_i \cdot b_i$. We define two thresholds α and β in unit of seconds for the playback time buffered. If the buffered playback time drops below threshold α video data is downloaded and the buffer is filled. If the playback time buffered exceeds β the download of video data is paused and the traffic burst ends. At the time video i is requested $t_i = t_{i_1}$, the first traffic burst i_1 is downloaded. The video playback starts after the playback time buffered exceeds threshold α the first time. The throughput ρ_{i_j} received for burst j of request i is determined randomly according

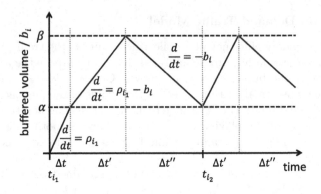

Fig. 3. Playback buffer in case of $\rho_{i_j} > b_i$.

to the access technology and its cumulative distribution function derived from the network performance data set described in Sect. 3.1. The time a traffic burst i_{j+1} is downloaded depends on the throughput ρ_{i_j} received for the preceding traffic burst i_j.

1. Case $\rho_{i_j} \leq b_i$:

   If $\rho_{i_j} \leq b_i$ the throughput is not high enough to increase the playback buffer. That means threshold β will not be reached, and the rest of the video data will be downloaded within burst i_j omitting burst i_{j+1}. In this case, the volume of burst i_j equals the volume of the remaining video data:

$$
v_{i_j} = \begin{cases} v_i & j = 1, \\ v_i - \sum_{k=1}^{j-1} v_{i_k} & j > 1. \end{cases}
\tag{1}
$$

   This also covers the case where the buffer runs dry and the video stalls, requiring a new pre-buffering phase for alpha seconds buffered video.

2. Case $\rho_{i_j} > b_i$:

   If $\rho_{i_j} > b_i$ the burst download can be divided in 3 phases with durations Δt, $\Delta t'$ and $\Delta t''$, c.f., Fig. 3. In the first phase, the video is pre-buffered, while the playback of the video is not yet started. This phase only exists for the first burst. Video data is downloaded with rate $\frac{d}{dt} = \rho_{i_j}$ until the threshold α is reached, i.e., $\alpha \cdot b_i = \rho_{i_j} \cdot \Delta t$ and

$$
\Delta t = \frac{\alpha \cdot b_i}{\rho_{i_j}}.
\tag{2}
$$

In the second phase, the playback buffer is filled until it reaches β while the video plays with bit rate b_i. Hence, the gradient of the buffer volume is $\frac{d}{dt} = \rho_{i_j} - b_i$ and video data with bit rate b_i is downloaded, containing $\beta - \alpha$ playback buffer. That means $(\beta - \alpha) \cdot b_i = (\rho_{i_j} - b_i) \cdot \Delta t'$ and

$$
\Delta t' = \frac{(\beta - \alpha) \cdot b_i}{\rho_{i_j} - b_i}.
\tag{3}
$$

In the third phase, the traffic burst ends and the download of video data is paused until the buffer drops below α. During playback the buffer decreases with gradient $\frac{d}{dt} = -b_i$, hence $(\alpha - \beta) \cdot b_i = -b_i \cdot \Delta t''$ and

$$\Delta t'' = \frac{(\alpha - \beta) \cdot b_i}{-b_i} = \beta - \alpha. \tag{4}$$

The time of burst i_{j+1} is calculated by adding the duration of the phases Δt, $\Delta t'$ and $\Delta t''$:

$$t_{i_{j+1}} = \begin{cases} t_{i_j} + \frac{\alpha \cdot b_i}{\rho_{i_j}} + \frac{(\beta - \alpha) \cdot b_i}{\rho_{i_j} - b_i} + (\beta - \alpha) & j = 1, \\ t_{i_j} + \frac{(\beta - \alpha) \cdot b_i}{\rho_{i_j} - b_i} + (\beta - \alpha) & j > 1. \end{cases} \tag{5}$$

The volume of burst i_j is calculated by accumulating the throughput during Δt and $\Delta t'$:

$$v_{i_j} = \begin{cases} \min(\alpha \cdot b_i + \rho_{i_j} \frac{(\beta - \alpha) \cdot b_i}{\rho_{i_j} - b_i}, v_i) & j = 1, \\ \min(\rho_{i_j} \frac{(\beta - \alpha) \cdot b_i}{\rho_{i_j} - b_i}, v_i - \sum_{k=1}^{j-1} v_{i_k}) & j > 1. \end{cases} \tag{6}$$

Given the arrival times t_{i_j} and volumes v_{i_j} of each burst i_j for video request i, we can calculate the energy consumption of the video requests based on the energy model.

3.3   Energy Model

In this work we focus on the energy consumption of mobile devices, which is most relevant for end-users, rather than also considering the energy consumed in base stations and access points. Due to the vast amount of mobile devices in use, small energy savings per mobile devices sum up to huge energy savings in total. As in [15] the energy consumption for the individual connections is determined by calculating the consumed energy based on power consumption models for the Nexus 5. The measurements were conducted in an office environment with good network availability and signal strength. The measured power consumption is expected to be similar for outdoor and indoor communication, as for commonly used power amplifiers in mobile phones the power consumption does not depend on the output power. For each technology, traffic flows with different data rates were received on the mobile phone while measuring the power consumption of the device using the built in voltage and current sensors. The power consumption of the interface is calculated by keeping the device configuration stable (e.g. display brightness, active components), and later removing the influence of the idle state by subtracting the average power consumption of this state. Such, the power consumption of the individual connections can be derived. The data rates were adjusted using the linux tool tc with a hierarchical token bucket (HTB) on the server. Hence, no bursty traffic was used for calibration.

The power models as derived from the measurements of Google's Nexus 5 are given in Fig. 4. The plot shows the lowest cost for WiFi connections, followed by

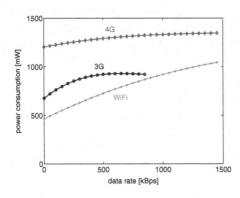
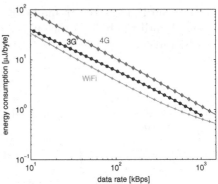

Fig. 4. Power consumption of the interfaces of the Google Nexus 5 at different data rates.

Fig. 5. Energy cost for receiving data on the respective interface of the Google Nexus 5 (excl. cost for ramp and tail).

the 3G and 4G connection. The derived model is valid for the typical data rates achieved on the respective interface.

Figure 4 includes the idle power consumption of the network interface, but not the idle power consumption of the mobile phone. The different offsets and slopes are caused by the different hardware components on the mobile phone. The average energy consumption per byte for a transfer of traffic with size S during time interval T is calculated by $\overline{E} = T \cdot \overline{P(r(t))}/S$, with power P at configured rate $r(t)$. This may be approximated by $E = P(r(t))/r(t)$ for constant bit rates, as in Fig. 5, which depicts the power while the interface is active converted to cost per byte transmitted.

The plot shows an exponential decrease of the energy expense per byte transmitted with increasing data rates. This depends on the fact that the idle time of the interface, which has little energy expense, increases with the data rate. The fraction of energy required to transmit one byte is particularly high for low data rates, as for high data rates the constant part is shared between a large number of packets. Analogue to Fig. 4, the cost per byte is lowest for WiFi, followed by 3G and 4G. Similar to the power consumption plot, the data rates for 3G approach 900 kBps. Higher data rates are only possible using WiFi or 4G.

The power model used in this publication includes the cost of connecting and disconnecting from the network. This is commonly referred to as ramp and tail energy. The power consumption and duration of these states was determined by evaluating the periods with higher energy consumption compared to the idle state before and after the data transmission. From this, the average power and duration of ramp and tail states is derived, and added to the total energy consumption. The power consumption of an exemplary connection is given in Fig. 6. The first 2 vertical markers indicate the begin and end of the ramp state (connecting to the network), while the second pair of markers indicate the end of the data transfer and end of the data connection, resembling the tail of the cellular connection.

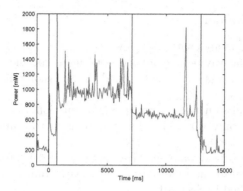

Fig. 6. Exemplary data transfer using the Nexus 5 on 3G. Indicated are the begin and end of the ramp state and begin and end of the tail state.

The resulting formula for a continuous data burst i_j with volume v_{i_j} is

$$E_{i_j} = E_{\text{ramp}} + E_{\text{tail}} + \frac{v_{i_j}}{\rho_{i_j}} \cdot P(\rho_{i_j}) = t_{\text{ramp}} \cdot P_{\text{ramp}} + t_{\text{tail}} \cdot P_{\text{tail}} + \frac{v_{i_j}}{\rho_{i_j}} \cdot P(\rho_{i_j}). \quad (7)$$

Further, $P(\rho_{i_j})$ is the interface power consumption during the transmission depending on the data rate ρ_{i_j}. The cost of transmitting at a given data rate is calculated based on the power models of the Nexus 5 as given in Fig. 4. For the course of this analysis, the power consumption and the data rate are considered to be constant over the duration of a single burst. The ramp and tail energies were derived from measurements for data transfers of finite duration. The measurements were repeated multiple times leading to the same results. Thus, the ramp and tail energies are considered as constants as given in Table 1.

Table 1. Ramp and tail durations and the derived energy consumption.

	t_{ramp} [s]	t_{tail} [s]	E_{ramp} [J]	E_{tail} [J]
3G	1.0	5.0	0.4	3.5
4G	0.1	2.0	0.1	1.2
WiFi	0.2	0.2	0.2	0.1

The individual connections and their duration are identified by iterating through the requested data bursts i_j. If the interval between two bursts i_j and i_{j+1} is smaller than the ramp and tail durations t_{ramp} and t_{tail}, the bursts are combined and the ramp and tail energies E_{ramp} and E_{tail} are added only once to the energy calculated for request i. This corresponds to the time-out for bearer release in cellular networks.

3.4   Simulation Model

As in [6] we consider an area with a set of way points W and a set of access points A. The location of the way points and access points is specified by longitude and latitude. Each access point $\alpha \in A$ has a fixed transmission range r and is shared with probability p_{share}.

For given transmission range r we define a function $\chi_r : A \times W \mapsto \{0, 1\}$, where χ_r returns 1, only if a way point $w \in W$ is in transmission range of an access point $a \in A$, else 0.

As set of way points W and set of access points A we use the way points from OpenStreetMap in the inner city area of Darmstadt and the interpolated access points described in Sect. 3.1.

The procedure of one run simulating n mobile requests is described in the following. A subset $A_s \subset A$ of shared access points is randomly chosen according to the sharing probability p_{share}. For each mobile request $1 \leq i \leq n$ a random way point $w_i \in W$ is determined. The mobile request i can be offloaded, if a shared WiFi access point is in range, i.e. $\exists a \in A_s | \chi_r(w_i, a) = 1$. With

$$off(i) = \begin{cases} 1, & \exists a \in A_s | \chi_r(w_i, a) = 1, \\ 0, & \text{else}. \end{cases} \tag{8}$$

the WiFi offloading potential is calculated by the amount of offloaded requests:

$$\overline{off} = \frac{1}{n} \sum_{1 \leq i \leq n} off(i). \tag{9}$$

If the mobile request can be offloaded, WiFi is used as access technology. If the request cannot be offloaded the request is served by the cellular network which uses 3G or 4G access technology, where, according to Sect. 3.1, 4G is available in approximately 4 out of 5 connections, else 3G is used. The throughput ρ_i received for request i is determined randomly according to the access technology and its cumulative distribution function derived from the network performance data set described in Sect. 3.1.

The model is limited in not considering temporal and spatial dynamics of users and cell capacities. The throughput received for a request does not consider the cell load or the load on the WiFi access point and the distance to the antenna. However, the throughput received is derived from real traces, which mitigates these impairments.

4   Simulation Results

In the following we describe simulation results to show the WiFi offloading potential in an urban environment dependent on the WiFi sharing probability. The results can be used by operators to assess the feasibility of establishing WiFi offloading according to their cellular network coverage, or to estimate the

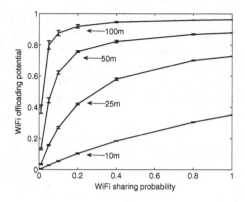

Fig. 7. Amount of mobile connections offloaded to WiFi dependent on sharing probability for different access point transmission ranges.

amount of users that share their access point, which is necessary to get a good WiFi coverage.

The results show mean values with 95 % confidence intervals of 10 runs with different random number seeds and $n = 10^6$ mobile requests in each run. We investigate the impact of the WiFi sharing probability on the WiFi offloading potential. As the transmission range of WiFi access points depends on the environment, the number of active connections and its configuration, we show results for different transmission ranges. Figure 7 shows the amount of mobile connections offloaded to WiFi $\overline{off}$ dependent on the WiFi sharing probability p_{share}. The WiFi offloading potential is depicted for different transmission ranges r. If a transmission range of only 10 m is assumed, the WiFi offloading potential is rather low and increases almost linearly with the WiFi sharing probability. Roughly every second mobile connection can be offloaded for a transmission range of 25 meters if 40 % of the access points are shared and 3 of 4 connections can be offloaded if every access point is shared.

If a WiFi transmission range of 50 m is assumed, a decent WiFi offloading potential is obtained if only 10 % percent of WiFi access points in an inner city area are shared. Hence, to obtain a good WiFi coverage, incentive mechanisms have to be designed, such that at least 10 % of WiFi access points are shared.

We use the traffic model described in Sect. 3.2 together with the energy model described in Sect. 3.3 to evaluate the energy consumption of mobile video requests for different access technologies. The buffer thresholds of the video on demand traffic model are set to $\alpha = 30$ s and $\beta = 100$ s, according to [21]. To compare the energy consumption of the mobile access technologies we generate 10^5 video requests for each access technology and calculate the energy consumption. Figure 8 shows the cumulative distribution of the consumed energy in Joule for mobile access technologies 3G, 4G and WiFi. Using 4G as access technology, generally less energy is consumed on the end-device as using 3G. The minimum energy consumption is achieved using WiFi access technology. However, WiFi

consumes more energy than 3G in more than 60 % of the requests and WiFi
consumes more energy than 4G in more than 80 % of the requests. This depends
on the fact that the energy consumption decreases exponentially with the data
rates and that the data rates obtained for WiFi in the measurements are very
poor compared to 3G and 4G. Hence, although WiFi is more energy efficient
than 3G and 4G for equal data rates, it consumes more energy in this case due
to lower data rates.

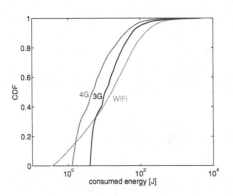
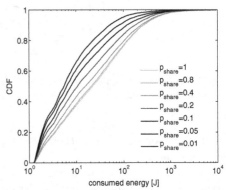

Fig. 8. Energy consumption for different mobile access technologies.

Fig. 9. Energy consumption for different WiFi sharing probabilities.

To investigate the impact of WiFi offloading on the energy consumption of
mobile devices, we conduct a parameter study on the sharing probability and set
the WiFi transmission range to 25 m in the following. We generate 10^5 requests
and determine the access technology according to the WiFi offloading simulation described in Sect. 3.4. Figure 9 shows the energy consumption for different
WiFi sharing probabilities. The energy consumption generally increases with the
WiFi sharing probability. The amount of requests that consume less than 10 J
decreases about one third if the WiFi sharing probability is increased from 1 % to
100 %. This depends on the fact that the throughput received for WiFi is rather
small in the underlying measurements. For high sharing probabilities there is a
saturation effect, because the increase of WiFi coverage diminishes due to the
fact that WiFi access points overlap.

Our results show that poor WiFi conditions lead to a higher energy consumption of mobile devices, which offload their video sessions to WiFi. However,
the minimum energy consumption for mobile video requests is achieved using
WiFi access technology by receiving a good connection with high throughput.
This suggests a high density of WiFi access points to reduce energy consumption of mobile devices and load on cellular networks by WiFi offloading. Here we
focus on outdoor users. In the end most video traffic is consumed indoors, where
strong WiFi rates and poor cellular rates occur. Considering this, the potential
of saving energy by WiFi offloading is even higher according to our results that
show low energy consumption for WiFi connections with high throughput.

5   Conclusion

The increasing number of mobile users and the growing popularity of video streaming puts high loads on cellular networks. To cope with this demand, mobile connections can be offloaded to WiFi networks. Especially in urban environments a high coverage of WiFi access points can be beneficial to stream video sessions to mobile devices while keeping their energy consumption low. To investigate the impact of WiFi offloading on the energy consumption of mobile devices during video streaming, we develop a generic model for traffic bursts in current video on demand services and model the energy consumption of current mobile devices for different access technologies. We use existing measurements to derive the throughput of mobile access technologies 3G, 4G, and WiFi in an urban area and develop a simulation model that generates mobile video requests. Applying our models, we assess the energy consumed by mobile video request based on the access technology and received bandwidth. Our results show that slightly increasing WiFi coverage has a high potential to take load off the cellular network. Due to lower throughput compared to 3G and 4G, derived in the provided data sets, the energy consumption increases with the amount of video connections offloaded to WiFi. However, minimal energy consumption is achieved by connections offloaded to WiFi that receive a high throughput. This could be achieved by a high coverage of WiFi access points.

Acknowledgement. This work has been supported in parts by the EU (FP7/#317 846, SmartenIT and FP7/#318398, eCOUSIN) and the DFG as part of the CRC 1053 MAKI. The authors would like to acknowledge valuable feedback by the reviewers and comments by their colleagues and project partners.

References

1. City of London WiFi network. https://www.cityoflondon.gov.uk/business/commercial-property/utilities-and-infrastructure-/Pages/wi-fi.aspx
2. OpenStreetMap. http://www.openstreetmap.org/export#map=14/49.8788/8.6628
3. Public Wi-Fi Berlin. http://www.visitberlin.de/en/article/w-lan-for-all-public-wi-fi-berlin
4. Wireless@SG. http://www.ida.gov.sg/Learning/Technology-You/Wireless-SG
5. Balasubramanian, N., Balasubramanian, A., Venkataramani, A.: Energy consumption in mobile phones: a measurement study and implications for network applications. In: Proceedings of the ACM SIGCOMM Conference on Internet Measurement, pp. 280–293. ACM, New York, NY, USA (2009)
6. Burger, V., Seufert, M., Kaup, F., Wichtlhuber, M., Hausheer, D., Tran-Gia, P.: Impact of WiFi offloading on video streaming QoE in urban environments. In: IEEE Workshop on Quality of Experience-based Management for Future Internet Applications and Services (QoE-FI). London, UK (2015)
7. Chen, S., Yuan, Z., Muntean, G.M.: An energy-aware multipath-TCP-based content delivery scheme in heterogeneous wireless networks. In: Proceedings of the IEEE Wireless Communications and Networking Conference (WCNC). Shanghai, China (2013)

8. Cisco: Cisco Visual Networking Index: Global Mobile Data Traffic Forecast Update, 2014–2019. Technical report, Cisco (2015)
9. Dimatteo, S., Hui, P., Han, B., Li, V.O.: Cellular traffic offloading through wifi networks. In: 8th IEEE International Conference on Mobile Adhoc and Sensor Systems (MASS). Valencia, Spain (2011)
10. Donelson, L.J., Sweet, C.W.: Method, Apparatus and System for Wireless Network Authentication Through Social Networking. US Patent App. 13/287,931 (2012)
11. Gladisch, A., Daher, R., Tavangarian, D.: Survey on mobility and multihoming in future internet. Wirel. Pers. Commun. **74**(1), 45–81 (2014)
12. Gonzalez, M., Higashino, T., Okada, M.: Radio access considerations for data offloading with multipath TCP in Cellular/WiFi networks. In: Proceedings of the International Conference on Information Networking (ICOIN). Bangkok, Thailand (2013)
13. Huang, J., Quian, F., Gerber, A., Mao, Z.M., Sen, S., Spatscheck, O., Qian, F.: A Close Examination of Performance and Power Characteristics of 4G LTE Networks. In: MobiSys, pp. 225–238 (2012)
14. Kaup, F., Jomrich, F., Hausheer, D.: Demonstration of networkcoverage - a mobile network performance measurement app. In: Proceedings of the International Conference on Networked Systems (NetSys 2015). Cottbus, Germany (2015)
15. Kaup, F., Wichtlhuber, M., Rado, S., Hausheer, D.: Can Multipath TCP Save Energy? A Measuring and Modeling Study of MPTCP Energy Consumption. In: IEEE LCN (2015)
16. Khadraoui, Y., Lagrange, X., Gravey, A.: A Survey of Available Features for Mobile Traffic Offload. In: Proceedings of the 20th European Wireless Conference. Barcelona, Spain (2014)
17. Lafuente, C.B., Titi, X., Seigneur, J.M.: Flexible communication: a secure and trust-based free wi-fi password sharing service. In: Proceedings of the 10th IEEE International Conference on Trust, Security and Privacy in Computing and Communications (TrustCom). Changsha, China (2011)
18. Mamatas, L., Psaras, I., Pavlou, G.: Incentives and algorithms for broadband access sharing. In: Proceedings of the ACM SIGCOMM Workshop on Home Networks. New Delhi, India (2010)
19. Paasch, C., Detal, G., Duchene, F., Raiciu, C., Bonaventure, O.: Exploring mobile/wifi handover with multipath TCP. In: Proceedings of the ACM SIG-COMM Workshop on Cellular Networks: Operations, Challenges, and Future Design. Helsinki, Finland (2012)
20. Panitzek, K., Schweizer, I., Bönning, T., Seipel, G., Mühlhäuser, M.: First responder communication in urban environments. Int. J. Mobile Netw. Des. Innovation **4**(2), 109–118 (2012)
21. Ramos-Muñoz, J.J., Prados-Garzon, J., Ameigeiras, P., Navarro-Ortiz, J., López-Soler, J.M.: Characteristics of mobile youtube traffic. IEEE Wirel. Commun. **21**(1), 18–25 (2014)
22. Rosen, S., Yao, H., Nikravesh, A., Jia, Y., Choffnes, D., Mao, Z.M.: Demo: mapping global mobile performance trends with mobilyzer and mobiperf. In: Proceedings of the 12th International Conference on Mobile Systems, Applications, and Services (MobiSys 2014). Bretton Woods, NH, USA (2014)
23. Rossi, C., Vallina-Rodriguez, N., Erramilli, V., Grunenberger, Y., Gyarmati, L., Laoutaris, N., Stanojevic, R., Papagiannaki, K., Rodriguez, P.: 3GOL: power-boosting ADSL using 3G onloading. In: Proceedings of the 9th Conference on Emerging Networking Experiments and Technologies (CoNEXT). Santa Barbara, CA, USA (2013)

24. Sastry, N., Crowcroft, J., Sollins, K.: Architecting citywide ubiquitous wi-fi access. In: Proceedings of the 6th Workshop on Hot Topics in Networks (HotNets). Atlanta, GA, USA (2007)

25. Seufert, M., Burger, V., Hoßfeld, T.: HORST - Home router sharing based on trust. In: Proceedings of the Workshop on Social-aware Economic Traffic Management for Overlay and Cloud Applications (SETM 2013). Zurich, Switzerland (2013)

26. Singh, S., Dhillon, H.S., Andrews, J.G.: Offloading in heterogeneous networks: modeling, analysis, and design insights. IEEE Trans. Wirel. Commun. 12(5), 2484–2497 (2013)

27. Sonntag, S., Manner, J., Schulte, L.: Netradar-measuring the wireless world. In: Proceedings of the 11th International Symposium on Modeling & Optimization in Mobile, Ad Hoc & Wireless Networks (WiOpt 2013). Tsukuba Science City, Japan (2013)

28. Vidales, P., Manecke, A., Solarski, M.: Metropolitan public wifi access based on broadband sharing. In: Proceedings of the Mexican International Conference on Computer Science (ENC 2009). Mexico City, Mexico (2009)

29. Wireless Broadband Alliance: WBA Industry Report 2011: Global Developments in Public Wi-Fi. Technical report (2011)

30. Wittie, M.P., Stone-Gross, B., Almeroth, K.C., Belding, E.M.: MIST: cellular data network measurement for mobile applications. In: Proceedings of the 4th International Conference on Broadband Communications, Networks and Systems (BROADNETS 2007). Raleigh, NC, USA (2007)

31. Zhang, L., Tiwana, B., Dick, R.P., Qian, Z., Mao, Z., Wang, Z., Yang, L.: Accurate online power estimation and automatic battery behavior based power model generation for smartphones. In: CODES + ISSS'10. ACM (2010)

On the Use of Emulation Techniques over the ns-3 Platform to Analyze Multimedia Service QoS

Juan Arroyo, Luis Diez[✉], and Ramón Agüero

University of Cantabria, Santander, Spain
jaarsolares@gmail.com, {ldiez,ramon}@tlmat.unican.es

Abstract. This paper presents an assessment study on the use of emulation techniques to evaluate the performance of multimedia services, in particular a video streaming application. The proposed methodology exploits the emulation functionality that has been integrated into the ns-3 simulation platform, as well as virtualization techniques. We describe the requirements and the main limitations of the scheme, in order to offer an appropriate accuracy. Last, and in order to assess the feasibility of the proposed scheme and its potential, we carry out a study of various QoS parameters of a video streaming application.

1 Introduction

The growing presence of advanced mobile terminals and the way they are being used are causing a great change on the mobile data traffic. According to the latest reports [1], video streaming sessions are believed to become the predominant type of traffic in the forthcoming years. This is of course posing several challenges to the mobile operators, that need to face an unexpected resource demand. Different algorithms, techniques and solutions, are being proposed to overcome this situation.

In order to assess the feasibility and efficiency of such proposals, the use of real implementations is usually not an option, since the available technology might not be able to provide the required functionality or simply because it is not realistic trying to emulate the conditions under which the assessment should be carried out. As a consequence, the use of simulation techniques is gaining more and more popularity. One of the criticisms about this approach is that in some cases, this simulation-based analysis is not realistic, especially considering the characteristics of the lower layers as well as the details of the real services.

In this paper we focus on this latter point, since we study an approach to enhance the realism of a simulation-based study, thanks to the recent advances in virtualization. The Network Simulator 3 (ns-3) framework [2] allows the use of virtual nodes, able to run real applications, which can be connected to the simulator so that they would use the network technology it provides. That would bring several advantages, since we could, for instance, better understand the effect that a particular type of errors might have over a multimedia-flow; it goes

© Institute for Computer Sciences, Social Informatics and Telecommunications Engineering 2015
R. Agüero et al. (Eds.): MONAMI 2015, LNICST 158, pp. 196–208, 2015.
DOI: 10.1007/978-3-319-26925-2_15

without saying that being able to reproduce similar conditions is one of the clear
limitations of carrying out a characterization over real testbeds.

The rest of the paper is structured as follows: Sect. 2 discusses some works
that have used the same simulation strategy to analyze the performance of
some services. Afterwards, Sect. 3 discusses the main conclusions that can be
extracted when exploiting the ns-3 as an emulation tool; first, we analyze the
constraints that are inherent to ns-3, and afterwards, the tool is used to study
the behavior of video services over multi-hop wireless networks. Finally, Sect. 4
concludes the paper, advocating a number of research lines that we will tackle in
our future work, exploiting the acquired know-how and the possibilities that are
brought about by the combination of a network simulation tool and virtualization
techniques.

2   Foundations and Related Work

Network simulation platforms have become a key tool for the scientific and
research community. In spite of the recent looming of various testbed initiatives,
simulation still offers a greater degree of flexibility, making it a very attractive
tool for the initial steps of the research of novel aspects and topics (for instance,
network coding). Among others, one of its main advantages is that it brings
about the possibility to analyze large and complex network topologies, on both
a cost and time effective manner. As a consequence, there are still a large number
of research works that involve the use of network simulation.

In any case, and despite the aforementioned advantages, the interaction with
the *real world* becomes in some cases an essential aspect. It is particularly relevant when the goal is to analyze the impact of specific networking technology,
entity or solution might have over specific services (e.g. real-time applications). In
order to address this need, ns-3 provides a set of capabilities that allow its closer
interaction with real entities at different levels [3], as it is depicted in Table 1.
As can be seen, depending on the selected configuration, different entities of
the communication system (final nodes or network infrastructure) can be simulated and afterwards integrated with real systems. In this work, we focus on the
interaction of networks that are simulated in ns-3 with real nodes (indicated in
Table 1 as **NS3-TAP**), exploiting virtualization capabilities; this configuration
brings about the possibility of running real applications over simulated network
infrastructures. In the remainder of the paper we will refer to this approach as
emulation.

Table 1. NS3 interactions with *real world*

	Networks		
		Real	Simulated
Nodes	Real	Host	**NS3-TAP**
	Simulated	NS3-EMU	Simulation

In order to interact with real nodes, ns-3 provides an interface between the simulated and the real systems, the so-called *NS3-TAP*, which can be connected to virtual bridges of the host computer. The most typical setup for this emulation entails Linux Containers (LXC) [4], which offers the possibility of including *light* virtualized nodes, where real applications may be embedded. From the host point of view, a virtual bridge defines a network within the host, and both the container embedding the application and the *NS3-TAP* are connected to it. Besides, the *NS3-TAP* is also attached to a simulated node, and the data sent by the LXC virtual node can be in fact forwarded to the simulated node. Furthermore, the interaction with real applications requires that the simulated time (that internally managed by the simulator) is aligned with the system clock. To achieve this, ns-3 provides a configurable scheduling mechanism, which can be configured to use the system clock (instead of the internal simulated time) when scheduling the various events happening during a simulation. Throughout the paper we will study the performance and the limitations exhibited by the simulator when using this configuration, paying special attention to the accuracy of the real time scheduling.

There are some works that have successfully exploited this emulation capability over different network technologies and using various applications. For instance, in [5,6] the authors use the ns-3 emulation capability to study the performance of video applications over LTE networks, focusing on the impact that handovers might have over the Quality of Service (QoS) perceived at the receiver application. Nevertheless, they do not discuss whether the simulator has any limitations to carry out such type of experiments or how it was configured.

Other works have focused on the applications. For instance, [7] developed, over an emulated environment, a tool to measure both the QoS and the Quality of Experience (QoE) of video applications with a modified version of the VLC player. In this case, the authors do mention the real-time scheduling limitations (in particular the *HardLimit* parameter that will be extensively discussed in Sect. 3), but the results they discuss are rather limited, restricted to the particular scenario they used.

Finally, other works specifically study the limitations of the simulator, but they do it from a different perspective. The authors of [8] propose a distributed ns-3 emulation, to share the computational load between a number of real systems. Although this approach is able to reduce the computation time, there exist some network topologies that would not allow the use of distributed systems. One important example are wireless networks, where different nodes share the same physical channel, preventing the nodes from being moved to different machines, since that would not allow emulating the interaction of the lower layer mechanisms in an appropriate way.

3   Experimental Evaluation

In order to assess the feasibility of the ns-3 platform to exploit emulation techniques (i.e. run real applications/services over simulated network topologies), this section presents some of the most relevant results that were obtained after an extensive simulation campaign that had a twofold objective: first, Subsect. 3.1 discusses, based on a number of topologies with increasing complexity, the limitations exhibited by the simulator. Afterwards, Subsect. 3.2 discusses an evaluation of real video traffic (in terms of QoS) that was carried out as a proof-of-concept, describing the impact that this type of applications might have on the simulator.

It is important to mention that all the results presented herewith have been obtained with a laptop ASUS $S500CA$, equipped with an Intel Core $i5 - 3317U@1.7$ GHz microprocessor and 8 GB of RAM memory. We have used Ubuntu $14.04LTS(64bits)$ as the operating system.

3.1 Impact of the Simulator Performance on the Real-Time Scheduling

We start by studying the impact of the number of devices over the validity of the methodology. We are therefore interested in finding the limit that might guarantee an appropriate accuracy.

In order to better understand the results that will be shown afterwards, it is worth summarizing how ns-3 can be configured to use emulation techniques. ns-3 is an event-driven simulator, where the different events that happen during an experiment are enqueued according to the *simulation time* they take place. In its normal operation, as soon as one event has been handled, the following one is taken care of. However, emulation purposes the simulator exploits the system clock, and the events are processed according to the actual time. In this sense, if a large number of events take place within a short period, the simulator might get overloaded and a delay between the time an event had to be handled and the moment it actually was differs; we call this difference Simulation Delay (SD).

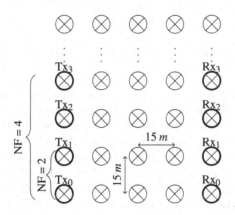

Fig. 1. Simulation scenario with a given number of traffic flows

The simulator allows the user to set a maximum value of SD by means of a configuration parameter called *HardLimit*; hence, if the SD exceeds this value,

the simulation is aborted. In this section, we study the evolution of the SD under
different network topologies. We pay special attention to the number of physical
devices that are deployed, since they share the same physical channel, and this
leads to a large number of events that are scheduled when a single packet is sent,
regardless a node is directly involved in the communication or not. In this sense,
all physical devices need to be checked when a packet is sent, which might lead
to a bottleneck at running time. It is worth highlighting that this circumstance
takes place at he physical layer, so that it could not be solved by using multiple
machines, and it has also become an important challenge for the parallelization
efforts that have been carried out within the simulator framework.

The topologies under study in this section consider a uniform grid structure,
see Fig. 1. The nodes have been configured to use Ad hoc On-Demand Distance
Vector Routing (AODV) as routing protocol, while the distance between the
traffic sources and the corresponding destination nodes is 4 hops. The traffic
flows are modeled as Constant Bit Rate (CBR) traffic and we have executed
simulations of 15 s.

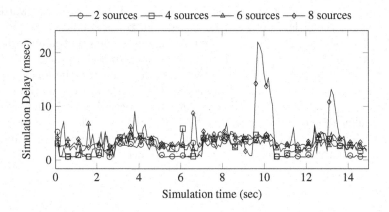

Fig. 2. Simulation delay evolution in a single experiment with 50 nodes

As an illustrative example, Fig. 2 shows the evolution of the SD value during
one simulation, for different number of flows and considering 50 WiFi nodes. The
results reveal that, in spite of the presence of delay peaks, the simulator is able
to maintain a low and constant difference with the real time. This peaky effect
at the beginning is due to the scheduling several of events at some particular
moments (e.g. when the nodes send the AODV *HELLO* message). It can be
therefore conclude that with an strict value for the *HardLimit* parameter some
scenarios would be considered as unacceptable for certain requirements, while
that particular threshold might be only exceeded at a particular time.

Figure 3 shows the Cumulative Distribution Function (CDF) of the SD value,
initiating different number of flows in the scenario. The figures have been
obtained by measuring the SD every 100 ms and for 20 simulations, yielding
a number of around 3000 samples per configuration. As can be observed, ns-3 is

able to appropriately simulate WiFi ad-hoc networks with up to 50 nodes with a reasonably good degree of accuracy. In this sense, Fig. 3a shows that more than 90 % of the samples showed a SD less than 5 ms, but for the scenario with the highest number of traffic sources, 8. In this latter case, the corresponding traffic jeopardizes the real-time accuracy.

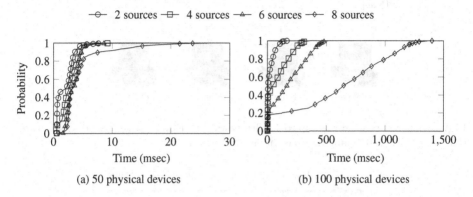

Fig. 3. Simulation delay with 50 physical devices for different number of traffic sources

On the other hand, an increase of the number of physical devices, see Fig. 3b, has a strong impact on the SD value. In this case, 90 % of SD values for 2, 4 and 6 traffic sources is below 500 ms (leading to a $\approx \times 100$ increase as compared to the previous scenario) while the observed values with 8 flows would not mostly be acceptable.

In light of the results, some interesting conclusions can be extracted. The first one is that a hard constraint of the SD might not be always desirable, since the value of this parameter fluctuates along time, and the simulator might be able to recover from temporary maladjustment. We have also seen that, for the studied scenarios, while the number of traffic flows does not have a strong impact over the methodology accuracy, the number of physical devices within the scenario can definitively limit the validity of the emulation capabilities.

3.2   Evaluation of Video Applications

This section illustrates the evaluation of a real video streaming application, by using the emulation capability of ns-3. To this end, we have embedded instances of VLC player within LXC virtual devices. In order to have a finer control over the network, the coverage range of the WiFi nodes has been fixed to avoid collisions between packets belonging to different flows; in particular, we have used a disc propagation model with a maximum range of 15 m. It is worth highlighting that the 802.11 protocol implementation within the simulator does not prevent the different devices from contending for the channel, even if they are outside the coverage range of the transmitter (within the carrier sensing range).

First, we have carried out a number of simulations to study the effects that real applications might have over the emulation behavior. For that, we have

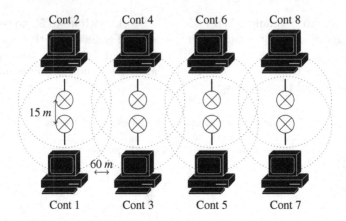

Fig. 4. General scenario with up to 4 video flows. The PCs represent Linux Containers that are attached to simulated WiFi nodes

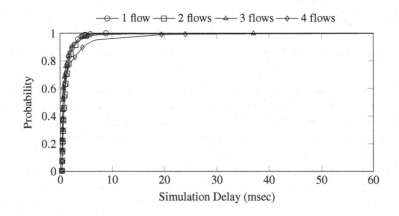

Fig. 5. Simulation delay with real video traffic

established a simple scenario in which the number of video flows is increased; Fig. 4 shows an illustrative example with 4 flows. As can be seen, each video flow implies a pair of LXC devices; furthermore, the various flows do not interfere with each other.

The performance metrics obtained from this scenario, but those corresponding to the SD, are always measured over the first pair of containers (1 and 2, see Fig. 4), allowing us to study the influence of the traffic load. Besides, 20 independent experiments of each configuration have been performed, ensuring the statistical validity of the results.

Figure 5 depicts the CDF of the SD parameter, considering different number of active flows. SD values have been again measured every 100 ms in each simulation. As can be seen, the simulator is able to carry out an appropriate emulation, with SD values below 30 ms up to when 4 traffic flows were active.

Comparing these results with those discussed previously, we can conclude that the number of devices deployed within the scenario has a stronger impact than the traffic load.

Once we have analyzed the performance of the proposed methodology when using real applications, i.e. with realistic traffic patterns, a number of illustrative QoS metrics are analyzed. First, Fig. 6 shows the application jitter, that has been measured as the gap between two consecutive packets at the receiver. The results reveal the shallow influence of the number of video flows over this metric, since all the values are very close to 0, as can be observed in Fig. 6a. Indeed, Fig. 6b, the zoomed version of Fig. 6a, shows that more than 90 % jitter samples are below 2.5 ms. The figure also yields the appearance of jitter peaks, that can be inferred from the small percentage of samples with values near 1 s.

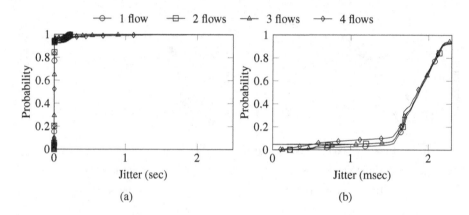

Fig. 6. CDF of the packet jitter upon different number of video flows

Afterwards, we have analyzed the end-to-end delay of the application packets, which is represented in Fig. 7. In this case, the results show that the delay increases as long as the number of traffic flows gets higher. As was previously said, all nodes generate events related to channel contention. This is clearly seen with the packet delay increase for the scenarios embracing 3 and 4 flows.

Finally, using the same scenario we have measured the data rate of the flows as they leave and enter the target containers. Figure 8 shows the CDF of the throughput experienced by the applications during one session; the throughput has been measured, alike the SD parameter, every 100 ms at both the transmission and reception sides of the first pair of containers. As can be seen, the presence of a larger number of video flows (more instances of video applications), has a clear impact on both the transmission and reception data rate. Since this particular parameter is measured at the simulator 'entry-point', we understand that the corresponding impact is due to the computer processing capacity.

So as to illustrate one of the advantages of the proposed methodology, we configure some of the wireless channels to induce errors. In this case, the scenario embraces a video server that, simultaneously, sends the same stream to two

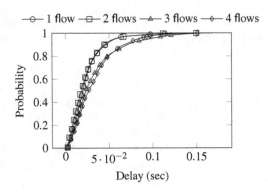

Fig. 7. CDF of the packet delay upon different number of video flows

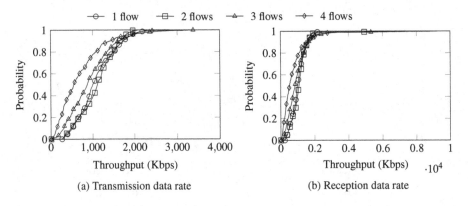

Fig. 8. CDF of the throughput of the first flow upon different number of video flows

clients. The scenario has been designed so that the channel conditions between
the server and each client are different. Figure 9 illustrates the particular network
topology; the video clients, **Client1** and **Client2**, require 4 and 2 hops to connect
to the server, respectively. Besides, the channel conditions, that are established
with the Frame Error Rate (FER), are worse in the route between the server
and **Client1**. In this case, in order to analyze the behavior in a more realistic
situation, we have carried out experiments lasting for several minutes.

Figure 10 depicts the throughput transmitted by the server and observed at
each client. The results show that the throughput value at **Client2** is slightly
higher than that measured at **Client1**; this is due to the more hostile channel
conditions in this latter case (the corresponding path has more hops and the FER
is also higher). Besides, the results also evidence that, while the throughput at
the clients is rather constant (tightly around 1 Mbps), the application throughput
at the server oscillates between 1 and 5 Mbps. It is worth highlighting that this
kind of metric, as well as the packets sent by the application from the clients to
the server, could not be correctly characterized using synthetic traffic models,

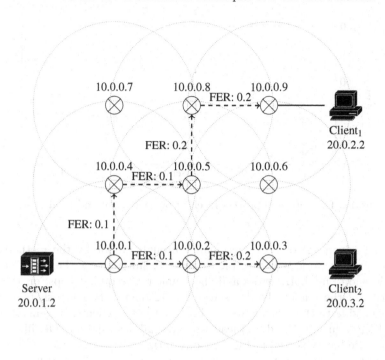

Fig. 9. Scenario with channel errors (FER)

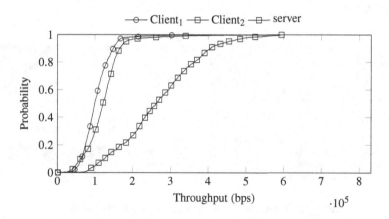

Fig. 10. CDF of the throughput experienced by the users and sent by the server

which are usually implemented in network simulators and traditionally used in various research works.

Figure 11 shows the percentage of packets that was received by each client, as well as the losses that were observed. As can be seen, in both cases there exists a significant packet loss, which is slightly higher for **Client1**, as a consequence of the worse conditions over the path it uses to connect to the server.

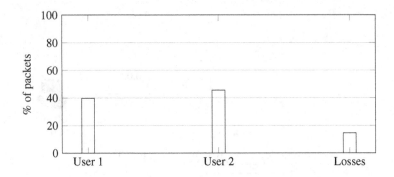

Fig. 11. Percentage of packets received by each client and total losses

Taking advantage of the functionality brought about by the methodology proposed in this work, it is possible to analyze, subjectively, the impact of the channel conditions, both errors and the number of required hops, on the user perception of the quality. In this sense, Fig. 12 depicts two snapshots, each of them belonging to the video flows received by the two clients, In general, moderated FER values (0.1 and 0.2) lead to a gradual degradation. The illustrative snapshots we have selected in Fig. 12 capture this general behavior, the quality of **Client1** is much worse. In general we can conclude that multi-hop wireless networks might have a rather negative impact over the performance of this type of applications.

(a) Client 1   (b) Client 2

Fig. 12. Example of video captures for both clients

4   Conclusion

In this work we have presented a methodology that promotes the use of emulation techniques to analyze video services over simulation platforms. It exploits the functionalities offered by the ns-3 tool, which allow its interaction with real systems. In particular, we have carried out an illustrative study on the behavior of real streaming video services when used over multi-hop wireless networks, using WiFi technology.

First, we have thoroughly studied the limitations exhibited by the simulator to appropriately tackle real-time emulation tasks, as well as other parameters that might impact the accuracy of the results that can be obtained. This first analysis yielded that, int he scenarios under study, the number of physical devices that are deployed in the corresponding scenario has a great impact over the capacity of the simulator to perform a real-time execution. On the other hand we have also observed that its influence is much stronger than the one due to a traffic load increase, since even those nodes not actively participating in the communications generate a relatively large number of events that the simulator needs to handle.

Besides, we have also seen some particular behaviors that might be attributed to the characteristics of the machine that was used to carry out all the experiments. In order to overcome them, a possible solution would be (when the number of active services is large) to transfer some of the applications to other (physical) hosts; this would help to alleviate the computational burden of the machine used to simulate the wireless network.

Finally, we have assessed the feasibility of the proposed methodology by studying the behavior of a real video service (using the VLC application), considering both ideal (error-free) wireless channels and the presence of errors induced by wireless propagation impairments. The obtained results show the behavior that might have been expected, validating the capability of the presented approach to carry out the evaluation of real applications over 'simulated' network deployments. We have indeed observed unexpected traffic patterns, which might not be reproduced with synthetic models (those traditionally used over simulation platforms), as another indication of the possibilities brought by this technique. It is important to mention that the approach ensures the possibility of systematically using a scenario with the very same conditions (reproducible in different experiments), providing it with a great flexibility, which was in fact one of the main pursued goals.

Regarding our future work, we are planning to exploit the proposed technique to broaden the analysis of different solutions over multi-hop wireless networks, including network coding, routing algorithms, etc., introducing real applications on top of them. On the other hand, as a more direct extension of the work presented herewith, we will also characterize the emulation capacity of the ns-3 platform, using other communication technologies, in particular LTE, due to its growing relevance.

Acknowledgment. This work has been supported by the Spanish Government by its funding through the project **COSAIF**, *"Connectivity as a Service: Access for the Internet of the Future"* (TEC2012-38754-C02-01).

References

1. CISCO: Visual Networking Index (VNI) Global Mobile Data Traffic Forecast Updateis part of the comprehensive Cisco VNI Forecast, an ongoing initiative to trackand forecast the impact of visual networking applications on global networks, February 2014
2. Network simulator 3. http://www.nsnam.org/
3. Howto make ns-3 interact with the real world. https://www.nsnam.org/wiki/HOWTO_make_ns-3_interact_with_the_real_world
4. Howto use linux containers to set up virtual networks. https://www.nsnam.org/wiki/HOWTO_Use_Linux_Containers_to_set_up_virtual_networks
5. Molloy, T., Yuan, Z., Muntean, G.-M.: Real time emulation of an lte network using ns-3. In: Irish Signals Systems Conference 2014 and 2014 China-Ireland International Conference on Information and Communications Technologies (ISSC 2014/CIICT 2014). 25th IET, June 2014, pp. 251–257 (2014)
6. Fouda, A., Ragab, A.N., Esswie, A., Marzban, M., Naser, A., Rehan, M., Ibrahim, A.S.: Real time video streaming over NS3 based emulated LTE networks. Int. J. Electr. Commun. Comput. Technol.(IJECCT) **4**(3) (2014)
7. Bustos-Jimenez, J., Alonso, R., Faundez, C., Meric, H.: Boxing experience: Measuring QoS and QoE of multimedia streaming using NS3, LXC and VLC. In: 2014 IEEE 39th Conference on Local Computer Networks Workshops (LCN Workshops), pp. 658–662, Sept 2014
8. Alvarez, A., Orea, R., Cabrero, S., Pañeda, X.G., García, R., Melendi, D.: Limitations of network emulation with single-machine and distributed ns-3. In: Proceedings of the 3rd International ICST Conference on Simulation Tools and Techniques, ser. SIMUTools 2010, ICST, Brussels, Belgium, Belgium: ICST (Institute for Computer Sciences, Social-Informatics and Telecommunications Engineering), pp. 67:1–67:9 (2010). http://dx.doi.org/10.4108/ICST.SIMUTOOLS2010.8630

Applications and Services

Analyzing the Impact of Delay and Packet Loss on Google Docs

Lam Dinh-Xuan[1]([⊠]), Christian Schwartz[1], Matthias Hirth[1],
Florian Wamser[1], and Huong Truong Thu[2]

[1] University of Würzburg, Würzburg, Germany
lam.dinh-xuan@informatik.uni-wuerzburg.de
[2] Hanoi University of Science and Technology, Hanoi, Vietnam

Abstract. Software as a Service allows end users to use complex software directly from their browsers, transferring heavy computation to servers in the cloud. One use of this paradigm is word processing, former a classic use cases of Thin-Client computing. Similar to Thin-Clint systems, the network parameters are an important influence factor for the cloud application performance.

In this paper, we study Google Docs as an example for online word processing tools. We consider a traditional single user scenario as well as a collaborative scenario with two users working on one document simultaneously. We identify multiple relevant sub-processes per scenario as performance metrics and use a testbed to automatically evaluate the performance of Google Docs under varying network parameters. The main contributions of the paper are (1) the quantification of the impact of network parameters such as delay and packet loss on application performance metrics for both scenarios and (2) linear regression models to derive the application performance for giving network parameters.

Keywords: Google docs · Network parameter · QoS

1 Introduction

Cloud Computing and Software as a Service (SaaS) have received considerable interest by both the research as well as the industrial community. In recent time SaaS solutions have begun to absorb markets traditionally occupied by Thin Client products. One such SaaS application is *Google Docs*, an Internet based word processor. While a traditional desktop word processing application such as Microsoft Word provides a more complete feature set, Google Docs is a lightweight utility with sufficient office features and high flexibility. As an additional feature, Google Docs enables users to share created documents with other users or even collaboratively edit them.

However, as Internet-based cloud application, the performance of Google Docs depends on the network quality between server and client. Our study evaluates the performance of Google Docs with regard to different network conditions

© Institute for Computer Sciences, Social Informatics and Telecommunications Engineering 2015
R. Agüero et al. (Eds.): MONAMI 2015, LNICST 158, pp. 211–224, 2015.
DOI: 10.1007/978-3-319-26925-2_16

in two scenarios. First, a *single user scenario* is studied. In this scenario, a user has to take several sub-processes such as *Login* or *Typing*. We consider the time required to complete the sub-processes as a metric for the performance of the service. In the *collaborative scenario*, two users login to Google Docs. The first user edits a document while the other user observes the editing. Here, we consider the time both users require to complete the total process as well as all composite sub-processes as a measure of the application performance. To evaluate the influence of different network conditions on the processing time in both scenarios, we emulate various network delay conditions and packet loss settings in a local testbed.

Increased network delay or packet loss can cause an increase of the duration of the whole process or certain sub-processes on client. Therefore, in order to perform a better service, it is important to know which network characteristic influence the total processing time on the client. Furthermore, different sub-processes may be affected differently by network conditions and it is necessary to know which sub-process is most sensitive to delay or packet loss. Specifically, this paper answer the following research questions:

1. How do delay and packet loss influence the duration of sub-processes if a single user interacts with Google Docs?
2. How do delay and packet loss affect the duration of sub-processes in a collaborative scenario?
3. How does the combination of delay and packet loss influence the total processing time in collaborative tasks?

To answer those questions, we use a local testbed at the University of Würzburg to measure the duration of processes when users interact with Google Docs in both scenarios. We emulate one or two users which automatically perform workflows relevant to the scenario and record the required time. In this study, the duration of total process or each sub-process is the main criteria to evaluate the performance of Google Docs regarding different network conditions.

The contribution of this paper is threefold. First, we introduce a testbed for the measurement of SaaS applications w.r.t. varying network parameters. Second, we analyze the performance of the Google Docs application regarding the identified performance metrics. Finally, we provide a model used to derive Google Docs performance metrics given a set of network parameters and quantify the goodness of fit.

This paper is structured as follows. Section 2 presents the background of this study and related work. The testbed setup as well as the methodology is described in Sect. 3. Then, Sect. 4 discusses results gathered from the measurements. Finally, Sect. 5 concludes this work.

2   Background and Related Work

In this section, we introduce Google Docs as well as the two use cases considered in this paper. Thereafter, we present an overview of related work.

2.1   Background

Google Docs is a web based word processing application [1] whose client side front end is based on HTML and JavaScript and can be accessed using any modern web browser. In contrast to standalone office software products, e.g., Microsoft Office or LibreOffice, Google Docs requires a permanent Internet connection as documents are not stored locally on the client but on the Google server infrastructure. Google Docs does not provide rich feature sets like stand alone office products, however, it offers an easy way to share documents and enable collaboratively editing with up to 10 users simultaneously by sharing a link to the document or granting explicit rights to other registered users.

We consider two scenarios, which are derived from common Google Docs use cases. First, we discuss the single user scenario with one user editing a document. Here, a session is divided in five steps, which we will refer to as *sub-processes*. In a first step, the user logs into the system to gain access to a previously created document or to create a new document (*Login*). In the next step, the user creates a new document (*Creating*). Then, the user starts typing while the client continuously sends updates to the server to stores entered text at the server (*Typing*). After entering the text, it takes a shot amount of time to save the last changes to the text (*Saving*). The session is then ended with the logout of the user (*Logout*).

The durations Δt_{login}, $\Delta t_{\text{creating}}$, Δt_{typing}, Δt_{saving}, and Δt_{logout} of the five sub-processes *Login, Creating, Typing, Saving,* and *Logout,* as well as the total time of the session Δt_{total} are considered as an objective metric to asses the impact of network conditions on the quality of service for Google Docs. While it is intuitive that most of the aforementioned metrics depend on the network parameters, Emmert et al. [2] showed that the effective typing speed of an user also depends on network parameters in thin client environments. We will refer to this scenario as *single user scenario* in the remainder of this work.

As mentioned before, one of the major benefits of Google Docs is collaborative editing. In this case, the user session is more complex than in the single user case. For this scenario, we assume that *user 1* is creating the document and shares it with a collaboration partner *user 2*. Therefore, the work flows of *user 1* and *user 2* are almost similar to the work flow in the single user scenario. However, to share the document, *user 1* sends a link to *user 2* which grants him access rights to the newly created document. In this scenario, we additionally define two waiting times: (1) the duration *user 1* has to wait until *user 2* is ready to receive text, (2) the duration that *user 2* has to wait until *Receiving* starts. After *user 2* accessed the document, *user 1* starts writing and the content is automatically synchronized with *user 2* via Google Docs. As *user 2* is not actively editing the document, he does not observe a *Saving* phase.

2.2   Related Work

The impact of network conditions on Internet applications and remote desktop systems has be widely studied. However, to the best of our knowledge, the evaluation of quality of service for Google Docs has not been taken into account so far.

Schlosser et al. [3] analyzed the behaviour of Microsoft Word and Excel running in a remote desktop environment under different network conditions. They considered the Microsoft's Remote Desktop Protocol (RDP) and Citrix Presentation Server (CPS) as possible thin-client solutions. Their results showed that delay $\leq$ 500 ms or packet loss $\leq$ 2 % does not have any influence. However, the combination of delay and packet loss results in measurable impairments.

In [4], the authors focused on how Input Buffer and Speedscreen options can improve the performance of Citrix Presentation Server (CPS) in a WAN scenario. The author performed measurements with a user typing a text, scrolling a text, and selecting specific sub-menus on Microsoft Word and Textpad, respectively. The test duration under different network conditions was the main criteria to evaluate the performance of CPS. From the results, the author concluded that with the increasing of network delay up to 500 ms in combination with packet loss $\leq$ 2 %, CPS with the combination of Speedscreen and Input Buffer took less time to finish the test than without these options.

In both studies, the applied methodology is similar to the one used in this work. However, we are not focusing on traditional thin-clients but rather study a web based solution. Further, we also consider a collaborative use case, which is not studied in previous publications. Other publications study cloud services and theirs network requirements. The authors of [5] focused on five fundamental challenges for wide adoption of cloud computing using the *OPTIMIS* toolkit. Amrehn et al. concluded that for general file storage services, the upload and download speed, financial aspects, privacy, and security are important QoE influence factors [6]. The authors of [7] used a prediction system to forecast the CPU demands for web based cloud services. Other studies evaluated the subjective user satisfaction, i.e. Quality of Experience, with cloud services [8,9].

These studies focus on different aspects of cloud computing. However, the authors did not evaluate a specific cloud application or investigate the impact of network conditions on the performance of cloud applications.

3   Methodology and Testbed Setup

We use a dedicated testbed including a network emulator to analyze the influence of different network parameters on the behaviour of Google Docs, allowing for an easy adaption of network parameters such as delay and packet loss. In the following we first detail on the test setup for the single user case in Sect. 3.1, thereafter we describe the setup for the collaborative scenario in Sect. 3.2.

3.1   Testbed Setup for Single User Scenario

The testbed setup for the single user scenario is schematically depicted in Fig. 1 and consists of one measurement server, one network emulator, and a control PC. The measurement server hosts the virtual machine VM1 used as Google Docs client for *user 1*. The virtual machine is connected to the Internet via another

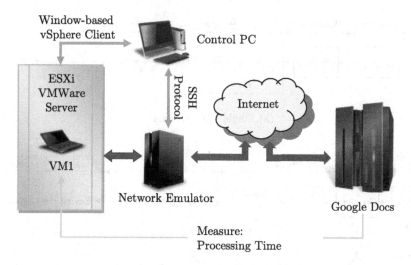

Fig. 1. Overview of testbed setup for the single user scenario

server running NetEm[1], which enables us to adjust packet loss and delay on the connection. To control the measurements, we use a control PC that is connected to the network emulator and the Google Docs client via a dedicated control network to avoid interference with the tests.

The measurement server and the network emulator are SUN FIRE X4150 servers with 8 CPUs 2.5 GHz, 16 Gb RAM, and 4 Ethernet 1 Gbps NICs. VMware ESXi 5.5[2] is used as virtualization solution and both the Google Docs client and the network emulator use Ubuntu 12.04 LTS as operation system. The testbed is connected to the Internet with a research network. We measure the baseline network parameters with a round trip time of 3.91 ms and no packet loss over 1000 packets. For later evaluation, we consider network delays from that baseline up to 1000 ms. Such high delay values can, e.g., occur due to long distance Internet access [10] or bottlenecks [11]. We consider packet loss from the baseline up to 4 % which may occur in a wireless link in urban area [12].

As discussed in Sect. 2, we assess the influence of the network parameters by measuring the duration of the sub-processes. To this end we use the Selenium Webdriver[3] to automatically generate user interactions. Figure 2(a) depicts the program flow of the measurement script and the recording of the time stamps used for measuring the duration of the sub-processes.

First the control PC sets up the network emulator with the desired configuration. Thereafter the Selenium script is started, which signs in to Google Docs and creates a new document. The content entered by the script is an English text taken from the introduction part of Selenium webpage. To evaluate the

---

[1] http://www.linuxfoundation.org/collaborate/workgroups/networking/netem.
[2] https://www.vmware.com.
[3] http://www.seleniumhq.org.

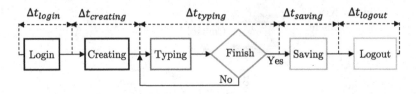

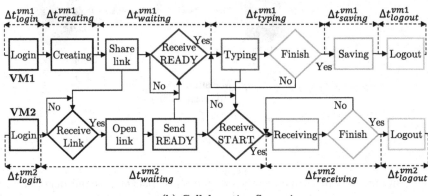

(a) Single User Scenario

(b) Collaborative Scenario

Fig. 2. Measurement workflows

influence of the length of the text of the duration of the typing process, we use a short text of 1548 characters, which corresponds approximately on paragraph in a document. Besides this we also use a long text with about 6189 characters, which corresponds to about two pages of A4 document. After the automatic typing is complete, the Selenium script waits until the document is saved and logs out of the Google Docs. For each network parameter setting we produce 50 replications within several days to avoid measuring diurnal effects.

3.2 Testbed Setup for Collaborative Task Scenario

In the collaborative scenario we consider two users working on the same document, with one user editing the content of the document and the other user reading the document. To analyze this scenario we extend the testbed configuration described in Fig. 1 by adding another virtual machine (VM2) as *user 2* on the measurement server. In this scenario we require synchronized clocks for both client PCs. While this is challenging when using two different physical machines, it can be accomplished using two virtual machines sharing the host clock. Similar to VM1, VM2 is connected to the Internet via the network emulator, so that both VMs share the same network parameters. VM2 is also connected to the control PC using a dedicated control network. Additionally a second control network is established between the two virtual machines to synchronize the workflows of the machines as describe below. In the measurement, we use short sample text from the single user scenario and the same network settings.

Figure 2(b) shows the workflow in the collaborative scenario. The upper and the lower part of figure represents the processes on VM1 and VM2, respectively. The workflow for VM1 is similar to the one in the single user scenario. However, after creating the new document, VM1 shared the document with VM2 by sending a link. The workflow of VM2 differs in such a way that VM2 does not create a new document itself, but just waits for the link to the shared document. In order to synchronize the workflows of the two virtual machines, VM1 waits after sending the link to VM2, until VM2 places a marker in the shared document. Thereafter, VM1 starts tying in the document and VM2 observes the changes.

In addition to the times measured in the single user scenario, we also consider the waiting times of the two virtual machines in this case. This is for VM1 the time between creating the document and the notification from VM2 that it successfully accessed the shared document, and for VM2 the time between logging in and observing the first changed by VM1 in the shared document. Moreover, we also measure the time it takes until all changes on the document made by VM1 are visible on the document seen by VM2.

4   Results

Based on the measurement setup discussed in Sect. 3 we analyze the scenarios introduced in Sect. 2.1. We study the impact of network parameters, i.e. packet loss and delay, and text length on the single user and collaboration scenarios, with regard to the sub-process and total durations introduced earlier.

All measurements were performed between February 12, 2015 and March 24, 2015. For each parameter setting 50 repetitions of the measurement were performed, in order to increase statistical significance. The measurement settings are chosen according to the values discussed in Sect. 3. In order to avoid measuring diurnally effects, we did not perform measurements with the similar settings consecutively, but distributed them over different times of day.

In Sect. 4.1 we evaluate the effect of individual network parameter on the single user scenario. Then, in Sect. 4.2 we extend the study to the collaboration scenario. Finally, in Sect. 4.3, we consider the impact of the combination of delay and packet loss on the collaboration scenario.

4.1   Impact of Different Network Conditions on Sub-processes in Single User Measurements

We first investigate the single user scenario, as described in Sect. 3.1 and show the results in Fig. 3. For all figures, the y-axis gives the sub-process duration with 95 % confidence intervals in seconds. For sake of readabilities the y-axis is cropped to 30 s, but the measurement values are given in the figure description.

In Figs. 3(a) and (b), we study the impact of different network parameters for different text lengths. Here, the x-axis in the left sub figures shows the different

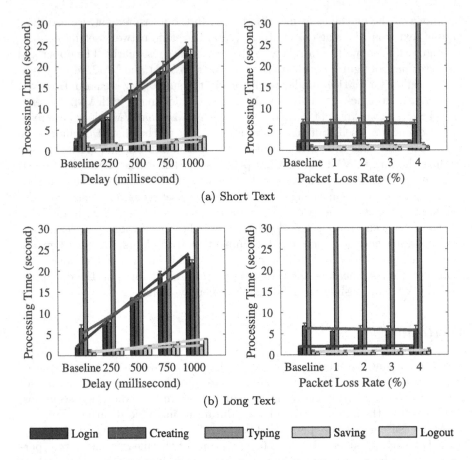

Fig. 3. Impact of network conditions on sub-process durations in single user scenario

delay settings in milliseconds, from the baseline unmodified delay, to an additional delay of 1000 ms in increments of 250 ms. The right sub figures show the impact of packet loss on the single user scenario. Here, the x-axis gives the additional induced packet-loss from the baseline setting without additional packet loss, up to 4 % in increments of 1 %.

All figures give sub-process durations as bars, colored depending on the sub-process type. Additionally, for each sub-process a linear regression is performed, which is shown as a colored line, depending on the sub-process type. Table 1 shows the detailed results of the linear regression depending on the delay, including the coefficient of determination r^2 as a measure for the goodness of fit. Figures 3(a) and (b) show the packet loss in the considered range up to 4% does not affect the processing time for any sub-process. However, the increase of network delay results in increased processing times for all sub-processes except the *Typing* time, with *Login* and *Creating* document being the most sensitive to network delays. When delay increases from baseline to 1000 ms, the *Typing* time remains

Table 1. Linear Regression of Sub-processes for Delays in Single User Scenario

Sub-processes	Short-text Measurement	r^2	Long-text Measurement	r^2
Login	$22.07 \times 10^{-3} \cdot x + 2.54$	0.99	$21.64 \times 10^{-3} \cdot x + 2.26$	0.99
Creating	$17.50 \times 10^{-3} \cdot x + 4.83$	0.96	$15.89 \times 10^{-3} \cdot x + 5.14$	0.94
Typing	$3.70 \times 10^{-3} \cdot x + 56.71$	0.49	$-4.95 \times 10^{-3} \cdot x + 247.35$	0.32
Saving	$0.84 \times 10^{-3} \cdot x + 1.29$	0.87	$1.41 \times 10^{-3} \cdot x + 0.95$	0.92
Logout	$2.70 \times 10^{-3} \cdot x + 0.65$	0.99	$3.16 \times 10^{-3} \cdot x + 0.71$	0.99

almost constant at 60 s and 247 s for the short and the long text, respectively. This is due to the fact that updates to the server are sent asynchronously and the typing process does not depend on the reply of the server. Particularly, the duration of the *Login* process is about 7 times longer than for a delay of 500 ms then for the baseline measurement and 12 times longer at a delay of 1000 ms. The duration of the *Creating* document process doubles and almost triples for the corresponding delay values in comparison to baseline measurement. This is due to the fact that the *Login* and *Creating* sub-processes rely on multiple communications between client and server which are executed in serial order. In contrast to this, the *Saving* time only slightly increases and the *Logout* time takes approximately 3.3s at 1000 ms delay compared to 0.60 s at baseline delay. Due to the synchronization of the typed text in a background process, the saving of a document relies only on few communications with the server and thus is not influenced by a large measure. In the measurement of the long text as shown in Fig. 3(b), the behaviour of the *Login*, *Creating*, *Saving*, and *Logout* sub-processes is similar to the behaviour observed for the short text. Table 1 summarizes the results of the linear regression for the sub-processes, both for short text and long text measurements for a given delay x. Packet loss is not considered, as the impact on sub-process duration is negligible in this scenario.

We observe that increasing delay results in a large increase of the *Login* time and *Creating* time, while the effect on the other sub-processes is less significant. The linear function of *Typing* time has small slope coefficient of 3.70 compared to its intercept of 56.71. Therefore, the length of text is primary factor changing the *Typing* time, not the network delay or the packet loss. The durations of the *Typing* sub-process vary non-lineary with increasing delay, resuling in a bad fit and a low r^2 value.

Our measurements show the in the single user scenario, Google Docs is robust against packet loss. However, delay affects the system negatively, especially during processes depending on multiple serial communication between client and server, e.g. login or while creating new documents. The actual typing process, which represents interaction between the user and the client, is insensitive to the network conditions, as it is basically a background process, which does not affect the user directly. The measurements show that the duration of the typing process is mainly depending on the length of the text.

4.2 Impact of Different Network Conditions on Sub-processes in Collaborative Task

We now analyze the influence of different network conditions on the sub-processes in the collaborative scenario. As described in Sect. 3.2, we use two virtual machines. The document is edited by VM1 while VM2 observes the creation process. In Fig. 4, the y-axis shows the duration of each sub-process in seconds, while the x-axis in the left figures shows the network delay and the packet loss rates in the right figures. Bars are colored by sub-process time and give the mean and 95 % confidence interval of duration, the lines show the linear regression.

Similar to the results from Sect. 4.1, Figs. 4(a) and (b) indicate that a packet loss of less then 4 % has no influence on the observed sub-process durations. Increasing delay results in an increasing duration of almost all sub-processes in both VM1 and VM2, with *Login, Creating* document and *Waiting* being the most sensitive processes. In contrast to this, the *Typing* time on VM1 and *Receiving* time in VM2 are only slightly fluctuating around 60 s even for higher delays. Again, this is due to the fact that synchronization between both VMs occurs asynchronously and does not depend on the responses of the server. As expected, the *Login* times are similar for both machines, because both experience the same network parameters. Furthermore, we observe that the *Waiting* time for VM2 is approximately the sum of the *Creating* and *Waiting* time of VM1. This can be explained, by the fact that both machines start with the login process at about the same time but VM1 has to create the document first. Thereafter starts the synchronization process for both workflows, c.f. Figure 2(b), which ends with the start of the *Typing* process on VM1 and the start of the *Receiving* process on VM2. These process again mark the end of the waiting periods of both machines. Interestingly, the *Typing* and *Receiving* process take about the same amount of time on both machines, independent of the network conditions. Again the parameters for the linear regression models are summarized in Table 2. The missing values in the table indicate the sub-processes does not occur on the corresponding virtual machine.

Considering the r^2, we again observe that the *Login, Logout, Creating,* and *Saving* sub-process can be fit using a linear model, in contrast to the *Typing* and *Receiving* which do not show linear behaviour regarding the considered parameters. For the *Typing* and *Receiving* process the intercept is again much larger then the slope coefficient, which indicates that the network parameters again have only little influence on the sub-process durations. Again, we do not provide a linear regression concerning packet loss due to the negligible impact of the variable.

Our measurements show the in the collaborative scenario, Google Docs behaves similar to the single user case. It is rather robust against packet loss and more sensitive to delay. Processes depending on repeated communication between client and server are more affected by additional delay, then e.g., the typing process which uses an asynchronous communication pattern.

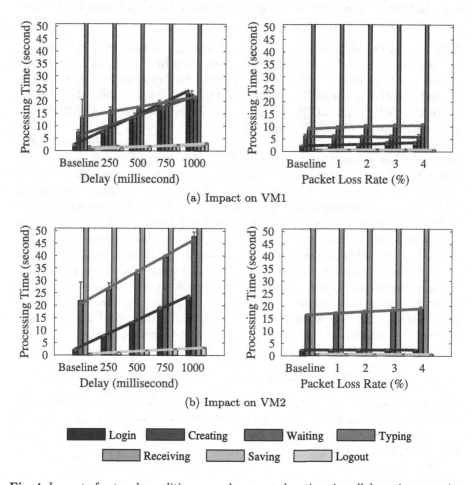

Fig. 4. Impact of network conditions on sub-process durations in collaborative scenario

Table 2. Linear Regression of Sub-processes for Delay in Collaborative Scenario

Sub-processes	VM1	r^2	VM2	r^2
Login	$21.53 \times 10^{-3} \cdot x + 2.51$	0.99	$21.47 \times 10^{-3} \cdot x + 2.41$	0.99
Logout	$2.39 \times 10^{-3} \cdot x + 0.59$	0.99	$2.50 \times 10^{-3} \cdot x + 0.58$	0.99
Creating	$15.56 \times 10^{-3} \cdot x + 5.95$	0.96	-	-
Typing	$-1.73 \times 10^{-3} \cdot x + 59.68$	0.29	-	-
Saving	$1.07 \times 10^{-3} \cdot x + 1.24$	0.83	-	-
Waiting	$8.16 \times 10^{-3} \cdot x + 13.57$	0.97	$25.94 \times 10^{-3} \cdot x + 20.56$	0.98
Receiving	-	-	$-2.81 \times 10^{-3} \cdot x + 60.08$	0.49

4.3   Impact of Combined Delay and Packet Loss on Total Processing in Collaborative Task

After analyzing delay and packet loss separately, we now consider the total process duration given packet loss and delay occurring at the same time. We consider total processing time Δt_{total} required for inputting the short text in the collaborative scenario. The results for the measurement show that the differences of $\Delta t_{\text{total}}^{\text{vm1}}$ and $\Delta t_{\text{total}}^{\text{vm2}}$ are negligible. Therefore we focus our discussion on obtained values for $\Delta t_{\text{total}}^{\text{vm1}}$ depicted in Fig. 5.

In Fig. 5, the y-axis shows $\Delta t_{\text{total}} = \Delta t_{\text{total}}^{\text{vm1}}$. The x-axis shows the different packet loss values from baseline to 4 %, different delay values are shows as grouped bars, including the 95 % confidence intervals for each measurement setting. We show a examples of a more general linear regression parameterized for the measurement parameters as lines colored according to the specific delay.

For the baseline packet loss and the considered delay values we observer that Δt_{total} increases, as discussed in the previous sections. We also see, that Δt_{total} is almost independent of the packet loss as long as the delay is small, i.e., at the baseline. This is intuitive, because in this case retransmission of lost packets can be considered as almost instantaneous and does not affect the transmission at all. However, in case of larger delays, the impact of packet loss starts to increase, as retransmissions take longer and consequently the time until information is successfully transmitted between server and client increases, as well.

This can be modeled using a linear regression with a r^2 value of 0.943 as

$$\Delta t_{\text{total}} = 62.247 + 0.077962 \cdot x + 809.54 \cdot y$$

for a delay x and a packet loss of y. Comparing the predicted results of the model with our measurements, we observe that while fluctuations up to 10 % occur at the bounds of our parameter set, the results are of sufficient quality to be used in general cases.

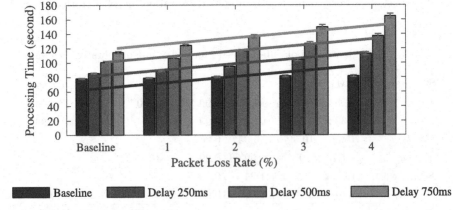

Fig. 5. Impact of combined delay and packet loss on the total duration of the collaborative task

These results show, that while packet loss alone has no significant impact on application performance, a combination of both packet loss and delay can negatively impact application behaviour. In real world scenarios, especially if WiFi or cellular access is concerned, both network parameters can be degraded noticeably. However, results from Sects. 4.1 and 4.2 show, that the impact can be mitigated by using asynchronous communication patterns between client and server.

5 Conclusion

Cloud services and SaaS products gained considerable interest recent times as a replacement for traditional centralized infrastructure and locally installed software products. Despite many advantages varying network conditions can significantly affect their performance. To assess the impact of network impairment, we analyzed the impact on a representative SaaS product, Google Docs.

In the first scenario, we considered a single user editing a Document, in the second one a collaborative use case, with one user editing the document and a second user observing the changes. To quantify the impact of network delay and packet loss objectively, we measure the time it takes to complete the whole process as well as certain parts of it, e.g., the login or the creation of the document. The measurements were performed using a local testbed which is connected to the Internet via a NetEM network emulator. The user interactions were automated using Selenium.

Our results show that in both scenarios, packet loss below 4 % does not influence the duration of sub-processes, if there is no network delay. In contrast to this, network delay negatively influenced the performance of Google Docs, even in the absence of packet loss. Hereby, the login process as well as the process of creating a new document are the most delay-sensitive sub-processes. Furthermore, we also analyzed the impact of combined delay and packet loss. Here the results show a significant degradation of the Google Docs performance even for small values of delay and packet loss, if both occur at the same time.

The results from this study can help to shed a first light of the behaviour of Google Docs as an exemplary SaaS solution under varying network conditions from an objective point of new. This in turn can later be used to evaluate the impact of this application behaviour on the perceived quality of the end-user (QoE). Here especially the obtained linear regression models can be used in analytical models for optimization and trade-off analysis network resources, energy consumption and QoE. In a next step, these model can be extend to other Google cloud services such as Google Spread Sheet and Presentation.

Acknowledgment. This work is supported by the Deutsche Forschungsgemeinschaft under Grants HO TR 257/41-1 "Trade-offs between QoE and Energy Efficiency in Data Centers".

References

1. Dan, H.: Google this!: using google apps for collaboration and productivity. In: SIGUCCS Fall Conference. St. Louis, USA, October 2009
2. Emmert, B., Binzenhöfer, A., Schlosser, D., Weiß, M.: Source traffic characterization for thin client based office applications. In: Pras, A., van Sinderen, M. (eds.) EUNICE 2007. LNCS, vol. 4606, pp. 86–94. Springer, Heidelberg (2007)
3. Daniel, S., Andreas, B., Barbara, S.: Performance comparison of windows-based thin-client architectures. In: ATNAC 2007. Christchurch, New Zealand, December 2007
4. Daniel, S., et al.: Improving the QoE of Citrix Thin Client Users. In: International Conference on Communications. South Africa, May 2010
5. Ferrer, A., et al.: OPTIMIS: a holistic approach to cloud service provisioning. In: Future Generation Computer Systems, vol. 28 (2012)
6. Amrehn, P., et al.: Need for speed? on quality of experience for file storage services. In: Workshop on Perceptual Quality of Systems. Vienna, Austria, September 2013
7. Reig, G., Guitart, J.: On the anticipation of resource demands to fulfill the QoS of SaaS web applications. In: Conference on Grid Computing. Beijing, China, September 2012
8. Hoßfeld, T., et al.: Challenges of QoE management for cloud applications. IEEE Commun. Mag. **50**(4), 28–36 (2012)
9. Jarschel, M., et al.: An evaluation of QoE in cloud gaming based on subjective tests. In: Innovative Mobile and Internet Services in Ubiqui-tous Computing (IMIS), pp. 330–335. IEEE (2011)
10. O3B Networks. What is Network Latency and Why Does It Matter? White Paper. http://tinyurl.com/nv8agu8. 2008
11. Ningning, H., et al.: A measurement study of internet bottlenecks. In: INFOCOM. Miami, Florida, USA (2005)
12. Anmol, S., et al.: Packet loss characterization in wifi-based long distance networks. In: International Conference on Computer Communications. Anchorage, Alaska, USA (2007)

Analysis of Group-Based Communication in WhatsApp

Michael Seufert[1]($\boxtimes$), Anika Schwind[1], Tobias Hoßfeld[2], and Phuoc Tran-Gia[1]

[1] Insitute of Computer Science, University of Würzburg, Würzburg, Germany
seufert@informatik.uni-wuerzburg.de
[2] Chair of Modeling of Adaptive Systems, University of Duisburg-Essen, Essen, Germany
tobias.hossfeld@uni-due.de

Abstract. This work investigates group-based communication in WhatsApp based on a survey and the analysis of messaging logs. The characteristics of WhatsApp group chats in terms of usage and topics are outlined. We present a classification based on the topic of the group and classify anonymized messaging logs based on message statistics. Finally, we model WhatsApp group communication with a semi-Markov process, which can be used to generate network traffic similar to real messaging logs.

Keywords: Group-based communication · WhatsApp · Survey · Classification · Semi-Markov process · Network traffic model · Mobile instant messaging · Group chats · Mobile networks

1 Introduction

Today, our everyday life cannot be imagined without the possibility of mobile communication. On smartphones, especially text-based communication like Short Message Service (SMS) and Mobile Instant Messaging (MIM) is used by a large share of the population. Currently, WhatsApp is the most popular MIM application in the world having around 700 million monthly active users [5], followed by QQ Mobile and Facebook Messenger, which are both used by more than 500 million users [7]. The advantage over the traditional SMS is that MIM services are mostly free and not only text messages but also media like videos, images, and audio messages can be transmitted easily.

In contrast to SMS, MIM applications use the Internet to exchange messages. Thus, ubiquitous communication through MIM applications increases the Internet traffic and puts a lot of load on mobile networks. Therefore, MIM applications and their usage have to be investigated to efficiently handle the increasing traffic and provide a proper management of the cellular resources.

One of the most popular features of MIM applications is group chatting. WhatsApp, for example, allows users to communicate in a group with up to 100 members. In contrast to regular chatting, a post in a group has to be transmitted

© Institute for Computer Sciences, Social Informatics and Telecommunications Engineering 2015
R. Agüero et al. (Eds.): MONAMI 2015, LNICST 158, pp. 225–238, 2015.
DOI: 10.1007/978-3-319-26925-2_17

to multiple recipients, and thus, multiplies the traffic on the network. In order to develop new mechanisms, which cope efficiently with the increasing traffic but also guarantee a high user satisfaction, it is necessary to understand group-based communication in detail.

The goal of this paper is to analyze group-based communication in WhatsApp, to classify WhatsApp groups, and to model the communication in groups and the resulting network traffic. Therefore, this work is structured as follows:

First, relevant related work will be presented in Sect. 2. Section 3 will describe the user study and present results about the participants' WhatsApp usage and the ratings of their groups. In Sect. 4, anonymized group chats logs are analyzed, and first approaches to classifying WhatsApp groups are outlined in Sect. 5. Finally, Sect. 6 presents a semi-Markov process for generating realistic WhatsApp conversations in groups, and Sect. 7 concludes.

2   Related Work

In this section, recent research papers are summarized, which relate to our work. They include a comparison of SMS and MIM, studies about mobile group-based communication, and works investigating WhatsApp and its impact. Nevertheless, our study is the first work to analyze group-based communication in WhatsApp based on a survey and the analysis of messaging logs.

Comparison of SMS and MIM. To understand the reasons for the success of WhatsApp, it is important to relate it to other types of communication. Church and de Oliveira [1] compare MIM behaviors with traditional SMS communication. Their research focuses on the motives and perceptions of the usage of WhatsApp and what this service offers above and beyond traditional SMS. By conducting interviews and a survey, they worked out that neither technology is a substitute for the other. SMS costs significantly impacts people's frequency of usage and is, together with social influence, one of the main reasons for today's migration to MIM applications like WhatsApp. According to the authors, WhatsApp messages tend to be more social, informal, and conversational in nature, whereas SMS is seen as more privacy preserving, more formal, and generally more reliable.

Group-Based Mobile Messaging. Considering research about group-based communication, Counts and Scott [2] demonstrate interesting results. In their paper, the authors develop a group-based mobile messaging application called "SLAM", which offers features comparable to group chats in WhatsApp. Afterwards, they analyze the communication in relation to its social impact. It should be kept in mind that this paper was published in 2007, two years before WhatsApp was released. The paper shows in which ways and to what dimension group-based messaging improves the social and leisure aspects of communication. They found out that participants used group-based messaging for roughly the same purposes as one-to-one messaging. However, by analyzing the message volume, it becomes clear that participants sent significantly more messages in groups than in one-to-one conversations. In a survey conducted by the authors, participants state that mobile communication is more fun in a group than in one-to-one communication.

Research about user satisfaction with mobile messaging applications was published by Park et al. [6] in 2014. By conducting a survey with 220 users of MIM apps, the authors analyze factors affecting user satisfaction. They found out that self-disclosure, flow, and social presence significantly affect user satisfaction. Nevertheless, the feeling of being together everywhere and at any time is specified as the most important factor of satisfaction by the respondents.

WhatsApp. Network-related aspects of communication were covered by Fiadino et al. [4] in 2014. In their paper, they analyze the traffic behavior of WhatsApp. According to the authors, WhatsApp is a fully centralized service. It is hosted by the cloud provider SoftLayer in the United States. They work out that WhatsApp is mainly used as a text-messaging service, with more than 93 % of the transmitted flows containing text. However, 36 % of the exchanged volume in uplink and downlink are caused by video sharing, and 38 % by photo sharing and audio messaging.

There is also research about the impact of WhatsApp on its users. In 2014, Yeboah and Ewur [8] investigated the influence of the use of WhatsApp on the performance of students in Ghana. According to their paper, the application makes communication easier and faster, but 76 % of the interviewed students think the use of WhatsApp has rather negative than positive effect on their studies.

3   User Study on WhatsApp Usage

In order to obtain reliable data, we conducted a study on the usage of WhatsApp. Therefore, more than 200 people were consulted during three days in the end of November 2014 on the campus of the University of Würzburg, Germany. The participants answered the questions of the survey in a separate room using personal or laptop computers. On average, this took 15 min. The survey was divided by topics into three different parts. Each part contained various questions that were presented on individual pages. Questions had to be answered using text fields, single choice, or multiple choice options.

After collecting demographic data about the participants, they had to specify details about their usage of WhatsApp in the first part. The next part dealt with the network usage statistics that WhatsApp collects automatically on every device. Finally, the focus of the questions was moved to the individual WhatsApp group chats the participants had on their devices.

After taking part in the survey, the participants were also asked to send some of their messaging histories from WhatsApp group chats. The results of the analysis of these messaging histories will be discussed in Sect. 4.

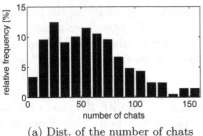

(a) Dist. of the number of chats

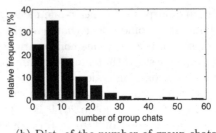

(b) Dist. of the number of group chats

Fig. 1. Distribution of the number of chats and the number of group chats of each participant of the survey

In total, 243 participants took part in the study. Because of invalid answers to some questions, the records of 34 people were removed for the following analysis. Invalid answers were, for example, implausibly high values in the network usage (i.e., more than ten times the average network usage) and a negative value or zero in questions, in which only positive numbers could make sense. After filtering out participants with invalid answers, 209 participants remained – 106 (50,72 %) female and 103 (49,28 %) male. The youngest participant was 17 and the oldest 29 years old; the average age was 21.4 and the median age was 21. The relatively low average age can be explained by the fact that most of the participants were students. The following paragraphs show the most important results of the statistical evaluation of the answers.

Usage of WhatsApp. In the first part of the survey, the participants had to count how many chats in total they had on their devices and how many of these chats were group chats, i.e., chats with more than one partner. Figure 1a shows a bar plot of the binned distribution of total number of chats per user. The width of each bar is ten. It can be seen that only 3.35 % of the participants had ten or less chats and 12.44 % of the participants had more than 100 chats. The maximum number of chats was 158, the minimum was 3. The average number of chats, i.e., the average number of people with whom messages were exchanged, was 59 (median 56). It follows that WhatsApp is an important means of communication for many people as they use it to send messages to a large number of different people.

Figure 1b shows the binned distribution of the number of group chats per user. Here, the width of each bar is five. The mean number of group chats was 10 (median 8) and the maximum was 59. Only 1.91 % of the participants had no group chats at all. Please note that it is possible to delete group chats and the participants indicated during the study that they had already deleted on average 7 groups (median 3).

Looking at the share of group chats among all chats, only 6.7 % of the participants had less than 5 % group chats in all chats. Most participants (83.28 %) had a ratio of group chats in all chats between 5 % and 30 %. All in all, it

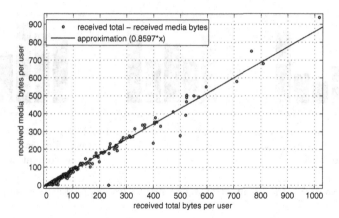

Fig. 2. Relation between received media bytes and received bytes in total per person

can be assumed that the group chat feature is used frequently by nearly every WhatsApp user, which makes it a key function of WhatsApp.

The next set of questions was about the frequency of the participants' usage of WhatsApp and SMS. The evaluation of the answers showed that WhatsApp is used significantly more often than SMS. 85.17 % of the participants indicated that they use WhatsApp at least every two or three hours, whereas only 6.69 % use SMS so frequently. Most participants (80 %) use SMS at most one or two times a day. This leads to the conclusion that WhatsApp communication was preferred considerably to SMS communication by the participants.

Network Usage. In this part, the participants were asked to copy the numbers of WhatsApp's network usage from their device. On an Android device, for example, these statistics can be accessed from the menu at Settings – Account – Network Usage. On average, the participants sent 11936 and received 17753 messages, which includes both media and text messages. The average amount of the sent media data is 86.88 MB and that of received media data is 141.69 MB. Also, on average every person sent 33.46 MB and received 69.82 MB in text messages. In total, 78.27 MB were sent and 348.99 MB were received by an average participant. It must be taken into account that the time of WhatsApp usage is different for each participant and that statistics of WhatsApp's network usage can be manually reset and also start from zero when changing the device.

Considering the relation between received media bytes and received bytes in total, a high Pearson correlation coefficient of 0.92 can be determined. Figure 2 shows this correlation by representing each participant by the number of total bytes (x-axis) and the number of media bytes (y-axis) he or she received. The relation between received media bytes and received bytes in total can also be approximated by a linear function. In this case, $f(x) = 0.8597 \cdot x$ provides a very good approximation indicated by the very high coefficient of determination $R^2 = 0.9739$. Thus, nearly 86 % of the bytes sent can be attributed to media

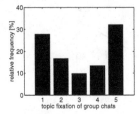 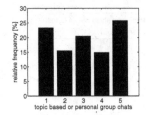 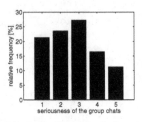

(a) Topic fixation of a group, (b) Distribution of the an- (c) Distribution of the an-
from one single topic (1) to swers if the group is topic swers whether the group has
multiple topics (5)   based or personal   serious content or not

Fig. 3. Analysis of the content of the groups with ve-point Likert scale ranging

posts, i.e., photos, videos, or audio messages. This indicates that media posts
cause the largest part of WhatsApp's network traffic.

WhatsApp Groups. In the last section, the participants had to answer several
questions about every WhatsApp group chat, up to 20 group chats, they had on
their phone. First, the participants were asked about the number of members
in each group chat and how many of these they did not know. Note that the
creator of the group chat has to invite each partner to the group chat individually
from the contact list of his device. Although WhatsApp allows to create group
chats with up to 100 members, the majority of group chats analyzed in the
survey contained only few members (mean 9, median 6). In terms of unknown
members, the group chats had an average of 1 per group and the median was 0.
This leads to the assumption that WhatsApp group chats are mainly used for
communication with specifically selected members who knew each other.

In the following, the topic of the group chats was investigated. At first, the
participants had to indicate whether the subject of each group chat was a unique
event, a repetitive event, or no event. 21.96 % of the group chats dealt with a
unique event, 21.47 % with a repetitive event, and 56.57 % with no event at
all. Next, the participants were asked to rate the topics discussed in the group
chats on a five-point Likert scale from single topic (1) to multiple topics (5).
Figure 3a shows that most of the group chats had one single topic (27.75 %) or
multiple different topics (32.16 %), but rarely something in between. Figure 3b
shows the distribution of the answers whether the group chat is focused on the
topic (e.g., a birthday present) or on the persons (e.g., a soccer team). Here, the
five-point Likert scale ranges from topic based group (1) to personal group (5).
It can be seen that the distribution of the answers is nearly constant. Only the
extremes, topic based (23.04 %) and personal (25.78 %), are slightly increased.
Figure 3c shows the distribution of the seriousness of the group chats. The bars
of the chart represent a Likert scale from trivial and amusing content (1) up to
serious content (5). It becomes obvious that while very few groups had serious or
mostly serious content (27.55 %), most groups had either both serious and trivial
content (27.25 %), mostly trivial (23.63 %) or very trivial content (21.37 %).

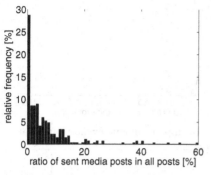

(a) Dist. of ratio of media in all posts

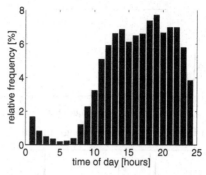

(b) Distribution of posts over the daytime

Fig. 4. Distribution of the ratio of media posts in all posts of a group chat and of the interarrival time of all posts

4   Analysis of Group Chat Logs

After taking part in the survey, the participants were asked to send some of their messaging histories from WhatsApp groups. In order to protect the users' privacy, these histories were anonymized. For each message, we only kept a time-stamp as well as a unique user ID, the number of sent characters and a hash value of the message. Some participants gave their consent to also keep their original data for further investigations. In that way, 271 anonymized and 131 original messaging histories have been collected.

General Information About the Messaging Histories. First, we present a short statistic about the collected data. In total, the 271 group chats had 224 658 posts. The maximum number of posts in a group chat was 16 202, the minimum 3. On average, a group chat had 832 posts and the median was 186.

72.76 % of all posts consist of less than 40 characters. Furthermore, 8.26 % of the text post consist of only one ore two characters or emoticons. Only 1.84 % of the text posts consist of more than 160 characters. It shows that long messages, which are an advantage of MIM considering the limited length of SMS messages, are rarely sent. This leads to the conclusion that the participants mainly used WhatsApp similar to SMS and rarely sent completely formulated sentences.

Ratio of Media Posts in All Posts. Fig. 4a shows the distribution of the ratio of media posts in all posts of a group chat. 59.32 % of all group chats have less then 5 % media posts in all posts, 28.70 % have less than 1 % media posts in at all posts. The distribution of the ratio decreases very fast between 0 % and 20 % and then approaches zero. This leads to the conclusion that group chats in WhatsApp are mainly used to communicate via text posts, while media posts were only used to some extent. However, as Sect. 3 shows, media posts cause the largest part of WhatsApps network traffic.

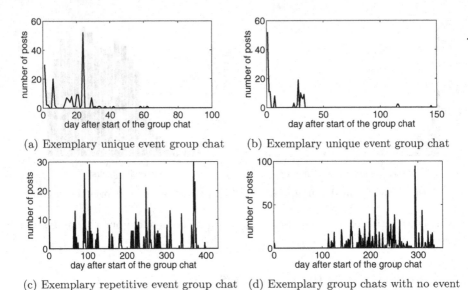

(a) Exemplary unique event group chat   (b) Exemplary unique event group chat

(c) Exemplary repetitive event group chat   (d) Exemplary group chats with no event

Fig. 5. Examples of the distributions of the number of posts per day

Temporal Evaluation of the Chat Histories. First, the frequency of posts at a particular time of day was investigated. Figure 4b illustrates the daytimes in hours (x-axis) in connection with the relative frequency of posts (y-axis). Mosts posts were sent between 7 pm (7.72 %) and 6 pm (7.38 %), fewest between 5 am (0.20 %) and 6 am (0.24 %). The chart shows the trend that only 18.35 % of the posts were sent in the morning or noon between 6 am and 1 pm.

Next, the interarrival times of messages in group chats were analyzed. 59.32 % of the posts were immediate responses and had an interarrival time of less than one minute. 80.90 % of all messages have an interarrival time of less than 15 min. Moreover, only 15.10 % of all interarrival times are 30 min or longer. These findings supports the statement that WhatsApp constitutes a very fast communication.

5   Classification of WhatsApp Groups

In this section, we investigate different characteristics of groups, i.e., whether different categories exist in which WhatsApp groups can be classified. Therefore, we follow a naive approach and use the *Density-based spatial clustering of applications with noise (DBSCAN)* algorithm [3] to compute clusters based on the group characteristics, which were reported by the participants of our study (cf. Sect. 3). Three clusters could be observed in the answers of the participants. The main distinctive feature of these clusters was whether the topic of the group chat was a unique event, a repetitive event, or no event. In the following, the properties of the clusters (mean ratings on the respective Likert scale) are presented:

Unique Event. Group chats belonging to this class deal with a unique event. Therefore, on average these group chats had mainly one single topic (1.53) and were rather topic based than personal (2.09). On average, the content was neither very serious nor trivial (2.23). In total, 222 (21.81 %) group chats described in the survey fit into this class.

Repetitive Event. All group chats in this class deal with a repetitive event. On average, the group chats in this class had rather a single than multiple topics (2.18). They also were rather topic based and their content was neither very serious nor trivial (2.17). 216 group chats described by the participants (21.22 %) belonged to this class.

No Event. This class contained group chats which deal with no specific event. They had on average rather multiple topics (3.96) and are also rather personal (3.67). The seriousness of the group chats were rather low (1,35). Of all group chats described in the survey, 577 (56.68 %) were allocated to this class.

To classify groups in an automated manner, further properties had to be determined from messaging histories. Therefore, some of the original, non-anonymized messaging histories were selected according to their group name and analyzed. This means, if the group name clearly indicated that the subject of the group was a unique event (e.g., a birthday party), a repetitive event (e.g., a regular social gathering) or no event (e.g., a group of family members), this group was used to find further properties.

Figure 5a and b show two exemplary distributions of the number of posts per day of unique event groups. Here, every day after the creation of the group chats was labeled on the x-axis and the number of posts per day on the y-axis. It is noticeable that both have a very short duration (shorter than 150 days). It can also be seen that both plots have one distinct maximum and otherwise a mostly low number of posts per day. The left figure has its maximum at 52 posts per day. The second highest number of posts per day is 30, which is only 58 % of the maximum. Similarly to this, the right figure has one clear maximum (52 posts per day) and has a great distance to the second highest number of posts, which only has 40 % of the maximum. This characteristic distribution of the posts was visible at all original messaging histories classified as unique events.

In Fig. 5c, there is an exemplary plot of the distributions of the number of posts per day of a repetitive event, while Fig. 5d shows an exemplary plot of a no event group chat. Here, no distinct maximum can be found. The left figure shows two maxima with 29 and 30 posts. The right figure has a maximum of 94 posts. The second highest number of posts per day is 66, which is 70 % of the maximum. By comparing them using this distribution, no significant difference of behavior can be determined. Both classes have a longer duration than group chats dealing with unique events (about 400 days) and also several spikes. Surprisingly, no obvious regularity can be found in the plot of the repetitive event. Contrary to the expectations raised by the answers to the survey, the original messaging histories showed no differentiation between group chats dealing with repetitive events and no events.

In the following, a classifier for the detection of a unique event group from anonymized messaging histories will be presented. Based on the properties observed above, we classify a group chat history as a unique event when the following conditions hold: A group chat, which deals with a unique event, has a maximum duration of half a year. It also contains one day on which the most posts were sent and the second highest number of posts is not more than 60 % of the maximum. By checking all collected anonymized messaging histories, 87 (32 %) group chats were classified as unique event groups. Compared to the classification on the basis of the survey, about 10 % more unique events were detected than expected. As the participants only sent a limited number of messaging histories of all of their group chats, they certainly had selected consciously which history they wanted to send. Thus, the participants might have chosen less personal and less private group chats with a higher frequency, which could be the reason of the higher rate of unique events in the messaging histories. Nevertheless, the presented approach can be seen as a first step towards classification of group chats, although its performance has to be validated based on more original messages in future work.

6   Model of Group Communication

The previous sections evaluated the answers of the survey and the collected messaging histories. In this section, these results are used to create a communication model of a group chat history, based on a semi-Markov process. This model could, for example, be used to estimate the network traffic of WhatsApp group chats.

In this model, only media posts and text posts are considered. Figure 6 illustrates the activity model of the WhatsApp group communication. The probability that a media post is followed by another media post is 30.55 %, which means that the probability that a text posts follows is 69.45 %. With 94.71 %, a text post is followed by another text posts; thus, it is followed by a media post with a probability of 5.29 %. These probabilities have been obtained from the analysis of the messaging histories by counting the frequency of occurrence of each transition.

This activity model can be transformed into a semi-Markov process by converting each transition into a model state and additionally taking the corresponding interarrival times (IAT) of the messages to account how long the

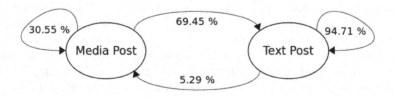

Fig. 6. Activity model of WhatsApp group communication

Table 1. Percentiles of the interarrival times of the different transitions in minutes

Transition	90 %	99 %
text post - text post	63	1066000
text post - media post	1244	613600
media post - media post	129	35670
media post - text post	81	302300

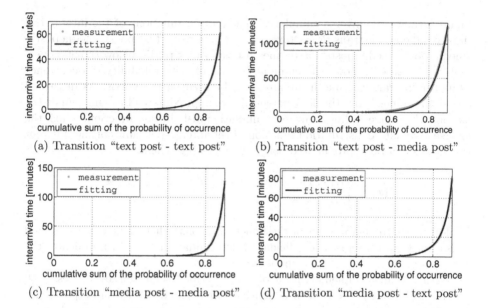

(a) Transition "text post - text post"   (b) Transition "text post - media post"

(c) Transition "media post - media post"   (d) Transition "media post - text post"

Fig. 7. Inverse cumulative distribution function of the interarrival times of the different transitions

semi-Markov process will stay in the respective state. We excluded IAT values above the 99 % percentile, which are unrealistic and were caused, for instance, by message log modifications when changing to a new smartphone. Moreover, we split the measured interarrival times at the 90 % percentile. The observed IATs below this percentile can be accurately fitted, however the IATs above do not show regular behavior, which is due to phases of inactivity during the group conversation. To approximate these phases, we use a uniform distribution for the 10 % of IATs which can take values from the 90 % percentile to the 99 % percentile. The respective percentiles are listed in Table 1. Note that phases of inactivity in the groups, which are usually modeled as on/off-processes, are not considered explicitly in this work. However, the presented approach can be easily extended, e.g., by adding a state for inactivity.

We implemented a Java discrete event simulation to generate realistic network traffic for group conversations. To create random numbers, which follow the interarrival time distribution, inverse transform sampling was applied.

Table 2. Approximation of the interarrival times of the different transitions

Transition	α_1	β_1	α_2	β_2	β_3	γ	R^2
T – T	$6.756 \cdot 10^{-4}$	11.99	$1.763 \cdot 10^{-12}$	33.79	41 670	37 441	1
T – M	$3.899 \cdot 10^{-3}$	14.11	0	0	110 550	98 251	0.9984
M – M	$1.207 \cdot 10^{-15}$	42.41	$3.196 \cdot 10^{-7}$	21.51	41 890	37 572	0.9984
M – T	$3.224 \cdot 10^{-5}$	15.99	$4.672 \cdot 10^{-20}$	52.99	29 250	26 244	0.9996

Figure 7 shows the inverse cumulative distribution functions of the interarrival times of all possible transitions "text post - text posts", "text posts - media post", "media post - media posts", and "media posts - text post", below the 90 % percentile. The x-axis shows the cumulative sum of the probability of occurrence while the interarrival time in minutes can be seen on the y-axis. As described above, the values above the 90 % percentile are approximated by a uniform distribution, which gives a linear inverse cumulative distribution function. Thus, the inverse cumulative distribution function of the interarrival times of the different transitions can be approximated using the following scheme:

$$f(x) = \begin{cases} \alpha_1 \cdot exp(\beta_1 \cdot x) + \alpha_2 \cdot exp(\beta_2 \cdot x) & x \leq 0.9 \\ \beta_3 \cdot x - \gamma & else \end{cases}.$$

Table 2 shows the parameters of the four transitions, where T is a text post and M is a media post, and the coefficient of determination R^2, which indicates the goodness of the fitting of the exponential part.

With the Java implementation of the described semi-Markov process, 150 group chats with a duration of 3 months were created. As a counterpart, also 150 extracts of the original messaging histories, with a period of 3 month, were randomly selected. The only condition for these extracts was that they had to be active parts of a group chats, which we defined as a minimum of 30 posts in 3 months. According to the results of [4], media posts have on average a size of 225 KB and text posts a size of 6.7 KB. Thus, every post was weighted on the basis of these results. Note that this is the traffic as observed by an individual user without any distinction between uplink and downlink traffic. For better comparison, the average cumulative sum of the bytes per day was calculated, which is shown in Fig. 8. The x-axis labels the number of day from day 0 up to 91 (three months), while the y-axis shows the cumulative sum of sent KB. The black graph shows the average cumulative sum of KB per day of the original messaging histories, the brown graph shows the average cumulative sum of the simulation model. On average, an original messaging histories generated 11 545 KB and the simulation model 11 711 KB network traffic per group member within three month. The difference is therefore only 166 KB. The maximum difference of the cumulative sum of the bytes per day is 1 044 KB on day 30. Therefore, the presented communication model constitutes a good way to simulate network traffic generated in WhatsApp group chats.

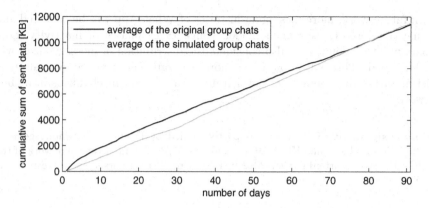

Fig. 8. Cumulative sum of sent KB per day of the original messaging histories and the simulation model

7   Conclusion

This paper investigated group-based communication in a popular MIM application. By conducting a survey and evaluating messaging histories, statistics of group chatting in WhatsApp were obtained. Moreover, a classification of group chats was presented and a model for group communication was developed. These insights and results lay the foundations for future research on group-based communication and can help to efficiently handle traffic generated by MIM applications.

It could be confirmed that WhatsApp users utilize this application significantly more often than SMS. The survey also indicated that, for many people, WhatsApp has become an important means of communication in many conditions of life. It became clear that the main distinctive feature for the classification is whether the topic of a group chat was a unique event, a repetitive event, or no event. By applying these classes to the messaging histories, further properties of the classes could be determined.

A classification method was created, which is able to decide whether a messaging history deals with a unique event or not. According to this method, approximately one third of the collected messaging histories deal with a unique event, and thus, have a limited lifespan. These results came close to the findings from the survey.

Finally, a communication model of a WhatsApp group chat based on a semi-Markov process was developed. Its transition probabilities are based on the probability of occurrence of certain message sequences and each transition takes the respective interarrival time distribution of the subsequent message into account. This model was used to simulate network traffic of WhatsApp group chats. The evaluation of the simulated traffic showed similar properties to network traffic caused by original messaging histories. Thus, this simple model can already be used for the performance evaluation of the WhatsApp service in mobile networks.

In future work, more messaging histories of WhatsApp will be collected and evaluated. Moreover, a refined model, which takes phases of inactivity more explicitly into account and also considers the distribution of message sizes, will be developed. This will allow for a more accurate performance evaluation of existing or the development of novel traffic management mechanisms in mobile networks.

Acknowledgement. This work was partly funded by Deutsche Forschungsgemeinschaft (DFG) under grants HO 4770/1-2 and TR257/31-2, and in the framework of the EU ICT Project SmartenIT (FP7-2012-ICT-317846). The authors alone are responsible for the content.

References

1. Church, K., de Oliveira, R.: What's up with Whatsapp? Comparing mobile instant messaging behaviors with traditional SMS. In: Proceedings of the 15th International Conference on Human-computer Interaction with Mobile Devices and Services, pp. 352–361 (2013)
2. Counts, S.: Group-based mobile messaging in support of the social side of leisure. Comput. Supported Coop. Work **16**, 75–97 (2007)
3. Ester, M., Kriegel, H.P., Sander, J., Xu, X.: A density-based algorithm for discovering clusters in large spatial databases with noise. In: Kdd, pp. 226–231 (1996)
4. Fiadino, P., Schiavone, M., Casas, P.: Vivisecting Whatsapp Through large-scale measurements in mobile networks. In: Proceedings of the 2014 ACM Conference on SIGCOMM, pp. 133–134 (2014)
5. Koum, J.: Facebook post (2015). https://www.facebook.com/jan.koum/posts/10152994719980011?pnref=story. Accessed on 26 January 2015
6. Park, S., Cho, K., Lee, B.G.: What makes smartphone users satisfied with the mobile instant messenger? Social presence, flow, and self-disclosure. Int. J. Multimedia Ubiquit. Eng. **9**, 315 (2014). Please check and confirm the edits made in Ref. [6]
7. Statistica: Most popular global mobile messenger apps as of December 2014, based on number of monthly active users (in millions) (2014). http://www.statista.com/statistics/258749/most-popular-global-mobile-messenger-apps/. Accessed on January 26, 2015
8. Yeboah, J., Ewur, G.D.: The impact of Whatsapp messenger usage on students performance in tertiary institutions in Ghana. J. Educ. Pract. **5**, 157–164 (2014)

A Novel Data Dissemination Model for Organic Data Flows

Anna Foerster[1], Asanga Udugama[1](✉), Carmelita Görg[1],
Koojana Kuladinithi[2], Andreas Timm-Giel[2], and Alejandro Cama-Pinto[3]

[1] University of Bremen, Bremen, Germany
`adu@comnets.uni-bremen.de`
[2] Hamburg University of Technology, Hamburg, Germany
[3] Universidad de la Costa, Barranquilla, Colombia

Abstract. The number of computing devices of the IoT are expected to grow exponentially. To address the communication needs of the IoT, research is being done to develop new networking architectures and to extend existing architectures. An area that lacks attention in these efforts is the emphasis on utilisation of omnipresent local data. There are a number of issues (e.g., underutilisation of local resources and dependence on cloud based data) that need to be addressed to exploit the benefits of utilising local data. We present a novel data dissemination model, called the Organic Data Dissemination (ODD) model to utilise the omni-present data around us, where devices deployed with the ODD model are able to operate even without the existence of networking infrastructure. The realisation of the ODD model requires innovations in many different area including the areas of opportunistic communications, naming of information, direct peer-to-peer communications and reinforcement learning. This paper focuses on highlighting the usage of the ODD model in real application scenarios and the details of the architectural components.

Keywords: Internet of Things · Opportunistic networks · Organic Data Flows · Reinforcement Algorithms

1 Introduction

The ubiquity of computing devices is growing rapidly. Omnipresent computing devices form the basis of the Internet of Things (IoT). The International Data Corporation (IDC) predicts that by 2020, the total number of connectable devices in the IoT will be above 200 billion [1]. Predicting further, IDC estimates that by 2020, the digital universe (DU) will consist of 44 ZB of data. 10 % of this data will be contributed by IoT based computing devices and 27 % will be created by mobile devices. To address these growth predictions, new networking architectures have to be proposed that focus on areas such as information centricity of networks, resource restricted nature of the computing devices of the IoT and large scale network based services.

© Institute for Computer Sciences, Social Informatics and Telecommunications Engineering 2015
R. Agüero et al. (Eds.): MONAMI 2015, LNICST 158, pp. 239–252, 2015.
DOI: 10.1007/978-3-319-26925-2_18

The networking architectures proposed for Information Centric Networking (ICN) address the information centricity of communications [2]. A number of enhancements to current architectures are attempting to address the resource restricted nature of the devices of the IoT (e.g., Constrained Application Protocol [3]). Another set of enhancements to existing computing architectures attempt to address the enablement of large scale network based services (e.g., Virtualisation [4]).

Though these new architectures and architectural changes address a number of issues, none of them place an emphasis on the use of the omnipresent data in a local context. Therefore, we foresee the following as being key issues to be addressed for the deployment of localised solutions of IoT.

– **Non-availability of Information Locally.** While the cloud paradigm allows for more flexibility on the server and infrastructure side, collecting all data into common repositories allowing a range of services to be deployed poses additional issues for the system architecture at the edge of the network. Most information is local by nature, but with cloud based solutions it must be transferred to the cloud, creating requirements dependent on always having the reliable connection to the cloud [5].
– **Pull Style Communications.** Current communication architectures require users to initiate communications to retrieve data (e.g., IP networks, where the communicating parties require the knowledge of host addresses to establish a communication session or in ICNs, where the named data is requested for by a user) or register to receive data when they are created. Further, these architectures are highly dependent on reliable communications and when failures are experienced, complete data are re-requested. This kind of communication architecture hinders probing and sensing of the environment for already available data locally.
– **Vertical Systems.** State of the art IoT applications are typically designed, implemented and deployed based on specific application requirements and for specific use cases. They tend to be largely proprietary and their maintenance cost is often included in the price of the installation itself or carried out based on expensive maintenance contracts that often create difficulties in the long term if the supplier is not the same as the organisation that maintains the systems afterwards. The adoption of this process has resulted in a myriad of isolated systems, all working with different communication standards, and using different applications and data storage solutions. These isolated systems are destined to never interoperate with each other, unless very costly integration efforts are made, sometimes costing more than a new, more advanced system installation.
– **Underutilised Local Resources.** The proliferation of smart mobile devices hosting heterogeneous communication technologies, considerable memory and processing capabilities together with sensory capabilities has brought about an environment in which service provisioning could be done anytime/anywhere. These devices together with the omnipresent resource constrained devices, such as sensors, collectively provide an exploitable environment to deploy

a multitude of services even without the support of infrastructures. These omnipresent resources cannot be utilised in a flexible manner mainly due to the above mentioned issues in the current communication architectures.

Therefore, we are motivated to solve some of the aforementioned issues by proposing a solution that creates an omnipresent distributed local knowledge base among the interested parties. The users will collaboratively sense their environment and opportunistically exchange and merge their data in a localised context, even with the absence of infrastructure networks.

In some scenarios such as environmental monitoring, data can be collected and utilised in an ad-hoc manner where the data has higher importance at its origin and decreasing importance after some time.

The data sources we refer to could range from human carried devices (e.g., smart phones, tablets and wearable sensors) to stationary devices with smart homes and smart cities (e.g., static sensors and actuators) and many more in between (e.g., mobile autonomous robots and autonomous cars).

The objective of this paper is to discuss a novel data dissemination model called the **Organic Data Dissemination (ODD)** model, inspired by human communications, in which the flow of information occurs based on application needs and feedback. Therefore, we propose a radically different communication paradigm, compared to the state of the art of networking approaches. The primary features of this communication paradigm are the non-existence of dedicated endpoints (sources/sinks), leading to a destination-less and thus connection-less communication paradigm, where data is propagated opportunistically allowing a node to self-learn based on the reinforcements received through feedbacks (reinforcement learning [6]).

This paper is structured as follows. The next section provides the details of 2 application scenarios where deployed devices can use the ODD model. The third section details the architectural components of the proposed ODD model. The fourth section builds the story board of one of the application scenarios providing details on how the reinforcement learning based self learning process operates in the ODD model. The last section concludes the paper.

2   Application Scenarios

The Organic Data Dissemination (ODD) model has a number of application areas. This section provides the details of 2 real world scenarios that are considered for deployment of ODD based devices.

2.1   Notifications of Natural Fires at VIPS

Barranquilla is a city in the north of Colombia in South America. It is home to over 1 million inhabitants. The city lies to the west of the river Magdalena which flows into the sea at the north of the city. On the west side of the river, facing the city is the nature reserve called the "Via Isla Parque de Salamanca" (VIPS). This nature reserve is home to many wild animal species unique to Colombia.

During the dry season, which falls between December to March, the soil and the vegetation becomes extremely dry in the VIPS nature reserve and becomes prone to natural fires [7]. These fires, when stated and without any interventions may last between 3 to 5 days. Annually, there are around 30 such fires.

These fires result in destruction to the nature reserve and its species. Additionally, the smoke that is generated by these fires is blown away and results in the city of Barranquilla being blanketed by a thick cover of smoke (Fig. 1(a)). The smoke results in breathing problems for children and older people, and furthermore, results in eye problems for many of the residents.

(a)   (b)

Fig. 1. The blanket of smoke affecting Barranquilla and a map providing information of the fire

Finding solutions to the above mentioned problems requires answering 2 questions. *How are the fires detected and communicated in a timely manner?* and *What actions can be taken when the fires are detected?*. When identifying a solution, the following aspects must be considered.

- **Developing country** - Colombia is a developing country. Therefore, the solutions must be cost-effective to deploy and maintain.
- **Climate** - Barranquilla has a tropical savanna climate. It is a hot weather with an all-year-round average temperature of 28 degrees with day temperatures sometimes rising up to 32 degrees. Solutions in such climatic conditions require reliability in terms of operations with minimum downtimes.
- **Deployment effort** - Access to the VIPS nature reserve is very limited due to the harsh terrain. Therefore, a solution must consider the ease of deployment.
- **Interest in community** - Inhabitants in Barranquilla are very keen on having a solution as they are directly affected by the smoke. Therefore, the adopted technologies must include components that allow the inhabitants to get involved in influencing the decisions of the authorities.

There are different sources from which data can be collected for detection in this scenario. This data cannot only help in detecting the origin of the fire, but also assist in the firefighting effort and reduce the impact of the fire (e.g., provide data to families vulnerable to such fires). Directly involved individuals such as forest rangers or government officials, and other parties such as trekkers are able to collect and propagate data about the forest fires due to their proximity to the origin of the fires. For example, air conditions and smoke sensors could be carried by government officials or fire fighters or pictures of air conditions (smoke) could be taken by tourists or residents. This data can be used to build a map of the current fire origin and the wind direction (Fig. 1(b)) to inform the government departments responsible for taking action and also the public.

2.2   Uni Recycler

Another application area of the ODD model is for the "Sharing Economy" [8]. There are many household items that people wish to dispose of, though these items may still be usable. In the context of the University of Bremen, it has been found that there are many freshmen who require such items when they commence their academic lives.

The *Uni Recycler* application is a Smartphone based application for people who wish to make any item available to give away (or for a nominal fee) to anyone who is interested. Figure 2 shows a view of the Uni Recycler application.

Fig. 2. Uni Recycler application

The application uses the ODD model to propagate information like in a *Grapevine*. The operations of this application are as follows:

- A user makes information of a recyclable item available in the Uni Recycler app.
- This information is propagated to a selected set of users in the neighbourhood of the original user.
- The neighbourhood users may have differing interest levels for the said recyclable item. This interest may range from liking this type of recycled items to complete dislike. The actions of the user in the app for this particular

item may result in different types of reinforcement leaning messages being generated about the app.

- These reinforcement learning messages are used to compute the relative popularity of the item by all users using the app (popularity is identified numerically by a value called the *Goodness* value in the ODD model).
- The popularity values are used by all users using the app to propagate messages to other users.
- The user who wishes to buy the item may contact the owner through another communication means.

In the remainder of this paper, we will use the UniRecycler application as our main scenario to explain and detail the envisaged ODD model.

3   Overview to ODD Model

In this section, we will introduce the Organic Data Dissemination (ODD) model in detail and define all its main functionality and components. The general model overview is presented in Fig. 3. In the next paragraphs, we will explain the functionality of each individual component. Section 4 will give a detailed example of how ODD works in reality.

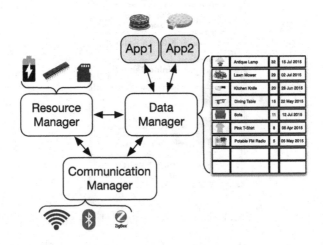

Fig. 3. The complete ODD model and its internal interactions.

The ODD model consists of four main components:

- Communication Manager takes care of the communications of the model. This includes scanning the neighbourhood for new connections, sending and receiving messages and evaluating whether the neighbourhood has changed significantly or not.

- Resource Manager takes care so that the ODD model does not drain the resources of the device. The main assumption here is that the device has some primary usage, such as for telephoning or browsing the web and that these primary applications should not be disturbed. The Resource Manager dictates to the ODD model how often it should scan the neighbourhood, how often and how much data should be exchanged, etc.
- Data Manager organises the data cache of the device by the quality of the data items. This quality can also be seen as the popularity or the *Goodness* of the cached data and is simply a number, which reflects how interesting and valuable this particular data item is for all users.
- Applications are sitting in fact on top of the ODD model, but they do implement one key functionality of the ODD model: the evaluation of the *Goodness* value of the data items. Only the applications can say whether a particular data item is interesting and valuable or not, and only they can observe the interactions of the user with the data items.

3.1   Data Manager

The *Data Manager* (DATAMANAGER) is responsible for all operations related to the cache in an ODD deployed node. It is aware of the size of the cache that it has to manage and uses this cache space to hold the different data items that traverse the node. The operations that the DATAMANAGER performs are as follows:

- Ordering data items in an ascending order based on the computed *Goodness* value. The ordering assists in the process of timely access and transmission of data items when required.
- The reinforcement learning model is used to calculate (re-calculate) the *Goodness* values associated with each of the cached data items. The reward function on which the *Goodness* values are computed **reside in the application** that uses that particular type of data (e.g., Uni Recycler). The reward function determines the value of the data based on user interactions or application requirements.
- The *Goodness* values of the data items "age" with time and loses their relative importance. The data manager defines and implements the ageing function.
- The data in the cache are purged using the *Goodness* values. If no space is available for new arriving items, the items with the lowest *Goodness* values are deleted.
- The data which are to be sent out next when a significant change occurs is determined within the DATAMANAGER by employing a double sided heavy tailed distribution over all data items. The maximum of the distribution lies where the focus of the DATAMANAGER lies (e.g., the focus is set to the highest *Goodness* data items when a significant change of the communication environment has been detected), see Fig. 4.
- When no significant change has been detected, the focus of the DATAMANAGER starts going down the data cache to the data items with lower *Goodness*

values, until it reaches the very bottom. The focus remains there until significant change is detected again and then, it jumps back to the top of the data cache.

- The actual selection of data items to be send out is performed in cooperation with the RESMANAGER, which defines how many items can be send out, and performing a stochastic selection based on the above heavy tailed distribution.

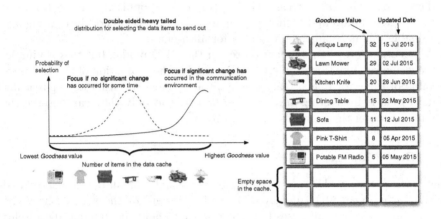

Fig. 4. Data manager operations

Figure 4 shows the structure of the cache populated with data from the Uni Recycler application. The data are ordered based on the *Goodness* value. The size of the cache (9 entries) is determined by the Resource Manager (RESMANAGER).

When determining which items are to be sent out, the following procedure is followed: First, the Communication Manager (COMMMANAGER) signals whether the communication environment (neighbours) has changed significantly since the last time or not. If yes, the DATAMANAGER places its focus on the highest *Goodness* data items. Placing its focus means that it actually defines a double-sided heavy tailed probability function over the whole data cache, with the maximum placed at the highest part of the data cache (where data items with higher *Goodness* values reside). This is shown in Fig. 4 (left of the data cache) where the focus lies approximately on the middle of the cache and the double-sided heavy tailed distribution spans the whole data cache. If no significant change has been observed in the communication neighbourhood, then the maximum of the probability function is moved down the data cache.

The reasoning behind this behaviour is that, if the environment has changed (or is changing fast continuously), the most important data items should be exchanged first. At the same time, we do not want to limit the selection to few data items, but also give a chance to the ones with lower *Goodness* values. Thus, we use a double-sided heavy-tailed distribution for selecting the data items, where the maximum of the probability is "focusing" on some part of the data cache at different times.

After setting the focus, the DATAMANAGER asks the RESMANAGER how many items it is actually allowed to send out. This number is typically small and the DATAMANAGER randomly (based on the double-sided heavy tailed distribution) selects the data items to send out.

This procedure makes sure that in changing environments preference is given to high *Goodness* data items, while not ignoring completely lower *Goodness* ones. At the same time, it also makes sure, through the random selection that if some of the neighbours remain for a longer time in the neighbourhood of the node, they will not receive the same data items repeatedly.

3.2 Resource Manager

The *Resource Manager* (RESMANAGER) is responsible for controlling and providing information related to resources in an ODD deployed node. Access to different resources such as caches, communication links, etc. have to be controlled due to the different characteristics that each of these resources have and the current conditions. Other parts of the ODD model is allowed (or disallowed) to perform actions only under the guidance of the RESMANAGER. Some examples include:

- The RESMANAGER may allow only a limited transmission of cached data items due to current communications being only possible over Bluetooth LE.
- The RESMANAGER hinders the use of the WiFi Direct network interface due to the battery level being below a certain percentage.
- The RESMANAGER allows only a very limited number of data items to be send out because of ongoing video streaming by the user.
- The RESMANAGER disallows any activity between 9 am and 10 am, when it has learned that the user heavily uses the system (e.g. for checking emails and reading news).

To perform these decisions in the RESMANAGER, it is armed with a collection of policies and a set of algorithms that employ scheduling and machine learning techniques. The algorithms use the policies to make decisions initially and the gained experiences are subsequently used to improve the quality of the decisions.

3.3 Communication Manager

The *Communication Manager* (COMMMANAGER) is responsible for two main tasks. The primary task is to send and receive data over the network interfaces that are currently usable in an ODD deployed node. The data sent by the COMMMANAGER are passed to it by the DATAMANAGER. Similarly, the data that is received by the COMMMANAGER is passed to the DATAMANAGER for further processing.

The secondary task that the COMMMANAGER has is the activity of making fuzzy-based decisions related to determining whether the communication neighbourhood has changed. Changes in the neighbourhood are required to be known by the DATAMANAGER to consider re-propagation of data.

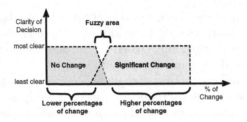

Fig. 5. Determination of neighbourhood changes by the communication manager

Figure 5 shows the fuzzy process of indicating whether a neighbourhood change has occurred or not. When the percentages of change are lower or if the percentages of change are higher, a clear determination is made to consider as the neighbourhood did not change or the neighbourhood changed, respectively. But the overlapping percentages require a fuzzy decision making process to take over. The fuzzy-based decisions assist in correctly and flexibly determining changes in the environment. A simple threshold is hard to identify and not flexible enough.

3.4 Applications

The applications sit on top of the ODD model and interacts directly only with the DATAMANAGER. They use the data in the data cache to represent it and interact directly with the user. They can also create new data items (e.g. sensor readings, pictures, messages from the user, etc.).

The applications also implement one of the most important, even if tiny, components of the ODD model, namely the reward function (shown as cakes in Fig. 3). The reason is that only applications can actually identify the *Goodness* of the data items by evaluating them and giving rewards to the DATAMANAGER. Different applications might give different rewards for the same data items and these rewards will be combined by the DATAMANAGER and its reinforcement learning model into the final *Goodness* value in the data cache. For example, the computation of the *Goodness* value for tapping the data item of the red sofa should be handled by the reward function.

4   The Story of the Red Sofa

In this section we would like to give an intuition of how our proposed ODD model works by relating the story of one particular announcement of the Uni Recycler application, i.e., a *Red Sofa* for sale.

In this story, there are two main actors, Alice and Bob, with their smart devices. Alice has a phablet with a quite large memory and good batteries, while Bob has an older smartphone with an unreliable battery. Alice has a red sofa to sell. She writes an announcement through her Uni Recycler application and saves it. From now on, the ODD model takes care of her message to be delivered to other users, such as Bob or others. The time behaviour of the system have been depicted in Fig. 6.

Now, the red sofa has been saved by Alice and the application passes it to the Data Manager to be saved in the cache. Its *Goodness* value has been set to some constant C, which means that this is a new data item worth spreading (e.g. to 10). The Resource Manager evaluates the usage of the device and sees that it is a good time to check around for new connections and to enhance some data. It fires up the Communication Manager, which scans the environment and decides that it has changed significantly and signals this to the Data Manager. Since the environment has changed, the Data Manager decides that its data items with the highest *Goodness* values should be sent first and puts its focus on the highest 25 % of the ordered cache, which happen to be exactly 20 data items. It also requests the Resource Manager how many items it is allowed to send and through which interfaces. The Resource Manager answers that it can send exactly 3 data items through Bluetooth. The Data Manager randomly selects three data items out of the 20 previously focused ones and the red sofa happens to be among the three selected ones. The Communication Manager sends out the data items and all of them happen to be received by Bob's smartphone (step A in Fig. 6).

The Communication Manager of Bob's smartphone saves the red sofa (and the others, but we are only interested in our red sofa) through the Data Manager to the cache. It also receives Alice's *Goodness* value of the red sofa - currently 10. Now, it needs to decide whether this data item is useful or not. The Data Manager sees that it is new. This is a sign that the red sofa is valuable, but it is still unclear whether it is interesting or not. Thus, it leaves the *Goodness* value as it is (step B in Fig. 6). In other words, it stays neutral towards this data item until more information is available. It asks the Resource Manager whether it is allowed to send out some data and gets a positive answer. It sends the new *Goodness* value of the red sofa plus some of its own cached items (selected as above for Alice) to all its neighbours and also to Alice.

Alice receives the new *Goodness* value which, for clarity, we call feedback, from Bob. Since the feedback is the same as her own value, the *Goodness* value stays as 10.

Now, both Bob and Alice have the red sofa, but they part and everyone goes on their ways through life. Let us first follow Alice for just a little longer. Next time she scans the environment the Communication Manager will signal to her Data Manager that the environment has not changed significantly (in fact, only Bob moved away). Thus, her Data Manager will, at this time, not focus on the highest data items in the cache, but will move its focus to the ones below to also give them a chance to be exchanged. Thus, in longer lived connections between devices, more data with all possible *Goodness* values will be exchanged.

Let us now follow Bob. Bob meets people on his way and pushes the red sofa also to them. He always receives neutral feedback from them, exactly as for Bob before. However, hours later Bob opens the Uni Recycler application and sees the red sofa announcement. He is interested and taps for more information.

He really likes the sofa and decides to call to check the availability of the red sofa later. He taps on the star next to the red sofa and closes the application again. Now the application has new information about how interesting the red sofa is for real users. It gives the red sofa 2 points for being tapped and 5 points for being starred. It passes these points to the Data Manager and the Data Manager re-calculates the *Goodness* value to 17 (step C in Fig. 6).

Bob continues to move around and time passes. Once in a while, the Data Manager re-evaluates the *Goodness* value of the data items and the red sofa gets 1 point off because of ageing. Next time, when Bob meets somebody else and sends the data of the red sofa, it will already have a *Goodness* value of 15, because two update periods have passed (step D in Fig. 6). For example, it might get to Charlie. Charlie will first receive the red sofa with a *Goodness* value of 15 (step E in Fig. 6). However, his Data Manager sees that the announcement is not very fresh any more and gives a feedback of 14 to Bob. Bob will re-compute his *Goodness* value to 14.5 to reflect the fact that the interest of somebody else is less important than the interest of himself (step F in Fig. 6).

Later on, when Charlie opens his Recycler, he will tap the red sofa, because it looks nice, but then he will immediately delete it, because he does not need a sofa right now. The application will evaluate his action and send -3 points (i.e. $2 - 5$) points to the Data Manager. Charlie's Data Manager will re-compute the *Goodness* value of the red sofa to 11 (step G in Fig. 6).

In this way, the *Goodness* value of the red sofa will continue changing over time and with different users. The tendency will be towards smaller values as time passes and the red sofa will start going down the data caches until it needs to get deleted because of space limitations and new data items coming in.

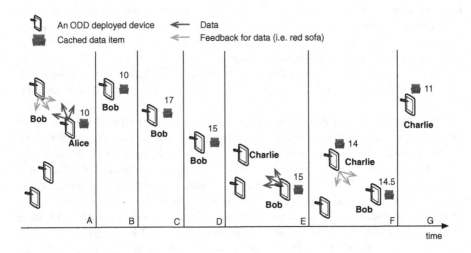

Fig. 6. Evaluation of goodness value for the red sofa (Color figure online)

5   Discussion of the ODD Model

Some interesting questions arise from the story of the red sofa:

- *Will the red sofa reach all users in the network?* Eventually yes, but it will not be flooded. The Resource Manager dictates how much data can be sent out and thus does not increase the traffic with increasing data cache size. Thus, with large amounts of data items in the network, not all data items will get everywhere. The data items with lower *Goodness* values will be deleted.
- *Can we ever delete a data item?* Not really. Instead, as any old rumour, you let it die. People will stop looking at it and the ageing function will make sure that it will slowly degrade its *Goodness* value.
- *Will we not start sending the same data item back and forth?* This can indeed happen, but the randomised selections keep this under control. Prohibiting it by, for example, saving information related to what went where, will introduce more overhead than actually saving resources. The Data Manager takes care of this as detailed in Sect. 3.

In the previous sections we have focused our discussion on one of the proposed applications, the Uni Recycler. However, the ODD model serves very nicely also other applications with similar properties. For example, in the natural fire notification system from Sect. 2, the data items are not things for sale, but sensory data, such as air quality, wind direction and wind strength. They are produced by either the authorities with deployed devices all over the city and the nature reserve, or by citizens with their smartphones, tablets and laptops. The application needs to implement its own reward function. This needs to take into account the freshness of the data and its geographical location. For example, a wind speed data item from 3 min ago is more valuable than something from the day before; tan air quality measurement from a location very close to where we already have a fresh measurement is less useful than from a new and far-away location. Similarly, problematic measurements, such as very high wind speed, fire detections or very bad air quality, are more important than data items which signal that all is good.

In summary, the ODD model offers us a novel way to look at data dissemination in very large distributed environments. It is not meant for targeted heavy-load communications, such as streaming services or phone calls. Instead, it focuses on the type of data which the IoT needs to serve: tiny pieces of information, produced continuously by billions of devices.

6   Conclusion

In this paper, a novel data dissemination model called the Organic Data Dissemination (ODD) model is introduced to exploit the benefits of utilising local data. The data flow in this model, inspired by human communications, is influenced by the data needs of applications and the feedback provided by these applications (i.e., the users of these applications). As application areas of the ODD model,

2 scenarios are considered. One of these scenarios, the "The Story of the Red Sofa" is used to elaborate the operations of the ODD model.

The focus of communications of the ODD model is on local data. Therefore, the underlying communications model that ODD uses is based on direct peer-to-peer communications where the nodes that are deployed with the ODD model is able to operate in networks without infrastructure. When considering a deployment in infrastructure based networks, the ODD model takes aspects such as the availability of the communicating parties into consideration when performing communications.

The next step of the development of the ODD model is to evaluate the performance. To evaluate performance, we are currently building a test-bed with hundreds of smart phones and tablets. The underlying communications are performed using WiFi Direct and Bluetooth Low Energy. To evaluate large scale deployments, a simulation model is being built in the OMNeT++ [9] environment.

References

1. International Data Corporation (IDC): IVIEW, Digital Universe in 2020, December 2012
2. Ahlgren, B., Dannewitz, C., Imbrenda, C., Kutscher, D., Ohlman, B.: A Survey of Information-Centric Networking (Draft), Number 10492. Dagstuhl Seminar Proceedings. Schloss Dagstuhl - Leibniz-Zentrum fuer Informatik, Germany (2011)
3. Shelby, Z., Hartke, K., Bormann, C.: IETF RFC 7252, The Constrained Application Protocol (CoAP), June 2014
4. Murray, P., et al.: FP7 SAIL Project, D-5.2 (D-D.1) Cloud Network Architecture Description, January 2013
5. Förster, Anna, Timm-Giel, Andreas, Görg, Carmelita, Giordano, Silvia, Kuladinithi, Koojana: DICE: A Novel Platform to Support Massively Distributed Clouds. In: Pesch, Dirk, Timm-Giel, Andreas, Calvo, Ramón Agüero, Wenning, Bernd-Ludwig, Pentikousis, Kostas (eds.) Monami. LNICST, vol. 125, pp. 273–286. Springer, Heidelberg (2013)
6. Sutton, R.S., Barto, A.G., Learning, R.: An Introduction. MIT Press, Cambridge, MA (1998)
7. Villadiego, K., Velay-Dabat, M.A.: Outdoor thermal comfort in a hot and humid climate of Colombia: a field study in Barranquilla. Elsevier Build. Environ. J. **75**, 142–152 (2014)
8. Sundararajan, A.: From Zipcar to the sharing economy. Harvard Business Review, January 2013
9. Udugama, A., Kuladinithi, K., Foerster, A., Goerg, C.: Federating OMNeT++ simulations with test-bed environments. In: OMNeT++ Community Workshop, September 2015

Using an Identity Plane for Adapting Network Behavior to User and Service Requirements

Pedro Martinez-Julia$^{(\boxtimes)}$ and Antonio F. Skarmeta

Department of Communication and Information Engineering,
University of Murcia, 30100 Murcia, Spain
{pedromj,skarmeta}@um.es

Abstract. The advent of Software Defined Networking (SDN) has opened the door to new network functions that were difficult or even impossible to have. This has been the case of typically complex network management operations, which now can be layered on top of SDN controllers in order to adapt network behavior to achieve some objectives or quickly react to network events so network consistence is unaltered by them. However, users and services have little to say in current SDN architectures. In this paper we discuss how to use an *Identity Plane* to carry user and service identities and requirements to network controllers, which would contact a management service that follows the management model proposed by Autonomic Computing (AC) to know the necessary changes to adapt the network behavior to such requirements.

Keywords: Future internet · Identity · Overlay network · Autonomic computing · Self-management · SOA

1 Introduction

In current networks, most network management operations are performed using certain mechanisms and protocols for monitoring and configuring network elements, from virtual to physical elements and from hosts to network equipments. Even though those mechanisms are normally used by specific applications that permits administrators to manage multiple elements from a central place, all tasks usually need human intervention. This behavior is also spread along the current Internet but, as the number of network elements grows, this task is becoming more and more complicated to accomplish. Therefore, a new management paradigm is emerging from the Autonomic Computing (AC) initiative. It will overcome future requirements on self-management of systems and services, which are key challenges for the Future Internet (FI) [1,17,19].

Apart from resolving the issue with the rapid growth of systems to manage, the AC also address the added problem found in the also rapidly growing computer systems complexity, dynamism, and heterogeneity. Thus, AC systems are defined as "computing systems that can manage themselves given high-level objectives from administrators" [12]. This definition encompasses the key

© Institute for Computer Sciences, Social Informatics and Telecommunications Engineering 2015
R. Agüero et al. (Eds.): MONAMI 2015, LNICST 158, pp. 253–265, 2015.
DOI: 10.1007/978-3-319-26925-2_19

principle behind AC: Administrators (humans) set the rules (policies) by which systems should be guided and those systems are responsible of enforcing them. This way, AC presents a good solution to add self-management capabilities to modern networks and services, and so is supported by the Future Internet Assembly [7] on its MANA position paper [8] on which autonomic network management plays a fundamental role, incorporating to the FI service model the main activities found in AC.

On the other hand, the Software Defined Networking (SDN) model is experiencing a huge growth, providing the necessary underlying mechanisms to implement control and management operations with little or no impact to underlying elements. Such model clearly separates control and data planes, which is an important feature, but also provides the necessary interfaces to build network services and applications on top of network controllers, which means the breaking of network ossification and the provisioning of huge flexibility to the network.

This has led us to define a mechanism that connects an *Identity Plane* [15] to the SDN controller and the necessary connection points for them to properly address management operations and reflect their results into the network. Intermediate network elements will not have to be changed because the connection is performed through the SDN control plane. This way, network entities will be able to declare their network requirements and the network will be able to respond to such declaration by taking the appropriate determinations to meet those requirements as best as possible. All of this will be done without human intervention but some humans, particularly the network administrators, have to define the policies to which management and control operations will be enforced to accomplish.

The remainder of this paper is organized as follows. First, we introduce the motivation of the present work and the challenges it exposes in Sect. 2. Then, in Sect. 3 we describe the proposed solution, composed of network management modules and the interconnection to the *Identity Plane* and the SDN control plane. In Sect. 4 we present an experimental instance of the proposed solution and discuss the experimentation results we have obtained with it. In Sect. 5 we briefly analyze the related work and, finally, in Sect. 6 we conclude the paper and introduce some hints for the future.

2   Future Identity-Based Network Management

The search towards future networks has exposed many challenges [11] that have promoted the design of new architectures that deprecate the current network models. Our vision is that many of them will coexist in the future so it is desirable to combine their qualities to provide the best service to network users. On the other hand, the advances in technology are merging our real lives with our digital lives, so user identities and contexts must not be only considered at application level but also at network level, allowing the establishment of zones of privacy (as in real life), as well as controlled identity linkability and information disclosure.

These challenges have motivated our work in a new identity-based network architecture [13–15] that builds an *Identity Plane* that interacts with users to know their intentions and willingness to use multiple devices in a communication, which requires more mechanisms than just network mobility. As user identities are delicate, every decision is taken with a maximal constraint: privacy and data protection. It leads us to avoid the disclosure of the relation of data and identities, the identification via IP or MAC address, and the ability to keep the privacy across layers, cross-layer security. Thus, it is mandatory to use identities to address communication parties, instead of using identifiers or locators.

To achieve these goals, the architecture we propose is heavily based on the overlay network concept and the possibilities offered by SDN. On the one hand, an overlay network is used to address entities by their identities, so entities themselves are the communication endpoints and they can reach each other without dealing with network location and keeping their privacy and overall security. On the other hand, the mechanisms provided by SDN are used to embed network sessions into the underlying infrastructures while ensuring they commit the necessary security and the requirements specified by communication parties.

Since this new architecture is not bound to any specific underlying network and since they can be combined during communication, the control mechanisms provided by SDN are used to establish, configure, and release communication paths among communicating entities. Such paths are defined by their communication properties or parameters that, among others, are: source and destination endpoints, represented by the rules accepted by the SDN, including the addressing scheme of the specific underlying networks; service type, or the operation that is requested to the network: send a file, ask for a file, web browsing, voice call, etc.; traffic behavior (variable/constant bit rate, rate + strength, etc.); maximum delay and throughput; and levels of priority, security, and privacy.

At the end, each underlying network will use these parameters when reserving the necessary resources to create the requested low-level communication paths. Moreover, these paths will not be static but dynamic, so they support mobility and other environment changes. However, path management must not cause a significant increase in complexity or disrupt the normal network operation. Finally, due to dynamic interactions, the complexity of the operations, and the number of elements that can be involved, the operations must not need the constant supervision of network administrators, just under enforcement of the policies they set.

These requirements have led us to opt for AC principles [12] to design the management blocks of the solution. AC can provide the required features by being stimulated by network control events and with very little disruption to end or intermediate network entities. As described in Sect. 5, current proposals for autonomic network management can not meet these requirements while being integrated with the *Identity Plane* and the SDN control. Therefore, as described in the following section, we have designed a simple management approach and included it into the integrated solution.

3 Proposed Solution

As introduced above, the *Identity Plane* promoted by our architecture is governed by the Domain Trusted Entity Infrastructure (DTEi) and connected to

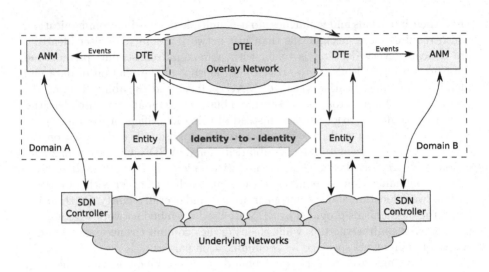

Fig. 1. Overview of the integrated architecture.

communicating entities in order to allow them to operate securely. This way, the DTEi is privately aware of both identities and objectives of the entities that communicate so it is in the precise position to determine the requirements of communication instances and ask the network to build the necessary paths. However, this task is out of the scope of the DTEi itself so an external component is introduced to perform it. This component is the Autonomic Network Manager (ANM), whose specific design is discussed at the end of this section.

The ANM is responsible of monitoring network operations by receiving events from the DTEi, determine which actions should be taken on response to such events, and communicate such actions to the SDN controller so it can enforce them to the network. Typical network events would be to establish new communication sessions or the movement of an entity from one network to another. In general, it would be required to change the network parameters very frequently in response of the dynamism of requirements specified by communicating entities but also in response of changes of the network. This also implies that the SDN controller will report to ANM the events related to the network paths it manages.

Instead of explicitly indicating the necessities to the ANM, it will be able to infer them by knowing what happens in the environment, like knowing when a network session is starting between two entities. To guide the whole management, the ANM will do an extensive use of policies, both to guess the reactions to certain events and to check if an operation is allowed or not. Those policies are set by network administrators, together with the necessary statements to match complex events from many simple events.

From now on we discuss how to integrate the ANM with the *Identity Plane* and thus how this solution meets the requirements commented in the previous section. Figure 1 illustrates how we propose to integrate them. It shows how

network elements from different domains interact to achieve the global autonomic management objectives. The elements and their functions are described
as follows:

– The DTEi, formed by the union of all its instances via an overlay network, is
  the main element of the *Identity Plane*. The overlay network is used to decen-
  tralize its operation across all identity/network domains. Its main function, as
  described above, is to mediate in communication negotiations for the entities
  (communication parties) of each domain. Thus, the DTEi manages, for each
  communication, the session establishment, the security aspects, etc. Thus, the
  DTEi is also in place to send the necessary events for the ANM.
– Entity represents a communication party. As commented above, entities can
  be persons, software, machines, things, etc. Each entity relays its network
  operations to its corresponding DTEi instance but the final data exchanges
  are performed through the data plane of the underlaying network.
– ANM is the element that watches its environment by receiving events from
  DTEi instances and the SDN controller. There is a different ANM deployed
  in each domain, connected to the DTEi instance of such domain. It receives
  the events, analyzes the environment, checks the policies, and decides what
  to do in response. Then, it will contact the SDN controller to communicate
  such decisions so the underlying network meets the necessary requirements.
– SDN Controller represents the controller of the current domain of the underlying network. It will report to the ANM the changes in the network regarding
  the communications it is managing. Also, it will receive requirements from the
  ANM to be enforced into the network. Those requirements are mainly represented by communication parameters, such as bandwidth, latency, security
  level, etc.

That said, the ANM is only coupled with the *Identity Plane* by means of the
messages (events) sent by the DTEi instance of its domain, so it respects the high
decoupling design principle, which is widely recommended in network architecture design. Thus, this point is the main and only point of interaction between the
two architectures. As it is totally asynchronous, the network operations are not
delayed or disrupted by the management operations. Finally, the inter-domain
nature of management and control architectures allows the integration and interaction of different domains. Below we discuss the internals of the ANM.

3.1   Autonomic Network Manager

As we will analyze in Sect. 5, existing proposals for autonomic network management are centered in the interior part of the network so they do not consider
entities into such task. Also, they do not use proper identification mechanisms
and they are difficult to connect to current SDN control plane in a lightweight,
non-intrusive manner. Therefore, in the integrated solution we have included our
own approach to autonomic management.

The management solution is designed as a service-oriented architecture.
Thus, it has a different service for each activity defined in AC, together with

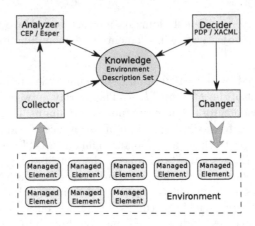

Fig. 2. Architecture of the management component, the ANM.

the necessary components to integrate them and help them to be integrated with other services or applications. These services are focused on genericity and flexibility. Instead of concentrated in the construction of certain solution, the services can be combined in many ways and with other services.

As depicted in Fig. 2, we have defined a different service for each AC task (collector, analyzer, decider, and changer). Also, we have defined a *knowledge* element that represents the knowledge that has the manager of its environment and that is built from the events received, the results of the analysis, the application of policies, etc.

Once we have defined the services we deploy them in top of GEMBus [16], a framework developed inside the GÉANT project to provide a new environment to enable users to create, integrate, and request service facilities on demand by means of the expansion of the current service model to produce the basic framework for a Multi-Domain ESB (MDESB). The inclusion of AC services into GEMBus framework may provide valuable capabilities to applications and services already deployed on GEMBus framework. Moreover, when the autonomic management solution is built in top of GEMBus it can interact with other management solutions, such as AutoBAHN [3] and PerfSONAR [10] as we show in the following section.

Below we show a brief description of each necessary component to assembly the whole solution but before we want to illustrate how it works:

1. The collector receives messages that can be sent from different sources containing one or more registers to describe (part of) the current environment state. These messages are used to build the environment description set (knowledge) and sent to the analyzer. If there is no message received from the outside, a special element built with the Quartz Service Engine sends periodic messages to keep the knowledge alive.
2. The analyzer is built with a Complex Event Processor (CEP) based on Esper [6] so it is capable to detect situations comprising several knowledge

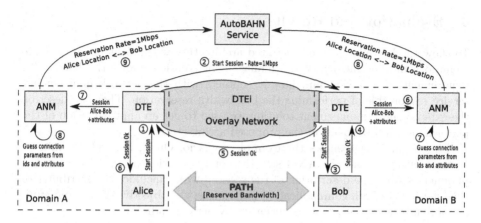

Fig. 3. Example scenario of interactions of the proposed solution with AutoBAHN service.

items. Thus, it analyzes the environment information and extracts new or updated items that are then sent back to the collector to complete the knowledge set.

3. For each received message, either from the outside, the *keepalive* service, or from the analyzer, the collector composes a new knowledge message and sends it to the decider.

4. With the knowledge it has received, the decider checks policies to know the environment correctness and with the result composes a new message to be sent to the changer. The policies are checked against a policy manager provided by an external service that implements a policy administration and decision point (PAP, PDP). It is based on XACML and here we decided to incorporate the implementation offered in XACML-Light [9]. This service is configured by administrators using its own interface to manage XACML policies.

5. The changer receives orders from the decider and communicates the actions (obligations) determined by the policies to the elements that should perform them.

This process shows that the key points of the architecture are the analyzer and the decider. They must be configured by administrators to determine the behavior of the manager but then it are designed to run by itself without other human intervention.

The services are deployed in an Enterprise Service Bus (ESB) which is used as service container and communication bus. It hosts the message router that is used to deliver messages among components. Here we use FUSE ESB because it is a standards based, free open-source software and is actively supported. Moreover, the service container offered by the ESB provides a complete component model and life-cycle management tool.

4   Evaluation and Results

To show the behavior of the integrated architecture we first define an example scenario that illustrates how the management solution knows the bandwidth requirement of a session and how it contacts with the network management service responsible of performing the bandwidth reservation. Then, we describe the experimental management solution we used to get an approximation of the performance and behavior of the proposed architecture.

First of all, Fig. 3 shows the example scenario. On it, two entities initiate a communication and the ANM sets the communication path, calculating the parameters from the description of the session, which includes the attributes of the identities of both communication parties and the objective of the communication, and the policies that has been set by network administrators.

In the example, steps from 1 to 5 are necessary to establish the communication through the *Identity Plane*. On these steps, Alice requests to start a session with Bob, specifying both identities and the aim of this session. Then, the DTEi instances talk to each other in order to negotiate the session. During this negotiation, Bob is actually asked to start the session and it accepts, so its DTEi instance accepts the negotiation and Alice's DTEi instance communicates it to Alice.

Once the communication has been accepted, the DTEi instances report to their ANMs that such session has been started, including the identities involved with their relevant attributes and the aim of the session. Then, the ANM checks the policies that apply to such identities and communication objective to determine the action to take. In the example, the action told and accepted by the policies implicated in such operation is to contact the AutoBAHN service in order to reserve a bandwidth of 1 Mbps between Alice and Bob. The AutoBAHN service here plays the role of the SDN controller because bandwidth reservation is performed on top of the SDN controller, as a network service or application running on it.

This also demonstrates the great benefit of deploying the management architecture in top of GEMBus, because it wins easy access to many network services, like AutoBAHN. We should notice that since the *Identity Plane* does not know the locators of the entities that start the communication until it has been accepted, the reservation request can not be fired up before receiving the *Session OK*. However, other scenarios may benefit from such action, so DTEi may be configured to trigger more events.

Once the scenario has been defined and the experimental implementation has been built, we have evaluated the solution by the generation of arbitrary events at different rates and the measurement of the time spent from the reception of a message (event) to the emission of a response (decision). We get the measures directly from the host where resides the management solution to avoid any latency that could be introduced by the network. The results are shown by Table 1 and we discuss them below.

In Fig. 4 we compare the average and total times spent to process each event while increasing the number of concurrent events. The average time is taken from the reception of the first message to the emission of the final decision, but

Table 1. Performance results (milliseconds).

Concurrent sessions	1	2	4	8	16	32
Average time	18.700	24.600	40.100	78.531	147.156	312.625
Total time, average	18.700	48.700	79.100	176.250	297.500	701.000
Total time, median	18.000	41.000	86.000	175.500	297.500	701.000
Normali. total time	18.700	24.350	19.775	22.031	18.594	21.906
Ses. estab. overhead	16.775	16.674	8.339	4.170	3.127	1.042

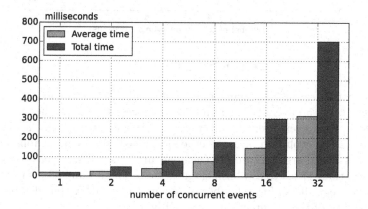

Fig. 4. Performance overview showing the average and total times spent processing each event.

the total time is the time spent in processing all concurrent events. Although the average time increases exponentially with the number of concurrent events, this does not mean poor scalability because the events are processed in series, thus there are many events processed at the same time but in different stage of the process. This parallelism is proved watching the total time spent in processing all messages. The total time does not match with the sum of the time spent in each individual event (or the multiplication of the average time spent processing an event by the total number of events being processed). On the contrary, we can see that the total time is around the double of the average time, what demonstrate the high level of parallelism and concurrent behavior of the architecture.

Finally, in Fig. 5 we show a correlation of the manager load, represented in number of threads, and the average time spent in event processing, from the reception of the first message to the emission of the final decision. We obtain this correlated time by dividing the average time spent in event processing by the number of concurrent events being processed at the same time. While concurrency level increases, the correlated time converges to 10 ms. This means that a manager processing 32 events at the same time is going to spend an average of 320 ms to each event, that is the product of 10 ms by 32 concurrent events.

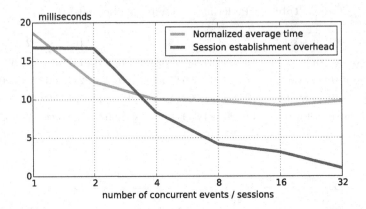

Fig. 5. Scalability overview.

Thus, we can infer that if a manager average load reaches 64 concurrent events, each event takes an average of 640 ms to be processed, if it reaches 128 concurrent events, each event takes an average of 1280 ms, and so on. Moreover, the figure shows the evolution of the overhead induced to session establishment by the identity-based architecture per each concurrent session, which states that it spends less than 17 ms to establish single sessions and around 33 ms in all parallel sessions, regardless of the number of concurrent sessions, thus demonstrating the scalability of the architecture proposed here.

5 Current Autonomic Management Proposals

In this section we discuss some interesting proposals for autonomic network management that were the starting point to design our solution. An important feature is the service orientation because SOAs are better suited for the specific requirements of our solution. Thus, we briefly comment their strengths and weaknesses, with special attention on the capabilities we require but they lack.

A proper autonomic management solution must provide, at least, transparent support to build distributed systems that involve many elements from different administrative domains, as well as the ability to easily integrate the architecture with existing systems, services, and applications, being or not service oriented and supporting different platforms. Moreover, it should exploit the control-loop concept of AC while offering fine granularity in management tasks. We have found and analyzed some reference solutions that meet most requirements, but with some lacks that justify the architecture presented in this paper.

First we have ANEMA [5]. It is an autonomic network management architecture that is driven by many types of policies and target goals. It follows AC principles and incorporates many network level elements and functions, but lacks the definition of specific mechanisms to involve multiple domains in the management process. Also, its mechanisms are not clearly provided as generic and reusable components, so it is difficult to customize it and make it interact with other external systems.

From the web service point of view, we have PAWS [2], that is a framework to build self-managed applications based on adaptive web services and following both AC and SOA principles. Its main purpose is to enhance business process execution language (BPEL) service composition adding self-configuration and self-healing capabilities. Although this architecture is generic and flexible enough to cover many management requirements, it does not offer a complete AC control loop nor the necessary mechanisms to extend the self-management capabilities out of the service scope.

MAWeS [18] is a new architecture for building service oriented systems that follows SOA principles to provide self-tuning capabilities using automatically generated performance predictions. Although it provides many interesting capabilities, it lacks the specific definition of AC tasks and misses the AC control loop. Also, this architecture does not define how to make services from different domains collaborate to reach distributed objectives.

Finally we have ASMF [4], a framework that follows SOA and AC principles to provide dynamic service composition and enforcement of SLA contracts compliance. Although this architecture is very interesting, it is very tied to service level management and lacks certain interesting features such as the component generalization to permit the customization of the self-management operations, the definition of a policy decision point (PDP) and policy administration point (PAP), and the definition of elements to achieve cross-domain management.

6   Conclusions and Future Work

In this paper we have discussed an approach to bring self-management features to the network by using a newly defined *Identity Plane* together with the management model defined by AC, both applied to SDN. Even though current architecture proposals follow AC principles in one level or another, they lack important features to build distributed systems in general, and cross-domain, federated systems in particular. Thus, we proposed to use our simple but complete solution to overcome the challenge but following the same AC principles as the other architectures.

Moreover, we have defined how to perform the integration, the connection points between the management functional block and the SDN controller, and the connection points between the *Identity Plane* and the management solution. In addition, we have demonstrated how the integrated architecture can be used and its good behavior by running an experimental implementation over an example scenario.

Our future work will be focused on the new features that the SDN may offer to the management solution, as well as the evolution of the *Identity Plane* in order to deepen its integration with SDN approaches.

Acknowledgments. This work is partially supported by the Ministry of Education of Spain under the FPU program grant AP2010-0576, by the Ministry of Economy and Competitiveness of Spain under the grants TIN2013-50477-EXP and TIN2014-52099-R (Edison project), and by the Program for Research Groups of Excellence of the Séneca Foundation under grant 04552/GERM/06. Finally, this work makes use of results produced by the SmartFIRE project, which is supported by the International Research &Development Program of the National Research Foundation of Korea (NRF) funded by the Ministry of Science, ICT and Future Planning (MSIP, Korea) (Grant number: K2013078191) and the Seventh Framework Programme (FP7) funded by the European Commission (Grant number: 611165).

References

1. Al-Shaer, E., Greenberg, A., Kalmanek, C., Maltz, D.A., Ng, T.S.E., Xie, G.G.: New frontiers in internet network management. ACM SIGCOMM Comput. Commun. Rev. **39**(5), 37–39 (2009)
2. Ardagna, D., Comuzzi, M., Mussi, E., Pernici, B., Plebani, P.: Paws: a framework for executing adaptive web-service processes. IEEE Softw. **24**(6), 39–46 (2007)
3. Bandwidth on Demand with AutoBAHN. http://www.geant2.net/server/show/ConWebDoc.2544
4. Cheng, Y., Leon-Garcia, A., Foster, I.: Toward an autonomic service management framework: a holistic vision of soa, aon, and autonomic computing. IEEE Commun. Mag. **46**(5), 138–146 (2008)
5. Derbel, H., Agoulmine, N., Salaün, M.: Anema: Autonomic network management architecture to support self-configuration and self-optimization in IP networks. Comput. Netw. **53**(3), 418–430 (2009)
6. Espertech Inc. and Esper contributors. Esper - Complex Event Processing (2010). http://esper.codehaus.org
7. European Future Internet Portal. Future Internet Assembly (2010). http://www.future-internet.eu/home/future-internet-assembly.html
8. Galis, A., et al.: Position Paper on Management and Service-aware Networking Architectures (MANA) for Future Internet (2010). http://www.future-internet.eu/fileadmin/documents/prague_documents/MANA_PositionPaper-Final.pdf
9. Gryb, O., et al.: XACML Light (2010). http://xacmllight.sourceforge.net
10. Internet2, GÉANT2, ESnet, and RNP. perfSONAR: PERFormance Service Oriented Network monitoring ARchitecture (2010). http://www.perfsonar.net
11. Jain, R.: Internet 3.0: ten problems with current internet architecture and solutions for the next generation. In: Proceedings of Military Communications Conference, pp. 1–9. IEEE Computer Society, Los Alamitos, CA, USA (2006)
12. Kephart, J.O., Chess, D.M.: The vision of autonomic computing. IEEE Comput. **36**(1), 41–50 (2003)
13. Martinez-Julia, P., Gomez-Skarmeta, A.F.: A novel identity-based network architecture for next generation internet. J. Univ. Comput. Sci. **18**(12), 1643–1661 (2012)
14. Martinez-Julia, P., Gomez-Skarmeta, A.F.: Using identities to achieve enhanced privacy in future content delivery networks. Comput. Electr. Eng. **38**(2), 346–355 (2012)
15. Martinez-Julia, P., Gomez-Skarmeta, A.F., Girao, J., Sarma, A.: Protecting digital identities in future networks. In: Proceedings of the Future Network and Mobile Summit 2011, pp. 1–8. International Information Management Corporation (2011)

16. Martinez-Julia, P., Lopez, D.R., Gomez-Skarmeta, A.F.: The gembus framework and its autonomic computing services. In: Proceedings of the International Symposium on Applications and the Internet Workshops, pp. 285–288. IEEE Computer Society, Washington, DC, USA, 2010

17. Pras, A., Schonwalder, J., Burgess, M., Festor, O., Perez, G.M., Stadler, R., Stiller, B.: Key research challenges in network management. IEEE Commun. Mag. 45(10), 104–110 (2007)

18. Rak, M., Villano, U., Mancini, E.P.: Autonomic composite-service architecture with mawes. In: Proceedings of the International Conference on Complex, Intelligent and Software Intensive Systems, pp. 1050–1056. IEEE Computer Society, Washington, DC, USA (2010)

19. Schonwalder, J., Fouquet, M., Rodosek, G., Hochstatter, I.: Future internet = content + services + management. IEEE Commun. Mag. 47(7), 27–33 (2009)

Wireless Sensor Networks and IoT Architecures

FESTIVAL: Towards an Intercontinental Federation Approach

Juan R. Santana[1(✉)], José A. Galache[1], Toyokazu Akiyama[2],
Levent Gurgen[3], Morito Matsuoka[4], Martino Maggio[5],
and Shuuichirou Murata[6]

[1] Universidad de Cantabria, Santander, Spain
{jrsantana, jgalache}@tlmat.unican.es
[2] Kyoto Sangyo University, Kyoto, Japan
akiyama@cc.kyoto-su.ac.jp
[3] Commissariat à l'énergie atomique et aux énergies alternatives,
Grenoble, France
levent.gurgen@cea.fr
[4] Osaka University, Osaka, Japan
matsuoka@cmc.osaka-u.ac.jp
[5] Engineering Ingegneria Informatica SpA, Palermo, Italy
martino.maggio@eng.it
[6] Acutus Software Inc., Kyoto, Japan
mrt@acutus.co.jp

Abstract. In the last years, in both Europe and Japan, several initiatives have been started with the aim of building and testing Internet of Things and Smart ICT architectures and platforms to address specific domain issues through designed solutions. FESTIVAL EU-Japan collaborative project aims at federating these testbeds, making them interoperable, allowing centralized data collection and analyzing societal issues in both cultures, all of it under a user privacy-preserving context. In this sense, FESTIVAL pursues a twofold approach: firstly, the intercontinental federation of testbeds in Japan and Europe using existing tools as well as developing new ones; and secondly, the creation of new services and experiments, to be performed on top of the FESTIVAL testbeds and experimentation facilities, associated to three different smart city domains: smart energy, smart building and smart shopping. Throughout this article the current status of the project (in its first year) is shown, describing the Experimentation as a Service federation approach to be implemented, with a first analysis of the platforms and testbeds that are included within the project. Furthermore, the paper also describes the services and use cases that will be conducted within FESTIVAL lifespan. Finally, next steps to be carried out in the coming years of the project are indicated.

Keywords: Federation · Testbed · Platform · Experimentation facility · Eaas · Smart shopping · Smart energy · Smart building

© Institute for Computer Sciences, Social Informatics and Telecommunications Engineering 2015
R. Agüero et al. (Eds.): MONAMI 2015, LNICST 158, pp. 269–280, 2015.
DOI: 10.1007/978-3-319-26925-2_20

1 Introduction

The Internet of Things (IoT) is an emerging paradigm that is radically changing the way we interact with daily life objects at various environments such as home, work, transportation and city [1]. By connecting the physical environment to the internet, it provides real-time information about the environment as well as possibility of controlling it with unexampled easiness. Having access to this cyber-physical environment by just clicking on the button of a smart phone is one step forward to human's dream of controlling everything.

IoT bridges the gap between the cyber and the physical worlds; therefore testbeds allowing verification of IoT solutions must be closely coupled with the physical environments where the experiments will be running. This is an important differentiation point with respect to traditional experimentation testbeds where the virtual resources can be everywhere on the planet and be shared among different experimenters. Real-life testbeds are thus necessary for validating Smart ICT services relying on IoT infrastructures. The experimenters have to be able to gather real-life environmental data, to have direct control to the environment and to interact with the end-users, as main actors for validating these ICT services.

However, IoT testbeds are not only expensive to setup due to the costs of experimentation material (sensors, actuators, communication infrastructure, etc.) but also difficult to deploy, setup and maintain in the physical world. For those stakeholders (researchers, SMEs, application developers, etc.), who do not have such opportunity of deployment, testbeds are crucial and the only way to verify their developments. Besides, if the developments cover several domains requiring different types of physical environments and/or user types, federation of those testbeds becomes the key concept for allowing the access to such valuable resources.

FESTIVAL [2] project's vision is to offer Internet of Things experimentation platforms providing an interaction facility with physical environments and end-users, where experimenters can validate their Smart ICT service developments in various domains. FESTIVAL testbeds will connect cyber world to the physical world, from large scale deployments at a city scale, to small platforms in lab environments, also including dedicated physical spaces simulating real-life settings. Those platforms will be connected and federated via homogeneous access APIs with an "Experimentation as a Service" (EaaS) model for experimenters to test their added value services.

There have been long years of research work in Europe and Japan on federation of testbeds and, more recently, on IoT testbeds. FESTIVAL will reuse as much as possible existing software and hardware components from Europe and Japan for building the EaaS federation. In the European side, several hardware, software and infrastructure enablers from various European Future Internet initiatives such as FIRE, FI-PPP and IERC could be reused, whilst Japanese side will offer hardware and software components from NICT's Smart ICT testbeds.

The paper will show the status of the FESTIVAL project within its first year of development, being structured as follows. In Sect. 2, it is presented the novel EaaS federation approach to be addressed by the FESTIVAL project, thus describing in Sect. 3 the different experimentation facilities, platforms, living labs and testbeds considered within the project to be federated under the aforementioned EaaS model. Section 4 will present the different use cases to be developed within the project scope, indicating the testbed(s) on top of which they will be running. Finally, Sect. 5 will indicate some conclusions derived from the work carried out, also indicating the next steps to be achieved in the next years of the project.

2 EaaS Model for Experimenters: A Federation Approach

As indicated in the introduction section of this document, one of the main objectives of the Festival project is to federate a highly heterogeneous set of facilities from Europe and Japan. For many years, over the FP7 program, the European FIRE initiative made an effort to move from individual or locally clustered future internet testbeds toward actual federation of testbeds. During these years, the federation technologies have matured enough to include a wide variety of tools such as resource discovery and provisioning, resource reservation, experiment control, resource and experiment monitoring, etc. FESTIVAL aims at going one step further by defining and applying the Experimentation as a Service approach. This concept is to be understood as the capability for a federated testbed to provide reconfigurable on-demand access to a set of virtual reusable resources allowing the set-up and running of traceable and reproducible experiments. The creation of this federation platform allows experimenters to rapidly deploy experiments based on new ICT services belonging to different smart city domains, such as smart shopping, smart energy, smart building, or participatory sensing.

The federation within FESTIVAL will take advantage of existing hardware and software components from Europe and in Japan, with the goal of creating APIs that will allow homogenous access to all existing resources in FESTIVAL. In order to guarantee the success in achieving these results, FESTIVAL federation follows a strict roadmap:

- Identify: this step identifies requirements for IoT experimentation testbeds, as well as the existing potential reusable assets in EU and JP ecosystems. The assets can be of different nature such as infrastructures, HW/software platforms, HW/SW components, etc.
- Analyze: once the candidate reusable assets have been identified, a deep analysis into the details to understand possibilities and limitations of the platforms will be carried out. Therefore, besides robust technical components, this part includes the documentation analysis to better understanding of the selected assets.
- Select: After analyzing the assets, a selection of those that are of interest to the project will be performed, also considering the requirements that will be identified at the beginning of the project and the results of the analysis performed in the preceding step.
- Integrate: The selected useful reusable components will be integrated into the existing target testbeds of the project, where the heterogeneity is a reality as consequence of technical, technological, operational and political specific constraints of each testbed. FESTIVAL will rely on an adaptation approach to make heterogeneous components work together.

- Federate: The testbeds enhanced with the selected assets will be federated by adopting an Experimentation Service Model. The EaaS platform will be based on commonly agreed standards and data models, in order to provide a homogeneous abstraction layer on top of the heterogeneous testbeds.

At the time being, FESTIVAL is finishing the second step in the described roadmap. Within this step, a wide set of interfaces, data formats, middleware entities and access policies have been identified. Furthermore, the analysis also considers other existing federation approaches addressed in other projects such as TEFIS [3] making available a set of testbeds, the TEFIS Testbed Federation, and offering a single access point to this federation for communities of experimenters, FED4FIRE [4] whose goal is to provide a homogenous access to the facilities built under the framework of the FIRE initiative, and FELIX [5], which is an EU-Japan collaborative project based on network infrastructure federation.

The three federation projects mentioned above are based in the existing Slice-based Facility Architecture (SFA) [6], in order to reach the maximum compatibility with other testbeds that use such architecture. The main component used with this federation philosophy, the GENI Aggregate Manager [7], is in charge of the discovery, reservation and provisioning of testbed resources, using their own format for describing the resources, namely RSpec. In spite of the fact that SFA is mainly intended for the management of fully controllable resources (e.g. ssh capable devices), IoT testbeds involved in FED4FIRE, such as SmartSantander [8, 9], are already implementing these tools as a wrapper of the native testbed tools for IoT device monitoring [10].

On the contrary, the FIWARE [11] initiative can be considered as a fourth federation approach, which has no link with SFA and is also more friendly with IoT-based testbeds. The use of FIWARE for IoT federation can be done through the available GEs (Generic Enablers), which allow fast deployment of different tools for managing IoT devices, as well as the storage of data retrieved by them.

3   Analysis and Classification of FESTIVAL Assets

This section aims at describing European and Japanese assets offered by the different partners within the FESTIVAL project, and will serve as basis for the identification of the best suited strategies for the federation goal.

It is important to make a clear differentiation between platforms, intended as the architectural and software elements that allow the management and use of the deployments; and testbeds, considered as the deployments and infrastructures that are available for external experimenters through a software platform. Apart from these groups, two additional ones should be also differentiate: the experimentation facilities, as the physical deployments and available areas for experimentation that can be used to experiment and retrieve data, but that are not still managed by a platform opened for external experimenters; and the living labs, oriented towards user-centric experimentation, involving the users in both the creation and the experimental processes.

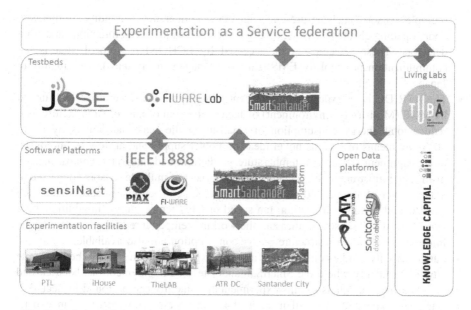

Fig. 1. Relationship between testbeds, platforms, experimentation facilities and living labs

Figure 1 shows the relationship among the different assets of FESTIVAL, all of them under the federation umbrella that will provide a homogeneous and uniform access.

3.1 Experimentation Facilities

As previously commented, experimentation facilities are conceived as playgrounds for experimentation, thus offering physical IoT deployments, including the possibility of adding new devices. The main difference between these experimentation facilities and the testbeds consists in the fact that the testbeds also include a software platform accessible from external experimenters to make use of the associated deployments. There are several experimentation facilities identified within FESTIVAL:

- The PTL [12], or the Connectivity Technologies Platform, is a facility to speed up the development of innovative products in emerging strategic fields of Health, Housing and Transport. The PTL is divided in three platforms: the "Connected Home" platform which is intended to evaluate interoperability of heterogeneous systems inside buildings; the "Connected Transport" platform to address mobility scenarios to improve safety and mobility connectivity in outdoor areas; and the "Health at Home" platform to retrieve and merge information from environmental, physiological and activity sensors. Higher-level information is transmitted through available communication networks to improve safety, comfort and autonomy.
- The iHOUSE [13] facility is an experimental smart house built by ISICO (Ishikawa Sunrise Industries Creation Organization). The iHouse facility is composed by

multiple sensors, such as presence detectors, temperature, humidity, luminosity, door opening/closing sensors, energy meters, wind speed/direction and rain detectors. These sensors can be accessed by ECHONET protocol, that is the communication protocol for EMS (Energy Management Systems), used mainly in Japan.

- The ATR DC is an experimental datacenter facility on the research project funded by MOE (Ministry of Environment) of Japan. The goal of this research facility is to reduce total energy consumption of small-to-middle scale datacenters by up to 70 %, by means of various novel ideas on power supply and airflow technologies, task assignment on servers, temperature prediction, and integrated control mechanism. The infrastructure of the facility is comprised of multiple sensors connected to a data center of around 400 servers with 8 racks. Each sensor can access data such as CPU and memory utilization, fan speed or CPU temperatures. In addition, data from around 100 sensors to measure the working temperature of the servers and the information of the infrastructure power consumption are also available.
- Santander City can be considered as an open experimentation space to be used. The city is the facility where the SmartSantander testbed deployment has been carried out. The specific details on this experimentation facility can be found in Sect. 3.3.
- The Lab, explained in detail in Sect. 3.4, can be also considered as an experimentation facility, thus offering its showrooms for deploying devices, including sensors, to perform the experimentation.

3.2 Software Platforms

There have been identified two groups of software platforms in FESTIVAL. On the one hand, the platforms that can be used to manage subjacent resources, such as virtual machines or IoT devices, thus supporting the control and management of the resources, including resource description, reservation or data monitoring. On the other hand, they are considered the platforms more oriented towards sharing information through open data policies.

In the first group, five platforms have been identified as candidates to be federated:

- The sensiNact Gateway [14] allows the interconnection of different networks with heterogeneous data formats and protocols, thus enabling the access and communication with embedded devices. It is composed of five functional groups and their relative interfaces: (i) the device protocol adapter, which allows abstracting the specific connectivity technology of wireless sensor networks; (ii) the Smart Object Access and Control, which implements core functionalities such as resource discovering and secure communications; (iii) the Consumer API, a protocol-agnostic API to expose services; (iv) the Consumer API Protocol Adapter, consisting of a set of bridges to translate the consumer API interface into specific application protocols; (v) the Gateway Management functional group, including all the components needed to ease the management of the devices connected to the sensiNact platform; and finally, (vi) the Manager Protocol Adapter, which allows adapting the Gateway

Management API to the specific protocols used by different external management entities.

- The FIWARE platform, which provides enhanced OpenStack-based cloud hosting capabilities plus a rich library of components including a number of added-value functions offered "as a Service". These components, called Generic Enablers (GEs), provide open standard APIs that make it easier to connect to the Internet of Things, process data and media in real-time at large scale, perform BigData analysis or incorporate advanced features for interaction with the user. Availability of open source Generic Enabler implementations (GEis) will accelerate availability of multiple commercial FIWARE providers, all supporting the same set of APIs. Of particular interest for the EaaS platform developed in FESTIVAL are two of the available GEs: the ORION context broker, an implementation of a Publish/Subscribe broker which allows registering context producer applications, and to subscribe and query context information; and the COSMOS big data, that allows the long-term storage of context information to be available later.

- The SmartSantander platform is the upper layer from the SmartSantander testbed. It is in charge of managing and control deployed resources in the city of Santander as well as external services that might use the platform to store and retrieve data. The SmartSantander platform provides a REST interface to register new producers and, once authenticated, inject data into the platform. It also exposes an interface for external experimenters and service providers so as to access real-time and historical data from SmartSantander. Both interfaces are provided by the IoT API component, which was created to support the federation within FED4Fire. Additionally, the platform also provides the functionality to manage the sensors and services registered in SmartSantander, making use of two components: the resource directory and resource register manager. Finally, the platform also provides the integration with FIWARE, allowing to inject the sensor data into the corresponding instances of the ORION and COSMOS GEs previously explained.

- The PIAX [15] (P2P Interactive Agent eXtensions) is an open source framework that integrates P2P structured overlay network and agent platform. PIAX is implemented by Java. PIAX can be used as a messaging platform for data gathering from the sensor network, parallel/distributed data analysis and delivering the analysis results to the actuators for facility controllers and visualization devices like digital signage. PIAX has its own testbed operated by NICT and it can be used to test PIAX Agent implementation easily.

- The IEEE1888 [16] is a standardized facility information access protocol (FIAP). IEEE1888 has a reference implementation of its communication protocol and data storage with standardized data format. Along with JOSE, it provides a platform which extends the IEEE1888 reference implementation to fit a large scale distributed computing environment. The extended implementation includes overlay routing function among storage instances of IEEE1888 (FIAP Storage) by using PIAX platform.

Regarding to the second group, the platforms more oriented towards sharing information through open data policies, next ones can be indicated:

- The Metropole of Lyon's Open Data [17] is a pro-innovation platform based on the Open Data paradigm. By providing wide-ranging access to public data such as the land register map for the conurbation, the surface area taken up by greenery, the availability of shared bikes (Vélo'v) or the locations of automatic car-sharing stations, the Greater Lyon SmartData platform is addressing the issues of data accessibility, which have been made objectives of the smart city. It includes a new series of data principally for the mobility sector, such as real-time traffic, highway events, traffic history or the number of available bicycles in Lyon.
- The Santander Open Data [18] is a platform deployed by the Santander City Council, offering official and public data in exploitable formats to the citizens, so they can reuse it for their own purposes, such as development of new services or the provision of added value to the existing ones. Among the data publicly offered, those related with transport, urban planning and infrastructure, shops, demography, society and well-being, culture and leisure events, are the most representative ones.

3.3   Testbeds

The testbeds within FESTIVAL are basically composed of a resource deployment, like the experimentation facilities explained above, and a software platform that supports the experimentation on top of them, allowing external users to perform their experiments, either deploying new software or making use of the data being produced in the testbed.

This section details the testbeds that belong to FESTIVAL and will be finally federated to be part of the EaaS platform. Among the testbeds we can identified two types: the Infrastructure provider testbeds that are the group of testbeds that provide infrastructure resources, such as virtual machines or SDN-based Service Orchestration, to perform experiments; and the IoT infrastructure testbeds.

Regarding the first type of testbeds, two can be indicated:

- The JOSE testbed [19], a Japan-wide open testbed which consists of a large number of wireless sensors, SDN capabilities and distributed "Cloud" resources along Japan. The facilities of JOSE are connected via high-speed network with SDN feature, aiming at accelerating field trials of "large-scale smart ICT services", essential for building future smart societies. JOSE has the following main characteristics: a huge amount of computation resources, a dedicated "sensor network" provision with SDN capabilities and a "takeout" sensor facilities for users' own experiments where many field trials can coexist.
- The Engineering FIWARE-Lab [20], stands as an instance of FI-WARE based on a cloud environment that allows the users to deploy, configure and execute a set of Generic Enablers. The cloud infrastructure is based on OpenStack, an open source software for creating cloud platforms and is directly managed by Engineering, which will provide specific computational resources dedicated to the FESTIVAL project. The FIWARE-Lab provides the possibility to create virtual machines and resources to deploy and execute the FIWARE Generic Enablers, with an existing set of preconfigured virtual images.

Regarding to the IoT infrastructure testbeds: they are composed of all the testbeds that offer a set of IoT devices that can be used to perform experiments either using their own sensor data or the data from deployed experiments in each device. In the case of FESTIVAL, the SmartSantander testbed provides an experimentation test facility for the re search and experimentation of architectures, key enabling technologies, services and applications for the Internet of Things in the context of a city. The SmartSantander is not just limited to the already deployed devices but it is flexible enough to add new ones.

3.4   Living Labs

As previously explained, this last category refers to those facilities where the user stands as the key issue of the experimentation, considering not only the useful data that the user can provide, e.g. giving feedback about a new prototype, but also as part of the co-creation process, making them participants of the actual research. The next two living labs are part of FESTIVAL and will be also part of the federation goal:

- Lyon Urban Data is an association based on a mixed consortium of public and private entities that operates a place named TUBA [21], which stands for "Experimentation Urban Test Tube". The TUBA is a 600 m^2 place dedicated to experimenting on new services and helping developing new projects (from startup, SMEs and large companies), based on available data. It is mainly composed of two spaces: The LAB, a 180 square meters showroom fully opened to the citizen, where they are encourage to contribute with their own ideas and feedback about what is being shown; and The Mix, a 420 square meters dedicated to show the last innovations advances from the TUBA partners as well as other public or private entities involved in the Smart City innovation.
- The Lab. [22] is the core facility in Knowledge Capital, an innovation space placed in the Grand Front Osaka building. The Lab. is a showcase where general public, such as researchers, creators, artists, students, senior citizens, housewives and children, can experience the latest technologies and have interactions with other exhibitors. The Lab. constitutes a space that attracts global prototypes and world-leading technologies, and is a hub from which the latest strains of culture emanate. Visitors not only get to see and touch ingenious inventions, but are also given the chance to participate in the creative process, fitting the description of this space as a laboratory.

4   Festival Use Cases

In order to exploit the potential of each of the testbeds as well as to take advantage of the additional features offered by the EaaS federation, several use cases and ICT services have been defined, mainly associated to three domains within the smart city context: energy, building and shopping. Use cases are framed in two categories: the application ones as those addressing services for end users under a real environment;

and the experimentation use cases, intended to specifically study the behavior of current and cutting-edge technologies over an outdoor testbed.

Apart from the aforementioned use cases are mainly intended on the one hand to be applied in specific testbeds or platforms for improving or generating new services such the use of cameras for different applications within the scope of smart building; and on the other hand, comparing behaviors associated to different testbeds and cities, such as those indicated for the smart shopping; others will be also described covering the use of the EasS model previously shown, thus taking advantage offered by the federation of several testbeds.

4.1 Smart Energy

Regarding to the application use cases, energy monitoring in buildings on top of PTL platform for metering consumed resources (water, gas, electricity), thus adapting the different parameters to the usage and presence in buildings, as well as study of energy management systems (xEMS) over different experimentation spaces such as The Lab, ATR DC and iHouse, in order to realize large-scale application service providers for various existing local xEMSs: HEMS (Home), FEMS (Factory), DEMS (Datacenter), CEMS (Community); and to contribute to global optimization of power consumption and overhead reduction of local EMSs. Apart from this application use case, regarding to the study of xEMS, two experimentation use cases are also planned on top of JOSE testbed and PIAX platform, thus allowing the experimenter to reserve several resources (sensors and VMs) according to an utilization plan sent to the administrator, connecting his own sensors and actuators and receiving the corresponding measurements retrieved by them.

4.2 Smart Building

From the smart building perspective, different use cases based on the use of smart cameras will be carried out thus considering on the one hand, the use of untraditional cameras that allows extracting some useful features of filmed scenes without the acquisition of "real images" and, on the other hand the use of traditional image sensors with dedicated image processing for extracting image features without storing image flows, over PTL space as well as TUBA and The Lab testbeds. The use of these cameras will be applied to queue management for counting people in a queue or a determined area (over TUBA and PTL), to adaptability issues in controlling media such as sounds, displayed videos and advertising (over TUBA) and to human- human interaction, thus capturing and streaming video in real-time for visually "connecting" people from separate places (over TUBA and The Lab).

4.3 Smart Shopping

Use cases on Smart Shopping are related with gathering different measurements, both environmental, presence detection and user tracking, within shops environment, thus accordingly processing the received data and offering context-aware incentives (e.g. specific discounts) to the users, all of them over the SmartSantander testbed. In the same direction, over TheLab testbed pedestrian flows will be captured, thus proceeding to recommend certain shops to the users according to their degree of crowdedness, as well as changing the background music, light, aroma for making shopping experience more pleasant to the user.

4.4 EaaS Specific Use Cases

Regarding to EaaS model, it is described the use of IoT-based experimentation, mainly based on SmartSantander testbed, thus reserving and accessing to the different IoT devices by sending/receiving commands or flashing them in order to run a specific experiment. For both accessing to the data and processing them accordingly to generate an application, the experimenter can access to the virtual machine resources offer within the Festival federated platform. Additionally to this use case, another interesting one consists on using FIWARE-Lab generic enablers (GEs), so that the experimenter specifies the objectives of the experiment, the duration, the needed computational resources and the GE that she wants to use. Once decided, the images of the GEs will be installed in the different virtual machines offered within the federated Festival platform.

5 Conclusions and Future Steps

As the technologies of the Future Internet move ever closer to the market, in an ever shorter innovation cycle, the need to validate the experimentation in "real life" trials with end user is becoming crucial. In this sense, the development of an open federation of testbeds enabled by the EaaS model, posed within the FESTIVAL project, will have a real impact on the number and quality of the experimentations that are run on the testbed(s), thus presenting both small and large scale trials over various application domains.

In order to achieved and assess (within the project lifetime) the aforementioned EaaS model, a set of testbeds, as well as platforms, living labs and experimentation facilities, have been described detailing their main characteristics and available resources, as the first step towards the federation of them under this EaaS model. Additionally, in order to show the potential of these testbeds, as enablers for real smart city applications, they have been presented the use cases to be carried out during the lifetime of the project, mainly associated to three main pillars: smart energy, smart building and smart shopping.

Finally, and considering that the FESTIVAL project is still in its first year of progress, the definition and implementation of a whole architecture (basis of the EaaS model) for accessing and managing of the testbeds in a homogenized and uniform way (common interfaces, APIs, access protocols, etc.), will be one of the main objectives in the second year of the project. Additionally, the translation of testbed-related use cases into commercial ICT services on top of the aforementioned architecture, will pose as another important challenge to be achieved.

Acknowledgments. This work was funded in part by the European Union's Horizon 2020 Programme of the FESTIVAL project (Federated Interoperable Smart ICT Services Development and Testing Platforms) under grant agreement 643275, and from the Japanese National Institute of Information and Communications Technology.

References

1. Botterman, M., Internet of things: an early reality of the future internet. In: Workshop Report prepared for European Commission, Information Society and Media Directorate General, Networked Enterprise and RFID Unit (D4), Prague (2009)
2. FESTIVAL project. http://www.festival-project.eu/
3. TEFIS project. http://www.ict-fire.eu/home/success-stories/tefis.html
4. FED4Fire project. http://fed4fire.eu/
5. FELIX project. http://www.ict-felix.eu/
6. Peterson, L., Ricci, R., Falk, A., Chase, J.: Slice-based federation architecture (SFA). Working draft, version 2.0 (2010)
7. GENI AM API. http://groups.geni.net/geni/wiki/GAPI_AM_API_V3
8. SmartSantander project. http://smartsantander.eu/
9. Sanchez, L., Muñoz, L., Galache, J.A., Sotres, P., Santana, J.R., Gutierrez, V., Ramdhany, R., Gluhak, A., Krco, S., Theodoridis, E., Pfisterer, D.: Smartsantander: IoT experimentation over a smart city Testbed. Comput. Netw. J. **61**, 217–238 (2014)
10. FED4Fire D4.5 – Report on second cycle developments of the services and applications community
11. FIWARE initiative. https://www.fiware.org/
12. PTL testbed. http://www.leti.fr/fr/layout/set/print/layout/set/print/content/download/2467/29637/file/3-SESSIONB3-Laurent-FrédéricDucreux.pdf
13. iHouse testbed. http://www.echonet.gr.jp/echo/example/pdf/example06.pdf
14. BUTLER Project. http://www.iot-butler.eu/
15. PIAX platform. https://piax.jgn-x.jp/pat/help/en/aboutPat/aboutPat.html
16. IEEE1888 reference implementation. http://fiap-develop.gutp.ic.i.u-tokyo.ac.jp/dist/
17. Metropole of Lyon's Open Data. http://data.grandlyon.com/
18. Santander Open Data. http://datos.santander.es/
19. Teranishi. Y.: JOSE: Japan-wide orchestrated smart ICT testbed for future smart society. http://cordis.europa.eu/fp7/ict/future-networks/documents/eu-japan/stream-c-teranishi.pdf
20. FIWARE LAB. https://fiware.eng.it
21. TUBA living lab. http://www.tuba-lyon.com/
22. The Lab. Knowledge Capital. https://kc-i.jp/en/

The Presidium of Wireless Sensor Networks - A Software Defined Wireless Sensor Network Architecture

Donna O'Shea[✉], Victor Cionca, and Dirk Pesch

Nimbus Centre for Embedded Systems Research, Cork Institute of Technology,
Cork, Ireland
{donna.oshea,victor.cionca,dirk.pesch}@cit.ie
http://www.nimbus.cit.ie

Abstract. Software Defined Networking (SDN) is emerging as a key technology to deal with the ever increasing network management burden created by our increasingly interconnected world. Wireless sensor network (WSN) are part of this interconnection, enabling to connect the physical world to the cyber world of the Internet and its networks. This connection of physical items, "Things", to the Internet in the form of an Internet of Things is creating many new challenges for the management of the Internet networks. SDN moves away from a distributed management approach that has been at the core of wireless sensor networks since their inception and introduces a centralised view and control of a network. We believe that the SDN concept as well as the general compute virtualisation enabled through infrastructure as a service can offer the required flexible management and control of the network of Things. While the application of SDN to WSN has already been proposed, a comprehensive architecture for Software Defined Wireless Sensor Networks (SD-WSN) is currently missing. This paper provides a survey of related work considering both SDN and centralised non-SDN approaches to network management and control, examines the challenges and opportunities for SD-WSNs, and provides an architectural proposal for SD-WSN.

Keywords: Wireless sensor networks · Software defined networking

1 Introduction

Wireless sensor networks (WSN) have emerged over the past 15 years as a key technology to interface computing systems with the physical world and being a central part of cyber-physical-systems and machine to machine communication systems. The community envisages WSN deployments throughout our environments, producing data for specific use cases such as environmental monitoring in buildings, traffic monitoring in cities, flood monitoring in river estuaries, and many more. The remote nature of WSN deployments requires unattended operation and a high degree of autonomy and self-configuration. From early on,

---

D. O'Shea and V. Cionca—The first two authors should be regarded as joint First Authors.

© Institute for Computer Sciences, Social Informatics and Telecommunications Engineering 2015
R. Agüero et al. (Eds.): MONAMI 2015, LNICST 158, pp. 281–292, 2015.
DOI: 10.1007/978-3-319-26925-2_21

the community traded centralised protocols for distributed, self-organising, self-healing, behaviour, sometimes with emergent properties inspired from nature [20]. In reality though, such deployments rarely functioned correctly and most deployments today are heavily monitored and controlled as nodes fail often and need manual intervention [4, 15].

Another application of sensor networks is in critical or real-time applications where there are strict timing and reliability requirements that have been addressed by implementing complex, application-driven protocols [17]. This may be a viable option for private, isolated and application-specific deployments, however it is less so if the WSN infrastructure is to be shared by multiple stake-holders, which is the case in virtualised WSN environments. In a shared WSN infrastucture, different occupants will have differing QoS requirements, which can't be addressed in an application-specific way but require a wide and detailed picture of the network state to make informed decisions about optimal traffic routing.

What the WSN community needs right now is increased control over the network to understand radio behaviour, diagnose and debug faults and ensure QoS. A relatively recent technology that provides increased control in networking is Software Defined Networking, or SDN. Software Defined Networking technology is under development as a mechanism to deal with the ever increasing configuration and management burden that large scale enterprise networks, data centre networks, and next generation mobile/wireless networks pose on network administrators. SDN simplifies network management by reducing the complexity of network elements (typically switches) to a rule table comprising match elements and actions, fully and directly controlled by a central manager that has complete control over the network [2]. The benefits of SDN are:

- a more programmable network where new protocols can easily be deployed;
- deterministic control that increases predictability of network behaviour over distributed protocols;
- optimal control enabled by a complete model of the network state.

While initial deployments in SDN were developed for wired networks, more recently it has excited the curiosity of researchers in wireless networks [12, 31] and WSNs (discussed further in Sect. 4.1). SDN has been a paradigm shift for network management, and it would probably provide an even more valuable shift for WSN, where resource constraints are as important as they are. Applying SDN to WSN however, represents a very different environment from what SDN was originally designed for in enterprise networks: low data rates, low performance and unreliable links. This paper joins an increasingly longer list of works that try to integrate SDN concepts into the WSN domain. However, the existing literature seems to be disconnected from previous WSN research and does not highlight previous forays into centralised WSN control, which, ultimately, is the core concept of SDN. This leads to an incomplete understanding of the challenges faced by an implementation of SDN in WSN and solutions that cannot work due to issues of scale and inconsistency. This paper proposes a possible architecture for Software Defined Wireless Sensor Networks (SD-WSN) and attempts to expose the challenges and opportunities that arise in this application of SDN, by analysing recent SD-WSN approaches together with older attempts at centralised WSN control.

2   Architecture for Software Defined Wireless Sensor Networks

The following section presents an architecture for Software Defined WSNs, called SURF (Service-centric networking for URban-scale Feedback Systems).

Typical SDN architectures consist of simple, "dumb", switches that are directly controlled by a logically centralised network manager. The manager has complete knowledge of the network topology and its state and therefore can run centralised algorithms for routing, load-balancing, etc. The controller talks to switches through a south-bound interface, the most common being OpenFlow [2]. The controller also exposes a north-bound interface for developers of network applications, such as routing algorithms, firewalls, proxies, etc., however, this one hasn't been standardised yet.

The SURF architecture acknowledges that sensor networks differ in many ways from the description above, the main difference being that nodes are not only switches (or routers, to be precise), but they also have one or more application components. In WSN we are not interested that much in network applications such as firewalls, but more in sensing applications, such as assigning a subset of the nodes to a single application (e.g. get the temperature in the city centre). Finally, the WSN case that is being explored is that of a large infrastructure shared by multiple stakeholders with different requirements.

The focus in a WSN SDN is on optimal resource sharing, from the point of view of sensing and communication. The SURF controller, presented below in Fig. 1 has the following capabilities:

- set up and manage data flows through the network that maintain a required level of QoS;
- find the optimal subset of nodes that can service an external sensing request, in terms of quality of sensing and communication;
- dynamically adjust allocations of data flows and sensing applications, by migrating flows or applications, in order to respond to external changes (e.g. interference) or reallocation requests (e.g. resources required by a higher priority application).

The SURF architecture can be described according to the following layers:

- **Network Applications.** This layer comprises of the business and network applications that monitor and control a set of resources managed by one of more SDN controllers.
- **Controller.** Through its northbound API and access to its Network Information Base (NIB) [1], the main responsibility of the controller is to faithfully execute the requests of the applications defined though this layer. It also is responsible for: resource monitoring and (re)optimisation; responding to and

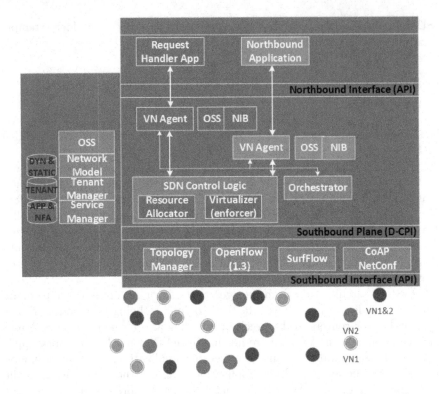

Fig. 1. Architecture of a software-defined wireless sensor network controller

generating events as a result of changes in the underlying network; and computing a collection of packet forwarding rules. These forwarding rules are then installed into the WSN nodes via the southbound API.

- **Physical and Virtual WSN.** This consists of the physical or virtualised network elements which can implement the decisions made in the controller layer issued via the southbound interface.

These layers are further described in detail below.

Northbound Layer. Within the northbound plane of the controller, programmatic interfaces also referred to as northbound Application Programming Interfaces (APIs) exist to create network services. Northbound APIs insulate the: applications from details of the network that are not needed; and the Network Operating System (NOS) (described further in Sect. 3.1) from applications allowing it to focus on its primary concern of dealing with application requests. Northbound applications can invoke external services potentially located in the cloud and may orchestrate applications from other SDN controllers to achieve its objectives. Applications at this layer receive events and notifications about the state of Virtual Networks (VNs) and can alter the state of VNs with varying levels of QoS and bandwidth. In the architecture described below it is important to recognise that we envisage that multiple physical SD-WSN deployments can be combined into a single virtual sensor network. In the case where each individual SD-WSN is controlled by a controller, we need to be able to have an over-arching control function that can deal with multiple controllers, perhaps with multiple owners. This control can be implemented as a client SDN controller or northbound application that invoke external services, applications or other SDN controllers to achieve its functional and business objectives.

Controller Layer. One of the key motivations behind our proposal for SD-WSN, is that the network can be virtualised to enable multiple users and use cases through multi-tenancy, that is multiple virtual overlays over the same physical network to allow multiple uses of the same physical infrastructure. This is also shown in Fig. 1 with two virtual networks overlaying the same physical infrastructure. To support this the SURF SDN control logic consists of a resource allocator, virtualizer and orchestrator the functions of which are further described below:

- **Resource Allocator** is the entity that is responsible for determining if a Virtual Network (VN) or Network Function Virtualisation (NFV) request can be accommodated by the network. In the event that the service request can be supported the resource allocator interacts with the virtualiser to allocate the physical resources that will form part of the VN.
- **Virtualiser** is responsible for creating an VN agent that represents the resources through a subset view of the NIB and actions available to the application. While this agent runs technically in the controller it should be noted that it is a trusted application to the client or application.
- **Orchestrator** To support NFV, service function chains which are used to compose network services, need to be flexibly compose network functions such as firewalls and data aggregation as independent services following Service-Oriented principles [5]. The orchestrator within the Surf architecture is used to provide this functionality. The orchestrator is also responsible for resolving conflicts between different applications and to ensure optimal performance in terms of resource utilisation, overhead, sleep schedules and routing is achieved.
- **Management** The controller also includes a management plane, which consists of a service manager, a tenant manager, a physical network model that keeps track of the physical infrastructure, and operation support services (OSS). The network model maintains a database of the network dynamics, the tenant manager has a database of tenant functions and the service manager maintains a database of virtual network applications and functions.

Physical and Virtual WSN. Communication between the controller and the physical/virtualised WSN nodes is achieved through the southbound interface, which is implemented through suitable protocols. Openflow is used in enterprise networks and a modified version such as proposed in [18] could be adopted here. However, we think that an extension of CoAP could also be a suitable alternative as it is already well established within the WSN field. We are also investigating alternative protocols that are tailored to the specifics of WSN. The southbound plane of the controller is expected to support multiple protocols that are designed bearing in mind the capabilities of the underlying infrastructure. In addition, this plane of the controller has a topology manager which updates the NIB for the SDN control logic. This layer also considers the modifications necessary on the sensor node protocol stack required to support communication with the controller via the southbound API, which is shown in Fig. 2. Through the separation of control and data plane, network nodes can have multiple data plane protocol stacks. In Fig. 2, two different data plane protocol stacks are shown. The control plane is implemented through a suitable control protocol as indicated above. The control functions configure the access to the physical communication medium via the MAC and physical layers. Depending on the services that are supported by the data plane application layers, the control plane needs to configure sleep schedules, medium access control, routing, and perhaps even data aggregation.

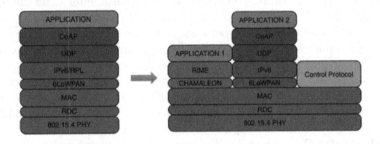

Fig. 2. Software defined wireless sensor node

3 Challenges and Opportunities

In the following we discuss the opportunities and challenges in migrating from the distributed status quo to a centralized management architecture as proposed for our SD-WSN concept.

3.1 Opportunities

This paper makes the case that there is a valid reason for adapting SDN concepts to WSN based on the main opportunities outlined below.

Network Operating System (NOS). In SDN, the NOS allows the decomposition of network operation into three distinct layers: the data plane, the management layer that is responsible for building and maintaining an abstract view of the network state, and the control logic that performs operations on network devices depending of its view of network state. These abstraction levels: "extract simplicity" from the network, reducing the need to "master complexity", make it possible to create network aware applications with the ability for expressive algorithms to reconfigure the underlying network in response to changing user applications requirements [25, 28]. In WSN this abstract view of network state (represented as a network model) could be used to provide optimal resolution over a number of WSN constraints such that in general, a maximization of resource utilization through optimal task scheduling could be achieved (with the aim of minimising packet loss and latency, redcing energy consumption and maximising network lifetime).

Network Virtualization. Applying virtualization to Wireless Sensor Networks (WSNs) has been proposed recently [14, 16]. WSN virtualization allows the evolution of sensor networks in their current manifestation, as isolated and application specific deployments. In this evolved view, the sensing abilities of WSN nodes can be shared among various federations and composed to form new applications and services beyond its original purpose or design. Separating the network infrastructure and its ownership also means that the traditional benefits associated with virtualization can also be leveraged in WSNs. These benefits include economies of scale, reduced cost of ownership and reduced cost to customers. While SDN is considered an enabler for network virtualization, it is important to recognise that the features offered by SDN were not directly designed to facilitate the creation of virtual networks, although SDN can be leveraged to facilitate network virtualisation in WSNs.

Tussle Networking. Tussle in networking is used to describe the contention among parties with conflicting interests. Within the context of WSN one of the tussles is the conflict between the irreconcilable network stacks that sit on top of the main standardized access technology IEEE802.15.4. These include: Zigbee, WirelessHART and RPL. As a result of these differences, situations may emerge that nodes cannot participate in the WSN even though all the devices use the same underlying access technologies. SDN provides mechanisms to deal with this tussle across heterogeneous WSN deployment by: defining routing functions through software that can be changed dynamically through a high level programming abstraction and facilitating layer 2 network virtualization.

3.2 Challenges

It is important to recognise that SDN is not a panacea in all situations and challenges exist in collecting data to provide a *consistent* and up-to-date network model to leverage the proposed opportunities. These challenges are further described below.

Out of Band Signalling. In enterprise networks there is either an out-of-band channel between the controller and each switch, otherwise secure tunnels are used that take advantage of the high data rates. The topology is static and the links are stable. Sensor networks have unreliable links, a dynamic topology and generally low data rates. An out-of-band channel could be obtained using dedicated higher power radios, but that would increase costs.

Dynamic Changes. Maintaining a consistent central model of the network when the network topology is dynamic requires periodic updates from each node. WSN attributes, such as the quality of links, can change quickly [3]. It is obviously impractical (if not impossible) to update the central model at each unit of change in a node's attribute set. The question is, then, *what is the smallest change in the sensor network that requires an update of the central model?* Obviously this depends on higher level policies, such as the range of QoS levels demanded from the network.

Low Data Rates. Another factor limiting the quantity of SDN control traffic is the generally low data rate of WSN. Wired networks have maximum transmission unit values in the order of kilobytes, and bandwidths of Gigabytes, whereas in WSN the MTU is usually around 100 bytes and maximum data rates around 250 kbps to perhaps 1 Mbps. The amount and rate of information sent by nodes to the central controller in a WSN should perhaps hold the same proportion as in wired networks. However, this may reduce the functionality and consistency of the central model and novel approaches for maintaining the network state will be required.

Distributed State Management. Running multiple SDN controllers physically distributed is necessary to ensure a responsive, scalable and reliable system. The challenge is ensuring that these physically distributed controllers act together to form a logically centralized one, to allow network refactoring through the control plane based on a global network view. The Ethane/Sane project [6], which is a predecessor to OpenFlow, proposed full replication across multiple controllers with a weakly synchronized state. ONIX [21], which was built on the work of Ethane, provides a general framework for dealing with distributed OpenFlow controllers and introduces the idea of a network information state shared by controller replicas. FlowVisor [26] supports multiple controllers by slicing the network resources and assigning control to one controller over the slice. HyperFlow [29] on the other hand, proposes a publish-subscribe mechanism where each controller selectively publishes events that are related to network state changes, and replica controllers use these events to construct the overall network state. More recently, Open Network Operating System (ONOS) [1] offers an open-source controller that also uses a publish-subscribe model to enable controllers to behave as a single logical entity. Other controllers that provide a distributed SDN architecture include Kandoo [11], DISCO [23] and ElastiCon [9]. The challenge of creating a logically centralized controller that integrates with the control of the core network for a future Internet of Things will introduce new scalability issues in terms of the number of devices connected and the need to be able to efficiently respond to the rate of change in network state from nodes (which are unreliable and could also be mobile). These are non-trivial problems that need to be addressed.

4   Related Work

In the following we present key recent work on both the application of software defined networking to wireless sensor networks and non-SDN based centralised management approaches in WSN.

4.1   Recent Work in Adapting SDN to WSN

To date rather limited research in the area of Software Defined Wireless Sensor Networks (SD-WSN) has been published in the literature. As indicated in the introduction, the majority of these proposals is disconnected from previous WSN research and focuses on issues of SDN that are specific to the core and enterprise network domains, without consideration for impact on WSN resources. With few exceptions, the papers do not provide results and overlook what is to these authors the most important problem in porting SDN to WSN: that the unreliable links, combined with the low data rate and energy constraints can lead to an incomplete or *inconsistent* network model.

Sensor OpenFlow [18] and SDWN [7] are two early adopters of SDN in WSN. Both papers propose architectures, highlighting potential issues such as what fields to use for matching rules and how to include additional functionality such as in-network processing. TinySDN [30] presents a similar architecture, where the CTP routing protocol is used to build the control path. Some results for overhead and latency as compared to basic CTP are presented; however, CTP only provides upward routing (nodes to sink) so it is unclear how the solution sends forwarding rules to individual nodes. The authors of SDWN have returned recently with SDN-WISE [10], a state-full WSN SDN controller that further develops the in-network processing capability. This paper also provides evaluation of latency and reliability, however the results are not related to control decisions but only to data packets, therefore the consistency of the central model is not addressed. Other approaches are by Qin *et al.* [24] that focuses on flow scheduling using a genetic algorithm and network calculus, and Jacobsson and Orfanidis [13], who propose an architecture where each node has a local controller.

4.2   Non-SDN Centralised Management Approaches

One of the key aspects of SDN is centralised network control. While Sect. 4.1 presented the related work in the field of applying SDN to WSNs, there are also significant contributions in the area of centralized routing and control for WSN, which none of the work on SDN for WSN considered. The following section highlights some of the main works in this area.

Estrin et al. in [22] were the first to point out the short-comings of distributed control and proposed instead the return to logically centralised control. Central control can be exerted over all the nodes at once, by disseminating commands, such as in SORA [19], where the network is seen as a price-driven marketplace. More fined grained approaches that target individual nodes also exist. For example the CentRoute protocol [27] exploits a multi-tiered network with devices of heterogeneous performance, where low-capability devices are "herded" into "flocks" by higher-performance devices, the "shepherds". Another example is the Flexible Control Protocol (FCP) which is used in the Koala [21] protocol suite. Both CentRoute and FCP, (re)compute the network model through periodic, bulk, downloading of data from the entire network and in order to save power the network lies dormant (from the point of view of the radio) for long periods of time and is then woken up by the base station and queried for new data. Both protocols assume a static topology and the centralised model built is used to install network routes and in the case of FCP also assigns radio channels and schedules the wake-up times of nodes along paths. It is important to note that Koala was found as the closest solution to SDN in WSN, even mentioning the separation of control and data planes. The paper also provides some results of the scalability of the central model. However there are several important differences - the central model is static (built on demand for each download session) and it is not used to enforce the optimisation of network parameters. A different, more generic, approach is taken with the Hydro protocol [8]. Hydro was the initial routing protocol for the TinyOS 6LoWPAN stack, only to be replaced later by RPL. Hydro and RPL both build upward and downward routes using beacons propagated from the root, and maintain a partial model of the network in the collection tree root. Hydro builds this global topology database by piggybacking statistics on data packets and addresses the need for efficient setup of peer-to-peer routes within the network, which differentiates it from RPL. To that extent, Hydro could be compared to OpenFlow in SDN where routes can be installed into nodes' forwarding tables which contain a traffic matching rule and a next hop. Hydro achieves good performance and relatively low control overhead even under heavy network failures.

5   Conclusions

In this paper we presented a proposal for applying the concept of software defined networking (SDN) to wireless sensor networks (WSN) and an architecture for software defined wireless sensor networks (SD-WSN). Our proposal is motivated by the need for improved management of large WSN deployments in use cases such as smart buildings and smart cities. WSNs are also a key part of the Internet of Things, which will lead to billions of wireless sensor nodes connected to the Internet over the next decade. As part of the Internet of Things, the concepts of multi-user or multi-tenant WSN is emerging, which will lead to virtualised WSNs similar to what is happening in enterprise or data centre networks. Our architecture is based on a central controller for the sensor network and a proposal for the split of data and control planes in sensor nodes. We also suggested how multiple SD-WSN domains, each controlled by a single logical controller, can be combined into multi-domain SD-WSNs. Implementing SDN for WSN also facilitates network virtualisation and multi-tenancy in a natural manner. In order to enable truly software defined WSN, a number of challenges need to be overcome in order to enable the many opportunities that this concept will facilitate. We highlighted some of these challenges and opportunities. Finally, we provided some related work on SD-WSN but also showed that the concept of centralised control in WSN is not new and that some of the prior work can be leveraged to solve some of the challenges ahead. We are currently working on a prototype implementation of our architecture with specific focus on the control protocols and challenges underlying network virtualisation.

Acknowledgements. This publication has emanated from research conducted with the financial support of Science Foundation Ireland (SFI) under Grant Number 13/IA/1885.

References

1. Introducing onos - a sdn network operating system for service providers. Technical report, ON.LAB
2. Openflowswitch specification. Technical report ONF TS-006, Open Networking Foundation, June 2012
3. Baccour, N., Koubâa, A., Mottola, L., Zuniga, M.A., Youssef, H., Boano, C.A., Alves, M.: Radio link quality estimation in wireless sensor networks: a survey. ACM Trans. Sen. Netw. 8(4), 34:1–34:33 (2012). http://doi.acm.org/10.1145/2240116.2240123
4. Barrenetxea, G., Ingelrest, F., Schaefer, G., Vetterli, M.: The hitchhiker's guide to successful wireless sensor network deployments. In: Proceeding SENSYS 2008, pp. 43–56. ACM (2008)
5. Blendin, J., Ruckert, J., Leymann, N., Schyguda, G., Hausheer, D.: Position paper: software-defined network service chaining. In: 2014 Third European Workshop on Software Defined Networks (EWSDN), pp. 109–114, September 2014
6. Casado, M., Freedman, M., Pettit, J., Luo, J., McKeown, N., Shenker, S.: Ethane: taking control of the enterprise. SIGCOMM Comput. Commun. Rev. 37(4), 1–12 (2007)
7. Costanzo, S., Galluccio, L., Morabito, G., Palazzo, S.: Software defined wireless networks: unbridling sdns. In: 2012 European Workshop on Software Defined Networking (EWSDN), pp. 1–6, October 2012
8. Dawson-Haggerty, S., Tavakoli, A., Culler, D.: Hydro: a hybrid routing protocol for low-power and lossy networks. In: 2010 First IEEE International Conference on Proceedings of the Smart Grid Communications (SmartGridComm) (2010)
9. Dixit, A., Hao, F., Mukherjee, S., Lakshman, T.V., Kompella, R.: Towards an elastic distributed sdn controller. In: Proceedings of HotSDN 2013, pp. 7–12. ACM, New York (2013)
10. Galluccio, L., Milardo, S., Morabito, G., Palazzo, S.: Sdn-wise: design, prototyping and experimentation of a stateful sdn solution for wireless sensor networks. In: Proceedings of the 34th IEEE INFOCOM Conference (2015)
11. Yeganeh, S.H., Ganjali, Y.: Kandoo: A framework for efficient and scalable offloading of control applications. In: Proceedings of HotSDN 2012, pp. 19–24. ACM, New York (2012)
12. Heming, W., Tiwary, P.K., Le-Ngoc, T.: Current trends and perspectives in wireless virtualization. In: Proceedings of MoWNet 2013, pp. 62–67 (2013)
13. Jacobsson, M., Orfanidis, C.: Using software-defined networking principles for wireless sensor networks. In: Proceedings of the 11th Swedish National Computer Networking Workshop (2014)
14. Jayasumana, A.P., Han, Q., Illangasekare, T.H.: Virtual sensor networks - a resource efficient approach for concurrent applications. In: Fourth International Conference on Information Technology, ITNG 2007, pp. 111–115, April 2007
15. Langendoen, K., Baggio, A., Visser, O.: Murphy loves potatoes: experiences from a pilot sensor network deployment in precision agriculture. In: Proceedings 20th IEEE International Parallel & Distributed Processing Symposium, pp. 155. IEEE (2006)

16. Leontiadis, I., Efstratiou, C., Mascolo, C., Crowcroft, J.: SenShare: transforming sensor networks into multi-application sensing infrastructures. In: Picco, G.P., Heinzelman, W. (eds.) EWSN 2012. LNCS, vol. 7158, pp. 65–81. Springer, Heidelberg (2012)

17. Li, Y., Chen, C., Song, Y., Wang, Z.: Real-time qos support in wireless sensor networks: a survey. In: 7th IFAC International Conference on Fieldbuses & Networks in Industrial & Embedded Systems-FeT 2007 (2007)

18. Luo, T., Tan, H.-P., Quek, T.Q.S.: Sensor openflow: enabling software-defined wireless sensor networks. IEEE Commun. Lett. **16**(11), 1896–1899 (2012)

19. Mainland, G., Parkes, D., Welsh, M.: Decentralized, adaptive resource allocation for sensor networks. In: Proceedings of the 2Nd Conference on Symposium on Networked Systems Design & Implementation - Volume 2, NSDI 2005, pp. 315–328. USENIX Association, Berkeley (2005)

20. Markham, A., Trigoni, N.: Discrete gene regulatory networks (dgrns): a novel approach to configuring sensor networks. In: 2010 Proceedings IEEE INFOCOM, pp. 1–9. IEEE (2010)

21. Musaloiu, R., Liang, C.J.M., Terzis, A.: Koala: ultra-low power data retrieval in wireless sensor networks. In: International Conference on Information Processing in Sensor Networks, IPSN 2008, pp. 421–432 (2008)

22. Paek, J., Greenstein, B., Gnawali, O., Jang, K., Joki, A., Vieira, M., Hicks, J., Estrin, D., Govindan, R., Kohler, E.: The tenet architecture for tiered sensor networks. ACM Trans. Sen. Netw. **6**(4), 34:1–34:44 (2010)

23. Phemius, K., Bouet, M., Leguay, J.: Disco: distributed multi-domain sdn controllers. In: 2014 IEEE Network Operations and Management Symposium (NOMS), pp. 1–4, May 2014

24. Qin, Z., Denker, G., Giannelli, C., Bellavista, P., Venkatasubramanian, N.: A software defined networking architecture for the internet-of-things. In: Proceedings of the IEEE Network Operations and Management Symposium (NOMS) (2014)

25. Rubio-Loyola, J., Galis, A., Astorga, A., Serrat, J., Lefevre, L., Fischer, A., Paler, A., Meer, H.: Scalable service deployment on software-defined networks. IEEE Commun. Mag. **49**(12), 84–93 (2011)

26. Sherwood, R., Gibb, G., Yap, K., Appenzeller, G., Casado, M., McKeown, N., Parulkar, G.: Flowvisor: a network virtualization layer. OpenFlow Switch Consortium. Technical report (2009)

27. Stathopoulos, T., Girod, L., Heidemann, J., Estrin, D.: Mote herding for tiered wireless sensor networks. Center for Embedded Network Sensing (2005)

28. Stuckmann, P., Zimmermann, R.: European research on future internet design. IEEE Wirel. Commun. **16**(5), 14–22 (2009)

29. Tootoonchian, A., Ganjali, Y.: Hyperflow: a distributed control plane for openflow. In: Proceedings of the 2010 internet network management conference on Research on enterprise networking, USENIX Association, p. 3 (2010)

30. Trevizan de Oliveira, B., Borges Margi, C., Batista Gabriel, L.: Tinysdn: enabling multiple controllers for software-defined wireless sensor networks. In: IEEE Communications (LATINCOM), pp. 1–6, November 2014

31. Wang, X., Krishnamurthy, P., Tipper, D.: Wireless network virtualization. In: International Conference on Computing, Networking and Communications (ICNC), pp. 818–822, January 2013

Author Index

Printed in the United States
By Bookmasters